THE EXTRAORDINARY KHOTSO

THE EXTRAORDINARY KHOTSO
Millionaire Medicine Man from Lusikisiki

by Felicity Wood

in collaboration with Michael Lewis

Part of the proceeds from the sale of this book will be donated to a trust fund for the Sethuntsa family.

First published by Jacana Media (Pty) Ltd in 2007
Second impression 2021

10 Orange Street
Sunnyside
Auckland Park 2092
South Africa
+2711 628 3200
www.jacana.co.za

© Felicity Wood & Michael Lewis, 2007
Photographs by Felicity Wood unless otherwise indicated

All rights reserved.

ISBN   978-1-77009-361-4

Cover design by publicide
Edited by Lisa Compton
Set in Stempel Garamond 10.5/16pt
Printed by Creda Communications, Cape Town
Job No. 003780

See a complete list of Jacana titles at www.jacana.co.za

Contents

Preface..ix
Acknowledgements...xi
Dramatis Personae..xiii
Prologue..xvii

PART ONE: 1898 – 1932
   1. In the Land of the Red Snow...1
   2. Into Nomansland...17
   3. Hunting for Dwarves and Jackals..27
   4. The Snake in a Whirlwind...41

PART TWO: 1932 – 1960
   5. The Wife Below the Water...63
   6. At the White House...82
   7. From Ibangalala to Ukuthwala..103
   8. Greater than God..131
   9. The Kruger Connection..139
  10. Verwoerd's Inyanga..159
  11. Hubris to Nemesis...174

PART THREE: 1960 – 1971
  12. Bantustan Fantasia..189
  13. Anger in the Hills...211

14. Sex, Drugs and the Broederbond 218
15. Tsotsis and Treasure 227
16. King of a Slippery Realm 235
17. Nkosazana and Bethinja 253

PART FOUR: 1971 and thereafter
18. The Last Days 263
19. Third Death and Final Party 277
20. The Boedel 285
21. Riches Are Like Mist 300
22. Life After Death 311
23. The Last Laugh 320

Glossary 325
Informants 329
Notes 333
Bibliography 352
Index 363

Photographs

Mount Nelson
Photographed by Obie Oberholzer
(between pages 196 and 197)
1. A statue of Khotso raised high on a pillar, riding a lion.
2. Lions guard the entrance to Mount Nelson. Khotso is astride one of them.
3. One of the sitting rooms in Mount Nelson. The herbs and concoctions that Thabo Sethuntsa uses in his medicines lie on the table.
4. Paul Kruger and his wife watch over a room in Mount Nelson.
5. A bust of Khotso awaits visitors in the foyer of Mount Nelson (detail). The eagle from the emblem of the South African Republic appears on his tie.

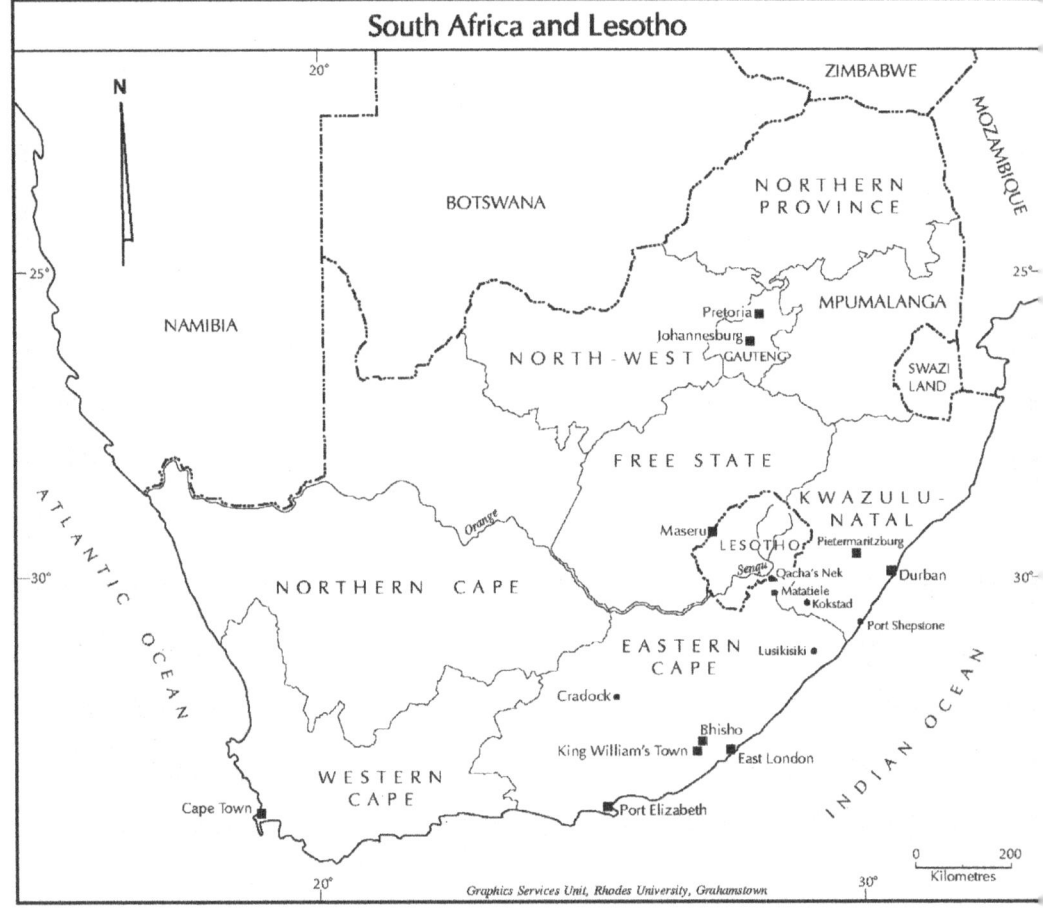

Preface

Felicity Wood wrote this book, drawing on the joint endeavours of herself and Michael Lewis. They have investigated the life of Khotso Sethuntsa for years.

Michael Lewis contributed a considerable quantity of the information upon which this book draws. In the course of his research, he acquired important documentation and conducted interviews with key informants who are now dead.

While the book was being written, Michael Lewis provided guidance, suggestions and editorial advice.

Both Felicity Wood and Michael Lewis entered the world of Khotso Sethuntsa and encountered one another in this world. In consequence this book was made possible.

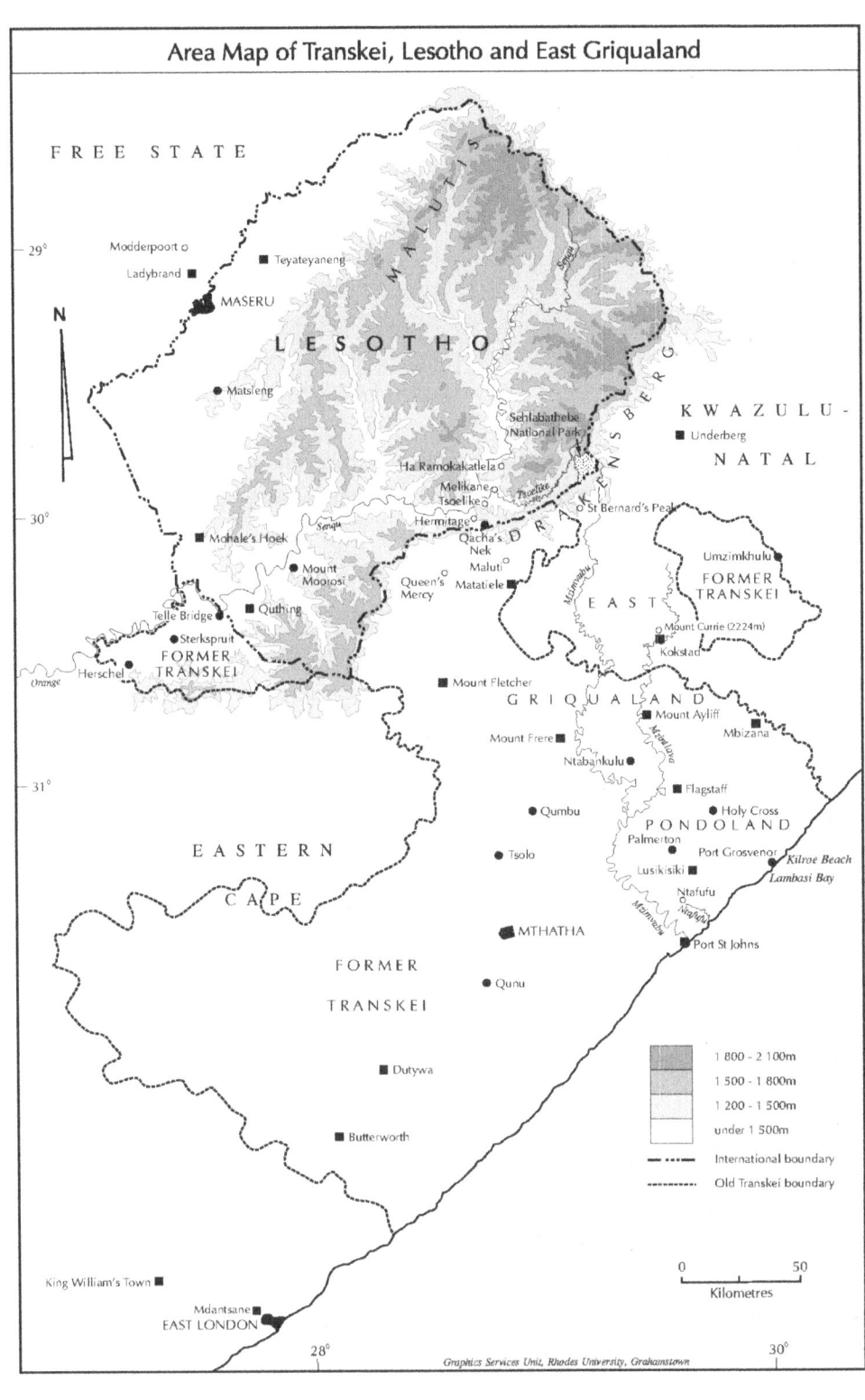

Acknowledgements

Special thanks are due to Sylvia Tloti, who has worked with Felicity Wood for years as her Research Assistant. Her energy, enthusiasm and unfailing good humour have helped carry this book along, and the investigation she has conducted into aspects of Khotso Sethuntsa's life and her liaison work with communities and key informants are highly valued. Above all, she has acted as a guide, not only through the hills of Pondoland and the mountain villages of Lesotho, but also through the world that Khotso Sethuntsa inhabited.

Felicity Wood and Michael Lewis are grateful to the people in East Griqualand, the Transkei and Lesotho who shared their knowledge of Khotso Sethuntsa with them. Moreover, they are indebted to the members of his family who assisted them in their research, and to James Lunika for all the information he provided and for his willingness to offer commentary on the manuscript itself.

The former journalist Jack Blades has made a significant contribution to this work by allowing Felicity Wood and Michael Lewis access to his own research into Khotso Sethuntsa's life. This includes some valuable oral material.

Dr Eva Hunter has played an important role, offering professional editorial guidance and moral support to Felicity Wood.

Felicity Wood appreciates the support she has received from her students and colleagues in her department. She is beholden to all the individuals at the University of Fort Hare who helped introduce her to

Khotso Sethuntsa and the wealth of stories surrounding him, starting with Fanele Sicwetsha and Anele Mabongo. Rina Flanegan in the Govan Mbeki Research and Development Centre has her gratitude for all the hard work she has carried out on her behalf, and her patience and understanding. She is also grateful to her Dean of Research, Andy Gilbert, for his advice and assistance, and the ongoing interest he has shown in her work.

Michael Lewis wishes to thank the following friends for their encouragement and insights: Tembisa Matolengwe, Mathabatha Sexwale, Nthabiseng Lewis, Dr Meso Letele, Dr Rafiq Surtie, Tsepo Letsie, Makhabane 'King' Moshoeshoe, Frank Leepa, Ellen Jones, Slokazana Makongolo, Lwazi Mahlaka, Elizabeth Brown, Peace Koko, Bangani Tsotsi, Thabo Letele, Bonner Seakhoa and Masechaba Sethuntsa.

This work would not be complete without the contribution of Obie Oberholzer, dedicated photographer, whose images capture essential qualities of Khotso Sethuntsa's world.

Felicity Wood and Michael Lewis extend their thanks to all the experts in their fields who have assisted them in their investigation. These individuals include Professors David Ambrose and Ben Machobane from Roma University, Lesotho; Stephen Gill, curator of Morija Museum in Lesotho; Professor Jeff Peires; Frans Prins from the Maloti–Drakensberg Transfrontier Project; Milner Snell from the Kokstad Museum; and the Kokstad attorney Barry Elliot. Mention should also be made of Geoffrey Wood at Sheffield University, an exacting critic and supportive brother who helped Felicity Wood make her way through the unstable terrain of Transkei politics.

The National Research Foundation and the University of Fort Hare provided funding for work on this book.

Finally, Felicity Wood owes a great debt of gratitude to her long-suffering and loving husband and Head of Department, Mathew Blatchford.

Dramatis Personae

Abraham, Hans: South African government official, Commissioner-General of the Xhosa in the Transkei.

Becker, Peter: popular historian and travel writer, who met Khotso in the late 1950s.

Blades, Jack: former journalist, who first met Khotso in 1970. He has conducted extensive research into Khotso's life.

Greeves, Francina: old friend of Ellen Jones. Now living in Ellen's house, the smaller White House, in Kokstad.

Jones, Ellen: met Khotso in 1946 and lived with him in Kokstad until 1952. Mother of Langa Lase-Afrika. Subsequently married to Victor Moyce. Lived in the smaller White House in Kokstad after Khotso's death, from 1974 onwards.

Khoapa, Julius: trader and ex-police sergeant from Matatiele. He knew Khotso from the days when they were both young men hunting jackal in the mountains.

Kruger, Paul: president of the South African Republic (the old Transvaal) between 1883 and 1900 and leader of the Boers during the South African War.

Lunika, James: Khotso's close friend and confidant until the late 1960s, the man Khotso called his prime minister. Lunika first met Khotso when he was a boy in the 1930s in Kokstad. Now living in Caquba, near Port St Johns.

Makeka, Pascal: a retired schoolteacher from the Hermitage, a village near Qacha's Nek. He remembers Khotso and MaDlamini from the early days.

Mancotywa, C. M.: principal of the St Andrews Secondary School in Lusikisiki and the master of ceremonies at Khotso's funeral.

Marsburg, Alf: Lusikisiki magistrate in the latter half of the 1960s.

Matanzima, Kaiser: first premier of the Transkei, after the region was given 'self-government' in 1963.

Moshoeshoe, Nthoa Bohlokhoa: Sotho herbalist, Khotso's principal source of herbs from 1930s onwards. Grandson of Moshoeshoe I.

Motumi, Lefu Ma-Thabo: Khotso's niece, born in 1919, the day Khotso's father, Motumi, died. One of the oldest inhabitants of Ha Ramokakatlela.

Ndzumo, Saul: Bethinja's lover, originally clerk in Lusikisiki funeral parlour, later minister in Matanzima's cabinet.

Newman, Bernard: travel writer who met Khotso in 1965, during his journey through the Transkei.

Ngcobo, Duke: Drum journalist, who wrote a substantial feature on Khotso in 1958.

Nogudlu, Meshack: current occupant of the White House.

Ramokakatlela, Mokholitsoane: Khotso's mother (sometimes known as Ma-Khotso, after her eldest son). The daughter of Maphasa, a chief in the Herschel district of the Eastern Cape, near the Lesotho border.

Ramokakatlela, Motumi: Khotso's father and founder of Ha Ramokakatlela, the village in south-eastern Lesotho where Khotso was born.

Sethuntsa, Four Boy: Selina and Khotso's son, born in 1963, cared for by Bethinja after her mother left Khotso. Towards the end of his father's life, Four Boy appeared to be Khotso's favourite son.

Sethuntsa, Langa Lase-Afrika: Ellen and Khotso's son, and heir to Khotso's estate. Born 1949.

Sethuntsa, MaDlamini (Catherine Qacha): Khotso's senior wife, known as Mhomkhulu (meaning senior mother). Daughter of Chief Qacha, from Qacha's Nek area, Lesotho. She lived in Khotso's house in Mount Frere in the latter part of her husband's life, moving back to his

Dramatis Personae

headquarters, Mount Nelson, in 1992.

Sethuntsa, Mametsi-a-Leoatle: Khotso's daughter.

Sethuntsa, MaMjoli (full name Eunice Nomantombazana Sethuntsa, née Faye): one of Khotso's principal wives, married to him in 1964. Formerly a teacher, living in Mount Frere, where she first met Khotso. Now residing in his house in Msikaba.

Sethuntsa, Masechaba: MaDlamini's daughter, otherwise known as Mary (and sometimes Likae).

Sethuntsa, Mosala Jack: Khotso's younger brother.

Sethuntsa, Nomalizo Grangxa (Bethinja): one of Khotso's best-known wives and foster mother of Four Boy.

Sethuntsa, Patricia: Khotso's eldest daughter, his first wife MaDzanibe's eldest child. Sister of Moticki (born 1924). She remained in her father's household after her mother left Khotso in the early 1920s. Later she became a nurse.

Sethuntsa, Selina (née Sithole): married Khotso in 1964 when she was fifteen and mother of Four Boy. She left Khotso in 1966.

Sethuntsa, Thabo: MaDlamini's grandson and Masechaba's son, now living in Mount Nelson.

Sicwetsha, Fanele: student researcher from a Transkei village near Mount Frere.

Sigcau, Botha: Paramount Chief of Eastern Pondoland, a friend of Khotso's.

Swartz, Chris (J. J.): Lusikiski lawyer, contacted by Khotso during the final weeks of his life. He drew up an inventory of Khotso's estate and was the administrator of the estate.

Tloti, Sylvia: University of Fort Hare Research Assistant from Sterkspruit, Eastern Cape. She lived in Flagstaff, Pondoland, for many years.

Verwoerd, H. F.: Minister of Native Affairs, thereafter prime minister from 1958 to 1966. Known as the architect of apartheid.

Yako, Lala: retired businessman, originally from Duncan Village, East London, who regularly visited Khotso in the 1960s to purchase medicines for good fortune for his business.

Khotso in one of his robes, with diamond earring. (©Independent Newspapers)

Prologue

In 1954, an Eastern Cape journalist wrote of Khotso Sethuntsa: 'So prodigious is his wealth and so strange are the stories told about him that his name is spoken in awe throughout the territories.'[1]

The millionaire herbalist Khotso Sethuntsa has been dead for decades, yet in a sense he lives on. Many elderly people in Pondoland do not want to talk about him because they remain fearful of his powers. Sacrifices to invoke his spirit are still made in the yard of his old headquarters in Lusikisiki, and he continues to visit friends and family members in dreams. After Khotso's death, one of his bodyguards said: 'Khotso knows. He is not around where you can still see him, but he knows. His spirit is here and more powerful than ever.'[2] Khotso's spirit endures, above all in the stories surrounding him, which continue to unfold to this day. Most people simply refer to Khotso Sethuntsa by his first name, Khotso, denoting an individual who moved through his remarkable life surrounded by an aura of mystery and magic that set him apart from all those around him.

At his funeral in 1972, Khotso's spirit seemed very much alive, mocking any attempts to explain exactly who he was and or to unravel some of the riddles surrounding him. Indeed, more than anything else, the speeches at Khotso's burial served to fuel some of the more astounding tales about his capabilities. Rather than resolving any of the mysteries, the addresses delivered by each of the speakers tended to reinforce uncertainty about him.

'Who was he?' asked the master of ceremonies, C. M. Mancotywa, the principal of St Andrews Secondary School in Lusikisiki, the Transkei town in which Khotso had lived for the last twelve years of his life. The question resonated throughout the funeral, as Mancotywa himself, and speaker after speaker who followed him, declared themselves mystified by Khotso's enigmatic, idiosyncratic character and the extraordinary twists and turns of his life.

Mancotywa described Khotso as a magnetic personality who drew many different people to him from nearly all walks of life, from inside and outside Africa.[3] The rural poor, traditional healers and diviners, Broederbonders, the heads of prominent African churches, white spiritualists, scientists, philosophers, tourists, treasure hunters and entrepreneurs: these were only some of the people who came thronging to his mansions. Most of all, however, visitors came to Khotso not as sightseers but as supplicants, believing that he somehow had access to astonishing powers that could work miracles in their lives. At the same time he was feared, precisely because people believed so profoundly in his supernatural capabilities. There are countless tales of the terror and calamity that Khotso visited on the lives of those who disobeyed or displeased him.

Khotso remains an enigma: charismatic, controversial and contradictory. He was an illiterate man with a limited command of English who became a millionaire, rising to the zenith of his wealth and influence during the apartheid era, the origins of his fortune and the exact nature of his powers surrounded in mystery. Decades after his death, the riddles surrounding Khotso Sethuntsa persist. This is perhaps one reason why Khotso, who attained such fame in the course of his career and shaped the lives of so many others in dramatic ways, still appears to belong to the shifting, hazy terrain of legend, rather than historical records.

In his funeral oration, Mancotywa spoke of one unanswered question that continues to hover, fascinatingly unresolved, whenever Khotso's name is invoked today. 'Khotso may be a puzzling character to many of us and the secret of his wealth will not be known, but his wealth was achieved probably not only through herbs, but through a secret he died with.'[4]

Stories abounded of the cellars under Khotso's houses crammed with coins, banknotes and diamonds. But despite the way he loved publicly flaunting his wealth, Khotso believed that his fortune was better protected if he retained secrecy around its origins. Some said that this was also because his wealth had been acquired through dark and dangerous means that Khotso preferred to keep undisclosed.

Time and time again, accounts of the strange occurrences that took place in Khotso's presence have been recounted, generating another series of questions in their turn. According to many of these accounts, Khotso was a remarkable worker of wizardry. Was he really a wielder of the mighty magic that even some of the most pragmatic of his friends and followers remain convinced he was? Or was his empire based on outrageous fabrications, unscrupulous manipulation of human weakness and shameless hucksterism?

Stories and riddles, then, are part of Khotso, the man of mystery and magic about whom so much has been told and so little has been written, apart from newspaper and magazine articles, often sensationalistic, dealing for the most part with episodes from the latter period of his life. Khotso loved stories, and he offered different versions of his life history to eager listeners while increasingly fabulous accounts of his wealth and powers arose around him. His history comes to us mainly in the form of tales – some of them even verifiably true – and it is into this labyrinth of narrative that we must venture if we wish to follow the path of his extraordinary career. Somewhere out there, within all the tales, Khotso Sethuntsa lives on.

Let us begin at the time when such stories were at their height.

It is February 1970, and a bus packed with tourists is making its way through the Transkei heat to a large blue and white house on the outskirts of Lusikisiki. The occupants of the bus chatter excitedly, even nervously, as they draw closer to an ornate, sprawling mansion surrounded by strange statuary. They have almost reached their destination: a place known as Mount Nelson, the headquarters of the person said to be one of the greatest workers of magic in southern Africa, the medicine man Khotso Sethuntsa. Some of the tourists are South Africans; others come from the United States. Khotso's fame has spread far.

Not far behind the bus, a car is also heading towards Khotso's house, carrying two journalists and a photographer. The Sunday newspaper for which they work has commissioned them to produce an article about Khotso's marvellous medicines, such as his elixir of life, which enabled him to return from the dead twice: in 1924 and then again in 1956. Or so Khotso has claimed. Then, there is his ever-popular remedy, *ibangalala*[5], the means by which men can soar to seemingly superhuman heights of virility and sexual prowess. Khotso declares that he himself is living proof that ibangalala works. He has boasted that he has hundreds of children and twenty-three wives. Although he says that he is now in his nineties, he has even more wives in the offing and an ever-expanding circle of concubines.

Above all, however, the journalists are interested in Khotso's special medicine for wealth and good fortune. It is widely said that many successful Transkei businessmen went to Khotso for this, one journalist observes. The other journalist is quick to remark that it is not only Africans who have made use of this medicine. There are a number of white entrepreneurs who owe their prosperity to Khotso too. For instance, in King William's Town, where he lives, there is one white businessman whose bottle store took a striking turn for the better after he visited Khotso. His brother, who works on a sugar cane plantation near Port Shepstone, knows of one white mechanic on the farm who sought help from Khotso. Shortly after he returned from Mount Nelson, he was promoted to foreman and then to assistant manager.

A fortress of a place, Khotso's property is ringed with a high fence, while his men stand guard at the imposing gates. Not everyone is permitted to pass through the gateway into Khotso's kingdom, yet as the bus draws to a standstill, the great gates, with the giant gold letter *K* in the centre of each of them, are dragged back. The tourists disembark and stream through, into a world the likes of which they have never seen before.

Their eyes are dazzled by the blaze of colours. The house and its numerous outbuildings are painted bright blue, with the outlines of bricks sharply delineated in white. Large panes of stained glass gleam jewel-like in the windows. The buildings and the yard are dotted with a multitude of statuettes, picked out in bold enamel paintwork. The first-time visitors to Mount Nelson do not realise that, inside the house, there is a riot of gaudy colour and clutter on a less imposing but equally grandiose scale.

It is the statues in particular to which the eyes of the many visitors are drawn. Wherever they turn, they find statues watching them, lined along verandas, guarding doorways, or perched on walls or the tops of pillars. The wild diversity of subject matter and the startling juxtapositions give Khotso's sculpture collection a weirdly compelling quality.

In one way or another, most of Khotso's statues embody power. There are mighty beasts: a concrete menagerie consisting of lions, leopards and elephants files away towards some of the outbuildings. The lions, regal beasts on sentry duty for Khotso, are accorded prime positions near the front door and on the gateway. Eagles stand sentinel on rooftops and walls. Busts of people of power are positioned one behind the other on the steps leading up to the front door. These include Khotso's ancestors, his father and his grandfather. But, above all, there is statue after statue of a mighty ruler and leader to whom Khotso is drawn: Paul Kruger, transformed into the household god of Mount Nelson. He perches on the tops of walls and pillars alongside the eagles, rests on a special plinth or waits near the front door to scrutinise Khotso's visitors with his solemn eyes.

Some of the tourists have come to Mount Nelson because they have read about Khotso in newspapers and magazines. Many of them are enticed by one particular feature that the newspapers return to time and time again: the Kruger connection. It is said that Khotso's parents worked for Paul Kruger and his wife, and Khotso maintains that his name was chosen for him by Oom Paul himself. Khotso often claims that, since his adulthood, he has been in regular contact with the spirit of the deceased president. He likes hinting that through his special bond with Kruger he may have been led to the long-lost Kruger millions. This leaves many speculating that his luxury cars, numerous farms and peculiar palatial dwellings may have been funded by the treasury of the old South African Republic.

The people Khotso calls Paul Kruger's children are present too. One of the visitors peers at a statue in surprise. He is staring at the heavy visage of Hendrik Verwoerd, as stony-faced as he had been in life, with his small, sinister smile. Verwoerd himself is not smiling any more, not where he is now. He has been dead for more than three years. Not everyone is startled to meet Verwoerd in Khotso's yard, however. It is no secret that Verwoerd had visited Khotso.[6] The politician who would become known as the architect of apartheid would travel to the man his people regarded as a 'witchdoctor' to obtain medicine for political power, the guide tells the tourists.

Verwoerd is accompanied by other Afrikaner prime ministers, a brigade of Broederbonders arrayed around the house, as if to watch over it. One especially noticeable feature of the yard, apart from the many watchful Paul Krugers, is a shining black Cadillac, which is being scrupulously polished by one of Khotso's minions. As a backdrop, there is a garage filled with a long row of vehicles. The tourists glimpse the large sleek shapes of a Chevrolet, a Dodge, a Pontiac and a Ford, so glossy and well cared for that, at a distance, they all appear brand new.

The tourists' guide and interpreter comes from the area and has visited Mount Nelson before for reasons of his own, so he knows well how much Khotso's cars mean to him. His black Cadillac is one of his most prized possessions, because it is a symbol of all that Khotso has managed to achieve in life. Its imposing, gleaming shape is a testament to the lustre that surrounds the very name of Khotso. When people in the Transkei and East Griqualand see this vehicle gliding by, they know that a great presence is passing before them.

One of the journalists is scrutinising the Cadillac and notices that the car's windows are dark-tinted. So Khotso travels closed off from the public gaze by smoked glass, just as he conceals himself behind impenetrable secrets and riddles.

The tourists are outnumbered by a crowd of Khotso's customers, some on edge, others filled with anticipation, but all eager for their encounter with the great *inyanga* endowed with the ability to bestow health or wealth and happiness on them. More customers come thronging in as the tourists wait. Some of the tourists, especially the white South Africans, feel that this is surely a testament to the deep-seated nature of black superstition. They have merely come to goggle at the famous 'witchdoctor'. One of the tourists nudges the guide and asks him to find out why some of the people have come to see Khotso. The guide approaches the crowd and begins addressing individuals. The first two people he addresses respond effusively, others tersely, while some appear evasive. He returns to the tourists and points to the woman and the man to whom he first spoke:

> She – that one there – says that the white madam she works for has been ill for a very long time. So she asked this person to go to Doctor Khotso for her, saying that the white doctors hadn't been able to find a cure for her, but she was sure that he would. And that man just next to her, he's a farm worker and a lot of animals have been stolen from the farm. So the farmer has asked him to come here to get Khotso's special medicine to stop stock thefts. He said that he knew that once people heard he'd got muti from Khotso, no one would dare steal anything from him.

While the tourists continue to peer around, the customers shift and murmur to one another. The whispered words '*zinyoka zikaKhotso*' hang in the air: Khotso's magical snakes, invisible, yet present in the imaginations of so many of the people clustered in the yard. The thought of these creatures strikes fear deep into those who venture into Mount Nelson; yet it is these very same serpents that have lured many into Khotso's kingdom. It is, after all, through the terrifying *ukuthwala* ordeals that involve encounters with Khotso's great snake that the very greatest wealth can be obtained. The most powerful of these trials take place in Khotso's special pools in the Mzintlava River, which flows past his weirdly imposing white house on the outskirts of Kokstad. Deep beneath these dark waters, Khotso's snakes lurk, people say.

There will always be those who simply want to gaze at the man who can bend to his will the *inkanyamba*, the giant storm snake that whips through the sky. Even in his mid-twenties, he was able to turn it against the white farmer who had punished him. Other, fantastically hybrid snakes surround Khotso, such as the creature with a serpentine body and a horse's head that he sends out at night after his enemies. Some of the customers, terrified as they are by the thought of such creatures, are gripped so tightly by curiosity that they are overwhelmingly eager to catch a glimpse of them.

A group of women appear, all wearing identical high-necked, full-skirted orange gowns. They are Khotso's wives. Their antiquated orange dresses stand out strikingly against the blue and white paintwork: a deliberate colour choice on Khotso's part, so that he can display the colours of the old South African flag. Under the remote control of an unseen presence deep inside the house, the women line up in a row in front of the tourists and journalists and then begin singing monotonously and continually, as if to lull visitors into a dreamlike daze. However, some members of their audience feel that they are already in this state.

Men in white glide past. Their heads are clean-shaven, polished to a mahogany sheen and encircled with bands of white beadwork. Khotso's fondness for smooth, immaculate surfaces is not restricted only to the exteriors of his cars. The white-clad men are Khotso's disciples, his trainee herbalists. They have come to him to acquire a working knowledge of plants and animal and mineral substances and their uses, seeking to become skilled not only in the art of healing but also in the ability to prepare medicines that will bring about much else, such as protection, strength, love, good fortune and success. Because of their special, privileged relationship to the person for whom everyone is waiting, these men appear to be lifted above the frenetic and curious crowd.

Then, like underwater currents shifting, the air of serenity and detachment that the white-clad disciples and the choir of orange-gowned wives brought into the yard with them begins ebbing, as the sound of drumming begins and a band of men surge, shouting and whistling, into the yard.

Beneath their great horned and plumed headdresses, these men are arrayed in an odd hybrid combination of commonplace modern garments and traditional accessories. They are clad in old faded shirts and shorts, over which they sport beads and fur armbands, buskins and kilts. Their shields are leopard-spotted or bear the face of a roaring lion: the creatures of which Khotso approves. The men carry themselves proudly, for they are about to pay tribute to the great Khotso Sethuntsa himself. In the centre of the yard, they launch into a dance that, through its forcefulness, evokes some of the qualities of the personage in whose honour they perform.

There is a sudden, slight movement within the main building. A figure has been sitting inside, half hidden, watching the dancing through one of the windows. This onlooker has been so still that the people in the yard notice his presence only as he starts slipping away into the cavernous depths of the house. For a moment, the crowd falls silent. Then there is a drum roll and the warriors leap high into the air before prostrating themselves in the dust of the yard, shouting the royal salute: *'Bayete!'* The wives fall silent and the disciples in white incline themselves in the direction of the front door, soundlessly clapping their hands. The customers press forward eagerly. The master of the house is about to appear.

But before we see Khotso at the height of his fame, let us turn back, to the place from which he began. Otherwise, like many of the first-time visitors to Mount Nelson, we may emerge from our encounter feeling as if we have been left with a kaleidoscopic collection of fantastical fragmented impressions. Let us travel back in time to the years just before the turn of the nineteenth century. We must then journey across the verdant, undulating Pondoland terrain, the high, exposed plains of East Griqualand and the mountain wall that sets the rock-hewn heart of southern Africa apart from the hills and plains that surround it. Here, in the soaring, storm-sculpted rockscapes of south-eastern Lesotho, at the feet of some of the greatest mountains and beside one of the mightiest rivers in southern Africa, Khotso's story begins.

Part One
1898–1932

Chapter 1

In the Land of the Red Snow

January 7, 1898: the year of the red snow. Strange things were possible in the year Khotso Rapitso Sethuntsa was born. Or so Khotso liked to tell those who asked him about his birth.[1] Unlike many of the astounding stories that he spread about himself, a rational explanation is possible for red snow. The tawny dust devils spiralling upwards mingle with flakes swirling down from the icy Malutis, thousands of metres up, in a starkly spectacular mountain realm, where the high peaks were citadels and sanctuaries for the heroic chiefs Moshoeshoe and Moorosi, from whom Khotso was descended. At any rate, this was a kinship that he liked to claim.

The elderly people in the village deep in the Maluti Mountains in Lesotho where Khotso was born do not know whether there was red snow in 1898.[2] They have heard stories of it from long ago but have never seen it themselves. Yet Khotso's tale of the strangely coloured snow that fell in the year of his birth has an appropriate ring to it. Firstly, red snow represents a combination of diametrically opposed substances: one coloured by the summer earth, the other a pale emanation from the winter sky. Also, with hindsight it could be viewed as symbolic, as if it heralded the arrival of someone who would thrive on paradoxes and contradictions. The unexpected presence of dust within snow calls to mind Khotso's surname: Sethuntsa, meaning 'dust raised up' in Sotho.

Khotso's name itself has a contradictory quality. His first name means 'peace' in Sotho, but his surname carries with it the suggestion of turbulence. Khotso was indeed a human whirlwind, a force of concentrated energy sweeping through the white farming communities of East Griqualand and the towns and villages of Pondoland, creating amazement and disruption, and turning conventional preconceptions upside down. And he had control over the elements: Khotso's fame began with the tale of the tornado that he called up to wreak havoc on the farm of the man who had dismissed him from his employment.

Lesotho, the country in which red snow has fallen, Khotso's ancestral land, is a country where the scenery is as extreme and overwhelming as the weather. The earth tilts and lists like a ship in a tempest, trying to break free from gravity and become one with the sky. The hills rise like waves to shatter in piles of broken rock and boulders against the mountainsides. From Quthing to Qacha's Nek – the route which Khotso's mother may have followed as she journeyed south-west to south-east across Lesotho, from her father's homestead near Herschel, just west of the Lesotho border, to her husband's village deep in the Malutis – the road rides the mountains like a crazy switchback, climbing up and up until the altitude and the kilometres of empty air below leave one giddy, and then plunging sharply down towards the faraway floors of valleys and canyons. No wonder the weather is so wild when the sky is constantly disrupted by the mountains, fracturing the horizon with their peaks like twisted knife blades, surreal fragmented castles for the cannibal giants of Sotho and Phuthi tales or huge shrouded heads leaning into the tempests. The workers of the most dangerous magic in Lesotho can turn the storms to work their will. Beware of angering the mountain magicians, people say, for they can hurl lightning at you.

The rivers are as weird and perilous as the weather. There are the great rivers, churning earth-red, that wind themselves around the feet of the Malutis, carving out valleys and floodplains on their way downhill into South Africa. The foremost of these is the Senqu (known as the Orange outside Lesotho), which draws the country's major rivers into it. At various points, the Senqu becomes one of Lesotho's many hidden rivers.[3] Tumultuous and treacherous, these snake their way far, far below the jagged convolutions of the mountainous terrain. These are hazardous places, not for bathing or washing, with flood-smoothed cliffs, crevices and boulders, where even the sure-footed can slip. The safest time to explore such rivers is during the arid winter season. But even then the deepest pools do not dry up. Snakes and leguans live there; also, it is rumoured, in the *ledumela*, the caves under the waters, dwell the river beings *mamolapo* and *khanyapa*. Many of Khotso's occult powers were connected in some way or another to water. It might be fitting that he should have come from a country of rivers that are as mysterious and dangerous as they are powerful.

Khotso was born in the village of Ha Ramokakatlela in south-eastern Lesotho, a child of the turn of the century, although at the height of his fame he preferred people to think that he had been born twenty years earlier. Ha Ramokakatlela lies high in the Malutis, a journey of many hours into the mountains north of Qacha's Nek. There are no roads that lead all the way to the village, so it can be accessed only by foot or on horseback. Even today it remains remote, a place where the villagers could be living their lives in much the same way that the inhabitants did when the village was founded. Many Lesotho mountain villages are situated in spectacular surroundings, but Ha Ramokakatlela must surely lie in one of the most striking settings of all. From the summit of the pass over which the track to the village trails, you gaze across at a panorama of the high peaks of the Malutis, their slopes silvered with snow in winter, then down at the village with its traditional rondavels, their curving walls constructed from tightly packed, rough-hewn yellowish mountain stone. Peach trees grow around the homesteads and in clusters along the watercourses, while poplars, alien trees adept at endurance in the highest, coldest parts of southern Africa, shiver their leaves in the winds that sweep off the summits. The villagers subsist for the most part by cultivating whatever is hardy enough to survive the altitude, poor soil and exposure to the unpredictable icy weather of the

Ha Ramokakatlela. The Senqu flows below the village, hidden in a canyon.

heights. The nights are so pure and cold and the village so high in the mountains that sometimes it seems as if one might be able to stretch out a hand into the blackness and touch the large bright stars hanging just above.

Far below the village the Senqu flows, cutting canyons through the landscape. Wherever possible, Khotso chose to live near water and, appropriately enough, he began his life near one of the greatest rivers in southern Africa. There are caves and rock shelters above the river where San people lived – and it was to these caves near his birthplace, the stories go, that the boy Khotso was drawn.

One place that Khotso certainly visited was the Duma-Duma cave,[4] on the path to Ha Ramokakatlela, near the village of Melikane. The walls of the cave are adorned with fading rock art of people and creatures, some of which do not quite belong to the familiar physical world, partly because their delicate, subtle quality imbues them with a sense of the mysterious. Although the San no longer frequent the cave, the place still holds mystical significance and local *dingaka*, traditional

Sotho doctors, still carry out rituals there, as is the case with many other San caves in the Malutis and the Drakensberg.[5] A mournful ghost is said to call out to travellers passing the Duma-Duma cave, asking them if they are going in one direction, to Ha Ramokakatlela where there will be feasting when the initiates return to the village as men, or in the other direction, to the St Francis Catholic Mission where the peaches are sweet. The ghost cannot journey to either of these places to attend the feasts or eat the fruit; it is trapped in the cave. One elderly man, a relative of Khotso's who still lives in Ha Ramokakatlela, described how, when Khotso visited the village, he would sometimes accompany him on the path from the Tsoelike River to Ha Ramokakatlela. Khotso would stop at the cave, go in, look around, then continue on his way.

Turn to a map of Lesotho and trace the course of the Senqu on its journey west through the Malutis, from Qacha's Nek to Telle Bridge, just beyond Quthing, where the river enters South Africa. The valley formed by the path of the Senqu not only contains some of the most dramatic scenery in southern Africa, but was once the home of many San communities. As late as the 1920s, when Khotso would already have been an adult, the San were still carrying out their rituals in rock shelters and caves along the Senqu. Now all that remains are the paintings in the rock shelters and the clicks in the names – Qacha, Quthing and the Senqu itself – that mark the south-westward trajectory of the river through Lesotho. But some people in the Qacha region believe that the fact that Khotso was born deep in the mountains, in the heart of a region that had once belonged to the San, gave him access to the elusive San themselves and the unique supernatural expertise they possessed.

Visit Ha Ramokakatlela today and you will still find members of the Sethuntsa family. Some old people remember Khotso as a young man who set off over the mountains towards great fame in another land, while for others it is almost as if he has not completely left the village. Not only does he live on in certain people's memories, but some individuals say that he continues to visit them in dreams. Khotso has been dead for decades, but praise songs in his honour remain alive in Ha

Oldest remaining members of Khotso's family in Ha Ramokakatlela. Khotso's niece Lefu Ma-Thabo Motumi in centre foreground.

Ramokakatlela. One of them begins in this way:

Tau ea lomo sa phuthing
Rea u lumisa morena.
Mahla a hlahileng Khotso
Terene tsa mathatha Maholimong.
Da nteka-tekane, phakisa kapele
Phakisa ka pele u eo bolela
u bolelle bo-Motumi
nore ka lapeng ho hlahile Mohale.

Loosely translated, the meaning is as follows:

The lion from Phuthing hill
we salute you, king.
The day Khotso was born
trains raced in heaven.
Messenger, hurry up,
hurry up and report,
report to Motumi
that a warrior is born.

Khotso's father, Motumi Ramokakatlela, founded Ha Ramokakatlela. The prefix *Ha*, which forms part of the names of many villages in Lesotho, simply denotes 'the place of'. Motumi was born around 1850 in the village of Ndawane, in the Underberg area in what was then Natal, in the foothills of the Drakensberg. During the late nineteenth century he crossed over the mountains deep into the Malutis, to found the village that bears his name. 'They were running away from some wars that were being fought at the time,' said Khotso's niece Lefu Ma-Thabo Motumi. Her bright, alert face and her upright carriage belie the fact that she is one of the oldest inhabitants of the village. Her name Lefu, meaning 'death', was bestowed on her because she was born in 1919, the year Motumi died.

Khotso belonged to the Phuthi, the people of the blue duiker, or *phuthi*. In the above song, the word *Phuthing*, meaning 'the place where the Phuthi live', denotes Khotso's origins. Today, the Phuthi live in the mountain valleys of southern Lesotho and in adjacent regions in South Africa, such as Herschel, Mount Fletcher and Maluti, near the Lesotho border. Their ancestors moved from the present-day Mpumalanga–Swaziland region into KwaZulu-Natal and from there into Lesotho in the sixteenth and seventeenth centuries.[6] Their language, primarily Xhosa with a strong Sotho flavour, is spoken today in Lesotho and, to a limited extent, in the northern Transkei.[7]

As they drew higher and higher into the mountains, the Phuthi established a connection with the San peoples. The Phuthi became intermingled with the San over the centuries, and Phuthi beliefs became permeated by the spiritual world of the San – a point of some significance when we consider some of the features of the supernatural that Khotso claimed to be able to manipulate. Like the San, the Phuthi are a very old, long-standing southern African people. Their language is ancient too, comparable to the primordial language from which Sotho and the Nguni languages (such as Xhosa and Zulu) arose. The Phuthi are not easy to categorise. Although their connectedness to Lesotho goes back over several centuries, they are not completely Sotho, just as they are not Xhosa, although in some areas they have lived as part of Xhosa-speaking communities for generations. The Phuthi are relatively few and live dispersed over some of the more remote regions of South Africa and Lesotho. Khotso's Phuthi identity, then, formed an integral part of the rare and elusive quality that surrounded him. Just like the people to whom he belonged, there was something separate and indefinable about him.[8]

Khotso's Phuthi roots cast light on certain aspects of his life, partly because he was a person of the borderlands. He and his family moved back and forth between Lesotho, KwaZulu-Natal and the Eastern Cape frontier region as they made their way in life. But he inhabited another kind of border area too, a realm in which, many believe, the supernatural and the everyday flow into one another. Others who knew him maintained that he shifted so often between tall tales and the truth, fabrication and reality, that he and his life history could never be clearly situated within one or another of these territories. For these reasons, Khotso remained an outsider throughout his life, never completely at one with the communities he inhabited: among them, yet clearly not of them.[9]

There is a well-known figure in African tales who occupies precisely this type of position: the trickster who takes on many forms, both human and animal, yet possesses certain essential qualities. In a study of South African oral literature, Harold Scheub emphasised that the trickster 'is always on the boundaries, the periphery'. A zone of this nature suits the trickster well, Scheub continues, because it helps the trickster go about his or her sly and cunning business. A paradoxical being of the borderlands, he or she cannot be contained, controlled or pinned down, as would be the case with Khotso.[10] Khotso would reside in various places, but as an adult he would be most at home in the country of story. A real-life trickster, in his later life it would seem as if he had stepped out of the world of fable, to draw a diversity of individuals back into his domain with him.

From childhood onwards, Khotso went his own way. He was a lively, mischievous child, but every now and then, those who knew about his life during that period maintained, there were indications that there was something different, even mysterious about him. When Khotso was about ten, he would sometimes disappear for days on end. No one knew where he had gone. When the boy was questioned afterwards, he'd say that he didn't know what had been happening to him, but he hadn't felt cold, frightened or hungry. Even at that early stage of his life, the signs that Khotso would one day deliberately set himself apart from others were already there.

'As a child, Khotso had strange habits, because he refused to eat with the other children,' said one old man who has spent his life in Ha Ramokakatlela. 'When Khotso grew up and returned to the village, he still continued with that: he would eat a goat alone, and then only slaughter another one for his mother after he had had his fill.'

In the region in which Khotso was born and in the communities through which he moved as an adult, traditional beliefs in the supernatural and spiritual continued to exercise sway, juxtaposed or intermingled as they were with Christianity. While generalisations inevitably have their limitations, since southern African beliefs are varied, fluid and mutable, a few points can be made about certain aspects of the sacred and the paranormal in the areas that Khotso knew.

For Khotso's people, as for the Sotho- and Xhosa-speaking groupings around him, the dead remain present among the living, as the ancestors, omniscient guides and guardians, and protectors of an orderly, ethical system.[11] The ancestral spirits watch over their descendants, bestowing goodness and blessings when they respect them and live according to their ways. But the ancestors can withdraw their protection, allowing illness, suffering or misfortune to descend on those who displease them by not carrying out their wishes or by deviating from the moral edicts and codes of conduct for which they stand.

The presence of spiritual forces, in the form of the ancestors above all, in the midst of ordinary life is a key aspect of traditional world-views of the southern African peoples among whom Khotso spent his life. The otherworldly is believed to flow through physical actuality in the same way that rivers and streams wend their way through dry land. Together, they form a whole. Khotso would draw on this conception of reality as he sought ways of advancing himself in his career as a medicine man, and when he depicted himself as a physical person with extraordinary, even paranormal capabilities.

At this point, we could return to water, no longer as a metaphor, but in terms of the way in which it pervades the belief systems of southern African peoples: both as a liminal zone within which the otherworldly and physical intermingle, and also as a gateway into another dimension. Water is perceived as an element that is not only necessary for physical sustenance, but is also believed to be imbued with spiritual potency. Religious rituals take place beside water, and some of the most ancient known sacred ceremonies have been conducted to invoke rain. Among many southern African peoples, water plays a vital role in the training of spiritual healers and diviners. The initiation of a Xhosa *igqirha*, for example, is sometimes termed *ukuthwetyula* (to be called under the river) and it involves a real or symbolic submersion in water. As we shall see, Khotso would draw on these hallowed associations of water, bending them to his own purposes. He was not an igqirha or sangoma, and some of the magical presences and forces with which he would become associated were very different from the sources of deep spiritual power to which these practitioners were granted access. Yet Khotso would present himself as one comparable to such specialised, chosen and consecrated individuals, by claiming to be able to descend under the water to enhance his spiritual energies and by carrying out riverside rituals.

It is also believed that rivers and deep pools provide dwelling places for beings and creatures of mystical potency. Xhosa-speaking peoples, for instance, make mention of *abantu bomlambo*, 'the people of the river', spiritual personages sometimes associated with the ancestors, who live in the dry world at the bottom of pools.[12] There is another, contrasting dimension to water. This element is also inhabited by menacing paranormal presences, many of which are serpentine. A number of these would become important in Khotso's career.

A whole world of watery knowledge comes along with the San:

rain-making magic, ancient beliefs in the water people and mystical serpent-like beings associated with water. Fantastical hybrid forms, often associated with water, are painted in caves in the Drakensberg and the Malutis. Sometimes they have horns or horses' heads, such as the rain snakes invoked in times of drought. There was a great deal of cross-cultural exchange and osmosis of ideas, stretching over centuries, between the San and their Zulu-, Xhosa- and Sotho-speaking neighbours. In Xhosa-speaking communities, for instance, the abantu bomlambo and the inkanyamba (the tornado spirit that takes the form of a snake, known as the khanyapa in Sotho) were adopted initially from the San, but were altered by the different cultural and spiritual contexts of the groupings that have taken them up.[13]

In Khotso's life, unseen, mysterious presences and sources of power would become interconnected with various features of the landscapes he knew. At the outset, the region in which he spent his formative years played its part in shaping certain directions his life would follow. The Drakensberg, with their surreal, soaring vistas of spears, spires and towers, their moods and shades constantly and unpredictably shifting, seem to be reaching up from the physical world into a sphere beyond. In Zulu these mountains are known as the *uKhahlamba*, or 'barrier of spears', and in Afrikaans as the Drakensberg, meaning 'dragon mountains'. These names are suggestive of the forbidding, mystical qualities of the range. On entering the wildness and isolation of the Malutis, the name given to the mountains of Lesotho, this impression is enhanced. It is appropriate that some of the tales dealing with Khotso's early encounters with supernatural forces should have taken place in this area.

It also appears fitting that some of the stories about the young Khotso should be connected to the caves where the San once lived, in the vicinity of Ha Ramokakatlela and the Senqu. Some people in the Qacha's Nek area say that when Khotso was a boy he had a recurrent dream in which he saw himself in these caves, surrounded by rock art depicting states of being in which the physical and paranormal are intertwined, with the broad Senqu flowing below him. It is said that later he found his way to the caves, where he met the San themselves.

'As a herdboy, it was said that at times he would just disappear for some days. When he came back and was asked where he had been, he used to report that he had been taken by *barwa* [bushmen]. He used to meet these *barwa* because Ramokakatlela lies above the Senqu and just near the river there are big caves. So he used to go there and stay with *barwa* there,' said one elderly man in Qacha's Nek. A member of the tourism association in the town, he is interested in the history of his area and he has acquired insights into the San communities who used to live in south-eastern Lesotho. He is also intrigued by the stories he has heard concerning Khotso's childhood encounters with the San, although he only knew Khotso when he was an adult.

Once, this elderly man related, Khotso vanished for some time, and when he returned he claimed that he had been undergoing special training with the San and that they had initiated him into some of their secrets. He even showed incisions to prove this. Later in his life, Khotso became an expert hunter. Some ascribed his prowess in this area to the San, who are famous for their hunting abilities. 'I definitely think they did pass some powers on to him because *ba ile ba mophatsa mmele kaofela* [they had made small incisions all over his body],' this informant said. 'That is a sign that they did that to him.'

According to family members and old family friends in Ha Ramokakatlela, Khotso's initiation into manhood took place in the Malutis, in the vicinity of his home village. San rock art expert Frans Prins observed that Khotso could have had a San initiation master, since the Sotho and Phuthi did make use of the skills of the San in their initiation schools. During his initiation period, the San doctor would have made incisions in Khotso's face into which a herbal medicine called *intelezi* would have been rubbed to ward off evil. Khotso himself, of course, might in later life have been keen to spread the story of his private, childhood encounters with San magic, since the abilities of the San to communicate with and even manipulate mystical forces were

Ha Ramokakatlela, with the Malutis in the background.

renowned in Lesotho and South Africa. For some who knew Khotso or who later came to hear of his fame, it could have been appropriate that the first people, widely perceived as the repositories of ancient spiritual wisdom, should have been the very first of all to realise that Khotso was no ordinary person. In any case, it is probable that Khotso did meet the San as a child when he was alone, herding animals around the caves and rock shelters above the Senqu. If, as the stories say, Khotso did indeed spend time with the San in his youth, it is likely that his affinity to water and the potent snake-like beings inhabiting it, as a source of mystical power, was strengthened by his contact with them.

Khotso's mother, Motumi's second wife, was called Mokholitsoane, otherwise known as Ma-Khotso, after her eldest child. Her name, meaning 'lizard' in Sotho, has a certain aptness to it, bearing in mind the role the reptilian world, in the form of supernatural serpents, would come to play in her son's life.

Khotso's affiliation to water, especially in the form of rivers, is expressed in one of his favourite songs. As MaMjoli Sethuntsa, one of Khotso's later wives, related:

You know that all traditional doctors have specific songs that they sing when they want to invoke the spirits or are faced with difficult situations. My husband's favourite was 'Nonkala [The Crab]':

Uyadidiyel'unonkala;
Uyadidiyel'unonkala ngasemlanjeni!
Wenza ngabom'unonkala;
Wenza ngabom'unonkala ngasemlanjeni!

Loosely translated, this means:

The crab is staggering sideways;
The crab is staggering sideways near the river!
The crab is doing this on purpose;
The crab is doing this on purpose near the river!

Amphibious creatures such as crabs have a significance in supernatural terms, moving as they do between the underwater realm of spiritual forces and everyday life. Khotso liked to create the impression that, just like a crab, he moved back and forth between these two worlds. And like a crab, he slid 'sideways', his real intentions and the truth underlying his words and actions disconcertingly oblique.

One such instance of the disparity between words and reality is apparent in Khotso's apparently factual account of his Phuthi antecedents. He let it be known that he traced his lineage back to one of the most famous figures in the history of Lesotho: Moorosi, born in 1795, paramount chief of the Phuthi, and partly of San descent.

In 1879, one of Moorosi's sons was convicted of horse theft. The prison in which he was incarcerated was broken into and he escaped. When the British discovered that Moorosi himself had engineered the jailbreak, they mounted an expedition against him, confident they would be able to enforce their authority over him speedily, only to discover their mistake. Moorosi had miscalculated too: he had hoped that the other Lesotho peoples, rendered apprehensive by the threat of an impending policy of general disarmament, would be prepared to join the Phuthi in their rebellion. A year later, the Gun War would commence, but this would be too late for Moorosi and his people. In

1879, the Phuthi were on their own. Moorosi, by then in his eighties, with approximately four hundred of his troops, was entrenched on a mountaintop in the southern Malutis that now bears his name. He had fortified its precipitous slopes 'with a skill that caused the astonishment and despair of his adversaries'.[14]

Moorosi and his men defended the mountaintop from March until November 1879. Besieged by the British troops, bombarded by their artillery – the blackened, twisted remains of shells still litter the mountainside – and reduced at one point to eating the hides of oxen, the Phuthi refused to surrender. Moorosi declared that he and his mountain were one, and he would rather die fighting. 'You talk of peace,' he said, 'yes, peace for the Whites, but not for my people; you would not even let me die in my country, where I wish to end my days.' Finally, while a feigned attack was taking place, the British troops succeeded in reaching the summit of the mountain, using extension ladders to scale the cliffs and precipices. Moorosi and most of his men were massacred and the old chief's head was borne off to King William's Town as a regimental trophy.[15] Decimated by the rebellion, the Phuthi scattered, in many cases fleeing to remote mountainous areas. Every year, the Phuthi gather on Mount Moorosi to honour their great chief who lost his life defending his mountain and his people.

Near the summit of Mount Moorosi there is a rock face on which a number of names have been carved, including those of British soldiers who besieged the mountain as well as clumsier scrawls left by modern tourists. But one name is of particular interest as far as Khotso's own story is concerned. Almost obscured by the welter of graffiti surrounding it, the name *Paul Kruger* appears, along with a date, *20 November 1879*, the date of Moorosi's death. It is a striking coincidence that the name of the person who came to feature prominently in the stories surrounding Khotso should appear on the very mountain that had been defended by the man Khotso claimed as his ancestor.

Kruger had visited parts of Lesotho. In his memoirs, he described how in the 1850s he climbed Thaba Bosiu, Moshoeshoe's mountain stronghold, in order to negotiate a peace between that leader and the government of what was then the Orange Free State.[16] But at no point in his autobiography did he mention ascending Mount Moorosi on the very day that his opponents, the British, defeated the Phuthi chief who had risen up against them. David Ambrose, from the University of Lesotho, has maintained that Kruger's signature on Mount Moorosi may be a forgery.[17] However, Khotso may have cared little whether Kruger's signature was authentic. In his adulthood, Khotso would seek a means to draw two mighty leaders, Moorosi and Kruger, into his own personal legend. Perhaps he found it fitting that the two individuals that he depicted as his ancestors, the one in a physical and the other in a spiritual sense, were in proximity to one another on the mountain that had become special to his people.

To begin to grasp possible reasons why Khotso sought to establish ties with Kruger we will have to wait until the 1950s, when history has begun to close, like a fist, around the black inhabitants of South Africa.

Chapter 2
Into Nomansland

While we know some basic facts concerning Khotso's mother's life during his childhood and early manhood, his father remains a more elusive presence. Motumi's nephew, the same man who accompanied Khotso as he walked over the mountains on his visits to Ha Ramokakatlela, said his uncle travelled round the mountain villages, selling home-made bracelets and grain baskets. He also sold traditional herbal remedies in Lesotho, and he was a diviner, who threw bones to predict the course of events. He was, however, not as well known or as powerful as his son. Khotso's father died long before his son became one of the most famous medicine men in southern Africa.

Khotso spent the early years of his life in and around Ha Ramokakatlela. But while Lesotho has much to feed the spirit and the imagination, there is little to be had in the way of material sustenance in the mountain villages. As was the case with many southern African families, economic need drove Khotso's parents apart. His mother, Mokholitsoane, had three other children in addition to Khotso, and in order to support her family, she left her mountain home to seek work on South African farms. Crossing over the mountains at the Qacha's Nek pass, she and her children journeyed into East Griqualand.

The discrepancy between the South African and Lesotho sides of the mountains is striking. The land is dramatic in Lesotho, and it is harsh on its people. But as one descends on the South African side of the Qacha's Nek pass, especially in the rainy season, the landscape becomes gentler. The grass on the slopes is more luxuriant, bedecked with the protea bushes that can be found along the slopes of the Drakensberg. The rolling curves on the eastern side of the mountain range, rippling with long lush grass, contrast with the steep, weather-eroded rocky flanks of the Malutis.

East Griqualand, which Mokholitsoane and her children entered, is a place where three peoples meet, the Sotho-, Xhosa- and Zulu-speaking groupings. In the nineteenth century, the colonial name Nomansland was bestowed on this area on the grounds that it was isolated and sparsely populated. As the historian Jeff Peires has indicated, 'Nomansland' was a misnomer, creating the impression that the region lay wide open and virtually uninhabited, to await the coming of the white settlers. In fact, the territory was inhabited by a variety of peoples: the Hlubi, Bhaca, Xesibe, Ntlangwini and some Sotho settlers, among others.

The first South African town that Khotso and his mother encountered would have been Matatiele, huddling in the middle of the windswept veld below the Qacha's Nek pass. Racehorses are bred on the plains of East Griqualand and, as a boy and youth, Khotso was a keen rider in horse races. In his twenties Khotso would regularly visit the Matatiele betting shop. By that point in his career, he might have sensed that while life was a gamble, he was on a winning streak. But as a small boy passing through the town for the first time, dwarfed by the immensity of the mountains above him and the grasslands before him, with an alien town bustling confusingly around him, he could not have been aware of the curious authority that he would one day come to wield in this unfamiliar terrain.

For the small family venturing down the mountains from Lesotho, Matatiele would have appeared a thriving urban centre, but in the eyes of many South Africans, the place would have resembled a remote outpost. Despite bitter frosts and a lack of winter grazing, the grasslands below the escarpment are good country for cattle and sheep. But even today, a century after Khotso and his mother crossed the mountains into Nomansland, the uplands beneath the southern reaches of the Drakensberg still seem a far-flung, lonely wilderness. The terrain is for the most part treeless, the grass bleached and flattened by bone-chilling winds in the dry winter season. All along the western horizon stretches the jagged panorama of mountains that wall Lesotho off from the rest of southern Africa. In later years, Khotso would often pass through this area on his visits to his home country and during his forays into the border territory as a jackal hunter.

Khotso and his mother moved into a region in which white farming possibilities were being promoted. The Griqua[1] farmers who had moved from Philippolis in the southern Free State, crossing the Drakensberg and settling in Nomansland in 1863 to establish their own Griqua state in the east, had been beset by setbacks. Some lacked the economic wherewithal to establish farms of their own in this new region; others had been systematically losing their land since the Cape Colony took over their territory in 1874.[2] Occupying land that remained largely unproductive, dogged by debts and loss of livestock, the Griquas gradually vacated their farms. Some African farmers took advantage of the economic decline of the grouping that had formerly exerted a measure of authority over parts of the region. Africans could buy land cheaply or could reside on farms as tenants. But above all, white farmers began moving in to fill the void, to occupy the fertile farmlands that had once belonged to the Griquas, while keeping a wary eye on the black subsistence farmers around them. In the late nineteenth and early twentieth centuries, the whites in East Griqualand viewed themselves as an isolated rural community in a remote frontier area, ever anxious that 'native unrest' could erupt, and fearing that the African and Griqua communities would unite in an uprising against them.[3]

Khotso trailed after his mother as she traversed the dusty roads and the winter-bleached grasslands of East Griqualand, seeking work in the newly established white farming community. Mokholitsoane entered the service of the Scott family, who owned several farms. In 1904, she began work on Kingston Farm, situated at the base of the escarpment that leads up to the battlements and ramparts of the Drakensberg itself. The farm is not far from the present-day St Bernard's Peak Hotel. Khotso's mother was known by her white employers as Khaki, the name deriving from the utilitarian brown working garments she wore. The drab hue from which Mokholitsoane drew her name would be oddly at variance with the gaudy, jewel-bright colours with which her son would one day surround himself. Perhaps Khotso loved such colours not only because they served to express an inner flamboyance of character and out of a childlike delight in rainbow-brilliant hues, but also because they contrasted so vividly with the dull garb that his mother, and so many others like her, had donned as a token of servitude. But that would be in the future.

In 1919, Eric Scott, one of the scions of the Scott family, moved to Beaconsfield, a farm lying in the Nolangeni Hills outside Kokstad, off the national road leading to Mount Ayliff. Mokholitsoane and her son accompanied him, the latter working as a herder of livestock. She would remain on the farm with the family until 1928, but Khotso left Beaconsfield a few years earlier, a departure marked by so dramatic an event that East Griqualanders talk about it to this day.

Today Jill and Elizabeth Scott, the daughters of Hal Scott, Eric's nephew, and the only remaining members of the Scott family in the area, run both Beaconsfield and the adjoining family farm, Nolangeni. They can take you along winding dirt roads to a hillside on Beaconsfield and show you the place where a small dwelling once stood, situated in the lee of the hill, just above a stream. This is where Khaki and her family once lived, they say. Half overgrown by bushes are the remains of an enclosure, which was once her pigpen. Did Khotso, as a boy, stand outside his home and look down the valley towards Kokstad, where his future lay, and decide that there was to be more to his life than a quiet cottage beside a pigpen on a lonely hillside?

The Scotts were one of the most prominent Kokstad families and the large valley in which Beaconsfield and Nolangeni lie was known as

Kokstad and Mount Currie, with the Mzintlava River in the foreground, in 1901. (W. Dower, The Early Annals of Kokstad and Griqualand East)

Scott Alley. If you visit the archives of the *Kokstad Advertiser*, housed today in the town's museum, and page through copies of the newspaper from the early part of the twentieth century, you will encounter Scott family members at work and play, during peace and war, going through the various rituals of country-town life and the major rites of passage: birth, marriage and death.

Kokstad, a town founded in 1871, lies fifty kilometres east of Matatiele, in a hilly, almost alpine region at the edge of the southern KwaZulu-Natal farmlands and plantations. It appears to be a pleasant place, with tall trees lining many of its central streets. On the edge of the town, the Mzintlava River flows past into Pondoland. Nearby, to the north, Mount Currie rises, overlooking Kokstad, while the town lies cradled in the hills, contrasting with the wild empty plains around Matatiele. On 27 November 1925, the *Kokstad Advertiser* would quote a pamphlet issued by the Kokstad Publicity Committee, which depicted the town as a 'health-giving' summer holiday resort, 'with its rugged mountains and champagne air' for those weary of the heat of the coast.

Khotso, on the other hand, had a lifetime of hard work ahead of him, the very toughest years of which would take place in the town itself and in the mountains of Nomansland.

Certain large stores featured prominently in the business area of Kokstad, and the young Khotso might have admired such places, in part for the range of goods they stocked, but principally for the way in which they testified to the fact that sizeable entrepreneurial ventures were thriving in the town. He and Mokholitsoane would have visited stores such as R. R. Mundell's, where clothing and hardware could be purchased, or A. H. Williams, the self-styled 'Universal Providers' (according to advertisements in the *Kokstad Advertiser* in the 1940s), in existence since 1880. 'You could buy everything from an elephant to a tractor there,' one long-standing Kokstad local remarked.

Plenty of old buildings still line Kokstad's main roads, and although the town is situated just off the N2 highway, one of the country's national roads, which streams past towards the cities, and meticulously spruced-up old-world B & Bs beckon the visitor, it retains the air of an old-style frontier town. Behind the town, wild grassy hills roll away past Matatiele until they are stopped by the rock wall of the Malutis. The town's face, on the other hand, is turned hopefully towards the N2 and away from Bhongweni, the township that sprawls on the bare brown hillside above it.

Kokstad was the administrative and military hub of East Griqualand, as well as a focus for traders and farmers. According to the *Kokstad Advertiser*, in 1925 the Kokstad region contained 'a total population of 5 002 Europeans and 126 647 Natives'.[4] Yet the town's relatively small white population was in the process of displacing the African community. Some decades later, Kokstad's black inhabitants would be shifted up the hill into the settlement that became known as Bhongweni.

When Khotso was a teenager, an official distinction was made between fertile white farmland and the areas to which black South Africans were restricted. In 1913, the Natives Land Act was passed. In terms of the act, specific tracts of land that whites had not seen fit to seize from African communities were demarcated as reserves and were set aside for black occupation. Beyond them lay territory deemed suitable for whites. In 1964, Govan Mbeki described the Land Act as consolidating a state of affairs that had come to pass after several centuries of conflict between white and black South Africans. 'These areas [in which Africans could reside] became known as the "scheduled areas", but they mirrored no change in their new name. The Act merely defined a situation that had already been established when the last war for African independence was lost.'[5]

In addition to historical events, current economic factors had played their part in the passing of the 1913 Land Act. In 1886, gold had been discovered on the Witwatersrand and cheap labour was needed to sustain the growing mining industry as well as the agricultural sector. Thus there was a need to put still more pressure on black South Africans to become wage earners. Systems of taxation such as the hut tax, imposed on African households late in the nineteenth century, and the poll tax, first payable in Natal in 1906, were intended to force black South Africans to depart from their homes to seek employment. The territories to which black South Africans were consigned by the Land Act would fulfil a similar function. The reserves could not support a self-sufficient, independent livelihood for their populations, so the black South Africans inhabiting them would turn to the mines and farms to seek work.[6]

The Land Act was not implemented in the Cape until 1936. In terms of the provincial boundaries of that time, the Cape Province extended into East Griqualand. Thus, in Khotso's youth, the full force of racial separation and white hegemony still had to make itself felt in the part of South Africa in which he lived. More broadly, however, long before the Nationalist government's policy of racial discrimination, a system of racially segregated black territories had been established, foreshadowing the Bantustan areas into which South Africa's black inhabitants would be shunted under apartheid.[7] When he was an adult and had established himself in his career, Khotso would buy farms in the Matatiele region. Although these properties were in East Griqualand, they were located within a reserve area that would one day become part of the Bantustan known as the Transkei.

The landscape around Kokstad bears witness to this racially determined division of land. The first section of the road from Kokstad to Matatiele winds its way through a valley of farms. In the rainy season, it is possible to imagine, briefly, that you are in a highland region of Europe, with the gentle green vistas and somewhat enclosed prettiness that imbues certain north-western European landscapes. But cross the hills to the south into the Transkei and you find yourself back in a harsher part of Africa, in a setting that appears almost lunar by comparison. There is little to hold down the dust except the aloes and thorn trees that cling to the rocky hillsides. Dirt roads wind through straggling villages, many of which still lack running water or electricity. Walk through the centre of Kokstad, or stand in a queue at Rolyats Supermarket or the Kokstad Standard Bank or the Post Office, and all around you will see people stuck fast in rural poverty, on the cusp between the isolation of East Griqualand and the deprivation of the Transkei, struggling to scrape a livelihood out of the town and its environs. In Khotso's day, life would have been even harder. It is possible that many of the people around him felt that someone would be able to rise above his or her circumstances only with the aid of magic.

Khotso would have been aware that there were those who believed that the solution could be found in political activism. In 1914, he might have witnessed British troops moving into Kokstad, which was in a state of panic. All the available white men were armed, barbed-wire entanglements proliferated and the courthouse was hastily converted into a fort. People from farms and trading stores in the surrounding districts had fled into the town for sanctuary. Organised resistance to the compulsory dipping of cattle was intensifying. For instance, complicated regulations were imposed that restricted the movement of stock, whether for grazing purposes or for sale, and a compulsory fee had to be paid each time cattle were dipped. Dipping represented only one feature of a long process of rural 'betterment', promulgated by the white authorities on the grounds that it would promote more effective, modern farming methods. In reality, in the areas where rural 'betterment' schemes were imposed, already embattled systems of peasant agricultural production were undermined. Although resistance to dipping was eventually crushed by a display of force on the part of the British authorities, the anti-dipping movement represented an important stage in the development of rural politics in the Transkei, as ordinary rural people found themselves increasingly pitted against privileged, educated representatives of administrative authority.[8] But Khotso would have as little time for mass-based political protest as he would come to have for Christianity.

Kokstad may strike the casual visitor as a conventional enough country town, yet strange, even dark undercurrents have flowed through its life. Over the years, the *Kokstad Advertiser* has reported not only on local events and the weather, but also on accounts of witches and zombies. Today, some locals will tell you, there is a belief that malevolent spirits lurk by a bend in the road just outside the town, where accidents frequently take place. In 1995 Kokstad attained national notoriety because of a widespread local conviction that twelve schoolboys, victims of one such accident, had been turned into zombies. Three elderly women in Bhongweni were accused of being witches who had brought this about and were murdered by a mob of locals.

From the 1950s onwards, Khotso's name begins to enter the newspapers and stories about him start to spread through southern Africa. As his fame becomes widespread, it is easier to track his career. But far less is known about the shadowy, early years of his life, as he moved between East Griqualand and the mountains of Lesotho. We have odd, sometimes contradictory anecdotes from people with whom he had contact during that time. Although in later life Khotso loved to talk about his fame and wealth, he did not say much about his early days, preferring to let them fade into obscurity and become transmuted by the aura of legend that surrounded him.

According to the journalist Jack Blades, Khotso was sent to a Roman Catholic school, where he did not stay for very long. Blades first met Khotso in 1970. Captivated by the old man and the extraordinary stories surrounding him, he decided to write his biography, and conducted extensive research into Khotso's life after his death. Blades's book was not completed, but his fascination for his subject comes to the fore in his descriptions of Khotso and his life, and in the nature of the conversations he conducted with Khotso's family members, friends and acquaintances.

Blades observed that Khotso learned to sign his name and to count, an ability that he would need in later life, but not much more. As Khotso himself would indicate when he was an adult, formal education did not offer him the training he needed. He ran away from school, doing whatever casual work he could find, from herding sheep and cattle near Ha Ramokakatlela and in South Africa, to carrying out menial household tasks.

After Khotso's funeral, an elderly former Kokstad resident told a journalist that Khotso had worked for her late husband's aunt in the town when he was about ten or twelve, doing various odd jobs, such as polishing shoes. She and her husband later visited Khotso at his Kokstad home. She recalled:

> My husband used to tease him about his young days, spent polishing and cleaning, and Khotso would turn coy and say, 'Let's not talk about those times.' Unlike most millionaires, who like to talk about their poor beginnings, Khotso always wanted people to think he'd been rich all his life, born with a silver spoon in his mouth.[9]

By 1913, Khotso was herding livestock for Eric Scott, first at Kingston and later at Beaconsfield. The stage was being set for what would become one of the most remarkable careers in twentieth-century South Africa.

Chapter 3
Hunting for Jackals and Dwarves

While details of Khotso's early life remain obscure, he liked to create the impression that even then there were clear signs that he was set apart for greatness. While he resided with his mother in East Griqualand, Khotso regularly journeyed into his home terrain in the south-eastern Malutis. These visits allowed him to remain connected to his roots in Lesotho, and they enabled the boy to spend time with his father, who shared some of his knowledge of herbalism with his son. Certain informants from Lesotho said that Motumi instructed the boy to go to a mountaintop during a drought and burn a herbal concoction wrapped in an otter's skin to bring on rain.

A number of people in Qacha's Nek, Ha Ramokakatlela and the Transkei have told how in a cavern in the mountains the young Khotso met someone who passed special knowledge on to him: the Sotho prophetess Mantsopa, one of the most renowned spiritual practitioners in southern Africa. Some believe that her prophetic gift enabled her to foresee that the Phuthi boy she encountered would one day embark on the road to renown.

Mantsopa's full name was Mantsopa Anna Makhetha. She built up a huge following in the nineteenth century, during the reign of Moshoeshoe, and afterwards when she acquired significant status as an expert in traditional medicines, a rainmaker and a prophet.[1] It is said that Mantsopa was even able to predict exactly how much time had been allocated to her on earth, correctly predicting the date of her own passing away. From time to time, she would withdraw to a cave at Modderpoort in the eastern Free State that had become a place of private spiritual retreat for her. There she communed with the mystical powers to whom she owed her great wisdom and insight. Mantsopa's grave is located near this cave.

Mantsopa died around 1904, when Khotso was six years old, and many believed that she was then 111. Khotso would have envied her for this. In the final years of his life, when he was in his early seventies, he pretended that he was in his early nineties. Despite Khotso's talent for stretching the truth, he was never able to extend his age anywhere nearer the century mark, let alone beyond it. Even at an early stage in his life, Khotso would have been aware of how Mantsopa's fame was living on, keeping her name alive. So he might have found it fitting to concoct the stories that associate him with Mantsopa or with a wise old woman living in a cave in the mountains, who might, just possibly, have been her.

There was a line of traditional spiritual practitioners, many of them female, who continued Mantsopa's legacy for generation after generation, preparing herbal medicines for healing and throwing the bones to predict and interpret events. One of Mantsopa's daughters lived in East Griqualand, having married George Tlali Moshoeshoe, who established the village of Queen's Mercy near Matatiele, where Mantsopa's descendants live to this day.[2] While Khotso would not have encountered Mantsopa, he might well have met one of those who followed in her footsteps, or even this daughter. One of Mantsopa's direct descendants bore not only her name but also her gift of prophecy.[3] By letting it be known that some of Mantsopa's knowledge and powers might somehow have been passed on to him, Khotso could intimate that he was, in a sense, Mantsopa's heir.

Khotso would attain fame comparable to hers; however, Mantsopa was also well remembered for her acts of charity to the poor. The municipality of Ladybrand in the eastern Free State and next to the border with Lesotho now bears her name, partly in tribute to her generosity to those in her locality. She supplied food to the needy and, as an experienced herbalist, she assisted those around her, charging no fees for her acts of healing. Khotso, on the other hand, would offer food to poverty-stricken individuals, but his herbal remedies always came at a price, and he hugged his fortune to himself, securing it behind high fences and carefully guarded gates. Unlike Mantsopa, who eventually acquired the status of high-profile community builder, living on in official histories of the area and in contemporary civic nomenclature, Khotso would remain at a social distance from the communities he inhabited, his immortality residing predominantly in popular legend.

We now return to the meeting of two of the most famous and influential practitioners of the supernatural in modern southern Africa. Because Khotso was involved, this event makes for several good stories.

According to one account told by a man from Qacha's Nek, when Khotso finally left Mantsopa, he took with him her washing stone, an object that was more significant than it might appear, as is often the case when magical forces make their presence felt in the world of everyday things. Khotso had noticed that Mantsopa's powers were connected to this stone, and he wanted it for himself. But Mantsopa knew where Khotso had gone, and one day she turned up at the place in which he was staying in Kokstad, astonished that anyone could have had the audacity to steal her precious stone. Khotso took a great many risks in his life, but this was one occasion when he realised that he had overstepped the mark. He tried to return the stone to the prophetess, but she would not take it back. The object had now passed from her hands into his, she told him. Did Mantsopa feel that the time had come for Khotso to take on the stone, with all the weight and responsibilities that came with the supernatural potency with which it was charged? The narrator of this story had been a trainee herbalist at Mount Nelson in the 1960s. Thus he knew Khotso during the period when the development of the myths and mystique concerning him was at its height. In consequence, he may have felt that Khotso was capable of anything, even taking the great Mantsopa's special stone away from her.

This story also calls to mind some African trickster tales, in which one person or creature possesses an object of great value, which he or she uses wisely and prudently. But then the object is stolen by a trickster figure, who uses it excessively and heedlessly, coming to grief as a result. The fable thus ends on a moral note, censuring immoderate, incautious behaviour.[4] Some might like to claim that the young Khotso's theft of Mantsopa's washing stone helped him rise to fortune and fame, but he flaunted his wealth and led an extravagant life while using his powers recklessly, and this eventually brought about his downfall.

There are other versions of Khotso's encounter with Mantsopa. Khotso told others, including Ellen Jones, one of his better-known paramours, that when he was a boy herding cattle for his father in the Maluti Mountains, he came across an old, destitute woman living alone in a cave. She was so frail and sick that she could not even wash her own feet. Khotso described how he took pity on her and regularly visited her cave, where he would build a fire, boil water and bathe her feet in warm water scented with herbs and oils. The old woman told him which herbs to collect. When she sensed that her death was near, she wished to do something for Khotso in return for his kindness. So, from within the rags that she wore wrapped around her, she produced a stone. This, she told him, was a lucky stone that she had been given as a child, which she now wished him to have. This selfsame stone, Khotso told Ellen, was the secret of his wealth. Khotso liked to tell some of the women who became his lovers and wives stories in which he appeared as kind-hearted and caring, while highlighting his innate nobility of character. This may have been one reason why Ellen was told a tale of this nature.

A third version of the Mantsopa–Khotso story derives from a man called James Lunika, who would come to play such an important role in Khotso's life that Khotso would refer to him as his prime minister. Lunika is now over eighty years old and lives in the village of Caquba, near Port St Johns. Of the few remaining people who were close to

Khotso and are still alive today, it is perhaps Lunika who has the most to tell. He had known Khotso since 1936, and Khotso had told him a number of stories about his early days. Lunika remains an astute and sprightly man who exudes confidence. Traces of the handsome youth he had once been come to life in his face as he talks with excitement about his memories of Khotso.

Khotso told Lunika how he was hunting in the mountains in Lesotho when he met an old Sotho woman, a powerful herbalist. He told her that he wanted to be rich, and then she gave him some special medicine that set him on his path to wealth. But first, Khotso told Lunika, she offered him her two beautiful daughters. She only bestowed the medicine on him after he withstood their allure. The unusual part of this tale is that Khotso, who enjoyed sex almost as much as he delighted in money, succeeded for once in keeping his desires in check. However, as we shall see, he would find the element of sensual temptation useful to employ in his own practice later on. Lunika was close to Khotso at this point in his career. So Khotso might have told him this version of the Mantsopa story sensing that his prime minister might find it appropriate and convincing.

These stories offer us three different images of Khotso. There is the daring and unscrupulous youth, robbing his teacher of an object of great power, in his desire to wield control over the supernatural world; next, the kind, unselfish boy motivated primarily by concern for others; and finally, the young man who chose wisdom and wealth above fleeting carnal pleasures. Set side by side, these three versions provide insights into aspects of Khotso's nature: his overwhelming, perilous desire for personal gain; his exceptional thoughtfulness and generosity; his fascination with sexuality – but his stronger craving for material success.

Khotso might well have enjoyed each of these tales equally. He enhanced and expanded his horizons through the tales that he told concerning his life history, creating a world of multiple opportunities for himself. Moreover, he might have decided to make use of one specific version of a story to play on the emotions and imagination of the individual or individuals to whom he narrated it. He could, perhaps, pick whichever particular version of events took his fancy – or, if he felt like it, he might select several differing accounts at once.

Later on in his career, Khotso would make especial use of the accounts in which his praiseworthy accomplishments came to the fore to counterbalance the stories that cast a sinister light on him. One of the earliest of these dark tales dates back to Khotso's youth, told by an old man from the Flagstaff area who remembered Khotso from the early 1920s. This man's father and Motumi had lived close to each other near Matatiele. The man claimed that Khotso's father had apprenticed his son to a prominent herbalist named Macotha, who lived in a large house between Kokstad and Matatiele. Khotso's job was to drive around the district in a horse and cart, and capture dwarves wherever he could find them, loading them onto the back of the cart and bearing them off to Macotha's abode, where they were kept in a room until they were used for medicine. The old man relating the story averred that he had seen Khotso riding through the countryside driving a cart laden with dwarves.[5]

Various Kokstad and East Griqualand locals offer more mundane accounts, stating that Khotso spent a great deal of time working on white farms in East Griqualand in his youth. One of Khotso's tasks as a boy was to castrate bulls on farms belonging to the Scott family. In later life, when he boasted about his virility, he liked to refer to himself as 'Khotso the bull'. So he found it funny, friends said, that he had started off his career putting the sex life of real bulls to an end.

Khotso also worked with horses while he was a teenager. Racehorses were bred around Matatiele and the young Khotso, small and wiry as he was, would have been the right build for a jockey. He was reputedly a good rider, but black jockeys were relegated to training horses and stable work: it was the white jockeys who were accorded the excitement and prestige of riding in the big races themselves, which were organised by the white Jockey Club of South Africa.

When he took the young Khotso into his service, Eric Scott could not have predicted the way he and his farm would feature in one of the principal legends concerning Khotso. The young man's outward appearance gave no hint of the awe and fear that he would inspire later in his life. He was a stocky youth, less than five feet tall, with a lively, expressive face and a gap between his front teeth. As time went on and he smiled more often, this latter feature would give his face a mischievous quality.

But menial farm labour was not the path to wealth. According to Khotso, he began to amass his fortune with jackal hunting. He liked to speak about this activity, because jackal hunting allowed him to operate as an independent agent while making, he assured all his listeners, an impressive amount of money. In his analysis of the effect of jackals on farming in the Cape, William Beinart indicates why this was the case: 'Debates about improvements in the Cape pastoral economy were bedevilled by the shadowy presence of predators, and especially jackals, on farm boundaries. Jackals stalked the countryside and the imagination of farmers. It was the losses they caused, and the perceived losses they might cause, which were so often cited as a major reason for the kraaling system. Jackals were the enemy of farmers because they killed sheep.'[6]

Later in his life, when Khotso boasted about his wealth, he would sometimes mention how much he earned in his hunting days. He claimed that he sold a jackal pelt or tail for five pounds each. When questioned about this, Khotso was adamant: he hadn't been paid five shillings; it was definitely five pounds. In 1920, the government bounty for jackals was ten shillings, although some divisional councils offered far larger incentives, such as Bredasdorp in the Western Cape, which offered as much as five pounds per jackal.[7] But even if he was paid only ten shillings per jackal, in a remote stock-farming area such as East Griqualand, where predators could sneak down from the mountains at night, it is possible that a skilled bounty hunter could stand to earn a great deal. While bounty payment was earned from the jackals' tails, other parts of their bodies could be used to generate even more money. As Blades pointed out, 'The tail money was bounty, chiefs bought the skins to make into karosses and to decorate tribal dress. White men bought skins too.'

Blades and others have noted that Khotso's jackal-hunting days began in his teens and he operated in the mountains in the East Griqualand border area, using Matatiele as a base. He roamed the cold and desolate highlands with his pack of dogs, tracking down 'the pirates of the veld'.[8] This period in Khotso's life toughened him, making him able to work long hours. Possibly those years of deprivation sharpened his taste for some of the luxuries, such as expensive cars and ornate houses, with which he would surround himself in later life. While hunting, Khotso only wore a loincloth. When he was cold, he wrapped a cowhide around himself. Years later, he described his life as a jackal hunter to Blades. He would sleep on the ground beside a campfire, surrounded by his pack of dogs. Sometimes he hunkered down in the frost and snow, without a fire. 'It was c-o-l-d!' he shuddered. Blades said that although it was a warm summer day, Khotso huddled his shoulders deep into his sheepskin jacket as he recollected those nights in the mountains.

Khotso and his pack of dogs foraged for food off the land. There was not much to catch except rabbits and dassies. Julius Khoapa, a trader and ex-police sergeant from Matatiele, who had known Khotso when they were teenagers in the mountains together, recalled how he would share whatever he could with other hunters and herders. Sometimes Khotso was so proud of his ability to offer food to others that he behaved as if he was inviting them to a feast, in much the same way in which he would delight in hosting parties and banquets later in his life. Khoapa said:

> In 1917 I was herding small stock in the mountains. Khotso Sethuntsa was a very fine young man. In the rugged mountainside he would never stay in one place. He would move about. In those days, the jackal were a menace to our small stock. In that way he was actually helping people, killing these jackals. His home was in Matatiele. I remember one day he gave a loud shout on top of the mountains. He was accompanied by his dogs and he was shouting to the youths who were down below the mountains. 'Hey, hey, you – you'll find calabashes made of animal skins. Feast from those, I'll be coming.'[9]

Blades spoke to one white farmer from East Griqualand who met Khotso in his jackal-hunting days. In later years, the farmer and Khotso became friends and developed a long-standing business association. He described Khotso's hunting methods to Blades: 'The jackal used to hide in the crevices in the rocks. They would prey on the hundreds of sheep grazing on the slopes and they were a real nuisance. Khotso used to go around winkling them out.' The farmer added that Khotso had various ways of catching jackal. Sometimes he burned fat to attract them, and then poisoned them; on other occasions he used a small dog to nip in between the rocks and worry the jackal until it dashed out into the open, where his big dogs would be waiting. He even occasionally fished jackal out, using a long piece of wire with a hook on the end, which he poked behind the rocks until he hooked a jackal's thick, matted fur. Khotso was involved in jackal hunting, on and off, from the mid-1910s until the early 1930s. He would disappear into the mountains at intervals, then descend to Matatiele to collect bounty money and sell jackal skins.

As a jackal hunter, the young man who would become skilled in the art of illusion had to pit his wits against creatures renowned as tricksters. Beinart has drawn attention to the fact that 'the jackal often played the role of a person full of "tricks and cunning" in San, Khoikhoi and African folktales. The word "jackal" was used among Dutch settlers to denote a liar by the early eighteenth century. Its reputation for "cunning" was soon learnt by British settlers in the Eastern Cape.' As evidence, Beinart cites one farmer who maintained, in 1905, that 'the wily jackal has a trick of rendering himself invisible to the human eye'.[10] Decades later people would claim that Khotso could make himself invisible or change his shape at will, even adopting the form of animals, so that he could slip past unnoticed as he went about his risky, shadowy dealings. In such tales and in other aspects of his career, Khotso would surpass the cunning jackal of southern African oral tales in his ingenuity and wiliness.

Life in the mountains was not always cold for Khotso. On a number of his hunting trips in the 1920s and early 1930s, he had a companion: a

Painted photo portrait of Khotso, MaDlamini and Masechaba, c. 1950. (Courtesy of Mametsi-a-Leoatle Sethuntsa)

beautiful young woman called Catherine Qacha, who eventually became his second wife. They had first met in Matatiele, where Catherine, who later became known as MaDlamini, was working. She had been married to a man in Lesotho, but she had been widowed and was seeking to earn a living in South Africa, where she made and sold lovely traditional clay pots. These caught Khotso's attention and he became captivated by the woman vending them. He and MaDlamini became lovers and eventually she married Khotso according to traditional custom in 1932. Some years afterwards, Masechaba, MaDlamini's daughter, otherwise known as Mary, would come to live with Khotso and her mother.

Before he met MaDlamini, Khotso had taken a wife: MaDzanibe, née Jokazi, originally from Umzimkhulu. They had one son, born in 1924, known as Motiki because he was as small as a tickey coin,[11] and a daughter named Patricia. However, Khotso and his first wife had quarrelled and she had left him, the children remaining behind with their father. So Khotso turned to MaDlamini, and they embarked on a relationship that was to last a lifetime, in contrast with Khotso's fleeting first marriage.

Unlike many of Khotso's later wives and partners, MaDlamini came from his home territory. She was a mountain woman from a village in the south-eastern Malutis. Born in 1910, MaDlamini was only twelve years younger than Khotso. This was a small gap compared to the chasm between his own age and the ages of the youthful women with whom he began consorting later in his life. Unlike most of these paramours, Khotso and MaDlamini's relative closeness in age highlighted the extent to which MaDlamini appeared to be Khotso's equal in various noteworthy senses of the word, and even, in certain respects, more advanced than he was.

In later life, MaDlamini gave the outward impression of being grave, reserved and distant. 'She talked only when absolutely necessary,' her nephew Martin Qacha said. Solemn, reticent and devout, MaDlamini could be viewed primarily in contrast with her charismatic, flamboyant husband, as the austere, self-effacing senior wife who gradually became eclipsed by other figures in Khotso's household. Yet of all Khotso's wives, her status, forcefulness and expertise made her a pre-eminent presence in her husband's early career.

He was drawn to MaDlamini because she was young, lovely and the daughter of a chief. The town near MaDlamini's birthplace, founded in 1888, and the mountain pass leading up to it from South Africa are known as Qacha's Nek, bearing her family name. Khotso would like to pretend that he was of royal blood and the descendant of the famous hero of the Phuthi people, Chief Moorosi. Since MaDlamini was the daughter of Chief Qacha, a scion of the great Moorosi himself,[12] possibly Khotso felt that his connection to Moorosi's line, through his senior wife, was enough to transform him from a commoner into a member of a royal house. MaDlamini never forgot that she was a chief's daughter, and this, combined with her inner dignity and fortitude, carried her through the upheavals and calamities that beset her in later life.

Pascal Makeka, a retired teacher from the Hermitage, a village near Qacha's Nek, remembered MaDlamini as a young woman and observed: 'I know that Khotso Sethuntsa was interested in her because she was intelligent and she quickly and easily understood whatever Khotso wanted her to do. And on top of that, she was a beautiful woman. He was caught in a net!'

Khotso's much-vaunted capacity to win women over was not unfounded. MaDlamini allowed herself to be drawn into an adventurous love affair, but then the man with whom she became enraptured exuded a compelling sexuality. Certain individuals who knew MaDlamini have suggested that a key part of the attraction Khotso held for her also stemmed from the fact that she did not view him as a man from remote rural origins, trapped in the lowly place where he was born, his short stature somehow symbolic of his reduced, diminished position in life. Instead, it has been posited, she had the shrewdness to see him as a powerful, charismatic man on the move.

Many years later, when MaDlamini, as a decorous, self-contained old woman, alluded to her hunting trips with Khotso, it was possible to guess that these free, wild times of romance deep in the mountains, far beyond the reach of her family and of all those who might seek to restrict or contain her, were a daring, exciting experience. In a sense, a person who knew MaDlamini observed, she might perhaps have met someone of her own sort. Most of the men she had known until then, her former husband included, would not have condoned a wife embarking on adventurous forays into the mountains, instead of staying at home tending to the household fires. For his part, Khotso had the great good luck to team up with a regal, strong-minded woman alongside whom he would venture into the mountains, seeking the beginnings of his fortune. There were times during these hunting expeditions when Khotso related stories about himself to MaDlamini, partly, it might well be, in an attempt to charm her yet further. It appears that he succeeded in this. For instance, towards the end of her life, MaDlamini enjoyed recounting an anecdote, which she still thought was a sweet story, that had once been told to her by an endearing young man.

One night Khotso was sitting alone in front of the fire at his father's cattle post in the Maluti Mountains when he heard his dogs barking. Then a limping leopard came to visit him. The creature had a thorn stuck in one of its paws and Khotso sensed that the leopard wanted him to take it out. So he approached the leopard, took its paw and saw that the thorn was deeply embedded. As he was trying to remove it, the leopard would use its unwounded paw to tap on his shoulder whenever the pain became too much. Khotso succeeded in removing the thorn and the leopard went happily on its way. A few days later, the leopard returned, dragging a small phuthi buck, a gift with special significance. This was a thank-you gift for Khotso's kind attention.

Khotso told many striking, original stories, yet this one recycles the time-worn tale of a compassionate, helpful person, often from a humble background, who helps a majestic beast in its time of need. It may strike many as hackneyed and sentimental. But Khotso may have had no scruples about using a story of this nature to play on his lover's feelings and touch her heart. In terms of this underlying motivation, the leopard story is comparable to the tale that Khotso told Ellen of the lonely old woman in the mountain cave, whose dying days were eased by his kindness. Both these narratives have a fairy-tale quality to them as well, and Khotso may have felt that this would add to their appeal.

MaDlamini was used to highland conditions and, like Khotso, wore a loincloth and cowhide kaross when she hunted. Evidently she was an expert horse rider. Her experience as a hunter could also have toughened her, not only physically but psychologically. She outlasted most of Khotso's other major wives and, as future events were to prove, she would be a formidable opponent to take on, especially because she possessed staying power. She lived to see her grandchildren take occupation of Khotso's most important house, Mount Nelson.

'She was a very strong woman,' MaDlamini's grandson and Masechaba's son Thabo recalled admiringly. His grandmother's strength, he emphasised, lay not just in her outward physical capabilities but in her inner mental and psychological qualities as well. Thabo remembered how she would tell her children and grandchildren thrillingly frightening tales from Lesotho of the cannibal giants that strode across the highlands, where the rocks were as strong and sharp as their teeth, seeking fresh flesh and blood. These childhood stories took Thabo and his siblings far away from the gentle, green, undulating Pondoland landscape and into the wild mountain world where his family had once belonged.

Chapter 4
The Snake in a Whirlwind

Khotso's sojourns as a jackal hunter in an isolated, mountainous region were, in a sense, his time in the wilderness. He emerged from these periods of hardship and deprivation with – if he was to be believed – the foundations of his fortune. Gradually, he began to accumulate his wealth, buying sheep and cattle with the money he obtained from hunting and the various other jobs he took on. He saved his money, but never banked it. Instead he hid it, often underground.

But during the course of the 1920s, Khotso's real career would begin to take off. One specific event marked the beginning of his rise to fame and fortune. This took place in 1925, on Beaconsfield, Eric Scott's farm.

It appears that several things had gone wrong between Khotso and Scott. Firstly, when the fifteen-year-old Khotso was herding animals for Scott, some beasts strayed and he received a hiding for his negligence. There is another, more important reason why Khotso had a grudge against Scott. Years later, when he was working on Beaconsfield as an adult, Khotso would make periodic trips to Lesotho. There are allegations that he interspersed reputable activities such as bounty hunting for jackals with enterprises of a more dubious nature. He would head off to Lesotho, Scott said, and then return, leading horses that Scott had never seen before. According to a report in the *Kokstad Advertiser*, he

Tornado damage on Eric Scott's farm. (Courtesy of Campbell Scott, Eric Scott's grandson)

believed that Khotso was bringing stolen livestock onto his farm, and this led to growing tensions between them.[1] At one point in 1925, the police grew suspicious and visited Scott's farm, taking both him and Khotso in for questioning.

After the incident with the police, Scott grew angry with Khotso and told him to leave his employment. Evidently, Khotso told him as he departed, 'I'll come back on Monday at 2 p.m.'[2] On that Monday afternoon, 9 November, Scott received a visitor of quite another kind.

The *Kokstad Advertiser* ran an article entitled 'Destructive Cyclone Near Kokstad: Mr Eric Scott's Homestead Devastated'. Apart from a stone dairy that was left standing, the farm buildings were completely destroyed. Today, over eighty years after the event, the site of the disaster looks deceptively tranquil and bucolic, at first glance. Cattle graze in the shade of a spreading oak, and shrubs and trees flourish in the gentle dip of the valley, sheltered by the tall hills rolling away towards the Transkei. Then one notices large stones lying about, half overgrown by grass, and the remains of farm walls and buildings laid low and hurled far and wide, like toy blocks scattered by a careless child. Pieces of iron roofing, crumpled like pieces of paper, have been flung all over the nearby hills. These are traces of the devastation bearing witness to the violence of the tornado.

The reporter who covered the event, who obviously had served in the First World War, stated: 'Five minutes after the passing of the whirlwind, the scene of desolation everywhere was appalling, reminding one forcibly of a devastated Belgian farm after the passing of enemy troops. Sturdy oaks, that a man's two arms could not span, were snapped like matchwood, and all the laden fruit trees were broken and uprooted.' The roof of the house was ripped off and the walls caved in. Miraculously, no one was killed, although the Scott family and their servants went through a terrifying ordeal when the tornado struck. 'Hell's fury seemed to have been released in those brief moments,' Scott said afterwards.[3]

Not so much hell's fury, so the story grew, as Khotso's wrath. This, the *Kokstad Advertiser* stated many years later, was 'the cyclone which set Khotso on the road to success',[4] which many viewed as the inkanyamba, the snake in the sky. This being lives in deep pools, apart from the short periods when it sweeps through the air, wreaking havoc where it descends. It flies through the air in search of its mate, which resides in another deep body of water. Sex would come to represent a cornerstone of Khotso's life: in terms of his own libido, his clients' needs and as a key feature of the *mamlambo*, another potent serpentine presence with whom he would often be linked. Thus, the fact that the first mystical being with whom he would become associated should be driven by its sexual desires has a certain aptness to it.

The inkanyamba, it is said, can be controlled by someone with great occult power, a wielder of strong magic. If Khotso had this creature at his beck and call, then he was truly someone to be held in awe. This fear would have been intensified because of the belief, widely held in Pondoland, that witchcraft is associated with the ability to control the weather. We may recall that, according to popular beliefs in Lesotho, a land of violent mountain thunderstorms, meteorological destruction and dangerous magic are often interconnected. Moreover, there is the snake itself: the creature that manifests itself in many different forms in the traditional spiritual convictions and supernatural beliefs of Zulu- and Xhosa-speaking peoples. Khotso's association with the inkanyamba at this early point in his career helped pave the way for his association with other mystical, magical serpentine beings. Over and over again, we encounter stories in which his supernatural powers are connected to snakes, the most widespread, fearsome denizens of the southern African paranormal. In fact, one might say that serpents lie at the heart of the Khotso legend.

Rationalists will observe that tornadoes are not uncommon in parts of South Africa. But one of them just happened to coincide with Khotso's dispute with Scott and sweep right through the centre of his former master's house. When he was building up his business as a herbalist, Khotso would make productive use of coincidences, so it is possible that he began doing so at this crucial point in his life. Yet whether the tornado occurred by chance or whether there was – as Khotso boasted and as so many others believed – some form of supernatural agency involved, the growth of the conviction that Khotso was able to call up occult forces to work his will can be traced from this event.

Jill and Elizabeth Scott said that the family members were all very down-to-earth people. 'Even if Khotso did send the tornado, the family wouldn't have believed it,' Elizabeth Scott remarked. However, the sisters do agree that tornadoes are not frequent around Kokstad and, as Jill Scott added, it was strange that the tornado happened to pass right through the middle of the family farm.

Khotso's power over the inkanyamba takes us all the way back to the San, who were renowned for their ability to control the being that struck terror into their Sotho-, Zulu- and Xhosa-speaking neighbours. The practice of 'steering' the inkanyamba through the heavens during a storm by using two sticks – an indigenous version of air-traffic control – is rooted in San traditions. For instance, a descendant of the San from

Tsolo in the Transkei has been witnessed carrying this out.

After the tornado Khotso started to earn money as a herbalist and began tracking down traditional workers in the supernatural from whom he could learn. Various informants offer differing accounts of how he acquired his knowledge. Some mention the instruction that he may have picked up from his father, Motumi; others say Khotso may have acquired the information as Macotha's apprentice, when he was not out catching dwarves for him. Several individuals cite the stories in which Mantsopa appears as Khotso's mentor. However, Khotso's cousin, one of the oldest inhabitants of Ha Ramokakatlela, born in 1921, believed that a Sotho doctor called Peola was one of Khotso's most important teachers. He related how Khotso was probably in his early twenties when he went to Peola for training in traditional medicine. 'Khotso used to stay at the cattle post with my elder brother. Khotso took one of the beasts at the cattle post and gave it to Peola as payment. He then sent my elder brother to him to tell Peola that his beast had died at the cattle post.' Peola was the one who taught Khotso mastery over the khanyapa, Khotso's cousin continued. Eventually, the cattle owner found out that his cow had been used to pay off Khotso's debt. 'But he didn't and couldn't do anything.'

Julius Khoapa, on the other hand, described how Khotso met his grandfather from the Matatiele area while he was a jackal hunter. Khoapa's grandfather was a herbalist and he shared some of his special knowledge with Khotso. There was, for instance, a particular medicine for selling horses: 'My grandfather would burn a herb and those horses would jump over the fire,' said Khoapa, 'and then that day would be a big sale day for our horses.'[5]

There are many other explanations. According to one of Khotso's daughters, Mametsi, her father simply realised that he had special gifts and his powers came to him in dreams and visions. An alternative perception that several different people from the Kokstad and Lusikisiki area have expressed could also be worth considering. A Lusikisiki man who had once worked for Khotso posited that the latter had the capacity to swiftly, and sometimes unscrupulously, acquire skills and expertise from others:

> People came to Khotso from all over Africa, to get healed, maybe, or sometimes to acquire special powers for getting rich. But in fact he took from people who came to him. You see, there were those who came there who had powers of their own, but they wanted to acquire more spiritual powers for healing people. So he took their powers and used those powers.

One man who resided in Khotso's household for several years, observing him at close quarters over an extended period, held the view that Khotso's special ability lay in the fact that he was such a quick learner that he could easily create the impression that his knowledge was an inborn attribute. There are others who share this opinion. If this is accurate, it is likely that Khotso's learning process extended far beyond the early days of his youth, right throughout his life, even after he had become known as one of the greatest healers and teachers in southern Africa.

There is also the possibility that some of Khotso's knowledge of the uses of herbs came not so much from special training he had set out to acquire as from one source particularly close to him: MaDlamini herself. Sotho royalty are expected to have a sound understanding of a great many things, including herbalism. There are practical reasons for acquiring this skill, since there is always the fear that some enemy might seek to strike at the royal house by bewitching or poisoning one of its members. Training in the art of herbalism meant that members of royal families would be better equipped to protect themselves. As the daughter of Chief Qacha, MaDlamini might have acquired wisdom in such a significant area because of her lineage. This may also have been another reason why the young Khotso was drawn to her, perceiving her as someone with expertise in an area that could be turned to yield great financial benefit. Her grandson Thabo mentioned that in the days when she went hunting with Khotso, she showed him how the fat, flesh and pelts of the jackals could be used for healing and strengthening purposes.

Khotso would also watch her gathering medicinal plants in the veld and he learned much about their powers from her. One man in Lesotho who was Khotso and MaDlamini's principal source of herbs from the 1930s was Nthoa Bohlokoa Moshoeshoe, a grandson of Moshoeshoe I, king of Lesotho. He did not attach great importance to Khotso's skills as a herbalist. On the other hand, he appeared to have respect for MaDlamini in this regard.

Just as doctors today can profit from diagnosing ailments and dispensing medicines that may heal their patients' ailments, so a trained herbalist can stand to earn a good income provided he or she develops a reputation for being able – even if only sometimes – to solve customers' problems. And it is highly likely that when his medicines worked, Khotso broadcast this coincidence. One such example was the special muti that he sold to people going into court to make the judge acquit them. People used to wash in it and use it as a purgative to induce vomiting, James Lunika told Blades, before setting off to court. Inevitably, some of them went free and spread the word that Khotso's medicines worked.

Pascal Makeka recalled how Khotso went about setting up his business in the early days:

> The way he was advertising his medicines, he made them very much alive because he was giving examples of how successfully they worked. Some of these examples were exaggerated. But he always had an example! Now that's why many people went in with a lot of money to him. He knew how to give an example that could work immediately!

Khotso turned one of Makeka's experiences to his own advantage, pretending that a lucky coincidence that had befallen Makeka had taken place through his agency. Makeka recalled:

> Now Khotso was giving the example of stolen cattle. There were many people stealing cattle from Lesotho to Kokstad. So there were animals stolen from Lesotho, mine and from the mission, and we discovered them just as they were about to be driven out of the country. We stopped them from going. Khotso said, 'You see,

I'm just doing this for you; I don't even want you to pay.' It was so that I would come back home and advertise this to people.

A Sotho proverb states '*Ngaka e rutwa dihlare eseng mejo*' (A doctor is taught medicine, not business). This could be applied to Khotso. While he needed others to instruct him in the art of herbalism, he possessed an innate understanding of the craft of successful entrepreneurship. From the earliest days, he proved to be a shrewd operator, with extraordinarily sharp insights into his potential clients' fears, longings and desires. Some might have said that he possessed an uncanny ability, stemming perhaps from his skill in matters paranormal, to see into his customers' minds and gauge how best to bend them to his own commercial advantage. Added to this came what Eastern Cape anthropologist Manton Hirst bluntly terms the power of hogwash.[6] Many of Khotso's clients were eager to buy the potions and charms he had on offer because they had swallowed the tales concerning the wonders that could be wrought through his wares. Combined with his charisma, Khotso's stories seemed all the more convincing. To put it simply, he had the gift of the gab.

So Khotso sent his stories, like obedient children or faithful servants, out into the world to work on his behalf. In due course, he would discover that, like certain children and trusted retainers, stories have lives of their own and go their own way, not always in the direction of his choosing. But that lay in the future. And even then, as in the early days, Khotso's narratives could exercise a sway over those who heard them, because he had a sharply honed sense of the nature and the needs of his audience.

'The impression I have now is that it was psychology he was using,' Makeka reflected. 'But I want to go away from that and think of it in terms of that time. That time we thought Khotso Sethuntsa had very good medicine to stop thieves.'

There is another Sotho proverb, *Lehlohonolo hase lebelo*, literally meaning 'Luck does not depend on how fast you run'. In other words, good fortune does not arise from innate abilities, but is instead dependent on external factors. In Khotso's case, he was fortunate to have launched his career as a herbalist during a period when those around him were more inclined to believe his stories. Later, his listeners might have evaluated his tales more critically and sceptically, as indeed Makeka and many others do today. We will see too that Khotso was fortunate because he lived and worked in communities in which there was a great demand for certain medicines that he had on offer. He would derive substantial wealth from this. He would also be lucky enough to encounter coincidences that he could use to convince others that his magic worked. As Makeka indicated, he utilised these to advertise his medicines in his early days as a herbalist. Some are inclined to believe that the tornado that descended on Scott's farm may have been one of the most fortuitous coincidences in Khotso's career.

Although he had established himself as a herbalist, an *ixhwele* in Xhosa, Khotso did not always wish to be viewed exclusively as such. He liked to suggest that his powers extended far beyond a working knowledge of herbs and medicines right into the region where mighty beings like the inkanyamba awaited his command – much further, he would imply, than a straightforward herbalist might be capable of venturing. For this reason, Khotso preferred to be known as an inyanga. By using this term, he sought to suggest that he was not simply an ixhwele, but rather an individual with a special calling who had been initiated into mysteries that granted him the ability to exercise control over unseen forces.

Inyanga is the Zulu word for a herbalist, sometimes used by Xhosa-speaking peoples in the areas of the Eastern Cape adjoining KwaZulu-Natal, a region in which Xhosa and Zulu speakers intermingle. The term can take on additional meanings for non-Zulu speakers. For Khotso, and for a number of people who knew him, such as Lunika, an inyanga denoted a specialised and skilled traditional practitioner with a knowledge of herbalism and authority over various areas of the supernatural, rather than simply a herbalist. Thus, Khotso may have reconstructed the Zulu term, expanding its meaning to suit his purposes. Specific terminology is needed to indicate the nature of Khotso's profession, but in this regard, as in other areas of his life, he defies categorisation. Consequently, the term *inyanga* is utilised; and words such as *herbalist* and *medicine man* are also used at times, although their limitations in this specific context are acknowledged.

In this and in certain other aspects of his career, Khotso turned to mystification, a technique employed by a range of professionals in diverse fields. It can serve to enhance the status of a practitioner in the eyes of the general public, thereby increasing the influence that he or she is able to wield over those around them and making it harder for his or her authority to be challenged. One obvious example is the Western medical profession. Over the centuries it has been common practice for doctors to preserve a distance between themselves and their patients, emphasising their own superior wisdom and their clients' relative ignorance in the process, divulging only limited information about the exact nature of their patients' ailments. Another comparable instance occurs in academia, in which research findings can be encased in jargon so dense that it becomes almost impossible for a non-academic outsider to evaluate them.

Such practices seek to create the impression that the practitioner in question is an individual set apart, possessing a wealth of rarefied knowledge and expertise that is too extensive and complex for the layperson to comprehend. Consequently, it becomes difficult for outsiders to query the validity of a specific professional's judgement and insights. Instead, they are expected to be grateful for whatever forms of wisdom and assistance are bestowed on them from above. In like fashion, Khotso was inclined to present himself as a man who had gained special access to profound and perilous secrets inaccessible to ordinary mortals.

On a practical level, Khotso made use of a range of different plants and substances in his work. Some required a highly specialised knowledge of indigenous vegetation. Lunika, for instance, described how he was trained by Khotso's own herbalists, who took him into the veld to teach him about specific plants that could be utilised in herbal remedies.

Lunika said that Khotso himself remained cagey, taking care not to divulge all the ingredients of his own special remedies and potions.

The Qacha's Nek man who had received training at Khotso's house in Lusikisiki described how parts of plants possessing symbolic qualities, such as bark, leaves and resin, can, under the right conditions and with the correct preparation, be converted into active agents for well-being or prosperity. Strawberries, for instance, or the bark of a peach tree can be used to multiply riches, reflecting the way those plants themselves bear fruit. Sap from specific trees and shrubs can be used to generate fertility, because the milky fluid resembles mother's milk. Certain types of reddish resin call to mind blood, and so they can be used for protective purposes. 'But you need special training to understand this,' he said. 'And once you are trained, you can't disclose everything.'

Perceptions such as this draw on the age-old conviction that great knowledge and potency are founded on mystery. Divulge too much and you risk losing these attributes. In *Sundiata*, the thirteenth-century oral epic from Mali, the narrator concludes with these words: 'I was able to see and understand what my masters were teaching me, but between their hands I took an oath to teach only what is to be taught and conceal what is to be kept concealed.'[7] This was possibly another reason why Khotso preferred to surround himself with secrecy and why he encouraged his trainee herbalists to keep certain matters secret too.

Khotso made special use of intelezi, medicine for protection, purification and good luck. The flower beds outside his Lusikisiki house are densely packed with agapanthus – an indigenous plant that may seem commonplace because it appears in many public locations, such as on traffic islands and outside civic buildings. Yet it has special properties that not many know about. The bulb of the plant is ground, then mixed with other substances and water, providing one source of intelezi. If a customer had to appear before the magistrate, he or she could wash in water mixed with this potion, which could remove misfortunes in the same way it washed away dirt. Intelezi could be put to other uses, such as physical healing. For instance, it offers relief from stings and itches.

Another good-luck plant was *mapipa*. If the root was dug out and dried in the sun, ground into powder, then put in the bath, it could bring about success.

Khotso would also employ the concoction known as *isipili* in Xhosa (or *seipone* in Sotho) for certain rituals and procedures that became an important part of his work. It contains a herb that is known as *balao* in Sotho. As its name suggests, isipili, reminiscent of the Afrikaans word *spieël* (meaning 'mirror'), reflects the other world. It offers a way of communing with the ancestors and provides a doorway into the domain of the spirits, through visions, insights and answers to mysterious questions. Ask a question of the herb before taking the medicine, and it could give you the answer. 'If you wanted to find out the name of your worst enemy,' Lunika said, 'the medicine would tell you.' Isipili has hallucinogenic properties, and Khotso would take advantage of these.

Khotso also used certain stones. One person who was delegated to gather some of these for him was his niece Lefu. At the time of her birth, Khotso was already a young man. He would return to visit Ha Ramokakatlela, initially quite regularly. When she was a young woman, Khotso would ask Lefu and a few of her friends to collect mountain quartz for him. He would then grind up the stones into a powdery muti. Many others apart from Khotso believed, or have come to believe, in the healing power of crystals. For instance, they have been used as ritual objects by the San.[8] In Western society today, the perception that quartz crystals possess health-giving, restorative power has acquired considerable vogue, especially in New Age thought.

No discussion of Khotso's medicines would be complete without mentioning ibangalala, which is a muti for virility and sexual potency that is used on both people and livestock. Khotso offered some of this substance, which came in the form of a sweet-smelling yellowish powder, to Blades. Khotso wouldn't reveal what it consisted of, although he told Blades that it came from a plant his men gathered for him in Lesotho. Blades did try out the ibangalala Khotso offered him, admitting, 'It did give a sharp sexual stimulation.' Other informants have experimented with the plant and reported that they found it effective. The botanical name of ibangalala is *Corchorus asplenifolius Burch*.⁹

Although ibangalala was one of his best-known remedies, Khotso used a great many different substances in his work, and sometimes whatever was closest to hand became infused with his powers. His old friend Julius Khoapa told Blades how, in the early days, Khotso kept a number of black sheep on his first farm. Whenever he slaughtered a sheep, he kept the tail, smeared it with muti made from its fat and fastened it to a stick. This became his favoured method of keeping hail at bay. 'Khotso never had hail on his farm,' said Khoapa. 'He would wave his stick here and there and hail would go back to where it came from.' The hail sticks weren't cheap, but they proved popular, even among white farmers, according to Blades. In an area where hailstorms posed a problem, Khotso could, and did, claim that when people's crops were damaged by hail it was because they hadn't bought one of his special sticks.

Later in his career, Khotso would find another, more ambitious way of turning the hailstorms that beset East Griqualand and adjacent parts of Pondoland to his material advantage. Someone who knew Khotso described him as a racketeer – and one of his most lucrative and elaborate rackets was his hail insurance. Local farmers were reminded of the ever-present threat of hail and were encouraged to pay protection money to Khotso as a means of guaranteeing that their lands would remain hail-free. The idea caught on, and a substantial number of locals could be seen making regular payments, secure in the conviction that they were safeguarding their farms. Inevitably, hailstorms would strike indiscriminately and every now and then a dissatisfied client would summon up sufficient courage to complain. Khotso did not like being told that his medicines had failed; yet all the same, he had learned to master the art of smooth, reasonable explanations by means of which he could prove that the problem lay with the client rather than with the medicine. There was someone in the district, he would tell his dissatisfied customer, who had not paid for hail insurance, which meant that the area was not secured against hail. And if there was one unprotected chink through which the hailstones could fall, in the natural order of things they would move on, so that even those farmers who had behaved responsibly, by seeking protection against hail, would be at risk. So it was in their interests, he told his clients, to make sure that everyone around them had taken out hail insurance.

Like the lamb's tails used to shoo away hailstones as if they were impudent flies, some of the ingredients Khotso used would hardly be associated with magic under ordinary circumstances. But as Fanele Sicwetsha, a University of Fort Hare student researcher from a Transkei village near Mount Frere, once remarked, 'Nothing connected to Khotso was ever ordinary.'[10] Khotso was particularly fond of lavender oil, procured at Goodwin's Pharmacy in Kokstad, which he used as a base ingredient in a number of his potions, including one of his most popular concoctions: special muti designed to make people attractive to those around them. The lavender oil was probably the source of the perfumed aroma that hung around him, according to various people who knew Khotso well, including Lunika.

But there are also tales of the rare and strange ingredients forming part of Khotso's potions that could be procured only with great difficulty and danger. The Sotho herbalist Nthoa Bohlokoa Moshoeshoe, who would one day become one of Khotso's suppliers, told of two occasions in his youth when he plunged himself into grave peril while searching for a rare plant that Khotso required.

In 1932, Nthoa Bohlokoa was called to the great palace of Chief Dibopuoa in Queen's Mercy, near Matatiele, where he found the chief in the company of Khotso. He was instructed to assist the herbalist, and since nobody challenges a chief's command, least of all an eighteen-year-old boy, he departed with the visitor. Although Khotso was older than the young man, the youth noticed that he was strong in body. 'But I was no weakling!' Nthoa Bohlokoa declared. 'For my age I was regarded as one of the best in the district in stick fighting, horse riding, diving and swimming.'

He discovered that Khotso had come to hear of his expertise in swimming and consequently required his services. 'Khotso told me that he wished to go to a deep pool, to find a special plant that grew only deep under the water, in kingfisher droppings. We set off to the nearest river and I dived into first one pool and then another, but without any luck. It was only much later in the day that I saw, right at the bottom of one very deep pool, a plant growing in what appeared to be bird manure.'

Nthoa Bohlokoa had learned about flora and their various uses, but this species, with its flat broad leaves about the size of a hand and tapering to a point, was something he had never seen before. He gripped the plant and tried to yank it out, but it was rooted too firmly in the riverbed. Then he grabbed a small axe fastened at his waist and began hacking at the base of the stem. As he severed the plant, the water began to churn around him. What would normally have come naturally – to surface and gasp for air – became a desperate battle as the pool heaved and tossed, forcing him downwards.

'Eventually,' Nthoa Bohlokoa said, 'I managed to fight my way to the surface, still clinging to the plant, only to find Khotso had vanished!'

He set off homewards and it was not long before he saw Khotso in the distance, hurrying along as if the devil himself was at his back. Khotso glanced over his shoulder, saw the youth hastening towards him and stopped. Silently, Nthoa Bohlokoa handed him the plant. In much of southern Africa, it is believed that deep pools are inhabited by spirits and supernatural snakes that can become enraged if they are disturbed. In making off with the plant, Nthoa Bohlokoa realised that he had aroused the fury of the being in the pool. Khotso must have known that the expedition was fraught with hazard and decided to put as much distance as possible between himself and the river as soon as the water started to swirl.

Nthoa Bohlokoa's work did not end there. 'Before the year was out, I was summoned by the chief and told to accompany Khotso to another pool, much further away. What could I do? He was my chief, so I felt it would be disrespectful to say no.'

The pool in question was situated near a village called Ha Mapote in Lesotho, in the gloom of a deep gorge at the foot of the Malutis. Nthoa Bohlokoa dived into the icy mountain-shadowed waters and, almost immediately, he saw the plant below. As soon as he took hold of it, the waters began to close around him, seeking to clench him in their grasp. This time, the struggle was even more terrifying, but eventually he managed to break free of the pool. Thick mist shrouded the gorge and, once again, Khotso was nowhere to be seen.

'As I scrambled upwards,' Nthoa Bohlokoa said, 'I made out an eerie picture on the ridge of the mountain: the silhouettes of people peering downwards at me. When I drew closer, I could see they were gazing at me in awe and disbelief.'

After he had located Khotso and given him the plant, they were invited to the village. There, Nthoa Bohlokoa was told that the pool he had just escaped from was the dwelling place of a tremendous snake, which defended its turf with unearthly violence. 'So in the locals' eyes, I must have been very brave – or very foolish – to have ventured into the pool,' Nthoa Bohlokoa concluded. 'And I must have had very strong ancestors to have been able to escape from it again. Thankfully, that was the last time that Khotso wanted me to assist him.'

During the Second World War, Nthoa Bohlokoa was commended in an official dispatch for having performed valuable service against the enemy. But he maintained that no foe that he ever encountered in the white man's war could be compared to the enemy he did battle with at the bottom of the Senqu River. He learned later that the plant that Khotso so desperately wanted was called *ntekwane*. Both Nthoa Bohlokoa and Lunika agree that it is one of the luckiest of all the plants in southern Africa.

But it was not only through rare herbs, sometimes acquired at a potentially dangerous cost to others, that Khotso established himself in his profession. Many people who knew Khotso claim that he was able to accomplish this because he did have access to extraordinary powers, the exact nature of which remains the subject of some debate.

'A lot of the legend was just that,' Lunika admitted to Blades. 'But,' he added enigmatically, 'Khotso did have some supernatural powers. Inyangas do.'

Lunika is now a preacher in the Anglican Church. 'Because I am a Christian,' he reflected, 'I know that some of the methods Khotso used are against Christian principles. But I also know that if one believes in muti and snakes, he will get the power that he wants.'

Lunika's belief in Khotso's ability to exercise control over the paranormal is shared by Lala Yako, a retired businessman who initially lived in Duncan Village, East London, then later in the township of Mdantsane, an area twenty kilometres outside East London, to which Africans living in the city would have to relocate. In the 1960s, Yako regularly visited Khotso to obtain muti for good fortune for his business. 'I'm an educated man, but in my opinion, Khotso had genuine magic. If you've never seen it, you can't believe it,' he said.

Meanwhile, back in the 1920s, Khotso's reputation for possessing magical powers was still taking hold. Initially, Khotso would sell his herbs and potions as he moved around hunting jackal and carrying out other jobs. Then, towards the end of the decade, he worked from a tiny rented room in Kokstad. Khoapa, by then a policeman, described how he met Khotso in 1928. 'He had just a small house, a small room big as this mat. . . . I went into his house. I was shocked, I found five-shilling pieces, crowns all over the table and people getting their medicines.' In those days, five shillings would have been a lot of money for someone in Khoapa's position. '*Hau!*' said Khoapa. 'How Khotso laughed when he told me: "Now I'm making money!" '[11]

Not only as a teacher but in other respects as well, MaDlamini played an important part in helping Khotso build himself up as a herbalist. Once Khotso had launched his business, he used her to attract people to his practice. Makeka said: 'In fact, Khotso was very clever: MaDlamini was very beautiful, so he would tell customers to first speak to his wife before coming to him.' Thus, many of Khotso's clients had been lured to him by the prospect of spending time in the company of a lovely woman, and his marriage was also a business partnership.

The fact that so few people today, apart from some in the south-eastern Malutis, know where Khotso was born suggests that, as his wealth and fame gradually increased, he separated himself more and more from the village of his birth. Various older inhabitants of Ha Ramokakatlela have said that Khotso's visits to the village became less frequent over time. One account that these old people recollect embodies Khotso's withdrawal from his birthplace in dramatic form. They describe how, when he had decided to settle in Kokstad, his family hut in the mountain village burned down. One such account came from Khotso's niece Lefu, who remembered playing beside Khotso's family hut when she was a small child and seeing the rondavel suddenly catching fire. Lefu was unsure why the hut should have burst into flames. Its thatched roof might have caught fire as a result of some accident inside the hut or maybe the summer heat helped trigger the blaze, which could then have been fanned by the high mountain winds. But some people think that Khotso's strange powers may have been at work.

There is a supernatural phenomenon known in Xhosa as *ukuvutha*, which means 'to be on fire'. This appears to be a form of spontaneous combustion and certain traditional doctors have been said to have the ability to bring this about. When ukuvutha takes place, specific possessions, even livestock, have been seen to suddenly and inexplicably burst into flames.[12] Some suspect that when the family hut caught fire, it might have been a long-range form of ukuvutha for which Khotso was responsible. This explanation could have seemed credible to those who believed that Khotso's supernatural powers were closely associated with various other elements. He seemed to be not only connected to the potent beings that resided in rivers and pools, but also able to control the path of the inkanyamba as it tore through the skies. Drawing as he did on water and air to work his magic, he might well have wished to claim to make use of fire as well.

Whatever its cause, the image of flames destroying the family home suggests symbolically that Khotso was, in one way or another, burning his roots as he turned his interests and energies more and more towards Kokstad. As he put his true past behind him, so he began constructing a new history for himself, based not so much in the stark, unyielding terrain of a Lesotho mountain village, but in the luxuriant, multi-hued landscape of story.

While Khotso's father passed away fairly early in his son's life, when Khotso was twenty-one, his mother died in the Kokstad area in 1936, when Khotso's career was in the ascendant. Like the burning of his family rondavel, the death of Khotso's mother also severed his roots with his past. As the person who knew most about Khotso's origins and his family history slipped away into the shadows, so did the possibility of penetrating the mysteries surrounding his origins and early life.

Part Two
1932–1960

Chapter 5
The Wife Below the Water

By the early 1920s, Khotso had embarked on the first of several marriages. But after a few years, his earliest bride, MaDzanibe, had returned to her father. According to MaDlamini, she died in the 1930s. Khotso's first wife's departure from his household was not surprising. As subsequent wives and concubines would discover, entering into a relationship with Khotso was rather like boarding an overloaded minibus-taxi today and traversing a bumpy landscape, destination uncertain, crowded by a stream of other passengers embarking and disembarking.

On the other hand, MaDlamini, who became Khotso's second wife in 1932, remained part of his extended household, through a roller-coaster ride of dramatic changes, family upheavals and her spouse's rampant promiscuity. Khotso's eldest daughter, Patricia, who remained in his household after Khotso's short-lived marriage to her mother, MaDzanibe, had come to an end, was of the opinion that her father could not successfully manage polygamy and was intrigued by wooing and falling in love. Patricia would eventually become a nurse, and one press photograph displays her in a starched white collar and cap, with a grave expression on her face as she reflects on her father's misdemeanours.[1]

Even in these early days of her marriage, MaDlamini would have been aware of the extent to which her husband would never fully understand or empathise with the belief system that gave a sense of purpose and meaning to her life. As a Catholic, she attended church services regularly and tried to persuade Khotso to accompany her, but he had little time for Christianity. Western religion did not offer the kind of powers to which he wished to lay claim. Diverging though they did spiritually, physically MaDlamini and Khotso were very close to one another, spending the initial years of their married life cramped together in a shabby rented living space. Then, from 1934 onwards they rented a house next door to James Lunika's uncle, in Hope Street, Kokstad.

There is one wife that many maintain was one of Khotso's earliest spouses and possibly the most significant one of them all. Lunika has a picture of her, on one of his most prized possessions: a personalised, intricately carved staff bestowed on him by Khotso. Undulating out from the middle of the staff is an image of a mermaid. Lunika calls her Nkosazana, saying that she stands for good fortune. He concedes that this is another name for the mamlambo: a being of such potency and peril that some find it preferable to refer to her by a title such as Nkosazana, meaning 'princess' in Zulu, rather than calling her by her actual name. The mamlambo is a supernatural snake able to take on the form of a beautiful woman. She is often envisaged as a mermaid: half woman and half serpent. She has the capacity to bestow wealth on her owner, but at a great price. As Khotso's fame spread and his fortune grew, so did the conviction that Khotso, from an impoverished background, illiterate yet fabulously wealthy, was involved in *ukuthwala*, the Xhosa term for the possession of a wealth-giving creature, frequently a snake.[2]

A man from Matatiele who was friendly with Khotso in the 1940s and 1950s recalled an event that took place when the latter visited him. At four o'clock, Khotso would announce: 'My wife is expecting me under the water, I must be going.' By hinting that he was 'married' to the mamlambo, was Khotso merely having fun at his host's expense? Many people who knew Khotso, Lunika included, maintain that it is possible that the rise and decline of Khotso's powers can be traced to his relationship with a key female presence in his life: his wife under the water, Nkosazana. The word *mamlambo* derives from the Xhosa word for river, *mlambo*. Because *u-Ma-Mlambo*, her full name in Xhosa, resides in deep water, she is known as 'the mother of the river'. In Sotho, she is known as *mamolapo*, which has the same meaning.

The mamlambo tends to be associated with Western forms of prosperity, like money, so the fact that she is sometimes depicted as a Western mermaid, as in the form on Lunika's walking stick, seems apt. It is also said that on occasion she manifests herself as a beautiful white woman. In contrast with other beings in traditional southern African beliefs, such as the abantu bomlambo, or 'river people', and the inkanyamba, the mamlambo is a relatively new presence. She has arisen in part from a sense of disconnection to a traditional, communal way of life, inequalities and imbalances in the social order, and the lure of Western materialism. The Westernised forms which she often adopts testify to this.[3]

There are a number of mermaid figures in African traditional belief, one of the best-known of these being the West African Mami Wata. With her curvaceous torso and long flowing hair, she bears a close resemblance to the image on Lunika's staff. Like the mamlambo, she is a dangerous, seductive figure, offering wealth and power but able to bring about terrifying ruin.

Essentially, the mamlambo is perceived as a being who exerts her seductive force over males, and thus she is sometimes referred to as *inyoka yamadoda*, or 'snake of men'.[4] Her shape shifts and changes. As a serpent, she has shining, hypnotic eyes and may have a brilliant jewel set in her forehead.[5] In exchange for the wealth she provides, the mamlambo demands offerings. These can include bread, banknotes, the blood of animals or even, it is asserted, the blood of those closest to the mamlambo's owner, such as family members. Someone in the Lowveld once observed to the anthropologist Isak Niehaus: 'If you don't feed it with a sacrifice, it will turn and kill you.'[6]

'It's like a motor car,' said one man from Mount Frere, in the Transkei. Like many others in his area, he had heard numerous stories about the mamlambo and the practice of ukuthwala. 'You've got to service that motor car. If you don't, the car will start giving you problems.' Appropriately enough, the Tswana use the same word for blood and money, *madi*, suggestive of the way in which money is the lifeblood of modern existence, yet may prove damaging when a craving for wealth ruins the lives of individuals and communities, sometimes at the cost of personal relationships. The belief that the mamlambo feeds on the blood of those closest to its owner is symbolically appropriate in this regard.

The peril of owning a mamlambo is that it will eventually control its owner – just as the desire for money can come to rule people's lives. It appears that Khotso adored his wealth. For instance, Ellen Jones remarked: 'Money just had to flow in, one way or another. He loved the smell and touch of it, coins and notes. No getting out of it. There were pillows of money.' Khotso's aversion to banks, of which he only made limited use in the latter part of his life, can partly be understood in the light of his wanting to have his wealth within easy reach, all the better to contemplate it. One journalist remarked: 'All too often, Khotso is taken seriously. But it is only in his attitude to money that Khotso is really serious. He likes money and is not ashamed to admit it.'[7]

The term *ukuthwala* denotes a special long-term medicine for wealth and good fortune, as opposed to various short-term medicines for material success and luck, including intelezi. We can bear in mind that ukuthwala can also mean 'to abduct'. Was Khotso so carried away by his obsession with fame and wealth that he lost touch with certain basic realities? He wove outrageous fictions around himself and he ran various risks. In addition to this, certain strange, even shocking practices were attributed to him and he would forge shadowy, dubious alliances with leading, much-hated political figures. Were these all the result of the fact that he was a man possessed – whether by the snake-like mamlambo itself, or by the heady, treacherous dreams of economic prowess she embodies? Moreover, ukuthwala can also mean 'to bear a large load on one's head', a burden so heavy that it cannot be carried by hand. In other words, ukuthwala suggests bearing a huge weight that one is not adequately equipped to transport. This, in turn, could indicate that the ownership of a mamlambo involves taking on a load its owner cannot carry properly through life.

As far as many locals in Kokstad, and later the Transkei, were concerned, stories linking Khotso with ukuthwala provided a means of levelling condemnation against him on the grounds of his wealth, which would come to constitute a controlling force in his life and which he flaunted in the midst of poverty-stricken communities. The notion that Khotso's fortune, which seemed to many to have dropped into his lap through the workings of some shadowy supernatural agency, could not possibly have been honestly obtained pervades many of the accounts of his association with ukuthwala. For instance, the student researcher Fanele Sicwetsha reported that one elderly informant from the Mount Ayliff area had commented on the attitudes underlying such perceptions: 'In a traditional set-up, people believe that you've got to earn what you've got, be seen to work hard for it. You know, people were poorer then, especially blacks at that time. But no one knew where Khotso had got all his money from. So some people thought he had got a mamlambo.'

Over time, moral condemnation would feature more markedly in some stories about Khotso. In later days, this would cause him some concern. But during the Kokstad era, he would have brushed aside the ethical judgements of others. Tales connecting him with wealth-giving snakes helped build up around him a sense of fear and awe. This was also good for business, especially since he was a dealer in such serpents himself.

Like the inkanyamba, the mamlambo is at the centre of the stories concerning Khotso and the empire he created around himself. Some Kokstad locals claim that if you know where to look, you can find images by the Mzintlava River which symbolise this. There is a rock by the river, with reptilian creatures facing each other carved on it: inkanyamba and nkosazana, some maintain. No one knows exactly who did the carving or when it was done. Khotso liked to claim that he was responsible for it, using the image to remind locals of the terrifying, destructive supernatural serpents that he could call on to work his will.

Whatever one thinks of the stories detailing the supernatural origins of Khotso's wealth, there is the indisputable fact that his fortune owed its origins to some prosaic realities: his capacity for intense activity and steady, determined, goal-directed labour, which was evident right from the outset. The bare, exposed plains and plateaux of Nomansland and the freezing, precipitous mountainsides that he traversed in his days as a bounty hunter are reminders of the hardship, isolation and sheer physical endurance that characterised the period of his life during which he laid the foundations of his fortune. Throughout his career, Khotso believed in the efficacy of hard work and sought to impress this on others.

In fact, Khotso was a workaholic. Ellen remembered how he would demand coffee at three o'clock in the morning so that he could start his day. Even in his old age, one of his daughters said, his working day started at four in the morning and he would expect the other members of his household, even his children, to follow suit. He would sometimes quote the Sotho proverb *Ha no khomo ya boroko* (There is no *lobola* [bride price] cow which is paid for a lazy wife). Ellen recalled:

> Khotso was a strict person. When he wanted something done you had to do it at once. He only gave luck to good workers who didn't delay. Khotso never sat still for long. I'd see him loading his truck with men to work in his fields and building dams on his farms. He loved to make people work.

Even at night, while everyone else was resting, Khotso still seemed to be active. You could hear him walking around the house, said Ellen. It seemed as if he hardly slept. She did remark, however, that occasionally someone would stumble across Khotso in the dark, taking a brief catnap on the floor. He was attached to his dogs and would sometimes lie curled up among them for warmth and companionship.

There is another Sotho proverb: *Phuthi e tsoha ka meso anyese* (The phuthi, or the blue duiker, wakes at dawn to suckle). This suggests that the Phuthi people rise early to go about the business of the day. In other words, they are hard workers. Khotso's brand of industrious, energetic application to the tasks at hand far exceeded that suggested by the proverb.

The growth of Khotso's fortune stemmed not only from hard work, but also from thrift. He tried to make those around him aware of the importance of saving money. Even in later life, this remained a special concern of his. His wife MaMjoli said:

> Khotso always instilled good values and habits in those who interacted with him, whether as family members, friends or patients. He taught my daughter Ma-Six how to save money at a very early age. He encouraged her to save all the money she was given in a special container and not to immediately run off and buy sweets with it. He taught the workers in his household the same thing. I would go to what was then known as Barclays Bank to deposit money in all their accounts on a regular basis. They would only have access to their money after they had gone home.

Khotso resided in one of the main roads in Kokstad, although at some distance from the centre of the town. Yet at least he had the financial wherewithal to live in the town itself, at a time when Kokstad's working-class black inhabitants were being shifted into an area set apart for them. In 1923, the ground had been prepared for this when the Natives (Urban Areas) Act was passed. This expanded on and entrenched the notion of racial separation contained in the 1913 Natives Land Act, by drawing on the 1921 Transvaal Local Government Commission. This body, otherwise known as the Stallard Commission, promoted the idea that the urban areas belonged to the whites, having been brought into being by them. An African person, on the other hand, was envisaged as a temporary sojourner, who should be permitted to enter and reside in such areas only when carrying out work for members of the white community.

The Natives (Urban Areas) Act turned the notions contained in the Stallard Commission into reality, making provision for African townships, which were set apart from the cities and towns adjoining them, and limiting black entry into these districts. The act was amended in 1930 and regularly thereafter, becoming more and more restrictive over time. One woman, who was born and grew up in one of the major streets in Kokstad in the early part of the twentieth century but ended up living in Bhongweni, the area set aside for black occupation, recalled what transpired when blacks newly arrived in Kokstad sought to live in the town itself: 'Because of the influx of black people, those blacks who could not afford to buy erfs in town were given sites in Bhongweni. This was especially so with migrant labourers.'

Thus, long before the onset of apartheid, an economic, class-based form of racial segregation, reinforced by legal proclamations, was falling into place. However, in the 1930s, money could still buy Kokstad's African inhabitants a degree of security and respect, which Khotso would have enjoyed, as he was in economic ascendancy. Little did he suspect what the future held in store for him.

Khotso delighted in displaying the money he was earning as his business expanded. From the outset of his career, he pinned banknotes to the walls of his practice. One man who grew up in Kokstad and remembered Khotso from his boyhood in the 1950s said that he had been told that this had led a couple of individuals into temptation, with unexpected results. Evidently two Griquas stole some of Khotso's money from the wall while painting the room. They felt that Khotso would not even notice that some of the notes were missing. But he took one look at the painters and said, 'Tell those chaps to put their hands in their pockets and see what they will get.' Instead of the money, the painters found small snakes coiled up. Khotso loved practical jokes, and he burst out laughing when he saw their horrified faces. 'Ask for money, don't take!' he said to the painters. This playful forgiveness was one of his characteristic reactions to would-be robbers that he had thwarted. Some narratives relate that this was combined with gestures of surprising generosity. Years later, someone who had lived in Khotso's Lusikisiki household told a story illustrating this:

> This woman took a pumpkin from his field without asking . . .

She just stole it and got that pumpkin to her home. She chopped the pumpkin, put it into the pot to feed her children. Then the pumpkin talked: 'Why are you chopping me? You didn't ask my father for me. So, get me home! I don't want to be cooked without consulting my father.'

Hey! This woman was afraid. Then the pumpkin said, 'If you don't want to go to my father, consult the police.'

She took the pot with the pumpkin and she got to the police station. They took her with the van and brought her to Khotso. He said to the police: '*Hayi*! No! Just go, I'll solve this problem.' Then he said to the woman, 'Why are you stealing from my field?'

'I'm hungry,' she pleaded. 'My children have nothing to eat.'

So he replied, 'Don't you ever steal again in my field. If you have nothing, just come to me, I'll help you.'

He gave her a tickey and this woman went to the shop and bought everything she needed with it, and then got the tickey back. She spent and spent and spent and never used up that tickey.

But Khotso was a disconcerting mixture of gentleness and vengefulness. One never knew what to expect from him, for he could help would-be thieves or just as easily bring calamity down on those who tried to rob him. Pascal Makeka related a story concerning a special medicine that Khotso had on offer to prevent people from stealing stock. It didn't come cheap; it cost one hundred pounds. If his medicine was sprinkled around the cattle post, Khotso said, vultures would come and eat the thief. Once, through a combination of circumstances, this worked to his advantage, resulting in fatal consequences for a small would-be felon. Makeka related the story:

Khotso had given medicine to one man, one very rich man. He told him, 'Anybody who will come and drive your animals away, there will be vultures that will chase him.' Now what happened is, there was this dead horse, and the vultures were flying to this dead horse. But the boy that was stealing the cattle, he was in the process of driving the animals, so he ran away and fell over a cliff and died. Then Khotso was proved right.

A white Catholic priest heard about this special medicine of Khotso's and was determined to challenge local superstitions. So he stole some sheep from the very same place and later returned them, having proved his point – or so he thought. Not long afterwards, he died. Makeka remarked: 'As I look now, it was not because of Khotso Sethuntsa's medicine. It wasn't. But in those days, because people were full of stories about Khotso, we believed it was Khotso.'

There are many similar anecdotes. For instance, MaDlamini and others described an incident in which Khotso went to the Kokstad Post Office to buy stamps and a tsotsi picked his pocket. 'Khotso's bodyguards wanted to grab the man,' she said. 'But Khotso just told them, "Leave him, don't mind." Then the tsotsi fell and broke his head and died.'

Tales like these, some of which were initially related and circulated by Khotso, fulfilled a practical function: they made people reluctant to steal from him. In poor communities, such as the areas in which Khotso lived and worked, people with money stand out and run the risk of being targeted by criminals, the impoverished and the desperate. Khotso used stories the way well-off people today use razor wire and armed security companies. Moreover, with tales like these in circulation, the belief that Khotso's medicines worked increased, and his business prospered.

Various white farmers made use of Khotso's services, reasoning that if potential thieves knew they had his muti, this might well put them off. For instance, one white farmer from Cedarville, near Kokstad, consulted Khotso when his sheep kept disappearing. Blades was told that after Khotso had visited the farm and conducted 'a little ceremony', no more sheep vanished. A long-standing Kokstad local, now in her seventies, has similar recollections. When tools vanished from her father's farm, he called Khotso in and shortly afterwards the missing items were returned.

With cash rolling in from both black and white customers, Khotso began moving up in the world during the 1930s. 'He would put on clean flannels and don a blazer,' said Julius Khoapa.[8] This did not mean, however, that Khotso was turning into a snappy dresser. On ceremonial occasions or when he was greeting special guests, he would don his lavishly ornamented robes, but most of the time, as someone later remarked, Khotso's driver was far better dressed than his employer. Whatever the season, Khotso liked to wear what became his trademark uniform: corduroy trousers, workaday shirts and, when necessary, a baggy jacket, often sheepskin. He favoured velskoens, although growing up in rural poverty in tough mountainous regions had hardened his feet and sometimes he went barefoot, especially in his younger years. As Khotso's daughter Patricia remarked to Blades, 'My father was never a fancy dresser, a dandy.'

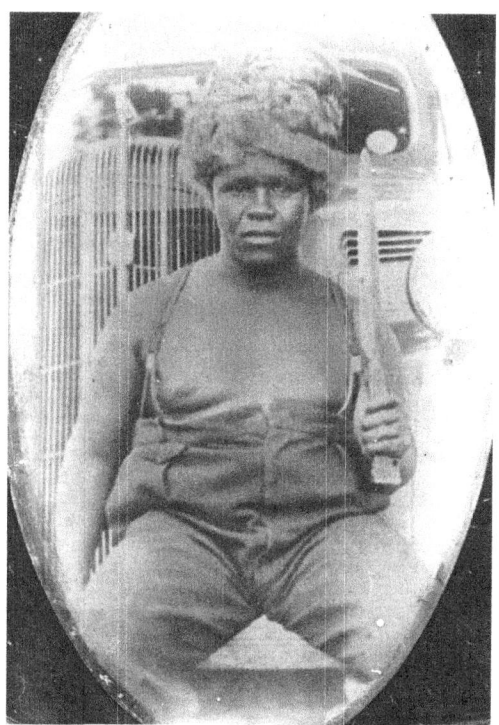

An early photograph of Khotso, in front of one of his cars. (Courtesy of MaDlamini Catherine Sethuntsa)

Khotso started working as a full-time herbalist only in the 1930s. Lunika first met Khotso when he became his uncle's neighbour in 1934. He did not remember money pinned to the walls, but what struck him were the fifteen-pint containers full of silver coins in the room that Khotso worked from – positioned just near the doorway, to impress the clients as they walked in. 'People who came into his room would see the silver and be frightened by the sight of such a lot of money,' Lunika said. 'Nobody would be bold enough to take any of the money.'

While Khotso worked hard to establish himself, the ancestors were working for him as well, MaDlamini maintained. She remembered what happened in 1936, when Khotso disappeared for a while, then reappeared bearing a traditional African clay pot of gold coins. The ancestors, he told his wife, had sent him to the top of a waterfall in Lesotho and shown him where the gold lay, waiting for him alone. MaDlamini was adamant that this was not a fanciful yarn. She had seen the pot of gold coins with her own eyes. Quite possibly, however, this pot of gold coins had as much substance to it as the article at the end of the rainbow. Not only was Khotso beginning to accumulate his wealth, but he was starting to weave a glittering web of stories, through which he wished to attract and ensnare those around him.

Accordingly, Khotso may well have wished to spread a dramatic tale suggesting that a substantial amount of his early wealth had come about through the agency of the ancestors themselves. Jackal hunting was all very well, but a pot of gold made a far more impressive story. Moreover, in Khotso's eyes spiritual and material blessings went hand in hand, so he would have enjoyed creating a fiction illustrating this. It is possible that MaDlamini was instructed to pass his yarn on. Even years after her husband's death, she continued to retell this tale, remaining loyal to him despite the difficulties he had inflicted on her in the course of their married life.

As a young wife in 1936, MaDlamini was already becoming immersed in the world of myth and legend that her husband was constructing around himself. Because his career was beginning to take off as a result of this, she may have felt duty-bound to assist him in this area, even though it was at odds with her own religious principles. The traditional clay vessel containing the gold coins in the story can also be perceived as a symbolic suggestion of the link between MaDlamini, the maker of beautiful clay pots, and her husband, the accumulator of wealth.

In the same year in which he claimed he had found the gold coins,

Khotso acquired enough money to buy his first car, a Packard. The year 1936 thus seemed a time by which Khotso had earned substantial wealth, but in the broader scheme of things it was a less promising year. Political developments that would later cast their shadow over his career were in the making. Firstly, the Native Trust and Land Act of 1936 was passed. This expanded on and consolidated the Land Act of 1913 and the Urban Areas Act of 1923, which had made provision for racially determined control and ownership of land. While increasing territory in black areas, such as in the Umzimkhulu district in East Griqualand, the 1936 act terminated the right still possessed by black South Africans in the Cape Province to buy land outside the reserves, binding them closer to the regions consigned to them. In consequence, it increased their dependency on the migrant-labour system. In the apartheid era, the 1936 act would facilitate the formation of the black 'homelands', which would be one distinctive feature of the rigid policy of racial separation propounded by the National Party. The 'homelands' would be based on the territorial outlines demarcated in the Native Trust and Land Act.[9] Also in 1936, the Representation of Natives Act was passed. This deprived suitably qualified Africans of their right to vote on the common Cape electoral roll. Instead, they were permitted representation only on a separate, communal roll.

But to outsiders, Khotso liked to create the impression that he deemed himself master of his own destiny. This would have been possible because at this stage the inequities in South African society did not impinge on his own little world.[10] In addition, the fact that he was becoming wealthy might have featured more prominently in his consciousness than did concerns that the new political legislation would affect his own career. During this period, conjecture grew concerning possible sources of his money. Khotso himself had begun to drop a few tantalising hints, which had the effect of compounding rather than avoid this window clarifying the puzzle.

'He was an elusive man,' said Lala Yako. 'He'd never tell anything straight.' Yako became so close to Khotso in the 1960s, when he

Khotso displaying what he described as 'diamonds that could buy half Jo'burg'. (©BAHA. Photo by Alf Kumalo)

regularly purchased good-luck medicine from him, that he maintained he was made to feel as if he was Khotso's son. Yet Khotso remained an enigmatic figure to him.

Possibly there were practical reasons why Khotso was so fond of secrecy. Start asking about possible sources of his wealth, and you will hear it alleged that, while Khotso's herbal practice was undoubtedly flourishing, he was also engaged in covert dealings in drugs and diamonds. His regular visits to Lesotho helped fuel such speculations. Lesotho has diamonds, and dagga (marijuana) is clandestinely cultivated in remote villages, as is the case in other isolated, poverty-stricken parts of southern Africa, such as the Transkei.

Just as the rivers spill down from Lesotho into the lower-lying lands encircling it, so many secret dealers in Lesotho diamonds flowed down the mountains into South Africa. One man from Matatiele remarked that during the 1940s and 1950s, when he owned a farm in East Griqualand, buying diamonds in that area was as straightforward a matter as purchasing dagga in a South African city today. If anyone wanted to buy diamonds, they just had to know the right contact people or simply put the word out and the stones would find their way to them. Even if you didn't want diamonds, you were likely to encounter them.

By the 1930s, Khotso was becoming rich, and in the region in which he lived illicit diamond buying could provide one means of acquiring wealth speedily. Thus the possibility of a connection between Khotso's wealth and secret dealings in diamonds began to take root in the minds of many individuals.

Yako described how Khotso once showed him a safe that was set into the wall of his house and was so big that it was like a chamber that one could walk into. He never unlocked his safe in front of other visitors, Yako said, but one day Khotso made an exception in his case. Yako saw masses of banknotes and piles of coins, both old and new, Kruger rands and a tray full of diamonds. Just next to it was another tray piled high with glass gems resembling diamonds.

'Where do people say I got my riches from?' Khotso asked Yako. The latter ventured: 'Some people say you got it from medicine and working strange things – but I really don't know.' As he often did with visitors, Khotso then showed him a great many press clippings about himself. Then he produced one item not usually put on display: a diamond digger's licence from Lesotho, made out in his name. 'He told me that he went to Lesotho at night to get diamonds,' Yako continued. 'He said that he got alluvial diamonds there, as well as diamonds from diggings.' Khotso's diamond digger's licence may have been there to help fend off awkward questions from official quarters.

Those who knew Khotso would have found it hard not to encounter diamonds, whether real or imitation, at some point or other. Sparkling stones sometimes dangled from the small gold hoops that Khotso wore in his ears, and apart from the diamonds, most probably fake, with which he bedazzled journalists, he even incorporated 'diamonds' into some of his remedies. 'He'd give glass stones away with his medicine,' Yako recollected. 'He'd tell people to wash with them.'

Lunika recalled that there was always one room in Khotso's main house at Mount Nelson that was kept secret, closed off from the rest of the dwelling. People – some of whom were wearing skins and appeared to be from Lesotho – would come and go, meeting Khotso inside the room and then quietly departing again, without the public fanfare and elaborate ceremonies with which Khotso usually greeted visitors. Even Lunika, his prime minister and confidant, was never told what went on in that room.

Blades noted that while the police had their suspicions about Khotso, they were never able to come up with any hard evidence in support of them. 'They wondered if Khotso was smuggling dagga and there would be an all-stations alarm every time his green car was seen on the road. But they never found any dagga in it. Was he buying diamonds from the workers in the Lesotho mines [or the Lesotho migrant mineworkers]? the police asked. Again, there was never a clue.'

Rumours spread that Khotso might have had not only the denizens of the supernatural world but also the forces of law and order under his control. Some allege that Khotso was involved in shipping consignments of dagga away from its source into richer areas where there would be a ready market for it. But it was said that he never did anything so publicly risky himself, that he would keep at a safe distance from the operation, dispatching one of his drivers to transport the consignment on his behalf.

Like Nthoa Bohlokoa, who was sent on perilous errands to pluck a rare herb from pools on Khotso's behalf, the drivers were embarking on a task that placed them in jeopardy, even if not risking their lives. But Khotso's men had much to gain if the venture succeeded. It was alleged that once Khotso's parcels had been safely delivered, the driver would return for his payment. If the expedition went wrong, it was the driver, not the master, who would take the rap. If he had to pay the penalty for illegal activities, he knew that such loyalty to his master would pay dividends. However, hearsay had it that the drivers were willing to embark on these excursions because they knew that Khotso's network of invisible connections extended as far as the local police.

The tales concerning Khotso's shape-changing abilities trace their origins back to these days. 'He could change into a snake, a donkey, a pig, any shape he wanted to be,' remarked one man who grew up in the

Transkei town of Lady Frere in the 1960s. The shape-shifting yarns offered one explanation why, despite rumours that Khotso was involved in illicit activities, the police never managed to apprehend him. Disguising himself by altering his appearance, Khotso could evade anyone he wished. One popular tale was that the police saw not the black millionaire passing in his Cadillac, but a white woman in a modest middle-class car, apparently carrying out innocent household errands around town.

The trickster in African oral narratives slips from one shape to another. Harold Scheub describes certain key qualities possessed by this figure: 'Disguise, deception and illusion are [the trickster's] tools and weapons.' Such devices, Scheub continues, are employed as the trickster 'moves through the universe undertaking to satisfy his basic appetites'.[11] This description fits Khotso, who drew on his resources of craftiness and guile to obtain that for which he hungered: money, fame, sex and material opulence.

As the stories that describe the diversity of shapes Khotso adopted suggest, he was becoming increasingly difficult to pin down. While this had been the case even in his early days, Khotso's tendency to slip from one kind of person to another in various different perceptions of him was to become more evident from the 1930s onwards. One bewildering incident took place in 1937 when Khotso's son Motiki fell ill and died when he was only thirteen. While Khotso was blessed by good fortune when it came to material things, his family life was touched by tragedy in various respects. None of his sons lived to see middle age, but his first-born son's life was the shortest by far. Throughout his life, Khotso avoided funerals, feeling that they were unlucky, but his son's burial was a different story. Lunika, who was more or less the same age as Motiki, describes the peculiar event that he witnessed: 'There was a beautiful, expensive white coffin. But before it was lowered into the grave, Khotso climbed into his boy's grave and lay down, in the earth. Only after he had finished whatever it was that he was doing did he let them put the coffin in.'

This was one of Lunika's earliest memories of Khotso, and his first realisation that the man who was his uncle's next-door neighbour in

Hope Street was unlike ordinary people.

'Sometimes it is necessary to lose a family member, to go through hell to get rich,' someone said when discussing Khotso and the practice of ukuthwala. Was his first-born son's death the price Khotso had to pay for the fortune that he so adored? Others too have hazarded the guess that Motiki's death might have resulted from his father's dealings in sinister magic. In time to come, some narrators would describe with ghoulish relish not only Motiki's death, but the other mysterious deaths and disasters that befell some of Khotso's children and, purportedly, his extended family, implying that by dabbling in darkness Khotso had brought calamity on his family. These tales about times when misfortune and sorrow visited Khotso and his household are suggestive of their tellers' own desires, while fulfilling a compensatory function. Even as Khotso became the subject of widespread fascination because he was achieving the riches that many yearned for, such stories reassured their narrators and listeners that because wealth such as Khotso's might have been attained at a terrible price, it could bring no lasting good. In the end, all Khotso could offer his beloved son was a costly, ornate coffin.

In some of these tales and especially in accounts of Motiki's death and funeral, allegations that Khotso was involved in the muti trade in human flesh were aired. Some believe that Khotso used his son's flesh for this purpose. 'So when he went into the grave like that, they say he was trying to pacify his son for what he had done to him,' one man said. Yet there may be a simple explanation for Khotso's actions at his first-born son's funeral. It is quite possible that Khotso was publicly displaying the extent to which he, as a father, was devastated by the loss of his child, by accompanying his son down into his grave and making it ready for him in the same way that a parent will prepare a child's bed for the night. But whatever the reason for Khotso's behaviour, his action at his son's funeral served to fuel the conviction that he was involved in perilous occult practices. Such opinions did not deter Khotso unduly. If people feared his powers, so much the better.

While Khotso's wealth was increasing, it was believed that Nkosazana was presiding as an unseen but all-controlling presence over him, his household and his fortune. Khotso had bound himself to her, people whispered, waiting to see what his marriage to his wife under the water would bring. Even after Khotso's death, it would be rumoured that the consequences of this illicit union were still playing themselves out.

Chapter 6
At the White House

As the retinue of servants, patients, clients and hangers-on increased, the Hope Street house was no longer suitable premises. Weary of what was beginning to feel like a cramped abode, MaDlamini took a firm stand, emphasising to her husband that since they were no longer struggling to make a living, it was time to move somewhere more in keeping with their new status in life. So in 1940 Khotso took the step of buying one and a half acres of land on the edge of town, between the railway line and the Mzintlava River. The cost was two hundred and fifty pounds. This was a considerable amount of money at that time, but Khotso had reasons of his own for wanting to purchase land beside the river. On his newly acquired plot, he built the first of his extravagant, eccentric mansions.

Khotso's house was said to be founded on money. 'My daddy used to tell us that when one of his houses was built, many wheelbarrows of coins were used to fill up the foundation,' recalled one Kokstad woman, a trained nurse who lives in Bhongweni. Her family's connection with Khotso went back a long way, because they knew him when he was young. Khotso was her elder brother's contemporary, and the two boys became friends.

Although he called it Melside, Khotso's house was generally known as the White House because the entire edifice was painted white,

The White House as it is today: derelict and stripped of its former glory.

the colour of purity. Khotso favoured the colour for this reason. Its counterpart in the United States housed the leader of a nation. Likewise, the White House in Kokstad was intended to be an impressive mansion for that town's most prominent citizen. At least, that was how its owner liked to regard himself. Like Khotso's later dwellings, the White House was a sprawling construction, designed to accommodate its owner and his ever-expanding entourage. It was unique, an edifice like nothing seen anywhere else in East Griqualand or, for that matter, in South Africa. It was part Gaudí, part Gothic and part Pep Stores, or, as some might have imagined, the product of a visitation by alien architects who set out to construct a Western-style mansion but then became carried away by images from the *Arabian Nights*. Later, as Khotso's kingdom grew, comparable houses would come to adorn the hills of a number of Eastern Cape towns.

One of the trademark features of Khotso's abodes was statues of lions, symbols of power and royalty. These were stationed in the yard to guard the White House. 'Now people believed that during the night those lions would have fire in their eyes and in their mouths and actually roar,' Pondoland student researcher Fanele Sicwetsha said.

Khotso loved bright glass, so bejewelled windows and doors gleamed between archways and colonnades. Inlaid all around the arch above one of the main entrance gates was thick, mirror-like glass, which dazzled approaching visitors. Coloured tiles were set into places in the walls and arches. Minarets perched on the tops of pillars, entryways and chimneys, and the two entrances were topped by archways and flanked by pillars and minarets. Between them was a small gateway that served as a sentry box. No one could enter Khotso's property without his permission. Large bay windows curved outwards on either side of the main porch, as if to embrace visitors entering Khotso's domain. The setting of the White House enhances its strangeness and singularity. It stands alone on the edge of town on an expanse of land by the Mzintlava River, the openness and simplicity of the grasslands and hillsides of East Griqualand a backdrop to the ornamentation and artifice of Khotso's fantasia.

Today many people in Kokstad prefer to steer clear of the White House. The stone lions are long gone, as are the bright panes of glass and the colourful tiles. But the minarets remain, like decayed wedding cakes or dovecotes for winged emissaries from the world of uneasy dreams. In many cultures, white is the colour of death, and there is something spectral about the White House: a bleached and empty shell with the hue of old discoloured bones. The windows are empty sockets with darkness behind them. Along the Mzintlava, the winter grass whispers secrets.

This, at any rate, is how the White House might strike some outsiders. One of its current occupants, Meshack Nogudlu, who practises as a traditional healer, feels differently. He never knew Khotso personally, only observing him at a distance during the latter years of his life, but Meshack says that he senses the presence of Khotso around him: 'Nothing bad can happen to me while I am in this house.'

The doors outside and inside the house are held shut with pieces of twisted wire, but there are stronger forces that keep some rooms closed off from outsiders. Before leading visitors into certain parts of the house, Meshack will speak to the *amakhosi,* the protective ancestral spirits who can manifest themselves as snakes, asking their permission to bring strangers into their space and explaining to them that these people mean no harm. The White House is not a place that most strangers would venture into lightly, however. Even if you don't believe in the spirit world, the memories that surround Khotso's former home have a force of their own. Besides, no one can tell who – or what – might be lurking in the darkened, decaying rooms, with their odd musty smell and their uneven earth floors. It is hard to imagine that these chambers were once full of colour and life.

In Khotso's day, the interior of the White House was packed with a rainbow-like assortment of sparkling glass and silverware, brassware, gilt ornaments, mirrors and china, making some visitors feel as if they had strayed into a gaudy, exotic bazaar or, some journalists would hint, a slightly tacky treasure trove. However, Khotso liked his living space to be a reflection of his flamboyant personality, and perhaps he was compensating for the spartan surroundings of his youth. One journalist's description of the interior of the White House gives us a sense of the vibrant, multi-hued nature of Khotso's domestic surroundings:

> [We] were shown into a verandah lounge forty feet long. Big windows shielded by lace curtains admitted plenty of light. The floor was covered from wall to wall with pale blue mottled rubberised material. Along the inner walls were big glass trays crammed with a brilliant array of ornamental mirrors and brightly coloured but tasteful glassware and crystal. The effect was an enormous, exotic splash of colour that lent an air of opulence to the room.
>
> Along the outer wall was a row of high-backed dining chairs. At one end stood a settee and armchair in contemporary style. We were shown to these. Presently the domestic brought us orange juice in brilliantly coloured glasses. While we sipped this we counted the chairs in the room. There were forty-two.[1]

Peacocks sauntered around the grounds, living manifestations of this opulence, complementing the towers, minarets and archways of the White House and leaving some with the impression that they had strayed into the fabulous riverside abode of some strange potentate. The forty-two chairs arrayed in the lounge of the White House indicated that Khotso was prepared for large numbers of visitors. Adjoining the main building was a guesthouse designed to accommodate many people and to impress them with its lavish decor. Apart from the numerous beds, there were two dining-room suites with thirty-nine formal, high-backed chairs. As if some of the tightly massed ornaments in the main house had overflowed into the guesthouse, the main surfaces of the rooms in this building were piled high with glassware.

Many of the writers and journalists who visited the White House allowed themselves to be carried away by its owner's extravagant vaunting. Overwhelmed by the mountain of wealth that Khotso poured out in front of them and thrown off balance by the extraordinary details of his personal history that he offered visitors, they could not be entirely blamed for depicting him as an extravagant eccentric at the heart of a wacky rococo empire. But others, like the popular historian and travel writer Peter Becker, who met Khotso in the late 1950s, realised that this was only part of the picture. 'Beneath this veneer of boastfulness', Becker insisted, 'was another Khotso, gentle, kind, considerate and generous. It was an alter-ego that generated a current of powerful love, that served not only to enliven his own personality but to bring joy to the lives of all who needed his help.'[2]

There were undercurrents to this liveliness. Khotso's love of fun could have a dangerous dimension to it, as is clear in the following anecdote related by a man from the Sterkspruit area. When he was a young man in the 1950s, he went to Khotso in order to grow rich. After undergoing ukuthwala, the long-term wealth-giving procedure that Khotso offered, he stayed on in the White House for some time as a member of the household. Later in life, he succeeded in becoming a wealthy bus operator. He described what took place on one occasion, when Khotso called him to his property in King William's Town, purchased in the latter part of the 1950s.

> We spent some time together on the farm, then one evening Khotso said that he wanted to drive back to Kokstad. He invited me to accompany him and drive the car. We got in the car and were about to leave when Khotso said:
>
> 'Let me give you a tip, my boy. If you want to show your bravery, always drive on the wrong side of the road. I promise you people will always give way, even the police.'
>
> So we drove all the way to Kokstad on the wrong side of the road, and indeed the oncoming traffic all gave way. Even the police did. So we arrived safely at Kokstad in the early hours of the morning.

Khotso displayed a perilous sense of bravado in his desire to be king of the road, even if only for one night. It is worth noting, however, that he invited the young man to take the greatest risk of all, by undertaking the driving during this hazardous expedition. As with Nthoa Bohlokoa, and on certain other occasions, he was instructing his companion to place himself in danger.

Despite the shady aspect of Khotso's character, Becker's fundamental point concerning the warmth and humanity that formed an essential part of Khotso's complex nature remains important and has often been overlooked in journalistic depictions of him. One of his wives who knew him best, MaMjoli, once said of him:

> Khotso was a man with two personalities. To those who did not know him well, he was a serious-minded person who lived a one-sided life as the world's famous herbalist.
>
> But once you knew him reasonably well, you would agree that he was an easygoing warm-hearted man.
>
> In his best element he exuded gaiety. He cracked many jokes which kept his audience in stitches. He was a simple man who loved to see people around him happy.[3]

Other members of Khotso's household remember him as a warm and fun-loving person. 'Khotso made people laugh, no crying,' said Ellen

Jones. She recalled how he liked fooling around, enlivening his jokes and stories with his imitations of other people and exaggerated dialogue, jumping around to demonstrate particular actions.

Khotso's facial appearance expressed his warm, jovial nature. 'You couldn't get a rounder face and he smiled a lot,' said a man who had been a farmer in Matatiele in the 1950s and had first come to know Khotso as a colourful local character. Later, the farmer was able to strike up a friendship of sorts with Khotso. The son of a trader near Mbizana in the Transkei, this man had grown up in a predominantly black area, was fluent in Xhosa and was thus able to chat to Khotso. In the 1960s, the farmer moved to the Transkei, where he worked as a building contractor. He maintained contact with Khotso, visiting him regularly at his house in Lusikisiki. One white Kokstad woman, an older resident of the town who grew up on a farm in the area, was struck by Khotso's essential amiability. 'Khotso was, well, just Khotso,' she said. He was eccentric, but always very civil and friendly. Many white Kokstad locals who remember Khotso from their childhood shared her opinion.

Khotso proved a genial, affable host, as one man, from Teyateyaneng in Lesotho, who worked at the royal court at Matsieng, discovered in 1946. He told of how, in his youth, he set off in a bus from Qacha's Nek, accompanying a team that was to play football in Flagstaff. The bus broke down near Kokstad and its occupants were stranded in an unfamiliar place. Night was coming on and the team was dismayed, but Pascal Makeka, the teacher who was presiding over the group, tried to reassure everyone. He said that he knew of a fellow countryman in Kokstad who might be able to help and he led them to the White House. When Khotso welcomed the footballers into his home, the Lesotho man was scared. He had heard a great deal about Khotso, though he had never met him. The amiable figure who greeted them in the doorway seemed far removed from the sinister master of the occult. Khotso served them all a full meal. How, his Lesotho visitor wondered, did he manage to cater, out of the blue, for sixty people? The only thing he found odd about the evening were the strict regulations: the guests all had to sit facing a certain direction, without looking behind them. After dinner, Khotso's guests were provided with accommodation for the night.

Like so many others, the man from Teyateyaneng discovered that visitors who entered Khotso's abode moved into a world set apart, where the master of the house ruled sovereign. There were fixed procedures and codes of conduct that had to be adhered to, however odd outsiders might find them. For one thing, the need for purity was emphasised through a foot-washing ritual, symbolically enacted through the washing of the soles of shoes. Foot washing was such an integral part of Khotso's household that even today at Mount Nelson a basin of water lies just outside the front door, in readiness for visitors' shoes.

A white medical doctor who practised in Kokstad from the early 1940s onwards remembered visiting the White House. He was ushered into the lounge and offered a cold drink. A servant with cushions attached to his knees entered and kneeled, bearing a tray of lemonade. In this way the floor could be polished at the same time as the visitor was served. Khotso demanded displays of respect and humility from his servants; at the same time, he was maintaining smooth polished surfaces around him.

Neatness and cleanliness, as an outward sign of spiritual purity, mattered a great deal to Khotso. He liked his surroundings and the people inhabiting them to be spick and span. The high premium that he placed on maintaining pristine tidiness – whether in relation to his cars, his clean-shaven followers or his domestic surroundings – made it one of the trademark features of many people and objects that belonged to him, in one sense or another. Describing the White House in 1954, a journalist wrote: 'The entire establishment is painted an immaculate white inside and there is not a smudge or speck of dirt to be seen anywhere.'[4] When wives and family members remember Khotso, they always recall, along with his sense of fun and his love of life, his emphasis on spotless, uncontaminated physical orderliness as an integral part of his personality.

By imposing purity and order on his domestic surroundings, Khotso could send out a clear signal that he was in control of all that he surveyed, albeit within the confines of a small kingdom. Also, he might have felt as if he was setting himself apart, even if only symbolically, from the squalor of poverty and oppression that increasingly contaminated the lives of black people in South Africa as the twentieth century wore on.

Besides foot washing, another of the formalities that guests were called on to observe was the removal of hats, right at the gate. Khotso's staff would bow low and, clapping their hands, would greet the guests. On Khotso's properties, hand clapping was always a gesture of respect. No drinking was allowed. Despite the extensive range of glassware and opulent decanters all over the house, Khotso became a strict teetotaller in the early 1950s and he did not permit any form of alcohol on his premises. Even at important functions, the most his guests could expect was orange juice.

Smoking was also taboo. 'Once a white man visited my farm to ask for some medicine,' Khotso told the journalist Duke Ngcobo from *Drum*. 'While I left him in the sitting room he took the liberty of smoking. Then the bees fled the farm, and now I have no honey to entertain my spirits and friends.'[5]

The rules, Khotso told Ngcobo, were there to ensure harmony and tranquillity on his farms so that the spirits would visit. They were also intended to instil respect. Lunika suggested to Blades that there may have been a practical reason why Khotso banned smoking. A driver might let a lighted cigarette fall on his car upholstery or a thoughtless visitor might burn the furniture. Alf Marsburg, who knew Khotso when he was the Lusikisiki magistrate during the latter half of the 1960s, related how the previous magistrate's wife and a female friend sneaked off to smoke in the toilet when they were visiting Mount Nelson. Khotso crept up to the door and locked them in.

Finally, there was the fact that, in the course of time, Khotso's followers would become identifiable by their clean-shaven heads. In this respect, they resembled their leader himself. A shaven scalp can have a shiny, immaculate quality to it, appearing tidier and more hygienic than an unkempt, tousled head of hair. Requiring that those close to him become 'clean-heads', as his daughter Patricia put it, would have tied in with Khotso's insistence on purity, and as Lunika pointed out, shaven heads were useful when Khotso and his disciples anointed their heads with muti. The medicine would spread better. Yet another advantage of baldness is that it does not show grey or thinning hair. This would have appealed to Khotso, for even in his declining years he liked to create the impression that he possessed an undiminished youthful vitality.

In the White House, as in Khotso's previous consulting rooms in Kokstad, money would always be on display. This was observed by one woman who now lives in Bhongweni but grew up in Kokstad. Her memories of Khotso pre-date his days at the White House. Not only did she hear a great deal about his background from her mother, but Khotso stayed in her mother's house in Kokstad for a while before he moved to his own abode. She described how she went to the White House as a little girl, along with her family. They were accompanying a relative who had come to Khotso for his special medicine for wealth. 'There was money all over the house, even in the dishes!' she exclaimed.

She didn't try to touch the coins, however. If you tried to take a coin, she was told, all the other coins would make a noise and alert Khotso. Her niece, also a Bhongweni resident who now works for the Kokstad Local Council, has her own childhood recollections of visiting Khotso's property in the 1950s. Recently she recalled the mixture of somewhat daunting hospitality and stringent adherence to strange rules that visits to the White House entailed:

> People were very scared of Khotso. On our way back from school we used to go to Khotso's place to watch people dancing and singing. On some days we would be given umvubo [pap and sour milk]. We used to go in groups and we would be hungry. We would be given food, but we were told that one of the rules at Khotso's place was that if you were given food you had to eat up – you were not allowed to leave food on the plate or in the dish. On certain special days we would be given braaied meat and brown bread. But before we ate, we had to wait until some men

had taken bread and raw meat and thrown them into the pool below the house, as an offering to Khotso's snake in the river.

As a child, she did feel that a sense of peril hung over the White House. But that did not put her and her friends off.

> But we still went to Khotso's place. The fruit at that place! The peaches were the most delicious. We would go there and ask for the fruit and we would be given more than enough. At other times we were told to stay away, not to go there. We never thought of stealing the fruit because we were always told that, when stolen, Khotso's fruit was poisonous. As kids we believed that, that's why we did not steal.

This description of curious and hungry schoolchildren being drawn towards the White House almost in spite of themselves conveys a sense of the uneasy fascination that Khotso exerted over many of those around him. The children only glimpsed Khotso briefly, at a distance. Those who spent some time in the White House and interacted with Khotso have described how they found themselves mesmerised and enthralled by the man. Reflecting on the time that he and the Qacha's Nek football team visited the White House, Makeka remarked: 'This man, as I knew him, I knew he was an uneducated man. But his surroundings captivated me so much that I believed everything that people used to tell me about him.'

Makeka was not the only commonsensical, practical person who found himself wondering whether Khotso might somehow possess extraordinary capabilities. 'Sometimes it almost seemed as if Khotso could be psychic,' said Alf Marsburg, describing events that had taken place much later, in the 1960s:

> I would be driving past someone selling bananas by the road, and my kids would want them. But I'd tell them no, we haven't got time to stop. And then we'd get back to our house and there would be Khotso's Cadillac parked outside and the driver would give us a big box of bananas from Khotso. Or my wife would say to me that I should get a sheepskin coat, for driving in. I'd say

yes, I'd really like one, but I'd forget all about it. Then Khotso would call me over to his house and when I got there, he'd have a beautiful sheepskin coat for me!

Marsburg recalled that once when he and his family were setting off on a trip, Khotso presented them with a massive tray of fried fish and fourteen roast chickens as food for the road – far more than they could possibly eat. Even in the White House days, there was something excessive about the nature of Khotso's gift-giving. One man, an octogenarian who still lives on the Scott family farm Nolangeni, where he used to work, remembered once returning from a wedding party with a group of friends, only to be stopped by Khotso, who insisted that they come to the White House for another, even bigger feast. He pressed huge quantities of food on his guests, leaving them feeling overwhelmed. It was as if Khotso was continually seeking to make the point that he could outdo all those around him in his hospitality and generosity. His competitive gift-giving could thus be described as a form of potlatching, as Khotso displayed his affluence in the very act of parting with some of it.

Duke Ngcobo became aware that Khotso was a mixture of opposites when he interviewed him for *Drum* in 1958. He drew attention to the way in which Khotso stayed ever watchful lest someone attempt to divest him of even a small amount of his money: a quality which was as much a part of his nature as his liberality. 'But he's too much a man of the world – this one and the next – to be always the uncalculating mountain of generosity,' Ngcobo noted. 'This same man who will think nothing about giving away a car can make an issue of a few pounds if he thinks someone is trying to take him for a ride.'

Almost perversely (in the eyes of various poverty-stricken individuals around him) Khotso would lavish expensive presents on people who did not appear to need such things, while bestowing relatively minor gifts on the poor. For instance, the Nolangeni farm worker got a free meal, while Marsburg received a relatively costly sheepskin jacket. Such actions represented a type of investment. By cultivating the goodwill of influential people, Khotso hoped that in the end he would be able to gain far more than he gave away. What he lost in the process, however, was the favour of certain members of local communities. From the early days on, Khotso began to develop the reputation of a tight-fisted man who hugged his wealth to himself in the midst of economically deprived regions. As racial divisions intensified in South Africa, it made matters worse that those people on whom Khotso heaped valuable presents were usually whites.

But Khotso was more concerned with the way in which his extravagant acts of largesse could serve his interests. From the Kokstad days, he was involved in charitable work. For instance, he regularly gave donations to the Carl Malcomess School in Kokstad. Undoubtedly, the more famous he became, the more he would have been aware that large, public acts of generosity, such as donations to schools and hospitals, were a way of highlighting his own munificence. However, Khotso's car-purchasing performances made a more lasting impression. To this day, accounts of these events are often cited as evidence that he must indeed have possessed a fabulous fortune.

The first such spectacle had been staged in 1936, when Khotso marched barefoot into a showroom in Mthatha, to buy a Packard. He didn't need shoes to buy the car – and neither did he need a chequebook. Instead, he was accompanied by an attendant carrying a battered suitcase fastened with string. He untied the case, displaying bundles of one-, five- and ten-pound notes, and the attendant laboriously began counting out the required amount.[6] Throughout his life, Khotso preferred to purchase cars in this manner. It took a while, but it gave him ample opportunity to exhibit his money.

As time went on, he preferred to buy vehicles in front of bigger audiences, such as the crowds at the annual Kokstad Agricultural Show. One year he outdid himself at this event: 'He had to point six fingers when he said, "I'll take the lot." What a chromium-gleaming haul it was: a Chrysler (price £2 128), Hornet V8 (£1 660), Jeep (mere £1 300), Mercedes-Benz (£3 960) and two tractors costing just over £2 000,' Ngcobo remarked. One year Khotso had been escorted to the Kokstad show by six attendants, all bearing large suitcases of money.[7]

In order to ensure that he always had sufficient cash at hand, Khotso apparently continued the practice, started in his jackal-hunting days, of burying money where only he could find it. One farmer and former motor dealer disclosed to Blades that when Khotso came to buy tractors from him, earth would fall from between the banknotes as he counted them. Also, two Kokstad lawyers told Blades that when Khotso visited them to sort out land deals, he would arrive with his trademark suitcase of banknotes, which often smelled musty, as if they had been buried somewhere. Another journalist would repeat the rumours that Khotso buried much of his fortune underground. This journalist had also been told that many of Khotso's banknotes had an 'earthy' smell and sometimes even had bits of soil adhering to them.[8] Where exactly Khotso's money was hidden gave rise to much speculation. Some believed that there were great dungeon-like vaults below the White House where he stored his wealth. Others maintained that on an isolated, virtually inaccessible rocky headland on the Wild Coast there was a cave in which Khotso's treasure was buried.[9] Not even his family knew where his fortune was concealed, and this would eventually come to perturb them.

While the spectacular way in which Khotso purchased his cars was fuelled by self-aggrandisement and while his impressive gift-giving could be carefully calculated, on the other hand it also sprang at least in part from an essential kindliness and a spontaneous, almost childlike delight in giving pleasure to people, as noted by informants such as Blades, Ellen Jones and MaDlamini. From the days when he was a hunter, sharing what he had with others in the mountains, Khotso loved giving presents. MaDlamini recalled: 'Someone said he was so hungry that he could eat a sheep. So Khotso gave him a sheep!' Ellen remembered how much he enjoyed giving gifts to children. 'Khotso was the children's friend,' she said. 'He gave them sweets and coins and they loved him for that. They got frightened when they heard about the snake. But they would soon forget those silly stories when they saw him again.'

Some were less quick to forget the 'silly stories'. Especially during the Kokstad days, when Khotso did not care if people feared him as long as they had heard of his name, there were those who were reluctant to take presents from him. In 1946, for instance, Khotso bestowed a gift of bread on the hospital in Qacha's Nek, but people were too scared to accept it. Who knows what strange magic Khotso's presents carried? The Teyateyaneng man described how Khotso went to the royal kraal at Matsieng to meet the queen of Lesotho and various chiefs in the 1950s. The queen refused to see him and the chiefs went into hiding. They felt Khotso was a strange and dangerous man.

On the other hand, there were large numbers of people who were prepared to overcome their fear. They believed Khotso could help them, and that was what mattered. Clients came to him not only for good fortune, but also to have their physical ailments treated. Ellen described how, in the days when she lived with Khotso and became his secretary, she would answer the letters of people who had written to ask for help, telling them to come to the White House so that Khotso could treat them in person. His customers would arrive early in the morning, usually on the train, from all over South Africa and Lesotho. In the evenings, people in Khotso's household would sing 'Bayeza'. One version of this song, in which Xhosa and Sotho words are intermingled, goes as follows:

Abagulayo,

Bayeza, hosasa, bayeza.

[The sick people

are coming tomorrow.]

This is an old song, which a number of traditional doctors have used to attract customers.

When clients arrived, Ellen went on, she would escort them to the waiting room and bring them tea and bread. Then they would consult Khotso in his office. Afterwards visitors would purify themselves by washing in river water containing intelezi, Khotso's special medicine.

The Bhongweni woman who had been a nurse and whose brother had been Khotso's boyhood friend, recalled: 'Respectable people used to come to Khotso's place and get into Khotso's uniform: just white overalls and no shoes. His policy was that you had to give him all your money first and then you would receive it back double-fold. That's how he got rich.'

However, when many of Khotso's clients offered all that they had, it was by no means enough to cover the costs of their treatment. Khotso would let them work it off. This was no doubt part of the reason why he always had a number of people labouring on his properties and farms without having to pay them anything, and why his lands and his houses began falling into ruin after his death. Hal Scott told his family of one farm worker who went to Khotso for healing. He didn't have money, so he had to repay his debt with his labour. He stayed on Khotso's property for a week. 'Dad said he was so exhausted that he almost crawled back to the farm. He had to work really hard!' Elizabeth Scott said.

In the evenings, the people who were working off their fees would sing and dance in Khotso's yard and then eat ox heads and pap before going to sleep. One Kokstad man, who was born in 1940, described how as a child he would peer from a safe distance at the festivities going on at the White House. He would see people playing accordions and drums and many people would come in, crowding together on the floor.

Some patients and trainees must have left bewildered and frantic families behind them, because on occasion people would depart for Khotso's house without letting those close to them know where they were going and, having arrived, they might stay there indefinitely. The Bhongweni woman whose brother had been Khotso's friend recalled one such case from her days as a nurse: 'This man from Namaqualand who was staying at the White House fell sick and was admitted to hospital. He had cardiac failure. He then gave his particulars to the hospital staff. When we realised he was going to die, we had to phone. We got hold of his son and he told us he had been looking for his father for a long time.'

Blades related a similar anecdote: 'An African journalist who went to see Khotso when he was living in Lusikisiki was shaken to find among the women the wife of an old friend, a teacher living near Johannesburg. She asked the journalist to tell her family she was well, but offered no explanation of her presence. It turned out that her husband had no idea where she was.'

In all likelihood, the teacher's wife had specific reasons of her own for abandoning her family. 'Khotso had a great attraction for women and when he treated them he used to form liaisons of short duration and liked to have a number of concubines around him,' his brother Mosala Jack once remarked.[10]

Mosala Jack's carefully deliberated formal expression was adopted because he was submitting legal affidavits during an inquiry into Khotso's estate and his heirs after his death. At the same time, language of this nature also creates the sense that Mosala Jack was primly distancing himself from his brother's promiscuity. Women who entered the White House often found themselves entering the jungle of its master's libido, since Khotso seemed to regard any female patient or potential trainee herbalist as a possible member of his large and varied harem, from which he could pick and choose at his fancy. It was not only Khotso's unashamed sexual rapacity that brought about this state of affairs, but also his capacity to draw women to him through a combination of personal charisma, sensual energy and smooth, skilled trickery, which involved being able to make others believe what he wanted them to. Ellen Jones herself entered Khotso's life in this manner. She was accompanying her mother, who had an eye problem and had come to Khotso for treatment, from East London.

Francina Greeves, Ellen's friend, now lives in the riverside house which Khotso called Waterfall, but which is also known as the White House. A smaller-scale version of the main dwelling, it is a little palace that Khotso built especially for Ellen. Francina can still be seen sprawling on the steps of the house in the sunshine, dredging up memories of Ellen when she was young: 'Oh – she was so, so pretty. She had a pale skin, and those blue eyes!' That was why Khotso liked Ellen, in Francina's view. Not only was she young and appealing, but her light skin carried with it a sense of status. Francina laughed loudly at this. Khotso couldn't marry a white woman, she said, but he could have a wife that looked almost white.

Khotso was also attracted to Ellen because of her youth and virginity. This was one of the few points in Khotso's life history when surface appearances not only provided an accurate reflection of underlying realities, but also hinted at the nature of future developments. Ellen was innocent, inexperienced and at the mercy of the events that befell her. She had vivid recollections of her early days in the house of the man who would, for some time, take control of the direction of her life. 'I first met Khotso in the winter of 1946. I remember because I used to tramp by the kraal and the cow dung was full of snow. When I first went to visit Khotso with my sick mother, we would wash ourselves in the grey steel drum by the river. If Khotso was peeping, you didn't know. He had thieving eyes.'

Khotso needed someone with reasonable writing skills to carry out secretarial tasks for him, as well as someone to act as an interpreter when whites consulted him, so he was pleased that Ellen was prepared to take on these jobs. But it wasn't only for practical reasons that Khotso wanted to have Ellen near him. She described what took place one day when she and the master of the White House were alone together. 'Khotso thought, "I must get hold of this woman" – so he did so there and then, on the floor of the office, and made a baby.'

In Francina's view, Ellen was overwhelmed by Khotso and she was not really prepared for life in Khotso's household, as yet another of his paramours. Just as others had been before her, she found herself enraptured by the man who had taken hold of her physically and emotionally. 'Love is blind!' cackled Francina.

On 17 December 1949, Ellen and Khotso's son was born. He came into the world at daybreak, so he was called Langa Lase-Afrika, his first name meaning 'sunrise'. His arrival symbolised a sunrise of another kind too. Never one to conceal his emotions, Khotso's joy on that day was overwhelming. Thirteen years after the death of his first boy, he had another son. Ellen was delighted at what appeared to be a great stroke of good fortune that had befallen her. 'Khotso was so charming,' she said. 'He looked after me well and I was happy to bear him a son, at a time when he was yearning to get one following the death of his first son by

Sarah Jane. It was as though a new sunshine was lighting his heart. He was himself when he said, "Now my name won't die."[11]

Ellen remembered how, when Khotso brought her and Langa home from the Kokstad hospital, people were lined up beside the house, clapping for the newborn baby. She argued that Khotso had made a lobola payment to her father, thus formalising a traditional union between them. Her sister, Ivy Jones, felt differently about the affair: 'After the birth of the child,' she said, 'Ellen accompanied by Khotso turned up at our home and gave my father R100 as damages [a penalty payment for impregnating Ellen]. Although we were most upset, we could not cause any trouble, as my whole family were afraid of Khotso, who was reputedly possessed of magical powers.'[12]

Ellen had some happy memories of her time with Khotso. 'He treated me like a princess. He built me a house,' she reminisced. Her dwelling was built in an attempt to maintain peaceful relations within the family, by giving Ellen and MaDlamini places of their own. But life in Khotso's household was hardly blissful. Ellen soon discovered that anyone who might be perceived in some way as an outsider and who occupied a prominent position in Khotso's household needed to be very tough or wily to stay the course. Ellen was neither. According to Francina, she was sweet-natured and happy-go-lucky. Someone else who knew Ellen felt that she was a lightweight personality. Unlike MaDlamini, she did not have the force of character that would enable her to remain a member of Khotso's domestic entourage.

When Langa was three years old, Ellen's father died in Mthatha and she went home for the funeral. She gave this account of the events that took place thereafter:

> While I was there I had time to think about my life with Khotso. I came to the conclusion that it would be best for me not to return to him. I did not seem to fit in with the rest of Khotso's wives and retainers. They seemed to resent the attention he showed me and they felt that because I was a coloured I was an intruder. I speak Xhosa fluently and I understood what was being whispered

behind my back by other people in Khotso's various homes. It made life unpleasant for me although I was very very happy with Khotso. He was a stern but kind man and he always treated me fairly. I had no complaints about him but I felt that I would not be able to go on in the atmosphere of suspicion and distrust.[13]

Ellen left Langa in Khotso's household when she returned to her family. 'She didn't want to break the old man's heart,' said Francina. Wives and concubines were within easy reach but, as Khotso was discovering, sons were harder to come by. Langa, who looked very much like Ellen, according to Francina, spent his youth being cared for by several wives, starting with MaDlamini and later MaMjoli.

Ellen moved to East London to find work. 'I did not tell Khotso I would not return to his place or to my son. I felt it better just to disappear,' she explained. Ellen eventually married a man named Victor Moyce in Pietermaritzburg. She only saw her son Langa again when he was an adult, after his father's death.

Some of Khotso's subsequent wives and concubines would possess more staying power than Ellen. One such example was Gloria Manuku Lesala, who visited the White House with her sister in 1954, to be cured of an ear problem. Gloria was still a teenager at this point and she appeared to be quiet, kind, young and innocent, all qualities that Khotso found appealing. In 1957 he signed a customary union contract with his new-found partner. 'Her parents, seeing Khotso's wealth, ended up agreeing to the marriage,' someone in Khotso's household later observed.

Gloria fitted into Khotso's substantial family in a way that Ellen had not. The other women liked Gloria, perceiving her as a considerate, helpful member of the domestic ménage, rather than an unwelcome outsider who had acquired a favoured position in Khotso's court. A year after her marriage, Gloria gave birth to her first daughter, Stella Mawana, otherwise known as Ma-One. Khotso sometimes liked to give his children names based on numbers. These numerical names tended to refer to the times of the day or night when his offspring entered the world. Later Gloria had another daughter, Rina Popie, or Ma-Five.

Gloria differed from Ellen in another significant way. Underlying her sweetness, innocence and self-effacement were qualities of assertiveness and determination that would come to the fore the longer she remained connected to Khotso's household. While many women passed through Khotso's life, certain individuals stand out more clearly than most, partly on account of the prominent places they occupied in the family or, like Ellen, because of the public attention paid to them after Khotso's death. Gloria is one case in point. Her voice still comes through forcefully in an affidavit she submitted in the legal proceedings after Khotso's death.[14] This hints at a toughness of character, which she shared with MaDlamini, and this perhaps is one reason why the women may not have got on in later life. Gloria may have disliked MaDlamini, and in all probability the older woman had little time for younger wives such as Gloria who were gradually supplanting her in the household.

During the White House days, Khotso's predilection for younger women gave rise to a remarkable encounter with a teenage schoolgirl who was to become one of the most famous people in South Africa. A biography of Winnie Mandela contains a description of an unexpected incident that took place when Winnie was on a school outing to Tsolo:

> The bus stopped at Flagstaff, and the pupils were stretching their legs when one of Winnie's friends pointed out that a dwarf was staring at her. He approached her and asked her if she knew how pretty she was. Winnie was dumbstruck and had no idea how to react, but when he gave her a ten-shilling note and said it was the first instalment for her lobola, she was near panic. Before he left, he told her she would be his wife as soon as she was fully grown. Afterwards, her friends told her the man was called Khotso, that he was wealthy and something of a legend in the district, and already had many wives.[15]

As we know, Winnie never accepted Khotso's proposal. But it is tempting to speculate what might have taken place in Khotso's life and during the tempestuous period after his demise if she had joined his household.

Chapter 7
From Ibangalala to Ukuthwala

During the White House days, and later when he lived at Mount Nelson, Khotso's domestic family consisted of wives, concubines and children, both real and symbolic. Some people stayed in Khotso's house for another reason. As Khotso's eldest daughter, Patricia, told Blades, they wanted 'to live in Khotso's shadow and become his children, his *isikwata*, or disciples'. These were apprentices, who flocked to Khotso's houses in Kokstad and Lusikisiki to be trained as herbalists. Their mentor liked to say, 'People who come to me are sent by their ancestors', and the Qacha's Nek man who went to Mount Nelson to be instructed in herbalism endorses this. He said that the spirits of his ancestors wanted him to go to Khotso and he could not disregard them. 'When I got to his house,' the man said, 'Khotso came out to welcome me – although I had not said anything about my arrival to him. He said to me, "I have been expecting you. I've been told of your coming."'

Ellen felt that Khotso owed part of his success to a special skill that he had with his fellow women and men. 'He took people equal,' she said, 'strangers or friends, rich or poor, black or white, sane or mad, man or woman ... he was a great teacher. Khotso was a good wizard: he helped many people and killed only a few.'

When Peter Becker visited Khotso in the late 1950s, his host told him: 'As news of my healing gifts began to spread, so too did the herbs

I sold turn into money. My home in Kokstad grew bigger and bigger, and I found myself surrounded by many followers.' The majority of Khotso's customers and pupils came from out of town. Local people tended to regard him with more awe and fear than those from further away, who were more concerned with what Khotso could do for them than what he might do to them.

Then there were the whites who flocked to Khotso's houses. Although this would become marked in the 1960s at Mount Nelson, white visitors were a feature at the White House too. Not all of them came merely to gawp at the colourful local 'magician'. Throughout his career, Khotso had a great many white customers including, as we shall see, some of the most influential figures in the land. And he liked his white customers. As Lunika observed: 'He said that whites tended to respect and obey his instructions far more than his black customers did.'

One white woman from the Kokstad area told Blades about a neighbour who turned to Khotso out of desperation, carried out his instructions meticulously and was miraculously cured. She had suddenly become weak, frail and querulous, losing all interest in life. Because no one was able to determine the source of her problem, her husband decided they had nothing to lose by consulting Khotso, who identified both the problem and the solution. His client had been bewitched by a servant, who had sprinkled powder over the threshold of the house. As soon as she had stepped over this substance, the woman had fallen ill. Khotso gave her a teapot in which she had to brew her own tea, a spoon to eat her food and some beadwork to wear around her neck. In due course the beadwork would disappear of its own accord, and this would signify that she had been cured. His customer did exactly as she was told. 'One day her beads weren't there any more,' her neighbour said, 'and Maria was cured. Now, when you ask her how she is, she's fine, just fine.'

By 1954, Khotso had become so widely known that when he produced his visitors' book for a journalist, it displayed names and addresses from far beyond the borders of South Africa. Some visitors hailed from the United States: from Beverly Hills, Minneapolis, Broadway, New

York, Chicago and at least fifty other places. Khotso's American guests frequently stayed for a day or two, and a member of staff was always on hand to interpret for him.[1]

Meanwhile, an extensive network of travelling salesmen were traversing southern Africa, promoting and peddling Khotso's wares. By the 1960s, Khotso told one journalist, he had more than two hundred agents at work in this way.[2] Pascal Makeka remembered how some of these individuals were hard at work in Lesotho. 'They were collecting people who were in difficulties and then sending them to Khotso. That's what actually made Khotso very rich, because he was getting a lot of money from Lesotho.'

What may have bestowed special potency on much of Khotso's merchandise marketed across southern Africa was the fact that some of his remedies and charms had his name emblazoned on their labels in huge letters. Others bore photographs of Khotso himself. He was using his name to promote his wares, and in turn his wares served as a form of self-advertisement.

Ibangalala would become the most renowned of Khotso's remedies and charms during the White House days. 'It is a great seller all over the country,' Khotso told Becker, 'so great that we often run short of supplies.' MaMjoli had assisted Khotso in the running of his practice, and she recollected this vividly:

> No medicine or muti was as popular as this one, because whenever people asked him how he was able to keep so many wives happy, he would tell them that he used this ibangalala. It became so popular that he would receive letters from abroad. It was actually quite funny! Some of these letters would be written in languages that none of us understood. So what we would do was to scan the letter until we saw the word *bangalala*, then we would know what to do. Most of these letters had dollars enclosed in them. That was why most of my husband's mail was opened by the authorities: they wanted to know what people from overseas were communicating with him about.

'I know I have a good product,' Khotso told the press later in his life, ever eager to promote his medicines. At that point, he was passing himself off as an octogenarian. 'I use ibangalala myself – and I'm more virile now than most men are at twenty.' He enjoyed telling a number of people that one of his wives had run off with his great-grandson, but she had returned within a week because her youthful consort couldn't satisfy her the way her husband could.[3]

Khotso's claims for his medicines were hyperbolic, but in the specific case of ibangalala, his protestations of miracle remedies appeared convincing because he radiated an energy and enthusiasm that made him appear youthful for most of his life. A number of photographs taken of him over the years capture his lively, frequently mischievous expression. It is as if Khotso's face never stiffened into the sober, time-worn lines of sedate elderliness. Visitors and journalists were often amazed at how much younger Khotso looked than the years that he claimed to be – but then this was hardly surprising, considering that he liked to add twenty years to his age. When asked if Khotso actually used ibangalala, MaMjoli merely smiled and shrugged. 'Your guess is as good as mine!' she quipped.

In the 1960s, Khotso displayed a list of some of the other potions he had on offer to the writer Bernard Newman, who met Khotso during his travels through the Transkei in 1965. Khotso recommended Yogomut, 'which Cleans the Bile and Gall out of your Body.' In addition, it 'makes you live longer and makes you stronger'. Then, there was his Stomach Specific (for upset or loose bowels and cramps); his Female Tonic, 'ideal for Maiden, Matron and Expectant Mothers'; and his Beauty Oil, which softened and soothed skin, offering 'an aid to beauty for courting couples'. 'No wonder the witch-doctors – and many shops – like the pharmacopoeia of Mr Khotso,' Newman marvelled. 'It cures or alleviates anything.'[4]

But the biggest money-spinners, according to Lunika, were Khotso's special medicines and charms for wealth and luck. These drew people to his premises from the Kokstad days onwards. Lunika described how

Khotso had a whole range of these medicines, including intelezi. There was, for instance, *isibunge*, which had to be burned outside business premises. As clients did so, they called for customers – and these would come. Lala Yako, who went to Khotso for this substance, said: 'I had a shop, a general dealer's shop, and I had no money then. I still remember, I paid twenty pounds for something he said would draw people to my business. Whether it's . . . er, psychological, I don't know, but when I used this stuff, people would flock to my business.'

Not only could Khotso's good-luck medicine bring riches and attract clients to a particular commercial establishment, but it could even build up churches. He wasn't a churchgoer himself, but Khotso viewed the spiritual and mercantile worlds as intertwined. He told journalists that the leaders of the two largest indigenous African churches in South Africa owed their success to him: 'Take Shembe and Lekganyane. They left their sons the legacy of two formidable sects, apart from living in clover. All the success that their fathers achieved they owe to my charms. Another is Bishop Limba, from Port Elizabeth.'[5]

The Church of the Nazarites and the Zion Christian Church (the ZCC) were established by Isaiah Shembe and Ignatius Lekganyane respectively. 'Bishop' James Limba was generally regarded as the founder of the Church of Christ, which originated in New Brighton, Port Elizabeth, in the 1930s with branches later springing up all over the subcontinent. Limba was viewed by his followers as God's chosen prophet.[6] Small wonder, then, that Khotso wished it to be known that he was associated with such prominent figures, ascribing their success to his own miraculous medicine rather than to the ineffable workings of God.

Despite the differences between them in terms of spiritual approaches, Khotso and Limba had some crucial features in common. Both men started their careers with very little, then came to believe fervently in what could be accomplished through the power of money. They also believed in the value of utilising their followers as labourers on their properties and as consumers in their various commercial enterprises. Members of Limba's church were some of his most important clientele in his stores and also the core of the workforce in his various businesses and on his farms. Moreover, he owned properties acquired with the help of substantial contributions from his church members. Like Khotso, Limba liked material possessions, especially large vehicles. It is said that he took pleasure in amassing cash and possessions for their own sake, and he enjoyed boasting about his fortune and luxuriating in the material comforts his wealth could buy.

Politically, there were further similarities between Khotso and Limba. In order to survive and grow, Limba's church depended on the approval of the government. To acquire this, it needed to appear to acknowledge the white political order as a legitimate form of authority.[7] Khotso would behave in a similar fashion, believing it would be in his interests to do so. If Khotso was indeed Limba's supplier, perhaps his special medicine for good fortune had the spin-off of making the consumer resemble the producer in these above respects.

While Khotso's quick-fix mutis for money and luck were widely used, he was most famous as a practitioner of ukuthwala, by means of which wealth could be acquired on a sustained basis. Large numbers of clients visited Khotso for ukuthwala, despite the risks and terrors that it was believed to entail.[8] In part, this procedure was feared because it involved encountering the supernatural serpents over which Khotso was reputed to have mastery.

'Khotso didn't wear beads and skins like other medicine men,' said Ellen, 'but people still flocked to see him without invitation, to get his lucky powder and be licked dry by the river snake.'

'The person who really wants wealth, he will contact Khotso. If a man comes from Khotso it means he has some sort of snake,' said one man from Mount Frere, now a university student, who had grown up surrounded by accounts of Khotso's prowess as an ukuthwala practitioner. These narratives arose during a period when the need for Khotso's medicines for wealth came to the fore.

In the 1950s and 1960s, Khotso's heyday, the white minority government was tightening its grip and the rural poor experienced a growing downward economic spiral, particularly in those areas that became the Bantustans. Even in the earlier part of the twentieth century, when the reserves were delineated under the 1913 Land Act, these territories had not been sufficient for a sustainable livelihood. Over the decades, conditions worsened. Khotso was situated on the edge of what would become the Transkei, which was fast becoming one of the most poverty-stricken regions in South Africa. The slide into environmental desolation and economic deprivation in the Transkei and the other reserve areas had become evident from the 1920s onwards.[9] There were several reasons for this, a major one being that traditional farming methods, whether pastoral or the cultivation of crops, were suited to shifting agricultural practices and required access to wide areas of land. The reserves, however, were limited, fixed territories.[10]

By the 1950s, historian Sean Redding observed, many people living in the Transkei were beset by a combination of debilitating factors: they lacked access to fertile land from which they could derive sustenance; there were few employment possibilities in their region; and a system of state influx controls impeded them from relocating to more prosperous areas. Migrant labourers earned very low wages and those who were able to carry out subsistence farming were confronted by worsening agricultural conditions.[11] In 1954, the Tomlinson Commission, set up by the government to investigate possible socio-economic development in the reserves, stated that the majority of the land in the reserves was eroded and that it was not possible for the inhabitants of these areas to cultivate sufficient food to sustain themselves.[12] In the 1950s, the deprivation and desperation in the Transkei gave rise to the escalating incidents of stock theft that supplied Khotso with a ready market for his protective muti designed to deter livestock thieves.

Adjoining the area where Khotso lived and worked was Lesotho, a state stripped of its most fertile land, which had been incorporated into South Africa in the nineteenth century. Out of what remained of the territory, the mountain poor came flooding, seeking a means of finding a livelihood in the country that had partially devoured their own. Finally, there was Nomansland itself. For many of the black inhabitants of East Griqualand, especially in the areas which would one day become outlying parts of the Transkei, the bite of economic hardship could be felt as keenly as the winter wind off the Malutis. When various older inhabitants of Bhongweni cast their minds back to the 1950s and the 1960s, and also the days before the authors of apartheid took political command in 1948, what struck them about those times was how little they were paid.

'The black people used to *nyamezela* [persevere],' said the Bhongweni woman whose family knew Khotso and who had visited him at the White House, 'because they couldn't do otherwise. Even before the Group Areas, things were hard, because they realised they were poor and nothing could make them rich.' Nothing except perhaps the tantalising dream of riches proffered by the most renowned medicine man in the region.

Taking Khotso's muti for short-term profit and good fortune was far less pricey – and dicey – than going through his full-length ukuthwala process, which involved endurance tests and frequently submersion in a pool in the Mzintlava River. Unlike baptism, or the traditional southern African religious rituals involving water that washed away inner contamination and offered spiritual upliftment, this descent into the realm of the river serpent came at a price for those seeking initiation into the occult mysteries of long-term wealth. 'Many people went there – of course, that was after they had paid big money,' remarked Lunika.

In general, the ukuthwala experience had a frightening, phantasmagorical quality. Decades after Khotso's death, one still hears tales all over southern Africa of what people are said to have undergone when they went to Khotso for this procedure. Although these ordeals often entailed a confrontation with snakes, the test could take a number of forms. Some of Khotso's customers were chased by a huge tyre (like a giant black snake that had curled itself into a hoop), made to swallow needles or face an oncoming train – a serpentine artefact of superhuman force.

'You'd see it coming at you, and you'd have to sit between the rails,' said a man who grew up in Kokstad in the 1940s and the 1950s. He spent some of his adult years in the 1960s at a Pondoland teacher training college in Flagstaff, not far from Khotso's headquarters in Lusikisiki. He had also heard about a paramount chief in Qumbu who went to Khotso. Khotso told him: 'Now you have to endure what's going to happen to you. I'm going to put you inside a grass hut and I'm going to burn it. You must stay there.'[13]

The district secretary of Qacha's Nek takes an interest in local history, not only in Lesotho but also in the adjoining regions in South Africa. He has heard a number of anecdotes about Khotso Sethuntsa, but recalls most clearly of all the accounts describing Khotso's ukuthwala procedure, related to him by people that he knows. For instance, the district secretary was told how one of his relatives went to Khotso for ukuthwala and was required to spend one night in the White House.

> And, as they slept, he was not alone, he was with friends, because they had come for a common purpose. People had many objectives to go there, but he would group them accordingly. Now, ultimately, they realised that the room they were sleeping in was full of water, whereas it was dry before they went to sleep. But then they discovered that they were covered with water and there was a big snake in this water. They had been warned that whether they feel anything or see anything they should not be scared. They should be brave enough. The snake started wrapping itself around them and at the start they enjoyed that. Then it pretended to swallow them, and they got scared and cried out. They tried to open the door and run outside, but somebody opened the door for them and there was nothing. [*Laughing*] So they were sent away because they had failed.

This description has a weirdly erotic quality to it, as the snake winds its body around those of the men and they find the sensation pleasurable. This sensual dimension of the ukuthwala experience was also emphasised by the man from Teyateyaneng in Lesotho who knew of many individuals who had been through ukuthwala in the 1950s and 1960s. 'There is the pool test,' he said. 'The snake winds around your body: don't panic. Mermaid, naked lady. Don't act, just stand. Don't be tempted. She will give you love kisses. Pretend nothing is happening.'

We are reminded of the sinuous, seductive figure of the mamlambo herself, who entices partly because to enter her dangerous embrace is to transgress established social codes. The attraction she exerts in this regard calls to mind the way in which sexual encounters can contain a particular thrill when they involve the breaking of rules, intertwining both pleasure and risk as they do so.

Fraught as they are with an alluring serpentine temptress at their centre, the ukuthwala narratives do not always stop short at the suggestion of perilous titillation. A number of them incorporate accounts of actual sex with the snake woman, who takes on a human female form for this purpose. Just as the word *thwala* implies abduction or the taking on of an extraordinarily weighty load, so sexual encounters with the being at the heart of the ukuthwala process can become a liaison too heavy to bear, during which the man – rather than the woman, as is the case in traditional practice – becomes the abductee, being swept away from those closest to him.[14] As has been noted earlier, the wife below the water demands that her consort put her before all others. Some narratives describe how a man's serpentine lover proves so insatiable in her sexual demands that she eventually drains him of his carnal energies. And so, it is said, he will neglect his wife's physical needs, leading all too often to the end of his marriage. 'Many men who go for ukuthwala divorce their wives, because that snake needs sex regularly. Wives get frustrated, and when the snake is satisfied it becomes a snake again,' someone who had heard many of these stories concluded.

But the mamlambo can have another type of damaging effect on her partner's sex life, as illustrated by the following description from Sylvia Tloti, a University of Fort Hare researcher and Pondoland resident who has conducted research into Khotso Sethuntsa's life. This account is based on her interviews with a member of Khotso's household and discussions with a Flagstaff inyanga:

> That the mamlambo is half fish and half human is a myth: she looks like an ordinary woman. She is strikingly lovely and has features that are completely beautiful. She is a demanding woman and is reputed to have an insatiable appetite for sex. One traditional doctor says that it is easy to see that a man has the mamlambo as his sexual partner, because *libhulukhwe zakhe ziyawa*, which literally means that his pants fall off his body, probably because of loss of weight. A man who has sex with the mamlambo is unable to have sex with an ordinary woman, because his penis eventually becomes the size that will satisfy the mamlambo, but which is obviously not suited to an ordinary woman.

Some people felt that even going for lucky powders and potions could have all sorts of disastrous implications for the lives and the family relationships of the individuals involved. A man who grew up in Flagstaff described what happened to his uncle, the principal of a Pondoland high school, who went to Khotso in the late 1950s because he wanted to buy a car:

> Khotso gave my uncle a small bottle and told him: 'Immediately you get your salary, put all of it in a purse with this bottle and put the purse under your pillow when you sleep. And don't tell your wife!'
>
> The following morning, my uncle opened his purse and counted the money and it was five times his salary, so he went to buy a car in Kokstad from the Weeks family. When he got home in his new car, he opened the purse and found double the amount he had used to buy the car. So he went out and bought more stuff, furniture and so on and every time he bought, the money came back, doubled. Then my uncle made the mistake of informing his wife. His wife told him: 'You know what, you are going to have a *tokoloshe* or a snake as your new wife and I will be driven away!'
>
> His wife forced him to throw the bottle into the sea and

he lost everything – no money and the car moved by itself and crashed into the house and everything was in chaos…. Then his wife deserted him! I believed my uncle's story and was forced to recognise Khotso's power.

Let us turn back to the full ukuthwala procedure itself and consider further descriptions of the ordeals, such as the following account related by the Qacha's Nek district secretary. He described what befell one of his acquaintances who went to Khotso for wealth:

> The other stages, he did not mention them, but he wanted to talk about this one, the final stage . . . it was more powerful. That is the stage if one goes through it, one has won. With him, it was in the final stage when he was asked to tell his wife to brew some beer. She had to carry it in a traditional clay pot to a place that was between two mountains in Lesotho, actually a pass.
>
> The man had to sit and wait near the clay pot and not look around. He had to stay there, and he would see a lot of things happening. He was also told not to react; he had to just let them happen and go by. And this story was said by him.
>
> He said he first experienced some poultry, chickens, hens coming and dipping their heads in the pot, drinking a little bit of beer and then passing by. And then there followed some livestock: sheep, goats and then cattle, horses – in groups, all drinking from the pot. What surprised him was that the pot remained full. And finally, he heard a sound coming from the east, and he saw a big light coming through the pass, as if the moon was passing over the pass. It was by then at night.
>
> He sat, he waited, and the sound grew louder and louder as it approached, and the light also grew wider and bigger, until it got to him. Then he realised the light was actually like a big eye. As it approached him, he realised that the body was that of a snake, a huge snake with one big eye. And when the body of the snake started wrapping itself around the pot, himself he got a fright and stood up and ran away. He had failed.

The mamlambo, we recall, is associated with objects that sparkle and gleam, and occasionally she manifests herself as a snake with a light emanating from her head, a diamond in her forehead or a single huge bright eye.

Sometimes the ukuthwala ordeals could take a more prosaic form. Nonetheless, such tests proved unpleasantly memorable for those who underwent them. Makeka recalled an account of one such ukuthwala trial. It took place in the midwinter of 1946 and it involved two men from Lesotho: James Tlali, from Maseru, who had an understocked café and a taxi, and a Reverend Mokoena, from Qacha's Nek, who had a café. At 6 p.m., just as darkness had fallen, Khotso sent his customers to his pool in the Mzintlava River.

Mokoena told Makeka how he and Tlali had stood right up to their necks in freezing cold water. They kept their shoulders hunched and their arms folded tight over their heads in an attempt to keep a small part of their bodies out of the river. Mokoena kept looking at his wristwatch; but after fifteen minutes, time had been passing so slowly that he felt that his watch had become stuck. After half an hour, he said that he could not stand it any more and departed. Tlali, on the other hand, was determined to stay in the water. Unlike many others who went to Khotso for ukuthwala, the ordeal of these two men was not surreal and hallucinogenic, yet it was an equally taxing endurance test. Given the choice, they might have preferred spectral terrors to prolonged immersion in the icy waters of a river in one of the chilliest parts of South Africa. The Kokstad winters can cut one to the bone.

In due course, having decided that the test was over, Khotso allowed Tlali to leave the river. He offered Mokoena a room in the White House for the night, but the latter made polite excuses and stayed overnight in the location. The following day, Tlali and Mokoena returned to Lesotho. Within three months, Tlali's shop was fully stocked and the following year he bought two buses.

Tlali became a very prosperous man, but both his sons died of sudden, surprising illnesses. 'If you want to get rich early by Khotso, then get rid of your heirs,' said someone who had heard of this. Tlali himself lived less than five years after he went to Khotso for ukuthwala. In 1951, he died in great pain and his business crumbled, leaving nothing for his family. Not only does this narrative offer a case history in which ukuthwala was seen as having disastrous implications for the life of the individual who underwent the process and the lives of those closest to him, but it embodies the belief that when those who have been through ukuthwala die, their wealth, obtained without the approval of their ancestors, goes to the grave with them.

There are relatively few accounts of people such as Tlali who stood firm throughout their ukuthwala ordeal. However, Lunika not only knows one such narrative, but was personally involved in the events that took place. He especially likes to tell how he witnessed someone undergoing the entire test when he took the man in question down to one of Khotso's pools.

In the days when Khotso was living in Lusikisiki, a white garage owner from Cradock arrived at his house, seeking help with his ailing business. Khotso introduced the man to Lunika and told him his name was Smith (possibly an assumed name that the man had adopted for the occasion) and that he should look after him. Lunika narrated:

> The following day, we went to one of Khotso's special pools, there on the Mzintlava. Khotso said that the white man would have to bathe there for luck. Actually, Smith would have to take all his clothes off, and step onto this stone, just in the water, near the bank of the river. Khotso gave me a rope. One end would have to be tied round Smith's wrist. I would have to hold on to the other end of the rope. Khotso went away and we did everything he'd told us to do.
>
> Then the stone Smith was standing on moved! It went right towards the middle of the pool. It sunk right below the surface. Smith disappeared underwater and then he'd reappear from time to time, looking terrified. I called out to the man – but I'd forgotten to hold on to the rope.

Afterwards, I thought that the stone this man had been standing on could have been the back of Khotso's snake itself, and that the snake was wrapping itself around Smith, under the water, cleansing him, to attract luck and money.

Next thing, Smith rushed out of the river. I suppose the snake must have finally let go of him. He ran off, straight into a thorn tree, then he rushed into town, towards the main street and disappeared. He didn't even stop to put his clothes back on. I tried to follow him. . . But I didn't know where he'd got to. As I was searching for Smith, I saw Khotso. He said, 'What's the matter with you? I told you to look after the white man, and now you've gone and lost him!'

So we were looking for Smith. And then we saw this police van, with two black policemen in the front and there was Smith in the back. They'd given him an old pair of white overalls to wear.

As soon as he saw us, he started shouting: 'There's the old devil! There's the young devil! They tried to kill me! They put me in the river with this huge snake!'

Khotso kept calm. 'Oh,' he said to the policemen, 'my son here was just taking him for a cold bath in the river. But then he started shouting things about snakes and ran away.'

The policemen must have decided that this was all Khotso's business and they shouldn't get involved. So they tried to calm Smith down, but he wouldn't listen. He just stormed out of town.

But six months later, Smith came back! He had a new car, he was wearing smart clothes and he had his wife with him. He was so pleased to see us. He introduced his wife to us and he hugged Khotso and called him his friend. 'Thanks to you, my business is doing so well that now I can afford to employ three new mechanics at my garage!' he said.

Lunika's account of Smith's ordeal is one of the better-known tales of Khotso's mastery over snake-like presences. It is also a story that many people have found entertaining. Lunika laughed when he described Smith's horror, and it is clear that the image of a naked white man charging in terror into a thorn tree as he fled from Khotso's snake in the water is one that will remain fixed in his mind for all his days. MaDlamini, by no means as dour as many believed, still giggled decades later when recalling what had happened on the day Smith went down to the river.

Lunika still retells this tale today with relish, and likewise many other ukuthwala stories are told and retold. In fact, they have come to constitute one of the most prominent groups of oral narratives in the Eastern Cape. In other parts of southern Africa, accounts of Khotso's ukuthwala process have acquired a special renown.

These ukuthwala narratives continue to exert a widespread fascination because of the promise they contain: that wealth could lie within any ordinary individual's grasp, despite his or her unpromising circumstances. The Lotto advertisements that we see today exert a comparable type of appeal. The ukuthwala accounts remain captivating, even to narrators and listeners who say that they do not believe in the supernatural, because these tales deal not only with what may or may not have taken place, but with that for which many people wish.

Yet it should be borne in mind that Khotso's clientele came not only from economically embattled black communities. The widespread, potent myth of economic betterment also dangled before the eyes of those who were less financially desperate, like Smith in Lunika's story. A substantial number of middle-class entrepreneurs, both black and white, visited Khotso. Like motorists running low on petrol visiting a garage, these people felt that their businesses needed the agency of magic to keep moving forward. Blades, for one, cites anecdotes about such individuals: a white butcher from Johannesburg who turned to Khotso and reaped financial rewards; and a white mine foreman from Germiston who went for ukuthwala, received promotion and declared that Khotso's magic had worked for him.

Lunika claimed that Khotso tended to overcharge his white clientele. In part, this was fuelled by a sense of devilish mischief on Khotso's part, but on the other hand, as Lunika had noticed from early on, Khotso liked his white customers because in general they did as he asked. So when Khotso demanded huge sums of money from them, chances were that they would dutifully hand it over. Lunika described one example of this to Blades:

> A white man would come to him and say: 'I have a butchery business in Johannesburg and it's not doing well.'
>
> Then Khotso would ask: 'But have you any money? How much?'
>
> And the man would say: 'A hundred pounds.'
>
> Khotso would tell him: 'Why, no, man, that's not very much. Bring a hundred and fifty because the more money you bring, the stronger the muti I'll give you.'

The client did as he asked, believing that his £150 was buying him powerful medicine that could bring about the economic solutions that he sought. But above all, Khotso's white customers believed in him because, like his black clientele, they had heard the stories describing Khotso's ability to bring about financial miracles in people's lives.

Another key factor behind the popularity and longevity of the accounts of Khotso's association with ukuthwala is the potency and durability of tall tales, and their tendency to proliferate. Thus a great many insubstantial narratives would have been fuelled by all the ukuthwala stories already in circulation. In his day, Khotso would have used this phenomenon to further his interests.

As had been apparent from the outset of his career, Khotso knew one of the central principles underlying the telling of tales: that stories, especially dramatic and extraordinary ones, give rise to yet more stories. He turned this to his financial advantage, relating colourful accounts of himself and his powers, including those displaying his prowess as an ukuthwala practitioner. Consequently, stories about him bred like rabbits. Wild and free, they sped over southern Africa, multiplying in profusion, overwhelming many of Khotso's clients or potential customers through sheer force of numbers.

Yako has his own theory accounting for the great many tales that have arisen concerning Khotso's ukuthwala process. 'People made up stories about Khotso,' he said. 'They would talk, talk, talk! People who described those tests didn't fail them – they were too scared to try going through the tests in the first place. So they made up stories about those tests to amaze other people.'

Indeed, as Yako intimates, part of the appeal and the staying power of the ukuthwala stories lies in their sensational entertainment value. This arises from the combination of their excitingly frightening and at times downright creepy atmosphere and their dramatic, suspenseful qualities, with the possibility of great wealth hanging in the balance all the while. Like people relishing a horror movie or children huddling together to tell ghost stories at night, the audience of many of the ukuthwala narratives delight in the dark thrills they contain. On one hand, they proffer an enticing prospect of sudden wealth; but on the other hand, like many horror movies and tales, the very distance between the ukuthwala stories and those who recount or hear them is reassuring. Both narrators and listeners might feel comforted that they themselves are not experiencing the events undergone by the protagonists. If they so choose, they can even feel satisfaction at being far removed from the horrors involved in the ukuthwala ordeals, because they do not personally believe in such a process.

These factors are perhaps part of the reason why a number of people laugh when discussing the ukuthwala stories or relating such tales themselves, just as the district secretary of Qacha's Nek did. Such ridicule could be an expression of spontaneous enjoyment evoked by a lively, action-packed yarn. But there could be nervous laughter too, springing from fear. Possibly some narrators and listeners feel uncomfortable at the way accounts of ukuthwala hint at sinister occult forces below the quotidian surface of ordinary experience. There are also the ominous, menacing implications of the ukuthwala process: the death and disaster it is said to bring in its wake. Even if they themselves do not believe in ukuthwala, some might resort to laughter in order to keep the darkness at bay. On the other hand, it is likely that this apparent ridicule may sometimes spring from underlying tension and embarrassment. While acknowledging that others may take the ukuthwala accounts seriously, the narrators and audience indicate through their dismissive laughter that they do not wish to create the impression of being credulous or superstitious themselves.

In contrast, those who recount how they visited Khotso for his short-term medicine for good luck and prosperity tend to adopt a more relaxed, straightforward approach. For instance, Lunika, among many others, still talks openly about the difference that Khotso's muti made to his life at the time. There is also a businessman in King William's Town who recently stated sadly: 'If Khotso were alive today, I wouldn't have the financial problems that I have now.'

Besides the individuals in the ukuthwala accounts related here, many other people who went to Khotso for this procedure did indeed experience considerable economic improvement in their lives. There are those who maintain that this could not be ascribed simply to Khotso's control over the paranormal. Instead, they argue that a variety of other factors were at work. For instance, Lunika, ever practical, believed Khotso's ukuthwala clients probably did experience something really frightening, because such tests made good business sense.

Firstly, Lunika pointed out that Khotso's ukuthwala medicine was a costly concoction, containing some expensive herbal ingredients. If he could withhold this from some of his customers on the grounds that although they had paid the high fee they had failed the test, he would save himself money. The medicine in his possession would last longer before he had to purchase the herbs needed to make more.

Also, Lunika added, Khotso was testing his clients' determination. If Khotso's customers could get through the test, quite possibly they would have what it took to make money for themselves. One person who endorsed this idea was a Lusikisiki man whose father had worked for Khotso. 'He was testing their courage,' he contended. 'It is said that what you see may be a figment of your imagination. It might not be a train, but when you see it, you think it is a train. And even when you're swallowing needles, you think it's needles, but it's just testing your character, how strong you are, to go through that process.'

In his ukuthwala business, as in other areas of his life, Khotso liked to back winners. Consequently, he preferred to bestow his medicine on those that he thought possessed the skill to become successful entrepreneurs – for example, clever, energetic, purposeful young men.

As far as Khotso's clients themselves were concerned, the power of suggestion played a role in strengthening their resolve to succeed in life. Clients who underwent various ordeals were strengthened in their belief that the remedies they were finally granted were so potent and efficacious that they could not simply be dished out to anyone who came asking for them. Various Pondoland locals share Lunika's view to an extent, sensing that the significance of Khotso's ukuthwala ordeals may have resided primarily in the psychological trials they entailed, rather than the uncanny dimensions they appeared to embody.

There is the possibility that some of Khotso's clients were fed hallucinogens in order to induce the weird phantasmic visions that characterised the ukuthwala ordeals. For instance, a herbalist in Matatiele recently described one concoction as 'Khotso's recipe'. This contains *isipili*, which summons up uncanny apparitions by inducing altered states of consciousness. One informant said: 'I took it once, and it was like things from dreams came alive and walked around me.' There are a number of tales of people who failed the ukuthwala test and then went mad. If these individuals had indeed taken a hallucinogenic concoction, then after their ukuthwala ordeals they might have experienced something comparable to the psychological and mental damage sometimes caused by LSD.

Khotso's remedies worked, Lunika said, because he made sure that his clients believed in them. His wealth-giving medicines were a case in point:

> A person would come to Khotso and he would take him to a
> bath. He would surround the bath with some incense and would

add some powdery muti in the water, with which the person would bathe. Khotso would talk to the spirits, the ancestors, and tell them that they must give the person some wealth. Then, those things would get to the man and he believed that he was going to be rich. And that faith would make the man strong. Khotso would also tell his patients not to drink or smoke, which was a good thing, you see, good warnings: *ungaseli, ungatshayi* and to avoid women. Today, that is the message that Khotso would have given people so as to avoid HIV/Aids, because he used to encourage abstinence. And the most important thing was that people believed that his muti would work.

Lunika's latter point is an important one. As he suggests, the all-important element of faith was required, whether belief in the medicine itself or a conviction that the stories testifying to Khotso's powers were true. To all appearances, there was solid evidence for this. Khotso himself was a conspicuously wealthy man, and people who had been to him for ukuthwala had become rich too. 'Whenever people saw a clean-shaven rich businessman, they were seeing Khotso-branded advertising,' someone remarked.

There was another, concrete reason why Khotso's ukuthwala procedure appeared to be effective. Successful clients might receive from him not only medicine but also business assistance. Long before the days of rural development agencies, Khotso helped a great many would-be entrepreneurs on their way. 'He'd give them good business advice,' Lunika recalled. 'He might even give them some money to get started.'

Khotso would go on to maintain a relationship with his successful clients, some of whom would call on him regularly and give him money. One such customer, the man who stayed in the White House for some time and drove Khotso on his perilous night ride from King William's Town to Kokstad, would give him several hundred pounds each time he visited him.

It could be argued that perhaps Khotso became a successful seller of ukuthwala because he hedged his bets and did not rely on supernatural

One of Khotso's pools on the Mzintlava.

forces alone. Yet, pragmatic considerations aside, it seemed to many that there might be presences in Khotso's pools that needed to be visited and propitiated. Even today, many approach those pools with caution.

An elderly white man, a local figure in Kokstad as the proprietor of Rolyats, a long-established supermarket, was friendly with Khotso from the 1950s onwards. Khotso would often come and visit him in his store and then buy loaves of bread to put in his special pool in the Mzintlava. Along with banknotes and meat, this was an offering to his snake. Lunika would sometimes accompany Khotso and a crowd of his followers. The steep banks and tangled trees give way to wide open grassland, allowing space for Khotso's followers to congregate beside their master. Part of the bank has been cut away, extending the pool and making it more circular in shape. 'We used to go there with Khotso's people,' Lunika recalled. 'We would form a circle around the pool and sing.' Lunika would at times just briefly glimpse a head in the water and something would take bread from Khotso's hand. But he couldn't make out what it was, Lunika said. It could have been a big snake or a fish, or a turtle – or anything.

The pool where this ceremony would take place and another pool that Khotso often liked to use are visible from the White House. Fort Hare researcher Sylvia Tloti described the impression that they made on her:

> The rambling structure faces east, as do most of Khotso's abodes. The river has two deep pools that are situated slightly to the right and to the left of the house. The location of these pools creates the eerie feeling that there are two big, dark eyes gazing forebodingly out into the world from Khotso's kingdom. It is with a feeling of unease that one approaches the pools; and Meshack the guide's obvious reverence for 'whatever' or 'whoever' is in the pools does not help ease this feeling. Before he takes you to the pools and discusses them with you, he first appeases their invisible residents.
>
> The pool to the left of the house is apparently the one that Khotso preferred to use and which, by implication, had more potent residents. The water in this particular pool is dark green and very cold. A logical explanation would be the tall and heavily branched willow trees. The guide, however, explains that the beings, which he calls amakhosi, that reside in the pool prefer it that way, because heat tends to make them apprehensive and not very cooperative. The mouth of the pool is surrounded by reeds. These reeds, the guide explains, were used by Khotso's disciples, customers and patients when they gathered around the pool to sing praises to the beings. They would hold the reeds high above their heads, whilst singing and dancing. Reeds, he says, are sacred.
>
> Although this pool has not been in use for a long time, one can still detect that a great number of people used to converge there, because the ground around the pool is still clean-trodden

and there is still evidence of discarded reeds nearby. The guide also explained that Khotso preferred this pool rather than the one to the right, because he was able to observe whatever was going on at the pool from his chambers in the White House.

As he incorporated water and reeds into his rituals, Khotso would have been drawing on their deep-seated spiritual significance, which goes right back to accounts of the creation. In the belief systems of Xhosa-speaking peoples, the term *uHlanga*, denoting both the creator god and the source of creation, refers to the place where people and cattle were brought forth. It was depicted as a marsh, overgrown with reeds, which hid the entrance to a huge cavern. Almost any river or deep pool could possibly contain an opening to uHlanga.[15]

A young Kokstad man, whose family was friendly with Ellen and who lived in the White House long after Khotso's death, said that outsiders would join in the rituals by Khotso's special pool: these were people who hoped that his snake would bring them luck. They would drop coins into the water as their offerings. Deep down at the bottom of the river, heaps of these coins still lie undisturbed. Kokstad is full of poor people, but it is unlikely that any of them would choose to plunge into the depths of the pool in search of these coins.

Local people tend to avoid walking along the river bank towards the White House for reasons that have as much to do with the practical as with the paranormal. For much of the way along the river, the area sloping down to the water is gloomy, overshadowed by large old trees and dense with tangled undergrowth. Although the Mzintlava is not far from the road leading out of town, this section of the river where Khotso carried out many of his rituals is hidden away from the everyday life of Kokstad. Rapes and attacks have taken place here, in the darkness under the trees. Then there is the water itself: black and deep and still. Pale dead leaves lie motionless on its surface, and it is easy to imagine that something could be lurking below. Standing beside the river, one shivers at the thought of accidentally slipping on the steep bank and falling in. A few years ago, two men went swimming there and one of them drowned.

Khotso's pool at Kilroe Beach.

The story goes that the man vanished, and some time later his body was found downstream. It looked as if he had been involved in a struggle of some kind. Had he known about this, it is possible that Nthoa Bohlokoa would have felt that he had once been engaged in a similar tussle deep in the Senqu. The Mzintlava and its environs do not feel safe. It is a relief to scramble up the bank, away from the river and into the dusty sunlit streets of Kokstad.

There were other parts of the Mzintlava that Khotso used as well, one of which is near Ellen's house. Francina now tells visitors that Khotso's inkanyamba once lived there. 'I once saw it going back into the water myself!' Khotso and his people would encircle the pool, she said, and feed bread to the being that resided in it. Today this spot is almost inaccessible, surrounded by reeds and blending into the flat marshy wetlands around it.

While the Mzintlava was the best-known place to which Khotso's clients were taken to meet his snake under the water, the ukuthwala procedure was carried out elsewhere too. One of his snakes was believed to reside in the most spectacular of all these pools, near Khotso's house at Kilroe Beach on the Transkei's Wild Coast, north of Port St Johns. Today, this place is known as Msikaba, deriving its name from a nearby village. As with his Kokstad property, it is likely that Khotso chose this particular site for one of his houses because of its proximity to a dramatically deep pool.

The Kilroe Beach house is one hundred and fifty yards from the sea. To reach it today, one travels from Lusikisiki, following a dirt road that winds over lonely hills, dotted here and there with isolated villages. Every now and then the road fords rivers, until eventually, on a hilltop, one has a vista of rocky coastline and wild wind-whipped seas below. There, where the rolling grasslands dip down to meet the ocean, stands a cottage, as solitary as it was in the days when Khotso lived in it. Today two women live alone there, with the seagulls and wandering goats for companionship: Khotso's wife MaMjoli, now over seventy years old, and her granddaughter Patricia. It is as if something of Khotso's presence still remains in the area around his little white house by the sea. Locals call this piece of coastline Khotso's Beach.

In Khotso's time, the Kilroe Beach house was his coastal retreat, to which selected friends and prominent acquaintances, such as Botha Sigcau, the paramount chief of Eastern Pondoland, and Alf Marsburg, the Lusikisiki magistrate, would be invited. Like his other dwellings, this house, small though it is, was crammed with brightly coloured glass and china. Most of the decorations are gone now, but visitors, both local and foreign, still journey out to Khotso's Beach. Some come because they want to visit the places where they believe Khotso's presence lingers. Others wish to commune with Khotso's spirit and seek good fortune. They stay overnight at the house, sleeping in the special bed where Khotso used to sleep, in MaMjoli's small, neat, whitewashed bedroom. The following day, clients trek over the hills with MaMjoli to the pool to which her husband once took his clients.

Looking up towards the hills from the house beside the ocean, one sees a waterfall spilling down a cliff face in the distance, the river below it tumbling steeply downhill through a series of rapids and pools into the sea. One scrambles up the rocky slopes, then pushes through lush subtropical bush and palmiet reeds and wades upstream through the river, towards the great circular pool itself at the base of the waterfall. The rocky banks ringing the forefront of the pool drop sheer down into the deep black waters, shadow-ringed by overhanging trees and the cliff wall. Here Khotso would have stood, invoking the being deep below the surface, while his clients waited beside him. Here too MaMjoli stands today with people who believe that Khotso's powers still flow on through the generations, and that the forces that brought him wealth and success can still be called on in places such as these.

When he visited Khotso's beach property, Yako felt that there was something lurking under the surface of the water, but just like Lunika, when the latter described Khotso's special place on the Mzintlava, he didn't want to assert categorically that the creature in the pool at Kilroe was a snake. Khotso, however, was far less equivocal. 'People say I have a snake here,' he told Yako. 'Do you believe it?' Yako, once again put on the spot by Khotso, simply responded, 'No, I don't.' This was Khotso's cue. 'I have a snake in the pool by the beach,' he told Yako. 'How big do you think the snake is?' He had two big oxen at Kilroe, he continued, 'but you could double those oxen and the snake will still be bigger.'

When it was misty, the snake would come out of the pool, Khotso went on. It would rise up, up and up, but its lower body would remain below, coiled on the floor of the pool. In the morning, it would rear up and start descending at midday, folding its body back upon itself, coil after coil. But this process would take the whole day and it would only be after nightfall that the snake would vanish below the dark surface of the water. Yako confessed that he would never dare to go to the pool alone. 'And,' he added, 'if you went to that pool with a cigarette, you would drown.'

Since Khotso's reputation as a commander of fearsome forces was so closely linked to his pools and the snakes they contained, it is hardly surprising that many people in East Griqualand and the Transkei felt that his powers were linked to water, especially the Mzintlava. People still make remarks like these uttered by Kokstad locals not very long ago: 'His snakes came out of the river. He stayed underwater, for long periods.' 'Ja,' said someone else, 'they reckon for hours. For two days at a time, and that's where he got his powers.'

Stories of this nature would have helped entrench belief in Khotso's ability to exercise authority in the supernatural world, given the spiritual importance attached to water in the regions in which he lived and worked. It is perhaps for this reason that Khotso saw fit to bestow a watery name on one of his daughters, Malewatle. She is also widely known as Mametsi. *Metsi* is Sotho for 'water' and thus the name *Mametsi* means 'mother of water', while *lewatle* means 'sea'.[16] Incorporating the ocean into his daughter's name, Khotso might have been calling to mind the very same waters that he could see from his Wild Coast home. As a whole, her name could have served as a reminder of his pre-eminence in matters monetary as well as mystical, as an African owner of a beachfront holiday house and as one able to wield influence over the supernatural presences in the rivers near his houses.

We have seen that water is revered as a sacred space within which communion with wise, benevolent spiritual forces is possible, and this element is also feared because it is believed that unseen dangers lurk below its surface. 'Most of the spirits that is witch spirits, they live in rivers,' said the man whose childhood in Lady Frere coincided with Khotso's days of glory in Lusikisiki. As he and others have indicated, various menacing otherworldly presences are associated with rivers and water, such as the dwarf-like tokoloshe, which lives in dongas and on river banks,[17] and the inkanyamba. As he went about building up his business, Khotso would harness this awareness of the ominous aspects of water and the frightening nature of the beings that inhabited it.

Chapter 8
Greater than God

Fear lay at the foundations of Khotso's empire. The influence he was able to wield over others was based in the final analysis on the fact that from 1925 onwards he encouraged the notion that he had called down a tornado to destroy Eric Scott's farm. People became frightened of incurring his displeasure. And as Khotso began getting richer, this sense of fear increased, since with the weight of both the material and spiritual worlds behind him there was no knowing what kinds of havoc he might be able to wreak if he felt so inclined. Repeatedly, people emphasised this when talking about the man. 'People were afraid of what he could do, you see,' one person said. 'He showed his powers by healing, but it was quite dangerous to be on the wrong side of Khotso, if he became your enemy.'

Today many South African homes carry signs indicating that dangerous dogs lurk within, and that twenty-four-hour armed-response guards are close at hand. The warnings displayed on these notices are easy enough to prove or disprove, but the accounts of the punishments that Khotso inflicted on trespassers, those who tried to probe too deeply into his secrets or questioned his powers, exuded a more insidious type of threat. Many individuals, while declaring themselves to be rational beings, carry within them an intuitive, irrational terror of offending supernatural forces. Some such people might, for example, avoid walking under ladders, feel a mild alarm at the prospect of Friday the thirteenth or shudder instinctively when an owl lands on the roof of their house. While such superstitions may differ qualitatively from overt belief in dangerous otherworldly beings and personages, they nonetheless suggest that those who entertain them might be inclined to endorse the possibility that certain misfortunes have their origins in the paranormal.

Until this day, those stories intended to deter interlopers continue to fulfil their intended function in certain quarters. 'If you released that information about Khotso to a person, maybe you get cursed or something,' one man from Lusikisiki said, echoing these widespread sentiments. He and many others maintain that they still feel cautious about enquiring too deeply into Khotso's life. The belief that Khotso controlled a number of snakes, both real and magical, fuelled this fear. Several informants cited stories of how Khotso would send his supernatural snakes after his enemies: a grouping that included those who tried to penetrate the mysteries surrounding him.

'People believed that he had apparently many creatures for particular functions,' one Pondoland informant remarked. 'They said Khotso had many snakes, and he would choose a particular type of snake, one for killing people, one for making people rich, you see.' He mentioned the specific serpent that Khotso sent out against those who sought to double-cross him or betray his secrets. Some said it was a huge horse-headed snake in the Mzintlava; others termed it Khotso's inkanyamba. Interestingly, there are two types of tornado spirit in the Transkei: the sky snake, familiar throughout southern Africa, and a winged horse, which appears to be specific to the area. Possibly, then, Khotso's horse-headed snake combined both these manifestations of the tornado spirit.

'They would come after you at night, you see!' declared the man who remembered Khotso from his childhood in Kokstad during the White House days, and later, in the 1960s, when he had been at a teacher training college in Flagstaff.

For many people, Khotso's snakes were just as much part of the

White House as the stained glass, archways and minarets. The snakes could not be seen, but many visitors were convinced that they were somewhere close at hand, watching them, biding their time, awaiting their master's command. Later on, people would feel much the same way about Mount Nelson.

Some tried looking for the snakes, Lunika included. 'You know, I'm an educated person,' he said. 'But because I'm a curious person, I wanted to find out whether I would see any snakes. I never saw any snake in Mount Nelson. I used to stay there, I slept there, but I never saw any snakes there.'

Some people went so far as to make enquiries. In the 1960s, Yako described how he heard a visitor to Mount Nelson asking where the snakes were kept and if he could have one of his own. Khotso brushed him off. 'Go to Durban,' he said. 'There's a snake park there where you'll be able to find a snake. There aren't any here!'

Sometimes, Lunika said, Khotso would plant a rubber snake in a conspicuous part of his house and play with it, roaring with laughter when wide-eyed visitors recoiled in horror. For family members, however, the tales of Khotso's serpents sometimes became too much. Later in Khotso's life, even as mundane and innocuous a dwelling as the family's outside toilet at his home in Mount Frere became transformed into a site of fascination and potential menace. Khotso's daughter Mametsi complained that because the outhouse door was always kept closed, people assumed that the family's wealth-giving snake had to be concealed inside the latrine.

The notion that one of the family lavatories did indeed harbour a wealth-giving snake was first established, then reinforced, by the potent weight of rumour. As was the case with a number of astounding tales concerning Khotso, this factor lent substance to opinions that could otherwise appear to be little more than fantasies for the ingenuous and the credulous. Khotso was partly responsible for the many far-fetched yarns that floated around him and his household, for, having embroidered on and even invented aspects of his life, he laid himself open to more elaborations and fabrications once his stories about himself and his life history had slipped beyond his reach. Also, rumours thrive on mystery and the more frequently and widely they are repeated, often with an air of solemn conviction, the more likely they are to seem plausible, moving from the flimsy, unreliable area of speculation and hearsay into the more solid terrain of fixed belief. The stories of Khotso's magical snakes gained an air of physical actuality, making them seem as much part of the physical world he inhabited as his Cadillacs and the statues of lions adorning his properties.

While some of the serpents in Khotso's world were terrifying presences, unleashing destruction, others were the amakhosi, or benevolent guardians, like the snakes on Lunika's walking stick. These were wreathed around the sides, front and back of the staff, just below the carving of the mamlambo. Khotso told Lunika that this would give him all-round protection, since they would be able to attack his enemies from all sides.

'Khotso warned me that I must never kill a snake when I saw one,' Lunika said. 'Never kill a snake because sometimes you might kill it only to find that it was a representative of the ancestors. It was a visit from your ancestors. Whenever I saw a snake I would just clap hands and let it pass in peace.' Likewise, when snakes appeared on Khotso's property, he respectfully escorted them off the premises.

Many may have wondered why Khotso never trained a son to follow in his footsteps. Indeed, the person most equipped to take over from him, in terms of his good working knowledge of the intricacies of Khotso's kingdom, was his prime minister, Lunika, who, as future events will indicate, was unable to take on this role. Granted, as Khotso's life unfolded, it was blighted by misfortunes and difficulties with his sons and there were cogent practical reasons why Langa, the son best positioned to follow after him, never received all the training he would need to take over from his father. Someone who knew Khotso, however, posited that it was possible that he did not want any of his children to carry on after him because Khotso could have done a number of risky, even frightening things early on in his career, when he was building up his strength and his fortune, and he did not wish any child of his to go through what he had endured.

In support of this idea, various informants cite the tale of Khotso's seven skulls. Were these proof of the darkness in his past? Khotso, it was rumoured, had these grisly objects arranged around his bath and he would pray to them at night. For some, the seven skulls were as much a feature of his household as his snakes. Even if you hadn't seen these relics yourself, many argued, they were certainly there, somewhere in a secret part of the house. Speculation abounded concerning the origins of the skulls. Had their owners perhaps fallen short in one of Khotso's endurance tests?

It was claimed that Khotso would light candles, bathe in intelezi and pray for wealth, focusing on the skulls. His prayer contained these words:

Izitha zam ndzinyathele ngenyawo
Indlela zam zibe mhlope.
[I must stamp with my feet on my enemies
Be my paths clear.]

Whether or not Khotso really used a prayer of this nature, surrounded by fearsome objects associated with death, to psych himself up and to build up the determination and ruthlessness he would need in his march towards greater wealth and power, one thing is certain. He had ways of letting people know that his vengeance would catch up with those who tried to thwart, rob or betray him.

'If you crossed his path, Khotso could be a dangerous man,' someone said. 'That's why people were scared of him.'

Khotso had one well-known method of instilling belief in his powers. In 1966 John Lennon triggered off international outrage when he claimed that the Beatles were bigger than Jesus. Khotso, however, went one better. Twenty years before Lennon's pronouncement, he began announcing: 'I am God and I will live forever.'

A number of informants describe how Khotso would gather his clients together and tell them to cry 'Khotso is greater than God!' What the staunch churchgoer MaDlamini made of these performances can only be imagined. One older woman from Bhongweni, who remembered Khotso's days at the White House, said: 'He was always asking people who was greater between God or himself. And, because people wanted to get rich, they used to say that he was greater than God. "It's you, *Morena*," those people would say. He was still asking people the same question, even when he was on the verge of death.'

The Sotho word *Morena* not only means 'Lord' or 'King' or 'Chief', but in the Christian context it also is the term for God. Khotso would have been aware of this fact. However, he was no fool. There were always two Khotsos: the outrageous public performer, who enthralled, shocked and bamboozled the world around him; and the other, private Khotso who – it may be imagined – contemplated with delighted amusement his own goings-on and the outrageous yarns that spread about his powers. How easy it is to take people in! As was so often the case with Khotso's apparently over-the-top performances, there were very practical reasons behind this public parading of his ability to outdo even the greatest spiritual presence of them all. As was the case with the tales alleging that he had entered into perilous pacts with sinister supernatural forces, Khotso appeared to believe that there was nothing wrong with publicity, even notoriety. If there were people out there who were really prepared to believe that he was greater than God, so much the better for business. Also, it is likely that psychological manipulation once again played a role. Customers who were prepared to take the step of avowing, in public, that they thought that Khotso was more powerful than God would probably have complete faith in his medicines. And given that degree of belief, the chances were that those medicines would have the desired effect.

In 1958, Duke Ngcobo, eager for some sensational material for his *Drum* article, tried asking Khotso if it was true that he was a miracle-performing god returned to earth. The herbalist confirmed this, even while pretending to deny it. 'Of course that's not true. Here I am alive and very much human. Perhaps they are referring to the fact that I twice died and came back. The first time was in 1924, two years after I had begun my practice. The second was in 1956. On the first occasion I was dead for three days, on the second for two days.'

Later, Khotso would seek to turn these kinds of stories into a source of profit. For example, in 1965 he told another journalist about his 'everlasting life offer', which had twice enabled him to return from the dead. His secret of eternal life could be purchased from him, although, as he told the reporter, it would be the most expensive medicine he had ever sold because it would cost one million pounds. It would be cheap at that price, however.[1]

'If a man came to me with that money,' Khotso assured his listener on that occasion, 'I would pass on to him the secret of eternal life. I would take him to the place where I pray with the spirits and he would stay there for two days. He would see the spirits and they would tell him the secrets of the world and the secrets of life. He would then depart with these spirits around him. They would protect him and guide him and tell him what to do. He would attract tremendous wealth, even as I do.'

One reason why Khotso might have emphasised his closeness to the spirit world on this and many other occasions was that it is difficult to be rich in a poor community. Envy at the good fortune of others is often the chief impetus behind accusations of witchcraft. Because of the tales alleging that he owed his riches to his dealings in dark and dangerous magic, such as the ones circulated after his son's funeral, Khotso created his own counter-propaganda. Sometimes he insisted that his wealth was based on sheer hard work, but on other occasions he would suggest that something more was involved. He used a number of different narratives, including the one above, to illustrate that wise, protective supernatural forces were on his side. Such stories also carried a warning. They implied that by attacking Khotso, whether physically or verbally, or by attempting to steal his possessions, one would be taking on the spirits too.

It was the spirits, Khotso said, that would enable him to live forever and, yet again, spiritual power, sheer luck and financial success were intertwined. He told one journalist: 'I have this secret and as long as people pay for my magic and for as long as I can have eternal life, why should I stop making money? . . . Why should I stop enjoying all this good luck?'

While he paid a great deal of attention to the practical side of things, Khotso always created the impression that he was a strong believer in the inexplicable, unpredictable workings of astonishing good fortune. His favourite English expression was 'Good luck, chief!' It is not surprising that Khotso invoked the idea of luck as often as he did, since it was something that mattered a lot to him and it seemed to follow him for a great deal of his life.

Makeka once described an event that he had witnessed which appeared to bear this out: 'In 1953, at the racecourse at Tsoelike [in Lesotho], the owner of a horse paid Khotso seventy pounds, so that he would have luck to win. Khotso just touched the horse's mane before it set off. At first it was in the rear, then it vanished from view – and then it was in the lead. I saw it win the race.'

According to Khotso, horse racing was one area where the amazing luck that followed him everywhere he went could be put to good use. Certain informants from Matatiele and the Qacha's Nek area who know about the earlier part of Khotso's career make reference to his racing successes. Makeka, for instance, remembered how Khotso could often be seen at the betting shop at Matatiele. 'And he was always winning,' another man said.

As with his ukuthwala trade, there were times when Khotso hedged his bets. One man from Matatiele claimed that on occasion Khotso would back the entire field. After the race, he would destroy all his tickets, except for the one with the name of the horse that had come first on it. This he would display as proof of his marvellous capability to predict the winner.

Chapter 9
The Kruger Connection

Khotso was interested not only in horses that won races, but also in those who emerged the victors in the race for political power. One of the most widely publicised aspects of Khotso's life, the stories of his personal connection with Paul Kruger, can be understood in relation to his desire to be on the side of the winners.

In order to display the importance he attached to this renowned Afrikaner leader, Khotso bedecked special rooms in his houses with Kruger memorabilia and flaunted Kruger rands and coins from the territory over which Oom Paul had presided, the South African Republic. On ceremonial occasions, Khotso would don an embroidered beaded robe in the colours of the *vierkleur*, the four-coloured flag of Kruger's republic: red, white, blue and green. At the back, coloured buttons spelled out the message 'God bless President Kruger'. Above all, there were Khotso's annual Kruger Day celebrations, which were to become the biggest and best-known parties that he would host.

Although much of this was to take place later, at Mount Nelson, Kruger can be said to have attained the status of a household guardian at the White House. He was present in the form of concrete busts – his heavy, solemn face and long flowing beard picked out with enamel paint – gazing poker-faced at the odd establishment over which he presided.

Ensconced in his strange white house, with tales of his remarkable wealth and powers spreading further and further across southern Africa, Khotso deemed it fitting to draw public attention to the position that he accorded to Kruger in his life. In this and other respects, 1954 was a momentous year for Khotso. On 17 July, he made his first major appearance in the newspapers, becoming the subject of an extensive feature in the *Daily Dispatch*, an Eastern Cape broadsheet. Khotso knew fame of this nature would reap economic benefits, as faith in his powers became reinforced by the superficially objective solidity of the printed word.

Khotso could have claimed, in all truth, that he owed his media breakthrough to Kruger. The headline of the *Daily Dispatch* article proclaimed: 'Transkei's Richest Native: The Incredible Dr. Khotso'. But it was the subheading 'He Prays to Kruger . . . and Gets Results!' that drew attention to the most sensational part of the feature.

The journalist from the *Daily Dispatch* had arrived at the White House accompanied by a government official, who acted as his guide and translator. From the headline onwards, the article served its subject's interests, making reference to him as 'Dr Khotso'. He encouraged the use of this title, despite the fact that it had never been formally bestowed on him. In Khotso's eyes, the appellation functioned as an honorific, enhancing his professional status and emphasising that he had access to special healing powers that could be acquired only through intensive training and inherent ability. A few years later, Khotso would feel compelled to find an unconventional way of formalising this title. In 1954, however, he let it be known that he was Dr Khotso Sethuntsa and, like so many others who would follow, his visitors took him at his word.

Then, as easily as a skilled magician drawing doves from a hat, Khotso produced a collection of tales that went flying effortlessly over the top, drawing the reporter after them. For his part, the journalist was provided with material for a colourful article that could feature prominently in his newspaper. In the following decade, other reporters would depart from Mount Nelson similarly equipped.

Khotso beside his Cadillac, with a Kruger badge pinned to his jacket. (©Independent Newspapers)

In a sense, the government official was in the front line, because he translated Khotso's words from Xhosa. The journalist describes his companion's state of shock during the course of the initial exchange.

> An incredulous expression appeared on my companion's face as Dr Khotso spoke about Kruger. After questioning the doctor in a way that suggested that he could not believe his ears, the official looked at me as though doubting whether he could repeat in English what the doctor had said.
>
> 'He says', he finally announced, 'that Paul Kruger lives in this house and at the moment he is supervising the Native servants who are cleaning the Packard outside.'

The visitors were led into the yard, where they beheld a singular spectacle. Two of Khotso's servants were busily cleaning a brown 1954 Packard. Beside the car, there was a chair with a bust of Paul Kruger resting on it, as if he was monitoring the work taking place before him. As if to protect Oom Paul from the chill of the Kokstad winter, a Voortrekker Monument scarf, secured with a Kruger sovereign converted into a brooch, had been wound around his neck. Khotso then drew his visitors' attention to two richly inlaid walking sticks lying on a chair in front of the statue. He explained that he himself had presented these to Oom Paul, after the latter had confided in him that he wished for just such a gift. Moreover, Kruger had a packet of sweets resting beside him. Khotso explained that these were intended not for Oom Paul but for the servants, who would receive the sweets from the president himself if they completed the job to his satisfaction. No doubt observing his visitors' expressions at this point, Khotso added that, as Kruger's representative, he would distribute the sweets on his behalf. This was Khotso's earliest recorded, carefully staged performance for the press and it displayed some of the signal features of many of his later productions, in its combination of wild inventiveness and sheer chutzpah of delivery.

The guests were then taken indoors for tea, where Khotso elaborated at leisure on what would become one of his favourite subjects: the nature of his relationship with President Kruger. Oom Paul helped him in many ways, he told his guests, and accompanied him wherever he travelled. While Khotso's domestic worker may have felt duty-bound to confirm this, it is possible that she had been primed as a member of the supporting cast who appeared in turn before the visitors that day. Whatever the case, she performed her job well, uttering the line that would make its way into the subtitle of the *Daily Dispatch* article: 'If Dr Khotso wants anything,' she said, 'he prays to Paul Kruger and he always gets what he wants.'

At this point, it appeared that both guests began smiling nervously, as if unable to believe what they were hearing. Seeing their expressions, the domestic worker asked: 'Don't you believe that we pray to Paul Kruger? Don't the Christians pray to their God?'

'Yes,' the government man responded primly, 'but we pray on a somewhat different basis.'

'And we pray to Paul Kruger in faith,' she said, 'and we get results, too.'

More results, she might have been implying, than Christians got when they prayed to their God. Khotso had, for instance, just confided in his guests that once, after praying to Paul Kruger, he was shown a vision in which he was given the name of the horse that was to win that year's Durban July, which had taken place several days earlier, on 5 July.

As a way of leading up to the grand moment when this revelation could best be shared with his visitors, Khotso had taken his guests on a guided tour of the White House. The highlight of the expedition was saved until the very end, when the two visitors found themselves in Kruger's room. This was in fact the dining room. The journalist observed that although all the major rooms were cluttered with glassware, a particularly large collection of brilliant, multicoloured glass had found its way into the dining room, a token, perhaps, of the way this room appeared to have become the heart of the White House. Here Khotso could astound his guests with the opulence of his surroundings and the magnitude of his hospitality, and here Kruger had taken up residence. Khotso showed his visitors a Voortrekker Monument scarf, which served as a type of altar cloth, upon which Kruger would rest when he was not monitoring the labours of his devotee's retainers. Here he would visit Oom Paul and pray to him, Khotso informed his visitors. Here too he would sit in silent, rapt contemplation of the concrete bust of the great man who had already begun to guide him towards wealth and fame.

It was at this point that Khotso revealed that Kruger had summoned him to this very chamber, so that he could receive the vision that would provide him with the name of the horse that was to win the 1954 Durban July, South Africa's premier horse race.

The reporter provided a heroically straight-faced rendition of Khotso's account of that event. One wonders, though, what the journalist's immediate reaction was as he listened to Khotso's description of his vision, which suggested that, having retired to the spirit world, Oom Paul had the leisure to devote some of his attention to horse racing. The sequence of events through which the winner of the Durban

July was revealed to Khotso Sethuntsa is taken from his Kruger House deposition, a document to which he would draw public attention a few years later:

> On the Friday night before the race Khotso was in his lower house in Kokstad. He received an urgent summons from Kruger, who normally 'lives' on the dining-room table at the top house, to appear at the top house. Dr Khotso arrived there shortly before midnight and told a domestic to prepare tea. He relaxed on the settee in the lounge. A few moments later the words 'C'est Si Bon – C'est Si Bon' appeared luminously before him. He retired to the dining room and prayed to Paul Kruger – the bust on the table. He returned to the lounge, had tea, relaxed again and shortly saw the luminous words floating before him once more. The next morning he placed a bet on C'est Si Bon and the horse brought him nearly £400.[1]

One memorable feature of this vision, which Khotso may have mentioned to his visitors, since it is also in the Kruger House deposition, concerns the way in which the name of the winning horse was initially manifested to him. In the deposition, Khotso described how he beheld the face of Kruger himself, with the words 'C'est Si Bon' shining before his eyes. It was as if the president was sending his disciple a sign to show that the mystical racing tip emanated from his prophetic insight into future events.

As proof of at least part of his tale, Khotso displayed the actual bookmaker's ticket that he had received when he placed his bet, with the name 'C'est Si Bon' scrawled on it. He had encased the chit in a brass frame, so as to preserve it for the gaze of future visitors. Even today, people who visit Mount Nelson are still shown this object. The ticket is yellowed and the ink is fading, but the name of the horse that helped carry Khotso towards greater wealth and renown remains visible.

In years to come, the story of Khotso's spiritual bond with Paul Kruger would be told and retold so often that when Khotso regaled journalists with this tale they would lap it up with the air of children being treated to a favourite bedtime story. The 1954 *Daily Dispatch* article has a different flavour to it. When the teatime meeting with Doctor Khotso Sethuntsa takes an unforeseen turn with the introduction of Kruger, there is an undercurrent of amazement and incredulity that is at variance with the apparently factual, straightforward tone of the article. In this respect, the piece takes on a unique entertainment value, since it is tempting to imagine the expressions on the faces of the reporter and, above all, the government man. From Khotso's perspective, the event could well have appealed to his sense of mischief-making.

The final act of the comedy would have been seeing the description of the visit in the *Daily Dispatch*. No doubt the episode left Khotso with a taste for fabrication at the expense of his visitors, since he had seen how easily such stunts could be pulled off. The pleasure in launching into enthusiastic flights of the imagination, overlaid with an air of solemn conviction that belied the playful trickery bubbling below the surface, was to remain an integral part of Khotso's character throughout his life.

Two years later, on 12 September 1956, Khotso set out to establish his connection with Paul Kruger firmly in the public eye, through his pilgrimage to Kruger House in Church Street, Pretoria. On that occasion, Khotso came equipped with a new prop.

He produced a document outlining not only his personal relationship with Paul Kruger, but also the way in which his family history was interwoven with that of the Kruger household. Before his journey to Kruger House, Khotso had dictated his parents' story to a Kokstad schoolmaster, C. J. R. Fortein. Part testament to the way his family's devotion to Paul Kruger had brought about marvels and miracles, part declaration of religious faith, all couched in Fortein's quaint, ornate prose, the document became central to the world of legend that Khotso constructed around himself.

When the journalist from the *Daily Dispatch* visited the White House, Khotso had simply stated that his father had worked for Paul Kruger. Two years later, he felt that the time was ripe to weave a grand tale

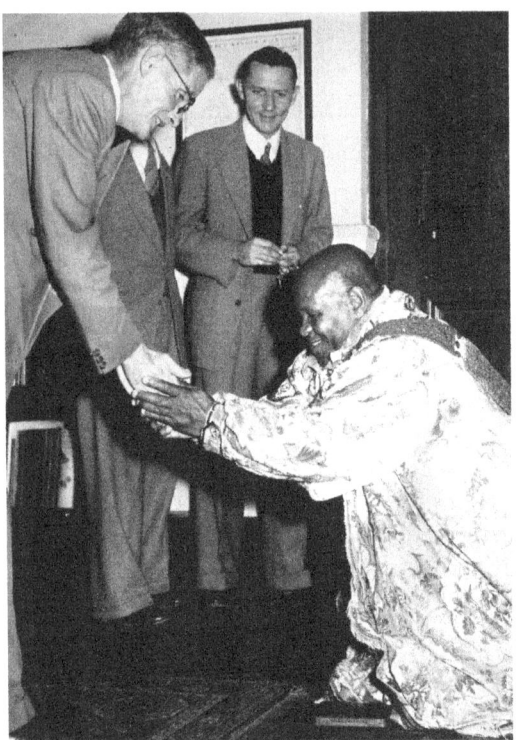

Khotso in Pretoria, kneeling before Dr V. FitzSimons, director of the Transvaal Museum, after making a donation of £100 for the preservation of Kruger House. (Courtesy of the Pretoria News)

showing how two loyal retainers transcended the status of mere servants and established a special connection with Kruger that took on the quality of a spiritual bond. Khotso bore his document, like a devotee bearing an offering to a shrine, to Kruger House, where the president had once resided and where it was deposited.

In the Kruger House deposition, the story unfolds as follows: Khotso's father, known as Speelman, was Kruger's coachman and trusted servant, eventually becoming his confidant. Khotso's mother worked for Kruger's wife, Gezina, and became known as Khaki. 'Mrs Kruger's tongue went lame whenever she had to say Mokholitsoane,' said Khotso. When talking of his parents to people outside his immediate family circle, Khotso generally preferred to use the names that he said had been given to them by Kruger and his wife, thus creating the impression that these names held a special significance for him.

Near the beginning of the deposition it is stated that 'Speelman and his wife Khaki shared the love and sorrow of the Kruger family'. One instance of this, Khotso claimed, took place when his parents played a crucial role in the history of the South African Republic by helping to foil the Jameson Raid. The incursion began as an attempt by Cecil John Rhodes to annex Kruger's South African Republic, but when he decided to call it off, the leader of the invasion, Leander Starr Jameson, decided to go ahead without Rhodes's support. According to Khotso, his mother had second sight and President Kruger always 'listened with great interest to [her] prophetic words' – especially on the occasion in 1895 when she announced that she had dreamed that the 'Rooineks' were taking over his country. Although the president was somewhat doubtful, as Fortein wrote, 'while stroking his flowing beard, he brooded over the matter in deep thought', and decided to investigate. Speelman and a fellow servant were sent on a reconnaissance expedition to the north. What they reported back was enough to alert Kruger. Jameson and his troopers were surrounded and compelled to surrender.

Khotso would have enjoyed relating this tale. His example of his family's devotion to Paul Kruger's cause made a good story in itself, one that drew attention to his mother's capacity to influence the path of history, and he liked to tell people that his own supernatural powers could affect political developments. The Kruger House deposition goes on to claim how, before the Jameson Raid, Khotso's birth itself resulted from his parents' loyalty to Kruger, 'a reminder to posterity of the singular nature and loyalty of the native inhabitants' to the Boers' cause'. A chief in the Herschel district, Maphasa, was proving an annoyance to the Boers in the eastern Free State, because he often raided their cattle. When he related this story to Peter Becker in 1958, Khotso was to remark: 'Maphasa was a clever man, very clever, for how else could he have become the biggest stock thief in those parts and survived the Boers' guns?'

The deposition relates that Kruger decided to send Speelman to mediate with Maphasa. In his conversation with Becker, Khotso would add a dramatic touch, telling him that initially the chief suspected that Speelman was a spy. Maphasa captured him when he approached his homestead and sentenced him to death. However, Speelman must have been a convincing talker, because Maphasa was won over and released him. As Khotso told Becker smugly, 'Like myself, my father was gifted with a way of speaking that caused men to listen and understand.' However, in the deposition, it is almost as if Speelman's arrival in Maphasa's territory magically brought about peace of its own accord, leading to a happy ending worthy of a fairy tale. Almost immediately after Maphasa met Speelman, he gave him the hand of his daughter Mokholitsoane in marriage as a pledge of his good intentions towards the Free State farmers. Kruger was so pleased by the successful outcome of Speelman's mission that when his trusted retainer's eldest child was born, he suggested that he be called Khotso, the Sotho word for 'peace'.

Before he presented the deposition to the domicile of the forefather of South Africa's political masters, Khotso embarked on a public display of his personal devotion to them. The *Pretoria News* began its account of Khotso's visit to Kruger's one-time capital with the following description: 'A short and powerfully built Native, dressed in a gown patterned with sequins and gold brocade, went down on his knees in the Transvaal Museum this morning and slowly counting out £100 in £10 notes, handed them to Dr V. FitzSimons, the director. Then he kissed his shoes.'[2] The money was intended as a contribution towards the preservation of Kruger House. Then, apparently overcome with emotion, Khotso wept.

In the month before Khotso visited Kruger House, Pretoria had received a visitation of a very different kind. On 9 August 1956, twenty thousand black South African women had marched to the Union Buildings, the administrative seat of government in Pretoria, to protest against the extension of the pass laws to women. This legislation was designed to control the movement of black South Africans to urban areas, the much-hated passbook indicating that its bearer was entitled to be present in a designated city or town because he or she was lawfully employed in that area. The women's march on the Union Buildings is commemorated to this day as a heroic act of mass-based resistance to apartheid oppression. Khotso, on the other hand, responded to the authoritarian white-dominated political milieu in which he found himself in a very different manner. In its theatrical quality, his pilgrimage to Kruger House was designed to attract press interest.

The Kruger House deposition depersonalises its two leading players. They exist primarily as loyal servants to the Afrikaner establishment of their day. Even Khaki's name, with its impersonal associations, appears in keeping with this. Khotso provides other accounts of his parents in which their individuality is similarly obliterated. He sought not only to continue but to expand on this claimed family tradition himself, as is emphasised in the latter part of his deposition, in which Kruger becomes a subject of spiritual devotion:

> Portraits of the President adorn the walls of [Khotso's] house. He explains this as follows: as the Roman Catholic Church worships the Mother Mary, so we worship President Paul Kruger, whose living spirit is always with us to bring us happiness and assure our prosperity.... So he maintains that his wealth and affluence can be attributed to the late President Paul Kruger, who is worshipped in a special room and signifies to him all that is worthwhile in life.

Whether the Calvinist Kruger would have relished the comparison with the Virgin Mary is a moot point. While the prominent position accorded to Kruger in the minds of many Afrikaners pales besides the apotheosis bestowed on him by Khotso Sethuntsa, the fact that Kruger acquired a mythic, iconic status among Afrikaners – the wise old patriarch, father of a heroic, beleaguered nation confronted with the might of British imperialism, a Moses driven away from the promised land – might have had some influence on the way he was perceived in certain sections of the African community. The traditional healer and diviner Credo Mutwa has commented on this. Like Khotso, Mutwa felt that it was in his interests to work within the prevailing political system and he enjoyed mythologising (although Khotso far outdid him on both counts). Mutwa made the following assertion: 'Paul Kruger . . . was worshipped by the Bantu of the Transvaal. And when I say worshipped, I mean literally worshipped – as people worship a god.'[3]

'The black people were traditionally closer to the Afrikaners than they were to the English,' Mutwa added in an interview. 'They lived together, they shared many things together. Of course it all changed from the 1930s on.' Both the indigenous peoples of South Africa and the Afrikaners felt the same closeness to the land, Mutwa maintained, and this formed a bond between them. He believed that Kruger spoke some African languages, had spent time in black communities and had access to traditional African knowledge. Mutwa cited one well-known anecdote. When Kruger was a boy, alone in the veld, he injured his thumb and was forced to amputate it. He shoved the bloody stump into the stomach contents of a freshly killed goat, an indigenous method of dealing with wounds. For all these reasons, Mutwa said, Kruger became revered as an ancestor figure by Africans.

Some of Mutwa's claims, reinforced by the similarities between his and Khotso's political positions in the days of National Party rule, might help explain why Khotso regarded Kruger as the foremost ancestor figure in his life. One journalist, in his account of Khotso's visit to Kruger House in the *Pretoria News*, lends support to Mutwa's views, making the following observation: 'To some Natives, especially the Sothos, President Kruger has great mythical significance. They call him Mmamelodi, "he who speaks sweet words".'

While on the one hand Khotso's accounts of his personal spiritual bond with Kruger make up yet another group of his tall tales, on the other hand there may have been a kind of truth to them. In other words, the events that took place on the day the reporter from the *Daily Dispatch* visited the White House may have amounted to more than a self-seeking prank on Khotso's part. Likewise, there may have been a certain sincerity underlying his display of emotion at Kruger House. On these and many other occasions, Paul Kruger provided Khotso with an opportunity to combine showmanship with spirituality. It is possible that Khotso indeed felt a kind of spiritual link with Kruger and accorded the latter a conspicuous position within his personal belief system, on account of Kruger's connectedness to money and power. We have already seen how Khotso's predilection to bedeck his home and his workplace with banknotes and cash stemmed in large part from his devotion to money. Khotso's reverence for power was expressed in the way he crouched on his hands and knees and kissed the feet of whites in positions of authority, from government officials to the bemused Dr V. FitzSimons on the day he visited Kruger House. In Khotso's eyes, whites were surrounded with the aura of power and privilege that he himself craved; when he abased himself before them, in a sense it was this very radiance that he was worshipping, rather than the all-too-often unremarkable pale-skinned individuals who exuded it. Ironically, however, by seeking to draw himself closer to the brilliance of power, Khotso was embarking on a course of action that would ultimately cast him into shadow.

While Khotso would have regarded Kruger as an appropriate focus of homage, as one of the founding fathers of the nation that had become South Africa's political masters, a special part of the attraction that Kruger held for Khotso relates to the former's association with wealth: the Kruger millions.

The Kruger House deposition ends with Kruger secure against his foes and, in return, symbolically blessing Khaki and Speelman's baby by bestowing a name on it. The infant, while not the actual bringer of peace, would symbolise it through his name and serve as its repository. Set against this, however, was the imminent historical reality of defeat and exile from which even Kruger's faithful servants, blessed though they were with second sight, courage and eloquence, would not be able to save him. But, enthusiastic storyteller that he was, Khotso rose to the challenge, taking it upon himself to create a memorable sequel to the deposition. At this point, Khotso shifted his parents from centre stage, to focus instead on an object that fascinated him: the Kruger millions, which provided him with the makings of an excellent mystery thriller, various forms of which were recorded by a number of writers and journalists. These led to repeated conjecture that Khotso had somehow succeeded in discovering where the greatest cache of bullion in South Africa, the legendary Kruger millions, had been concealed.

This famous South African legend has a historical basis to it. By 1900, during the Second Anglo–Boer War, also known as the South African War, the fall of the Boer capital, Pretoria, was imminent. As the British troops advanced on his city, President Kruger began his journey into exile.

As Kruger faded from South African politics, the rumour grew that the treasury of the old South African Republic had been carried away from Pretoria, along with the president himself. To add lustre to the legend, the coins and bullion that were believed to have been loaded onto the train that bore Kruger away were multiplied over and over, until they translated themselves into millions, most frequently envisaged as a fortune in gold. The story went that Kruger paused to bury this treasure before he fled the country. A number of people who might have had knowledge of this, the Boer commando leader Deneys Reitz included, deny that the Kruger millions ever existed.[4] Yet this did not stop the tale spreading that a fortune lay somewhere in the depths of the old Transvaal. There have been many attempts to find the hoard, all unsuccessful. Khotso, however, hinted that, through his special connections in the spirit world, he had been guided to the treasure.

According to Khotso, when the war between the English and the Boer republics broke out, he and his mother were sent back to Maphasa for safety, Speelman remaining with the Kruger household. Who, then, might be most likely to know of the fate of the Kruger millions but the old president's trusted servant who stayed with him right up until the end of his term of office? This was the impression that Khotso liked to create. As Speelman's fate and the whereabouts of Oom Paul's hidden fortune became intertwined, Khotso planted the seeds of the notion that he himself might have had access to the Kruger millions.

Rather than content himself with one story, Khotso embarked on several tales about the events that had befallen his parents after Paul Kruger left Pretoria. He told some people, including journalists, that Speelman had given Khaki a pile of Kruger sovereigns before she left Pretoria.[5] On other occasions, the pile of sovereigns transmuted into a loaded ox-wagon entrusted by the Kruger household to Khaki. The contents of the wagon were stored in a cave in Lesotho and people like the white Kokstad woman to whom Khotso told this tale were convinced that he would visit the cave, collect bullion and other valuables, and secretly sell them.[6]

By 1965, the story contained a strange and tragic twist. Khotso told some individuals that his father shared a grave with the Kruger millions. Speelman, Khotso told the journalist John D'Oliveira, was present when the treasury of the old South African Republic was hidden and he was shot and buried with it. In losing a father, he told D'Oliveira, he gained a fortune. 'I think that I could know where all this money is,' he said, 'but I would never tell and I would never interfere with it. . . . I have always believed that this is why money comes to me so easily. This is why the spirits bring all this money to me. This is the key to all my riches. The spirits are paying me back because my father is buried with all that money.'

None of these tales overtly states that Khotso's wealth was connected to Kruger's missing fortune. Instead, listeners were left to jump to their own conclusions, which they readily did. Khotso helped this process along through the collection of Kruger rands that he owned. He displayed these coins to visitors with considerable ceremony, as if his guests were privy to glimpses of items of treasure instead of objects that had been purchased. The Kruger rands Khotso presented to select individuals fulfilled a similar function. Lunika, for one, has a pair of cufflinks adorned with Kruger rands given to him by Khotso. When Khotso gave away such coins, those who received them would in all likelihood show them to others, as Lunika does to this day, thereby strengthening the connection in people's minds between Khotso Sethuntsa and the Kruger millions. This is so even though the Kruger rands could only function as a metaphor for the gold in Oom Paul's treasure trove, rather than wealth from the hoard itself. These coins were first minted in 1967, decades after Oom Paul's death.

One white woman from Ntabankulu, who described Khotso as

Khotso's face between two concrete busts of Paul Kruger and his wife. (Photo by John D'Oliveira, Sunday Tribune. © Independent Newspapers)

'an old family friend', thought that the story was a colourful way of accounting for all the gold Kruger sovereigns that he possessed. Khotso was an avid collector of Kruger coins, including gold pieces from Kruger's republic (issued between 1892 and 1900 as £1 and £1.10s coins), purchasing these wherever he could. 'He bought a whole kistful from my mother, and he paid her several thousand pounds,' the Ntabankulu woman recollected.[7]

Khotso's account of his family links with the Kruger household and his own mysterious connection with the Kruger millions represented one of his most impressive storytelling coups. It is likely that a degree of wistfulness, intertwined with an urge to transform himself and his personal circumstances, fuelled Khotso's extravagant tale-telling. He depicted himself as one directly related by blood to those who had been close to a person of great renown, even if they had not been famous themselves. He used the Kruger House deposition to portray his parents as individuals possessing such rare qualities that even the president of a mighty republic turned to them in his times of need. And thus he could imply that he partook of his parents' exceptional nature. Certainly Khotso's transformation of his and his parents' identities had the desired effect. Today very few people, apart from the inhabitants of mountain villages in the south-eastern Malutis, know Khotso Sethuntsa's birthplace. There are those who like to imagine that he was born in Kruger House and spent his first years there, under the gaze of Oom Paul, a distant, imposing, yet almost godfatherly presence in his early life. Khotso, however, did not bother to expand on the Kruger House deposition so as to incorporate a picture of his early years in the president's home. There were other, more important impressions that he wished to create. In the deposition, Khotso narrated how Paul Kruger came to be an ancestor figure in his life. The personal closeness between Kruger and his parents translated into a spiritual bond that continued into the next generation, incorporating their son.

The way we describe ourselves and our lives to outsiders can become a refashioning of our past, present and possible future. Khotso put more creative energy into this process than most of us do. For a range of reasons – professional, personal as well as political – reconstructing his identity was part of his life's work.

For the purposes of simple publicity, Kruger was a rich vein that could be mined for many tall tales. As the 1954 *Daily Dispatch* article indicates, he was the driving force behind another widely publicised group of stories: that the spirit of Oom Paul lay behind the financial success of Khotso Sethuntsa. When it came to economic matters, Khotso would declare, Kruger was his foremost adviser, offering assistance that encompassed both business concerns and horse racing,

In 1965, years after he had claimed to have predicted the winner of the 1954 Durban July with Kruger's guidance, Khotso was continuing to let it be known that, from his vantage point in the spirit world, Oom Paul was passing on racing tips to one favoured individual. 'Paul Kruger's spirit is with me always and it brings me luck,' Khotso explained to John D'Oliveira.

In 1958, Khotso told Duke Ngcobo that his wealth had arisen primarily through betting on horses. Ngcobo asked Khotso if it was true that he sold 'hot-tips' medicine for races and that he had been banned from big race meetings because of his absurdly heavy winnings. A master of the elusive answer, Khotso replied: 'Who doesn't want to see Khotso? Of course there would be a traffic jam if I went to any race meeting.' In 1967, Khotso tipped Sea Cottage, which went on to win the Durban July. The horse was an obvious favourite, and so some people correctly (and cynically) remarked that one hardly needed spiritual guidance to guess that it stood a good chance of winning.

It is quite probable that when Kruger and other spiritual presences were not providing Khotso with the names of potential July winners, Khotso's contacts, including some of the men working in the stables in Durban, were doing so. Blades, for instance, observed: 'They began to send him inside information, in the certain hope that they would receive his blessing in return.' That, at any rate, was the explanation some of Khotso's closest friends gave for his successes at the races.[8]

Then, in 1969, Khotso announced that he had been told the names of the winners of that year's Durban July. 'Can millionaire herbalist do it again?' asked *The Post* just before the race. Khotso predicted that Naval Escort would win the race, with Home Guard and Appointment coming second and third. 'I have consulted the wise ones, our ancestors, thrown the bones and the horses will win as I have predicted. I never go wrong,' Khotso announced. He added that he had such confidence in his selection that he had placed bets that amounted to thousands of rands on these horses. As with Sea Cottage two years previously, the first two horses were firm favourites.[9]

Khotso's predictions held true for Naval Escort and Home Guard, although Appointment came lagging far behind in fourteenth place. Several months later, he reproached Blades: 'Why didn't you back my selections? You haven't the faith, that's the trouble.'

Blades commented that faith wouldn't have stood him in very good stead in 1970, when Khotso, perhaps feeling the need to hedge his bets, tipped two different horses, Golden Jewel and Centre Court, as winners to two different newspapers. In any event, neither of these horses won, although Centre Court did at least manage to attain third place, with the odds at forty to one.[10] After this debacle, Khotso was far less willing to broadcast his racing tips in the press. But the fact remains that at least on some occasions it was as if he possessed the remarkable ability to predict which horse would be the winner.

Oom Paul's guidance in financial matters extended far beyond the area of horse racing. In 1958, Khotso confided to Duke Ngcobo that Kruger told him which farms to buy and which to avoid. His advice was fairly simple: 'Nothing cheap – only the best.' According to Khotso, one such example was his farm Mngqesha, near King William's Town. However, as someone who knew Khotso later remarked, not all his farms were purchased in compliance with Kruger's instructions. Some of them were little more than average-sized erven with a house on them.

In general, Khotso's houses tended to make more of an impression on outsiders than did his farms. By the latter part of the 1950s, he was building a dwelling on a piece of land he had acquired in Mount Frere in the Transkei, which MaDlamini would eventually occupy. Of all Khotso's houses, this is probably the one that most people saw, even in the latter part of the twentieth century, as it was situated beside the N2, just as the national road swoops through the town. With all its Khotso trappings – the lions on the gateposts, the pillars and stained glass, and what was to become his characteristic blue and white paintwork – the house looked uncanny. Even decades after its owner's death, it was as if it had dropped into the little town of Mount Frere, with its crowded bottle stores and fried chicken takeaway joints, like an edifice from a Gothic movie.

Fantastical though it may have appeared, Khotso's Mount Frere house was real. But how real was the story Khotso constructed around Paul Kruger? Khotso knew well that his accounts of the Kruger connection were bound to excite interest and generate publicity, especially in the white South African community, where the power and money lay.

It is worth noting that the *Daily Dispatch* journalist was treated to a description of Khotso's special relationship with President Kruger in 1954, six years after the Nationalists had become the ruling party in South Africa.

'We all know that Khotso of Kokstad had become the greatest friend of Afrikaners and other Europeans,' Khotso avowed in the Kruger House deposition. 'He learned to love Oom Paul Kruger's children from his mother Khaki.' Later on, he told a journalist that his mother had instructed him: 'My son, the Afrikaner Government should be your father in the same way that the Oubaas Kruger was father to your own father.'[11]

Not one of Khotso's family members in Ha Ramokakatlela have heard about the link with Paul Kruger, although they know all about how Khotso's father, Motumi, founded Ha Ramokakatlela. When asked about his own opinion on the Kruger connection, Lunika stated that he was not in any position to ascertain whether or not Khotso's parents had worked for the Kruger household. Someone who had been close to Khotso in the late 1950s and 1960s expressed this opinion: 'Khotso was a very clever man. He would build up a story to associate himself with the Afrikaner people.'

Marsburg has a candle given to him by Khotso. It consists of a plastic bottle with a protruding wick. The word *Khotso* appears in large letters on the label. 'He told me that it's meant to bring me luck,' explained Marsburg. One distinctive feature of his lucky candle is the orange, white and blue label, in the colours of the old South African flag. As the 1950s wore on into the 1960s, Khotso's fondness for these hues became more apparent. Most conspicuously, there were his blue and white houses, against which his orange-gowned wives would pose. The high waists and necklines and long sleeves of their dresses were reminiscent of late-nineteenth-century Pretoria fashion, and they could conceal their wearers' bodies from the intrusive gaze of outsiders. By adopting orange, white and blue as his trademarks, Khotso was, in effect, nailing his colours to the mast.

CHAPTER 10
Verwoerd's Inyanga

As the colours of the flag of Paul Kruger's children began to feature more noticeably in Khotso's life in a variety of ways, they became more marked than the red, white, blue and green of Oom Paul's vierkleur. This was a clear sign that Khotso did not rely on the workings of luck alone. The shadowy allegiances that he began forging with the white Afrikaner establishment extended far beyond the Paul Kruger stories.

Khotso liked to back winners. With horse racing, this might involve placing bets on the entire field; in the sphere of politics, it meant embarking on a programme of establishing links with a political party that would set itself up against the majority of the people over whom it presided.

In his everyday life, Khotso put considerable effort into staying on good terms with the white people around him. 'Khotso was accepted by whites and he was on the white people's side,' said one long-standing inhabitant of Kokstad, who was a boy in the 1950s, when Khotso resided in the White House. 'He made braais for them by the river.' For many decades, Khotso lived in a relatively remote corner of South Africa, where his wealth shielded him from many of the realities of racial oppression. In the latter part of the 1950s, as we shall see, apartheid legislation would begin to catch up with him. But earlier in his career, it was relatively easy for him to socialise in a relaxed, confident fashion with members of Kokstad's white community.

Khotso with Viscount Montgomery (left). (©Daily Dispatch)

In the days before the Kokstad Royal Hotel was demolished to make way for a shopping complex, visitors to the bar would behold the strange spectacle of a solitary gumboot fastened to the ceiling. The boot was Khotso's: he had left his mark in the bar, apparently as a gift to the owner, to make his bar a financial success. However, in a society which was steadily becoming more openly racist, his planting of his boot in a whites-only area meant he was asserting his right to take his place at the bar, beside the white inhabitants of Kokstad. He would drink and joke with the whites, it was said, while above his head the boot stayed fixed in its place. 'The one who pulls the boot down will see something. The whole town will be turned upside down. The boot must stay there,' Khotso warned.

In 1958, while visiting Khotso on his farm at Ntafufu, Duke Ngcobo heard Khotso's attendants chanting '*Staan reg, heyt bayete*, hip hip hooray'. This chant, he later heard, was repeated on all his properties. It reflected the type of jargon used by Khotso himself, since his speech patterns could be as heterogeneous as the interiors of his houses, especially when speaking to whites. He threw together bits of various languages, such as Xhosa, Sotho, English, Afrikaans and Fanagalo, in higgledy-piggledy fashion. The total effect could be intriguing and bewildering, Marsburg said, especially since Khotso had a tendency to get confused about the meaning of English words. Possibly, when white visitors dropped by or when he stood drinking with whites in the bar of the Royal Hotel, Khotso understood more English than he let on.

Most of all, it was whites in the government to whom Khotso was drawn. At various times, before or during their periods in office, the South African prime ministers D. F. Malan, J. G. Strijdom and H. F. Verwoerd, as well as other prominent Broederbonders, passed through the peculiar portals of the White House or Khotso's later abode, Mount Nelson. The representatives of a political party whose policy was based primarily on racial separation and the denigration of their country's black inhabitants did not usually come calling on black South Africans. We shall see that these politicians had complex reasons of their own for these visits.

From his vantage points in both Khotso's establishments, Paul Kruger watched his disciple's unorthodox guests come and go. During the 1950s, Kruger had some temporary competition from a source that would have been very unwelcome to him, had he been in a position to know about it. One Kokstad man described how he bought a statuette of Winston Churchill for five shillings in 1952. Khotso noticed it one day and asked who the statue depicted. 'I told him that it was Churchill, the greatest Englishman,' the Kokstad man said. Khotso pestered the man to sell the statue to him. Eventually, he agreed to part with it for twenty pounds. For some time after that, whenever white visitors came to the White House, Khotso would ask them whether they were English- or Afrikaans-speaking. If they were English-speaking, he would conceal the Kruger statuette and display the figure of Churchill; if they spoke Afrikaans, Churchill would be hidden.

Khotso's connections with prominent Afrikaners predated the National Party victory of 1948. Even before that date, the effigy of

Kruger predominated in the White House, since his children, the Afrikaner leaders, were poised to triumph.

Prior to the 1948 elections, Hendrik Verwoerd, who was to become minister of native affairs in 1950, visited Kokstad. According to Ellen, who was living in the White House at the time, he had a secret, late-night meeting with Khotso. Numerous conversations with Ellen allow a reconstruction of this curious encounter.[1]

It is 1948 and Verwoerd is electioneering in East Griqualand. He arrives in Kokstad in a light aircraft, his plane descending in a field belonging to a farmer supporting the National Party. After a political rally, Verwoerd is entertained with dinner and drinks. But he has one more meeting to attend that night: it has been arranged that he should visit Doctor Khotso Sethuntsa, at his home beside the Mzintlava River. Khotso is waiting for his important visitor. He has sternly instructed his closest disciples on protocol. On this occasion, there is to be no fanfare, singing, clapping or drumming. As usual, though, the visitors must not smoke or wear hats and the soles of their shoes must be wiped before entering the house. Verwoerd is to be quietly escorted to Khotso's consulting rooms, while the driver will be given tea in the kitchen. Why should Verwoerd, a political leader of the white supremacists, wish to visit a black 'witchdoctor' late at night in a small town in the rural backwater of East Griqualand?

The front door opens and Verwoerd sees Khotso for the first time: a sturdy, uncommonly short figure, radiating energy and enthusiasm. Khotso smiles broadly and his eyes sparkle in the dimly lit room. He is wearing an ornate gown of gold and silver, and he kneels to kiss Verwoerd's freshly wiped shoes. Verwoerd smiles thinly – if only all natives were so compliant. Khotso's magic is already working, for his visitor has started to dream.

Khotso knows the routine. It is not the first time he has received late-night calls from Afrikaner politicians. First, there will be mutual declarations of affection between the Afrikaner and the African peoples; then the conversation will turn to local politics, especially those of

Pondoland. At this point, Khotso will dominate the conversation and Verwoerd will listen attentively to his host's information and opinions. Finally, there will be talk of the forthcoming elections and Khotso will tell his visitor about luck and charms.

The meeting is over. Verwoerd puts one hundred pounds on the table and Khotso goes to his medicine room where he prepares a small bottle of muti: finely powdered ntekwane mixed with lavender oil from Goodwin's Pharmacy in Kokstad. He then hangs the small medicine bottle like a garland around Verwoerd's neck and stands back, admiring the effect. He wants to laugh and make jokes, for he is quick-witted and imaginative and very proud of his latest customer. Although he will boast of this visit in days to come, he is aware that Verwoerd himself will remain tight-lipped about the whole affair. Also, he senses that the latter is in no mood for laughter. It is time for him to leave.

Sceptics will say that it is a lie that Verwoerd visited Khotso, and Khotso was not uncommonly fond of the truth. Yet there were many people staying in his house that night, and on similar nights, who were not all asleep. There were accounts of silent witnesses in shadowy corridors and darkened rooms, listening to the two men's conversation, which lasted more than an hour. In the Transkei, East Griqualand and elsewhere in South Africa, the story ran that the National Party won the election in 1948 because they had Khotso's medicine.

Verwoerd met Khotso on several other occasions. In 1957, Verwoerd paid an unexpected visit to Kokstad and then to Matatiele. 'I met him with a retinue of about 100 of my men, all fully dressed for the occasion. The newspapers made a big noise about it,' Khotso said to Blades. (In fact, the press devoted only a few inches of column space to the event.) Dressed in his ceremonial robes with orange, white and blue beadwork, he presented bowls decorated with Sotho beads to Verwoerd, while his followers beat drums in the background.

Subsequently, Khotso dictated a letter of appreciation to his stepdaughter Masechaba, which was sent to Verwoerd. In part of the letter, he stated: 'I hereby wish to thank heartily His Honourable . . .

[f]or the honour he has done to us during the above-mentioned visits and it is something which will never be forgotten by our people. It is also a blessing for us to have such a minister who has great plans for our nation.'² In his enthusiasm, Khotso did not take into consideration the implications that some of Verwoerd's 'great plans' might have for his own way of life.

These are hinted at in the letter of response from Verwoerd, written and signed on his behalf by his personal secretary, in which he thanked Khotso for his appreciation of 'what he, in his capacity as the Minister [of Native Affairs], has done in the interests of good relations between white and Bantu, in accordance with the policy of separate development'. Verwoerd went on to provide Khotso with the following assurance:

> He is certain that along this road more and more Bantu out of experience will see that quite a lot of avenues have already and are being opened for their own people and more especially in Bantu areas. They will see and love these Bantu Areas as their homeland
> in which great developments will take place.

In his letter, Verwoerd alludes to his programme of separate development, a form of racial separation implemented several months later. Under Verwoerd's premiership, which commenced in the same year that he wrote to Khotso, separate development would give birth to the Bantustans, 'the old "Native Reserves" now dressed in new garb'.³ In the eyes of the white minority government, South African blacks 'belonged' to these regions, occupying other parts of South Africa only as temporary residents and labourers. Within the confines of the places that were termed their homelands, South Africa's black people were entitled to live freely and exercise full voting rights. In 1961, Verwoerd would outline the way whites stood to benefit from the homeland system in a speech to parliament: 'Separate Bantu states . . . [buy] for the white man his freedom and right to retain domination in what is his country, settled for him by his forefathers.'⁴

This marks a new stage in state ideology. Verwoerd was more optimistic about the homeland system and the pace at which it could

Danie Verwoerd as Khotso's guest, drinking traditional beer. (Courtesy of Danie Verwoerd)

be brought into being than were his predecessors D. F. Malan and J. G. Strijdom. He believed that with the aid of state intervention, the homeland system could be made viable; self-sufficient, racially segregated homelands could be used to build local and international support for his party. Internationally, the government could claim that it was granting 'self-determination' to its country's black inhabitants. Locally, the white electorate could be encouraged to view separate development as a solution to 'the Native question', giving rise to a South Africa with only white citizens, its African inhabitants securely contained within specially demarcated pockets of land, subjugated and controlled by official legislation during their sojourns in the land that belonged to the white minority.[5]

Verwoerd may have sensed that Khotso could be of use to him. The letter that he sent to him in 1958 is suggestive of this. With his prosperity, connections and capabilities, he might prove useful in various respects. Long after Khotso's death, MaDlamini and her daughter Masechaba would mention black vinyl recordings that had once been made by Khotso and Verwoerd, with both men talking. There was also some singing. What was it they recorded? Unfortunately, if they ever existed, the records have been removed or stolen from Mount Nelson.[6]

Not only prominent Broederbonders but their friends and family members came calling on Khotso. In 1957, Verwoerd's son Danie visited the White House while on a tour of South Africa. His host turned this event into an occasion that could be witnessed by the populace of the town. 'I garlanded Danie Verwoerd with a charm-necklace that had cost £100,' Khotso told Duke Ngcobo. 'He knelt before me in public view in Kokstad as I garlanded him.' Danie Verwoerd has a picture of himself as Khotso's guest, drinking traditional beer out of a clay pot.[7]

In a book containing her reminiscences of the twenty-four years she spent in Pondoland, when she and her husband were medical doctors in that region, Margaret Barlow describes an event that took place when she visited Khotso's house in the 1960s. It illustrates how seriously Khotso took his relationship with the Afrikaner government. The general manager of Chrysler Corporation was visiting South Africa and, keen to take in some local colour, he wanted to see the famous Transkei herbalist, Khotso Sethuntsa. Barlow, who knew Khotso, arranged the meeting. The American tycoon made the journey to Mount Nelson in an air-conditioned Chrysler with a built-in bar. At first, everything went according to plan. As the American entered Khotso's property, the Stars and Stripes was played. Khotso liked to treat foreign visitors to their own national anthems, although once, unfortunately, he played the American anthem to Viscount Montgomery. Khotso began kissing the American tycoon's feet. He greeted all important guests in this manner, with a peculiar mixture of obsequiousness (when it suited him) as well as braggadocio. Suddenly a black Cadillac appeared in the driveway, bearing the current commissioner-general of the Xhosa, Hans Abraham. Khotso took the situation in, and decided that, while American tycoons came and went, government officials were a fixture in his life. He left the American standing alone, to lavish all his attention on his latest visitor.

'He was always the smart little politician,' commented Barlow. 'It was an incredible sight to watch, especially the face of the Detroit multimillionaire, as obviously nothing like this had ever happened to him in the United States of America.'[8]

Today, decades after Khotso's death, the exact nature of his relationship with Paul Kruger's children remains as clouded by speculation as it was when he was alive. An informant who had been close to Boy Strachan, a Pondoland trader who owned a general dealer store in Lusikisiki in the 1960s, was asked to give his friend's opinion on this. Strachan had various memories of Khotso, who had been one of his best customers, possessing almost inexhaustible resources of spending power. Strachan had formed his own opinions of Khotso, and drawing on these perceptions, his friend said: 'Khotso was essentially a political opportunist. If the ANC had been in charge then, he would have treated them in the same way.' Many other informants shared this view. But unfortunately, as it would prove for Khotso, the white minority government, not the African National Congress, wielded political control. So literally and symbolically, he kissed the feet of his oppressors.

'Khotso never tries to fail to impress top political figures and senior government officials,' the journalist D'Oliveira observed in 1965. 'His letters pledging undying loyalty to National Party policies have brought him replies from men like the late Dr D. F. Malan', NP prime minister between 1948 and 1954. While Khotso had a fondness for a hyperbolic turn of phrase, this was not the case with his grandiose promise of 'undying loyalty'. In spite of, and also as a result of, the self-interest underlying it, this was a sincere expression of the extent of his devotion to the most powerful people in the country. In his letter of response, Malan wrote:

> Dear Friend, . . . it did my heart good to receive your letter and the kierie that I will treasure as a memento of your friendship, which I value highly.
>
> The golden Kruger pound, which is to-day so valuable, I will preserve as proof that our friendship is true and not just words.
>
> You and me are all children of the land. We need each other and must assist each other, each in our homes, to live in freedom, prosperity and happiness. I greet you. D. F. Malan.[9]

As events were to prove, Khotso and Malan, and the political party Malan represented, had very different notions of what this mutual assistance alluded to in the letter above would entail. With the benefit of hindsight, 'each in our homes' has an ominous undertone, hinting at the ideology of separation between members of different racial groups that Malan and his party were busy turning into law. In this regard, his letter calls to mind Verwoerd's letter of thanks to Khotso. Despite the superficial affection of the opening sentences, the letter closes with a subtle reminder of the sense of distance members of the Afrikaner establishment preserved between themselves and their devotee.

Khotso may have enjoyed associating with the ruling elite, the government representatives and the individuals with whom they were in cahoots because of the potency of associative magic, endorsed even by those who do not believe in any other form of the supernatural. But one spin-off from Khotso's connections with leading Afrikaner politicians would have been that it intensified the fear of his ominous, uncanny abilities, bearing in mind the assumption in various rural and urban African communities that whites had access to particularly strong magic.[10] Not entirely to Khotso's benefit, this came to be reinforced by the underground belief, post-1948, in 'government witchcraft', to borrow Sean Redding's phrase.[11] In its scale and malevolence, the malign power of the state became viewed as comparable to that possessed by forces of occult evil.[12] This perception was held in the northern Transkei and helped fuel the Pondoland Revolt, which would have a bearing on Khotso's life story.[13]

In her study of African oral narratives, Ruth Finnegan noted that one signal quality possessed by the many varied trickster figures in African oral tales is their adaptability: 'They are able to turn any situation, old or new, to their advantage,' she observed.[14] One of the most distinctive features of Khotso's career is the way in which he succeeded in drawing leading members of the ruling Afrikaner establishment to him, as he shifted, chameleon-like, into a figure who blended oddly into their political terrain. For their part, the white minority regime could use

Khotso as a showpiece. With his houses, cars and farms, he appeared to provide proof that blacks could make it under apartheid if they really tried. The South African government could display Khotso as a showpiece of another kind: a famous 'witchdoctor' with a large number of followers. This, one Transkei man remarked bitterly, provided the white authorities with an excuse to say, 'The "kaffirs" are superstitious savages, so how can they be entrusted with any responsibility in the "modern" world?' He adds that of course this is a notion which conveniently overlooks the number of whites who made use of Khotso's services.

There were further reasons why South Africa's white rulers might have thought that Khotso was worth cultivating. For one, it is likely that they tried to find out from him what the 'natives' were thinking, although Khotso's take on the country's history and politics was uniquely his own.

Over and above these considerations, one special reason for the Afrikaner political elite's visits to Khotso is repeatedly put forward by his family and his followers. One man who was part of the household in Mount Nelson during the 1960s and came to know Khotso well during those days expressed the following conviction: 'They were his clients. I can put it that way. They wanted power to lead.'

As with those who went through the ukuthwala ordeal, magic was mixed with psychology. Lunika suggested that Khotso might have sought to convince his guests that a degree of faith in his supernatural abilities was of practical use to them. He thought that Khotso might have succeeded in this. 'The Nationalists believed that Khotso had supernatural powers, but they did not want to be open about it,' Lunika maintained. According to this line of reasoning, influential Afrikaner politicians visited Khotso's establishments because they felt there was a constituency that he might be able to turn to their favour: the ward of the occult. His guests from the Broederbond might have departed from the White House or Mount Nelson believing more strongly in the possibility that political power might rest more securely in their grasp through the agency of a black 'witchdoctor' in a remote rural town.

It could also be posited that, political motives aside, many of the Afrikaner politicians who chose to drop in at the White House or Mount Nelson were indulging a private fascination with traditional magic.[15] Afrikaner links with indigenous belief systems go back a long way. As a great many people, apart from Credo Mutwa, have commented, before oppressive political edicts began wrenching them asunder the blacks and the Afrikaners had more in common than did the blacks and the English-speaking South Africans, many of whom, up until the later part of the twentieth century, spent a great deal of time looking over their shoulders to England, their true 'home'. The descriptive Afrikaans term for South African English-speakers, *soutpiel* (meaning 'salt penis': one foot in Africa, the other in England and the penis dangling in the sea), has a certain amount of accuracy to it. On the other hand, the Afrikaners' feet and other vital parts rest solidly on African soil. They have nowhere else in the world that they would wish to call home, and because of their history as a farming, pioneering people, they were closer to the world of the indigenous African supernatural than were the English. This is borne out by some of the oldest Afrikaans literature, which derives inspiration from African culture, traditions and belief systems. The tales told by itinerant pedlars, travellers and members of the trekboer communities often adapted elements from the lore of the African communities around them, while other aspects of indigenous wisdom became part of Afrikaans culture. As they ventured deeper into the unknown interior, for instance, Afrikaner communities needed to draw on local people's knowledge of plants and healing, incorporating these into their own remedies.

Or, on a superficial level, Khotso might have provided a spectacle of the exotic, colourful African Other for his Afrikaner guests, as he did for a great number of white tourists, both local and foreign. Today we have township tours, and the mandatory visit to the local sangoma (or igqirha perhaps) often appears to represent the highlight of the expedition for similar reasons. But given the austere, Calvinist nature of their own religious and cultural practices, Afrikaners might have seen Khotso as offering access to certain rich, mystical aspects of African culture and being from which their laws and traditions had walled them off. The Afrikaner Nationalist obsession with the Immorality Act (forbidding sexual relations across the colour line), and with the transgression of the act, represents another well-known instance of the fascination of the forbidden. Yet the appeal Khotso possessed for his white visitors had a contradictory aspect. He was too individual and eccentric to be viewed as straightforwardly representative of African culture. He had built his own world around him that was like none other, and this was part of the attraction (and also the alarm) that he evoked in many others, both black and white.

Khotso established links not only with the ruling Afrikaner elite, but also with the black politicians they controlled. During his time in Kokstad, he formed a firm friendship with Botha Sigcau, son of King Marelane of the Pondos. Botha described how he first met Khotso:

> I went to see him in Kokstad, where he then lived, because I had heard about him from people who wanted medicine to bring them luck in their cases [before the court]. I heard all about the money he was supposed to have around the house. The rogues who told me those things! There wasn't any money lying around. But Khotso and I became friends and we used to visit each other, always slaughtering cattle in honour of the occasion.[16]

Botha Sigcau may not have dropped by simply to socialise. It appears that he believed he needed Khotso's help to succeed politically. At any rate, Lunika claimed that this was what took place in 1939 when both Nelson Sigcau, son of King Marelane's senior wife, and his brother Botha, the king's first-born son but a child of the junior wife, wanted the paramount chieftainship of Eastern Pondoland. According to tradition, Nelson was the rightful paramount chief, but Botha was the candidate the white authorities favoured. They deemed that he could be bent more readily to their will. When the Nationalists assumed power, Botha indeed colluded with them, while Nelson sided with the struggle against white minority rule.

But it is possible that Botha felt that the weight of white official support was not sufficient to ensure that he would win the paramountcy in 1939. So he sought assistance from Khotso. Lunika recollected this:

> Botha went to Khotso. I remember that. I was in Kokstad then. Khotso told Botha that, in order to win, he had to go to a certain European guy who was very rich and get a gold coin. I have just forgotten the name of this man. I was there, because as a small boy in Kokstad, I used to go to Khotso's house to help chop and saw the wood so as to make some money. So when Botha's driver came up to Khotso's house, I saw smoke coming out of the car as if it was burning. When Khotso saw this, he said it was a sure sign that the driver had got the coin.

It is also possible that Khotso used his fame and his influence to mobilise support for Botha.

Botha's unpopularity rose to great heights when the network of Bantu Authorities was introduced into the Transkei in 1956. This system incorporated paramount chiefs and a hierarchy of underlings: a form of government which was nominally African, but which in actuality would facilitate turning the concept of separate development into a reality. For its part, the Bantu Authorities subordinated the paramount chiefs to white officialdom, thus serving as a conduit for Nationalist political control, by means of which it could permeate the territories that would become the homelands.

Botha Sigcau was an early adherent of Bantu Authorities, collaborating with his Afrikaner masters to advance their political programme. Govan Mbeki wrote that '[m]any Chiefs and headmen found that once they had committed themselves to supporting Bantu Authorities, an immense chasm developed between them and their people'. By 1957, the anger that Botha had aroused among the Pondos reached such a pitch that when he and a magistrate addressed a gathering, their voices were overwhelmed by shouts of protest. The rift widened between Botha and those he purported to represent as he appointed his own supporters to positions within the Authorities.[17]

Opposition to Botha's actions and those of the political party whose interests he served gathered force. In due course, the Pondoland Revolt was to erupt over Botha's head, and his friend Khotso would be touched by it too.

CHAPTER 11
Hubris to Nemesis

While political tensions simmered in the Transkei, Khotso's own position in Kokstad was becoming insecure. His public behaviour, however, belied this. When Khotso was proclaiming his ability to triumph over the greatest adversary of all, death itself, to Duke Ngcobo in 1958, he was also letting it be known that the authority and influence wielded by Khotso Sethuntsa surpassed even that of God. Ngcobo described how Khotso's followers, in frenzied fervour, chanted a paean when their lord and master, 'a stately figure, short and corpulent and wearing a skin jacket against the bitter cold of the morning', appeared at the door of his house, to bid him farewell: 'The Great One comes out to welcome you home himself. The One who is greater than any god we do not know, for having known him, what other god do we want to know?'

Yet Khotso was poised on the edge of defeat and humiliation. At the time of the interview with Ngcobo, it was being brought home to him that there were areas of his life in which he was powerless. This was something that Khotso sought to conceal from the outside world at all costs. Hence the performance he had his followers enact before Ngcobo. Moreover, throughout the preceding interview Khotso had kept trying to impress his visitor. For instance, he had boasted that, in 1958, he was probably the only black person in South Africa who owned a stretch of beachfront property, his land at Kilroe Beach. A photograph accompanying Ngcobo's article in *Drum* shows Khotso standing on the seashore at Kilroe in one of his characteristic poses, arms flung wide to indicate the extent of his possessions – as if he was embracing the ocean itself, as well as the beach on which his feet were planted. 'It's all mine,' he declared in the caption.

But Khotso had already discovered how unstable the ground under his feet could be. As Blades reported, he had two certificates testifying to his credibility as a traditional healer. The first, a South African Native Medical Certificate, had been issued in May 1945 by a commissioner of oaths and three inyangas. It declared that Khotso was granted a licence for 'Medicine Men and Herbalists (hereafter called Inyangas)', having successfully practised in this capacity for the last seven years. He also possessed a South African Native Medical Certificate that announced that he was a 'Full Native Medical', permitted to carry a licence as a herbalist and sell South African 'Native Medicines'. But neither these documents nor Khotso's chumminess with local and national political authorities had prevented him from being fined ninety pounds in April 1957 for contravening the Medical, Dental and Pharmacy Act by practising medicine for profit without the requisite licence.[1]

At the same time as the April 1957 court case, the *Kokstad Advertiser* also reported that eighteen 'Natives' (presumably some of Khotso's clients, trainee herbalists and followers) had to pay admission-of-guilt fines for contravening the Urban Areas Act by being at the White House for longer than the prescribed seventy-two hours. The fines were paid by Khotso. At the beginning of the 1950s, the *Kokstad Advertiser* had run an article entitled 'Petty Crime and VD on the Increase Due to Influx of Natives to the Town, says District Surgeon'. In the local official's opinion, the Urban Areas Act was not being properly enforced.[2] Such attitudes would have become widespread and entrenched as the 1950s wore on, reinforced as they were by apartheid legislation. With his followers and potential clients perceived as possible disease-bearing criminals, this had serious implications for Khotso's future in Kokstad.

The fact that all Khotso's qualifications and connections did not prevent his conviction was a clear sign that he could not expect special treatment from the authorities. Under J. G. Strijdom, who became prime minister in 1956, the notion of apartheid as purely *baasskap*, white domination, was entrenched. The Group Areas Act, introduced in 1950, was creaking into place all over the country, and Khotso was soon to suffer a far harsher fate than paying a fine for eighteen of his followers.

It appears that Khotso felt in need of additional official documentation around this time, and this is where his baptismal certificate came into the picture. He must have derived pleasure from being the owner of a baptismal certificate with the name 'Doctor Peace Khotso Sethuntsa' emblazoned on it.[3] Now he had legal grounds for bestowing a medical title on himself. Lunika told Blades how one of Khotso's white clients approached the great man in the 1960s, invoking this title as a sign of respect for his capabilities: 'Dr Khotso, I have only one mechanic working for me now. I understand you have some powers of helping me.'

According to certain individuals who knew Khotso well, the baptismal certificate was a fake, issued at some point in the 1950s (most probably after the 1957 court case) and not in 1922, as it claimed. It was MaDlamini, as well as Khotso, who was instrumental in this bit of deceit. This suggests that, despite the way in which they were gradually drifting apart, occasionally MaDlamini and Khotso operated as a team, something they had been accustomed to doing in the days when they joined forces to hunt jackal together. MaDlamini's involvement in the production of this document was an indication that, despite her devout habits, Khotso's most senior wife was not averse to occasional forays into the world of trickery in which her husband had taken up residence. Indeed, the woman who had derived great amusement from the tale of how a white garage owner had rushed naked into Kokstad after he met Khotso's great snake had a streak of mischief in her.

While Khotso's baptismal certificate was fuelled by practical needs, as well as by self-aggrandisement, there were times when he could put almost as much inventiveness and energy into acts of self-abasement. In

1959, he took it upon himself to wash the Cadillac belonging to M. D. C. de Wet Nel, the minister of Bantu administration and development. Early in the morning, Khotso and his retinue drove out to the hotel at Port St Johns where the minister was staying. While his attendants stood to attention, blowing horns and strumming a guitar, Khotso himself got to work on the Cadillac. As one newspaper put it, the minister's expression of surprise as he emerged from the hotel just as the finishing touches were being applied to his car 'was the best reward the millionaire herbalist could have had for his work'.[4]

There is a curious object in the Mthatha archives: a wooden rocking horse, a gift from Khotso to Hans Abraham, the prominent government representative who displaced the Chrysler executive in the herbalist's attentions. Khotso had the horse carved and painted himself, and the artefact bears some resemblance to a centaur. Abraham's head and torso (clad in a black suit and tie) rise out of the horse's body, just above two small handles that a child seated on the toy could hold on to while the steed rocked.[5] Was the gift a symbol of unusual power, intended as a tribute to Abraham? Alternatively, could the object be suggestive of the way in which Khotso may have felt that through his skills and cunning, his influence and his displays of obsequiousness, he could, in a sense, 'ride' the white political authorities, making them bear him where he wished? Or might the gift hint at the way in which its giver had, in certain respects, been taken for a ride?

By the mid-1950s, Khotso was becoming aware of the limitations of his own position and the widening gap between his own interests and those of the politicians he had regarded as his friends. This realisation may have lain behind a decision not to remain based exclusively in Kokstad and to switch his headquarters to his farm at Ntafufu, in the Transkei. Ntafufu was then little more than a single trading store. Peter Becker described a visit to Khotso's farm in 1958. After driving down an avenue of banana trees, he was escorted along a pathway bordered by rows of white stones to a red-roofed country house. What Khotso's Ntafufu abode lacked in splendour and spectacle, it compensated for in

Khotso and Langa at Ntafufu in 1958. (©BAHA. Photo by Peter Magubane)

ceremony and activity. Khotso was waiting to greet his guest, attired, Becker observed, in 'a silver robe, beautifully patterned with embroidered flowers and sprinkled with sequins which glittered in the morning sun'. Around him, attendants beat drums and blew whistles, while women he called his wives came forward, singing and clapping in greeting. Before Becker could enter the house, Khotso's son Langa was summoned, and he shyly kissed the visitor's hands. (His expression, Becker noted, was 'doleful'.) Although Khotso had changed his residence, it was still very much business as usual. Outside the house a row of white-clad women knelt, grinding herbs, roots and bark for medicine; and approximately thirty patients, seated on benches, waited for the great man to attend to them. Khotso showed Becker his students, who came from as far afield as Malawi, hard at work sorting, packaging and dispensing his medicines and charms. Naturally, foremost among these was ibangalala.

But Khotso's work at Ntafufu went beyond distributing herbal remedies from his home. He had not moved far from water. There are deep pools in the Ntafufu River, in which some of the serpentine presences that Khotso controlled waited to be summoned. Today, MaDlamini's grandson Thabo, now living at Mount Nelson, says that he continues Khotso's tradition, taking people to these pools for good fortune and prosperity.

While Khotso was in Ntafufu, a pretty young Pondo woman joined his household. She would later be remembered as one of the best-known figures in his life. The addition of yet another concubine was in itself hardly unusual, but in this case it led to an attachment that some felt would bring special joy to Khotso's declining years and that others, with hindsight, would believe had cost him dearly. Nomalizo Grangxa from Port St Johns, just down the road from Ntafufu, was brought by her husband to Khotso for treatment for infertility. She became better known as Bethinja. Later, some informants would claim that when Khotso saw Bethinja, he told some of those around him, 'I've been waiting for that woman to come here.'

It was not unusual for Khotso to inform people who came to him for training or treatment that he had been expecting them. One such example would be the man from Qacha's Nek who arrived at his house in the 1960s to be trained in herbalism. Perhaps at times he intended to impress the individuals who sought him out with his prescience, yet even if he had been responding predictably to the sight of an attractive woman within easy reach, there was nothing ordinary about the position Bethinja would come to occupy in his household.

Khotso told Mr Grangxa that he would contact him later to tell him how his wife's treatment was proceeding. But when he spoke to Bethinja's husband later, it was to tell him that he wished to marry his wife. Khotso had never before been deterred by the fact that some of his female patients happened to be married, and it did not discourage him in this case. In effect, Khotso bought Mr Grangxa off, repaying all the lobola cattle he had paid for his wife.

Bethinja was lively, energetic and skilled in intricate beadwork. 'This was what originally attracted Morena [Khotso] to her,' Lunika recalled. 'He asked her to come and stay at his place so that she would do beadwork for him. She then became his concubine – I'll put it that way.' Years after Khotso's death, the press put a more romantic spin on it, referring to 'the incredible love story of the world-famous herbalist Khotso Sethuntsa and his favourite wife Bethinja'. It was love at first sight on Khotso's side, and 'Bethinja repaid his love by rushing to obey his every command, and seeing to his every comfort'.[6]

Many, including Lunika, agreed that Bethinja was always willing to be of assistance. 'She did play an important role in Khotso's life because she was very diligent,' Lunika said. 'That is the point I know very well about her. When visitors came, she was always the first to get up and make tea for them. . . . And yes, he liked her very much.' As Lunika put it, Bethinja 'was easy to send around'. But was she really as demure and biddable as she appeared, or was she, like her new husband, a canny operator, biding her time and awaiting her chance? Opinions on this question remain divided.

'She was a nice person,' said Marsburg. When he met Bethinja in Lusikisiki in the 1960s, he and his wife would bring her flowers, which she loved. Her delight in flowers was almost childlike and it was as if she couldn't bear to throw them away, keeping them until the last petal dropped. But many others, including Lunika, have different opinions of her. More broadly, University of Fort Hare researcher Sylvia Tloti has described Bethinja as 'the legendary dark horse'. It would take a sequence of dramatic events to reveal her full character and capabilities.[7] At first, there were no hints of the turmoil that would later surround Bethinja. A range of people, even various outsiders who visited Mount Nelson, felt there was something appealing about her. 'She had such a round, pleasant face,' one person remarked. Similarly, the Transkei building contractor who kept in contact with Khotso observed: 'She was a well-built woman, with that pretty look that plump people can have.'

One person who joined Khotso's household later was struck by Bethinja's vitality and creativity, qualities also mentioned by some other informants. It appears that initially she appealed to some of the younger members of Khotso's family for this reason. One of his daughters, for instance, described Bethinja as very talented and friendly. She lacked formal education, but she possessed other special attributes. Not only did she produce the lovely, elaborate beadwork for which Pondo people often have a special flair, but she was also an accomplished singer and dancer. She was even skilled at preparing medicines. Her nickname Bethinja, meaning 'beat the dog', came from a song that she used to sing:

Nal'iyeza
[Here's the medicine]
Sela ukuba ufuna ukuphila
[Drink it if you want to get well]
Abany'abantu abafuni ukusela iyeza
[Some people don't like taking their medicine]
Sibathini?
[What should we do about them?]
Beth'inja! Beth'inja!
[Beat the dog! Beat the dog!]

In the song, as in Bethinja's nickname itself, the phrase *Betha inja*, 'Beat the dog', was abbreviated to Beth'inja. The fact that she should have often chosen to sing a song of this nature is significant on a number of levels. Firstly, the fact that Bethinja's nickname derived from what became her trademark ditty suggests something of her vibrant nature, expressed in part in her pleasure in song. Next, in its focus on the importance of medicines, her song indicates the path that she would come to follow in her life. Eventually, Bethinja would become a medicine woman in her own right. To a certain extent, she would take over where her husband left off.

There is also the chorus of the song which, it could be argued, hints at certain nuances in Bethinja's character. The closing lines express a determination, albeit interwoven with jesting, to beat some sense into those who refuse to behave in the way the singer deems appropriate. The song combines forcefulness and fun. A number of those who met Bethinja were first struck by her lively, playful nature; yet in time her underlying assertiveness and tenacity would become apparent. In time to come, when darkness descended on Khotso's household, she would set out to hunt for the prize that she deemed her due, proving to be a strong-willed personality and prepared to draw on weapons of her own. It is worth noting that there is another version of Bethinja's song, to which other lyrics could be added depending on the occasion:

Uboyibula'inja

[Kill the dog]

Yinja umntu ongenamali

[A penniless person is a dog]

This version has a ruthless, uncompromising edge to it. It also emphasises that a person's worth is measured in terms of money. Both these features, certain informants have claimed, became evident in Bethinja's character later on. Down the road that wound into the future, bitterness and conflict lay.

At this point, we turn back to the 1950s, before Bethinja came to feature prominently in Khotso's life. As indicated by the 1957 court case, in which almost twenty residents of the White House were convicted of violating the Urban Areas Act, life was becoming difficult for a black landowner in a South African town. While Khotso did move to Ntafufu for a while in the late 1950s, he did not wish to sever his ties with Kokstad, to which he returned periodically. It was the town where he had spent a large part of his adult life and established a thriving practice. Moreover, the part of the Mzintlava River that ran past his home flowed through the most momentous aspects of his work. But at this point in his career, Khotso was forced to realise there was no longer a permanent place for him in Kokstad.

In the light of this, the 1958 *Drum* article which celebrates Khotso's wealth, power and the extent of his empire, just at the time when he was being made aware of the limitations of that kingdom, is fraught with ironies. The opening image in the piece shows him at the wheel of his Cadillac, and the article closes with servants chiding the reporters for touching Khotso's car 'without the permission of the Great One'. But although he was the master of his own world, Khotso was a servant everywhere else.

Racial divisions may have been becoming entrenched, but nonetheless a number of Kokstad's white inhabitants would have preferred it had Khotso remained ensconced in the White House. After all, he had helped bring money to the town. In 1958, one businessman went so far as to lament to Duke Ngcobo: 'There has virtually been a slump since he left town three years ago.' Before Ngcobo's *Drum* interview, apartheid legislation was catching up with Khotso. As the 1957 court case indicated, his days as a herbal practitioner in his large house in a white part of town were numbered. The Group Areas Amendment Act had been passed that year, placing further restrictions on black freedom of movement in 'controlled' urban areas, designated for whites.

If Khotso had chosen, he could have moved to Bhongweni, the black township outside Kokstad. By the 1960s, as the Group Areas Act was being enforced in Kokstad, the area set aside as a black location would begin to expand. One elderly inhabitant of Bhongweni recalled this: 'Black people who stayed in town, who had properties in town, were moved without being compensated. Tin shacks were built for them and blacks were removed across the river, where Bhongweni is now. Along the river up to St John's Street were coloured people, and then further uptown there were whites.'

At that time, in order to reside legally in an urban area rather than being consigned to the territory deemed to be his 'homeland', Khotso, like other black people, would have needed to satisfy certain official criteria. These were detailed in the infamous 'Section 10' legislation of 1952, in one of the successive amendments to the original Natives (Urban Areas) Act of 1923. Khotso would, for example, have had to prove that he had been born in Kokstad; or that he had worked for one employer in the town for at least ten consecutive years; or that he had lived there for a period of fifteen years or more, having been granted official authorisation to do so. Or, he could remain in town provided he had been permitted to do so by a labour bureau official.

Khotso had built himself a palatial home and he did not want to leave it. Neither did he want to move away from his property adjoining his pools on the Mzintlava River, to which he took his clients for ukuthwala and where the being to which he made offerings resided. But although he did not meet any of the stipulations detailed in Section 10, with his cash, his cunning and his connections he might have found a way of remaining in Kokstad, in the black section of the town, had he chosen. But in all likelihood, he would not have wished to have been consigned to a tin shack in Bhongweni. He wanted to remain set apart in his unique domain, not surrounded by others, as merely one among many residents of a township. Under the circumstances, then, he opted for life in a territory that was neither his land nor his home: the Transkei, which would be the first Bantustan state to have 'independence' bestowed on it. There, Khotso could at least occupy an impressive estate, where he could set about constructing a new kingdom for himself.

He must have felt betrayed. He had lavished gifts on Strijdom, Verwoerd and their underlings and made heartfelt pledges of support and loyalty, and now the people he had regarded as his friends were kicking him out of his home. For a man as proud as Khotso, this must have been humiliating. He was being reduced to the level of just another second-class citizen, relegated to a rural backwater. When he left Kokstad, some said, he was so angry that a tornado swooped through the sky after him as he made his way into the Transkei.

Khotso relocated to the town of Lusikisiki in Pondoland, the region which lies in the north-eastern section of the Transkei, adjoining the sea. In 1958 Khotso purchased a trading site named Mount Nelson, but he moved there only in 1960. The original structure on the property was a small four-roomed house, so for several years Mount Nelson was under construction, being transformed into an ornate, rambling maze of expansive rooms and outbuildings, complete with enough fantastical ornamentation to rival Khotso's beloved home in Kokstad. At the turn of the decade, Khotso left his big white house by the river and a new phase in his life began.

Part Three
1960–1971

Chapter 12
Bantustan Fantasia

Mount Nelson rests on a hilltop outside Lusikisiki.[1] As with Khotso's Kokstad houses, which are situated on the periphery where the urban districts turn into grassland and bush, the location of Mount Nelson reflects Khotso's preference to locate himself on the borderlands, both literally and symbolically. Even today, those travelling past Mount Nelson can be reminded of the way in which Khotso was never entirely part of the places in which he established his abodes. The high fence and the imposing gates at this property emphasise the sense of isolation and exclusion with which Khotso chose to surround himself.

One of Mount Nelson's most distinctive features is its blue and white painted buildings. Deep inside these structures, safes were installed to hold sackfuls of banknotes, coins and diamonds. Underneath the main house, popular rumour had it, were the cellars where Khotso stored more of his treasures. It was whispered that some of the creatures that served him lurked there too, in the subterranean darkness. When Blades repeated some of this speculation to Khotso, he snorted with laugher.

Through the gates, one glimpses the large front yard, garages adjoining it, where Khotso welcomed guests and carried out all his important ceremonies, such as his birthday and the Kruger Day celebrations. The property is dominated by the edifice Khotso termed his 'palace'. This structure and its surroundings still bear witness to the fact that Khotso made Mount Nelson a space in which all his eccentric architectural whims held sway. Preposterous pillars prop up the blue Pondoland sky; like the archways that lead nowhere, they remind visitors that in Khotso's mansions a great many things exist primarily because the owner has decreed that they be there and not necessarily for any practical reason. The front gates, both adorned with the gold-painted letter *K*, are a reminder that even though the South African political landscape of the 1960s, with all its oppressive weight, surrounded the property, within the gates lay a separate realm, both fabulous and quirky, in which the dictates of the master of the house were law.

The part of Mount Nelson that visitors first behold has not changed substantially since Khotso's day. And inside the gates, brightly enamel-painted statuettes of people and creatures of spiritual and symbolic significance are still dotted everywhere, almost as if a slightly manic amateur sculptor had been allowed free rein. Some sculptures have found their way to the tops of the columns and arches, where they perch. As was the case at the White House, there are the lions, with their stone mouths agape, roaring at visitors. At Kruger House in Pretoria too, these beasts are present, positioned alongside the front steps, a gift to Paul Kruger from the mining magnate Barney Barnato. Was Khotso perhaps inspired by his 1956 visit to that hallowed building? But lions were not enough for him: leopards, elephants and eagles are also in attendance at Mount Nelson. Fabulous and unusual though it appeared, the White House was sedate in comparison with Khotso's new abode. The profusion of highly coloured statuary adorning this property would contribute to the flamboyant, almost circus-like quality that was to become the hallmark of Mount Nelson, both in terms of its outward appearance and the public events that were to take place there.

Khotso's new headquarters would not have been complete without Paul Kruger. Here he was accorded an even more prominent position than at the White House. His severe features peer from the tops of archways and pillars, through overgrown creepers and from below the branches of a cabbage tree in the main yard; indoors, he gazes at visitors in the lounge and down in the reception area of the main house. Concrete busts of Afrikaner premiers who came after Kruger – Malan, Strijdom and Verwoerd – line the steps leading down to the long, narrow banquet hall, eyeballing the effigies of Khotso and his family members. Statuettes of Khotso and his grandfather, riding white horses, flank the doorway. Above them on either side is the coat of arms of the old South African Republic, with the words *Eendragt maakt magt*, 'Unity is strength'.

For Khotso, those words would have possessed a certain resonance. Despite the way he had been treated by Kruger's people, the decor at Mount Nelson indicates how his allegiance, and a fundamental part of his status and the mystique that he had constructed around himself, remained connected to the Afrikaner nation and to Paul Kruger. Khotso assured visitors that Oom Paul was there at his side, just as he had been at the White House, offering guidance in matters financial and spiritual.

People have wondered why Khotso chose to paint Mount Nelson and his Mount Frere house blue, with white paint outlining, in sometimes wobbly squares, the imaginary shapes of brickwork. Family members are quick to point out that white and blue are the colours of purity, which would have appealed to Khotso. There is, however, a more practical reason why blue became the favoured colour of Khotso's houses. The canny Pondoland trader Boy Strachan, who had acquired large quantities of blue paint, managed to persuade Khotso that blue would be a good colour for his new house. Carried away with enthusiasm, Khotso turned blue and white into the trademark colours of his dwellings. Strachan was also behind the orange and blue uniforms worn by the group of women at Mount Nelson whom Khotso presented as his wives. Strachan had a large number of blue and orange dresses and cardigans in stock and he suggested to Khotso that his wives might look impressive attired in the South African colours. Khotso's wives kept their orange gowns for special, ceremonial occasions; for more everyday events they donned blue dresses with orange headscarfs.[2]

Khotso buying stained glass for Mount Nelson in Durban, accompanied by his entourage. Langa stands directly behind the pane of stained glass. (©Independent Newspapers)

To add to the profusion of colour, multi-hued glass windows glowed from the walls of Mount Nelson. Always one to present the most glowing depictions of himself and his career to outsiders, Khotso made sure that in turn he could survey the outside world through gaudy, jewel-like glass, some of it rose-tinted. He expended considerable time and effort selecting suitable stained-glass panes, preferably with vaguely art nouveau designs, for the windows of his new residence, far more so than he had done during his days at the White House. On 11 February 1964, in an article entitled 'Stained Glass for Transkei', the *Natal Mercury* carried this report:

> The millionaire herbalist, Mr Khotso Sethuntsa, came to Durban yesterday with a retinue of more than a score of beaded and fur-bedecked warriors on a shopping spree. His long grey Cadillac led a lorry and truck bearing his bodyguard through the streets.
>
> He is buying building materials and hardware for three new cottages at his home at Lusikisiki in the Transkei. Backed by his

retinue, he was photographed yesterday examining the pattern of 36 stained glass windows for the cottages with Mr S. Coutts, foreman of a Durban glass factory.

One is for visiting American tourists and another is for visiting Cabinet members of the South African Government and the Transkeian Territorial Authority.

In the accompanying photograph, behind the stocky figure of Khotso, who is attired in ornate robes and elaborate beadwork, stands a host of attendants wearing a heterogeneous assortment of traditional and Western garb: horns, T-shirts and fur buskins. Langa's small face is just discernible. The contrast between the faces of father and son is striking. Khotso is proud and ebullient; here, as in the majority of the photographs taken of him during his childhood and teenage years, Langa looks glum. In the midst of this, a slightly confused-looking factory foreman displays his wares.

Mount Nelson was Khotso's last home and his showpiece, and he made sure that his guests were treated to a show that they would remember. As visitors arrived, they would see dancers performing outside the house, which took place on a daily basis. In 1963, Leon Bennet, a journalist from the *Sunday Times*, described a typical pageant that Khotso liked to choreograph for his guests:

> As the car swings past the fluttering South African flag, through the huge white wrought-iron gates, each bearing a huge letter 'K', drums sound and a double line of Native warriors beat a cloud of dust into the air as they execute a dance of welcome. With a leap, they fall prostrate with a tremendous yell of 'Bayete!' Khotso's 12 wives file out of the house and line the sun-drenched stoep singing 'N'kosi Sikelele Afrika', 'Die Stem', 'God Save the Queen' and 'Jesus Loves Me'.[3]

The musical medley referred to above bears a certain comparison to some of the bets that Khotso placed on racehorses. At Mount Nelson, as at the betting shop, there were times when he liked to back the entire field. Khotso combined displays such as these with the idiosyncratic rituals and codes of conduct that had been a feature of his hospitality at the White House, such as foot washing. Beyond the entrance porch, its floor paved with silver coins, was a large reception room. In Blades's words, '[T]he walls were almost entirely covered with newspaper cuttings (about Khotso) and photographs (of Khotso) and letters of thanks (to Khotso) for gifts (from Khotso) to prime ministers and presidents.' These testified to the extent to which Khotso had become a figure of renown, his presence acknowledged by the mighty in South Africa and other lands.

Next, Khotso's guests would be conducted into the long, narrow dining room. A short flight of steps leads down into the middle of the area, which, as Blades observed, 'was so wide a view that we had to turn our heads from side to side at an angle of 180 degrees'. Even today, the row of tall windows, radiant with stained glass, still calls to mind the windows of a banquet hall in a historical mansion, or perhaps the windows of a church.

Khotso and his visitors would often settle at the end of a long table, awaiting refreshments. Khotso's guests could feel swamped by the scale of their surroundings and the quantity of food laid on for them. Bernard Newman, for one, described sitting at a table laid for sixty. Alf Marsburg has a photograph of his wife and daughter, with Khotso standing by as their host, seated at a table cluttered with whole roast chickens, joints of roast beef, and blue and white dinnerware.

Opulent though it had been, the interior ornamentation of the White House was restrained by comparison with Mount Nelson. Apart from the framed press cuttings and letters, a sparkling, enthusiastic juxtaposition of valuables and bric-à-brac constituted one of the principal features of the decor in the sitting room. 'It's like a giant magpie's nest,' Blades said when he first beheld the interior of Mount Nelson. 'Like OK Bazaars gone mad,' responded his companion, *Drum* photographer Alf Kumalo.

In the kitchen, one journalist was told, each wife had her own personal dresser, equipped with cutlery and crockery and topped with a large kitchen clock. There were no electrical items, however, for Khotso disapproved of many forms of modern technology – apart from expensive vehicles – and never bothered to install electricity in Mount Nelson. Nowadays, much of the kitchen is bare, dark and empty, so the room feels more like a mausoleum than a bustling working space. The memories of the preparations for the great feasts that once took place here have faded.

A memorable part of the extravaganza that Khotso staged for his guests – especially for visiting journalists – was his lavish, apparently casual displays of wealth, far more theatrical than they had been in the White House days. Khotso would send fistfuls of banknotes cascading around him and sackfuls of money would lie, like overstuffed cushions, in the corners of rooms. When the *Drum* team visited him, he brandished large sparkling stones at them – diamonds, he boasted (although they were so huge he could have been testing the limits of his guests' gullibility) and polished them in front of the photographer. The scale on which Khotso's flaunting of his wealth could take place is illustrated by the following description from one journalist:

> The millionaire strode into the room, his face beaming with delight, together with four wives struggling to carry a huge metal trunk.
>
> The contents were poured on the floor at our feet in one huge pile – thousands of South African coins (50c pieces). The herbalist commanded, pointing at us: 'Count it! Count it!'
>
> So we sat down and began counting, stacking the coins in lots of four, until an hour later, almost the entire floor of this section of the room was covered with gleaming piles of silver – in all, 4 396 coins, totalling R2 198. . . .
>
> While counting we had also discovered at least a dozen Kruger and Victorian coins, worth far more than their original value.
>
> To show us there was more money where this had come from, he returned with a pillowslip filled with bundles of R10 notes. These he spilled on to the floor and, with a queer sort of nose dive, he plunged into the pile and emerged with just his bald pate showing above the heap.[4]

As Khotso would have hoped, a photographer captured the heap of coins. A few days before, another newspaper had displayed him ensconced amidst his money.[5]

In general, Khotso cuts differing figures in photographs: often resplendent in elaborate beaded robes and headdresses or, going to the opposite extreme, an incongruous millionaire in drab workaday garb of corduroy trousers and baggy sheepskin jackets. Visitors sometimes glimpsed his large bulky farmer's boots protruding beneath the hems of his robes. A Pondoland Joseph, Khotso's multi-hued garments set him apart, as one earmarked for greatness from the outset. Apart from his vestments in Kruger's colours, he had a robe in orange, white and blue beadwork, to match the colours of his houses and the gowns of his wives. A photograph that still adorns the front room of Mount Nelson also shows Khotso in lemon yellow, turquoise and pink. The most opulent robe of all sparkled with sequins in silver and gold. In Khotso's day, it was magnificent; today, it hangs in a glass case in Mount Nelson, tattered, discoloured and moth-eaten.

James Lunika was often in attendance when people came calling on Khotso, as the latter's interpreter, secretary and adviser. At that stage, he was working as a clerk in the magistrate's office in Lusikisiki. As newspaper photographs indicate, Lunika had grown into a tall, handsome young man with an open, pleasant face. He described how he used to drink and smoke, but before his first visit to Khotso at Mount Nelson, he threw his cigarettes away and decided to give up alcohol. 'Khotso met me at Lusikisiki,' Lunika said, 'after knowing me from Kokstad. So he was glad to find me there and he had a lot of correspondence that he wanted me to help him with.' From that point on, a bond developed between the two men.

Lunika was trained in herbalism by traditional practitioners working under Khotso at Mount Nelson. He was also called on to assist when Khotso sought to make a good impression on influential individuals in the white community. As Lunika told Blades, if a new magistrate or police commander arrived in Lusikisiki, Khotso would ask him to take

Khotso and a row of 'wives' outside Mount Nelson. A bust of Paul Kruger rests on top of a pillar. (©Daily Dispatch)

some meat to that person. 'It was his way of advertising and of making sure the police didn't associate anything bad with him,' Lunika said.

Khotso referred to Lunika as his prime minister, but in personal conversations with Lunika, Khotso often called him Dlamini. This was Lunika's clan name; moreover, Khotso was also a Dlamini. Khotso was drawing attention to the connection between the two men, invoking the idea of family loyalty underlying their relationship. Yet future events were to show that this link would not be strong enough to forestall the growth of a rift which would force the two men apart.

However, in the early 1960s, all appeared to be going well for Khotso. He would have approved of the 1963 *Sunday Times* feature adorning the front page of the newspaper's magazine section and entitled 'Millionaire Medicine Man is Lord of Transkei'. During the course of such visits from the press, Khotso would delight in parading a long line of submissive women in front of visitors as his wives, as if they were designed to prove that his affluence extended into the area of his marital relations.

Some were merely passing sexual partners and others were women who weren't even connected to him at all. 'He'd do that with my wife!' Lunika complained. 'He'd tell visitors that she was one of his wives, and they would believe him!'

Small wonder that, in a number of the photographs taken of him in the 1960s, Khotso looks as if he has just pulled off an elaborate prank. While his fondness for behaviour that tested the limits had been taking place since the 1954 *Daily Dispatch* article, it became a distinctive feature of his life by the 1960s. And many of his fabrications were eagerly swallowed by listeners, then sometimes dutifully regurgitated as newspaper articles.

As MaMjoli, one of the most level-headed and perceptive of Khotso's wives, noticed, Khotso's delight in harnessing the opportunities for comedy that came his way had given rise to certain key features of the mythology surrounding him. She once remarked: 'Half the things he said, like having 23 wives and 200 children, were not true. You see, he was a practical joker who found capital fun in entertaining his guests and the Press with myth. I should know, because I was his wife. Many people could never tell when Khotso was serious or joking because he was a great leg-puller.'[6]

When it suited his purposes, Khotso could always maintain that other people had spread dubious tales about him, or simply claim that he had been misunderstood or misinterpreted. 'Newspapers print such lies!' he once said, all wide-eyed innocence, when challenged about some of his more barefaced inventions. The majority of Khotso's visitors, however, thought that his flamboyant public persona, reflected in his ostentatious, elaborate surroundings, was a true reflection of his inner nature.

'Come and see my Kruger Park!' Khotso would frequently tell visitors. Bernard Newman, and possibly many others too, expected to be shown a private zoo. What they found instead was a half-enclosed area full of tables and chairs, set out as if ready for a banquet. Here Khotso and his guests could relax and eat and drink tea while dancers would perform between Kruger Park and the main house. Kruger Park was situated directly facing the main gates so that Khotso could monitor them, since even more visitors might be likely to arrive. Today a long, ramshackle set of garages has been erected where Khotso's outdoor pavilion once stood.

Kruger Park was a source of pride to Khotso because it was here that he entertained cabinet ministers and other visiting dignitaries. And when flesh-and-blood VIPs were absent, Khotso produced notable guests of his own. Lunika has a photograph taken in the 1960s that depicts busts of Kruger, Malan, the South African state president C. R. Swart and their respective wives lined up at the table, as if seated and waiting to be served. Behind them, Khotso stands, as if waiting on them.[7]

The most special structure at Mount Nelson was a compact outbuilding near the main dwelling called Kruger House, an elaboration of the room devoted to Kruger in the White House. It contained several small interleading rooms filled with an array of Kruger memorabilia, the walls adorned with framed press cuttings about Kruger. An effigy of Oom Paul was placed in this building, which had been set apart as Khotso's sanctum: the shrine to Kruger himself. This was the place to which Khotso would retreat when he wished to commune with Oom Paul. Pictures of the president stared down from the walls at the concrete face of the bust and at the items of beadwork in the colours of the South African Republic flag. As at Kilroe Beach, where people slept in a special room beside a picture of Kruger, people who came to Khotso for ukuthwala might spend the night in Kruger House, lying in a bed beneath the coat of arms of the old South African Republic.

Kruger House would become Khotso's final resting place. His grave is housed in a private chamber at the back of this building. Although Khotso intended the building to be his private mausoleum, Bethinja's grave is in the main room, as is that of his youngest son, Four Boy. MaDlamini and her daughter Masechaba also rest here. It is hard to imagine that this building was once the heart of Khotso's empire. It is as if history has long since swept past Khotso, leaving him forgotten: his grave marked by a marble tombstone marooned in an unimpressive outbuilding on a dilapidated property.

By contrast, the festivities in Khotso's day were not only vibrant, they could be idiosyncratic. One incongruous little gathering took place when the National Party cabinet minister Frank Waring was in town and Khotso decided to impress him by organising a luncheon party for his young son, to which a number of the white children from the town were invited. One woman informant, who was ten at the time, was one of the little guests from Lusikisiki. She and the other children were taken to the house in Khotso's Cadillac. Many of the children were on edge; they were going to the house of a person that they had been told was a 'witchdoctor'. When they arrived at Mount Nelson, their shoes were washed at the front door, and Khotso's people dusted the floor behind them as they walked into the big sitting room, which made some of the children even more nervous. The woman who attended the lunch party remembered how everything shone brilliantly around them, even the red-polished floors under their feet. 'There were cabinets with mirrors, stained-glass windows and bright glass ornaments. The whole place seemed full of light and reflected light.'

To a ten-year-old child, Khotso himself seemed huge, towering over his guests and surrounded by servants who leaped to do his bidding. To the assembled children, he might have resembled a cross between a superficially benevolent but alarming, unpredictable, fairy-tale giant and a mighty ruler of an exotic kingdom. He pointed out objects in the house to the children and told them they had been given to his family by Paul Kruger. During lunch in the long dining hall, one boy was so tense that he dropped his potato. It was immediately cleaned away, leaving the floor as spotless as before.

In the White House days, Khotso mentioned in the Kruger House deposition that Kruger Day was a special annual occasion for him. However, at Mount Nelson he launched into his extravagant public Kruger Day celebrations. Each year, on the tenth of October, he held a party on a grand scale, to which everyone was welcomed: government officials and dignitaries, clients, tourists and people who just happened to be walking past the gates of his residence. Oxen and sheep would be slaughtered, Lunika said, and one leg of the ox was always sent to the local police station. Even today his family and followers, their distinctive shaven heads encircled with white beads, gather to continue this tradition. Family members visit Khotso's grave on the ninth of October to tell him that they will celebrate Kruger Day in his memory on the following day.

During this latter period of Khotso's life, he appeared to be the focus of more attention and excitement than ever before. Even when he went on a short excursion into Lusikisiki, he would be surrounded by people. 'You couldn't miss him,' someone said.

During his visits to Mount Nelson to purchase good-luck medicine, Lala Yako would sometimes travel around the Transkei with Khotso. He was struck by what happened on those occasions. 'That was funny, every time he went anywhere it was just like honey among ants! We would just stop somewhere: one, two, three! Within ten minutes, a whole crowd would have gathered around the car.'

The hordes came in part to goggle at the Cadillac. Yako added: 'You'd find a Cadillac in Johannesburg, but a Cadillac in the Transkei was another thing!'

It was not only the Cadillac that attracted people to Khotso. They were also eager to see acts of magic being performed. One man who had been a student at a college in Mthatha in the late 1960s believed he had witnessed exactly this on a day when the Pondoland millionaire herbalist came to town in his Cadillac. On this occasion things went too far, even for Khotso, with his love of public attention. He stopped at the General Motors car dealer and the word quickly spread that Khotso was in town. In no time at all, a large crowd clustered around the Cadillac to stare at Khotso. He wanted to leave, but the mob blocked his path. To make matters worse, many people were pressing against his car and he feared that they might damage it. He shouted: '*Sukani* [Scram]! I want to proceed on my way!'

Yet the crowd ignored him. Then a heavy shower of rain fell, just around the car. As people fled for shelter, Khotso drove away. Yako once said that onlookers did expect amazing things to happen when Khotso was around, so it is possible that they may have tended to view occurrences for which there might have been straightforward physical explanations as manifestations of Khotso's magic. But the Mthatha man who related this account is convinced that what he saw was proof of Khotso's ability to exert paranormal control over the elements.

But even if they themselves were not witness to extraordinary spectacles, a number of people came away from encounters with Khotso convinced it was quite possible that something of this nature could have taken place, in much the same way as individuals such as Pascal Makeka had felt decades before at the White House. Blades, for one, experienced this.

> Whenever I drove out through the tall gates of Mount Nelson after talking to Khotso, I knew that he had once again put a spell on me. I knew that this roly-poly man in his finery of ostrich feathers and beads, who bounded around with such superb confidence, shouting and marshalling his harem and polishing lumps of glass he pretended were diamonds, had the secret of making people believe exactly what he wished, at least for a little while.

Possibly, Khotso's ability to evoke responses such as this in many who encountered him fuelled press interest in him in the 1960s. The Mount Nelson period was, in many respects, the zenith of Khotso's career. His fame and his wealth had reached their height, and journalists, tourists and clients came thronging to Mount Nelson on a greater scale than ever in the Kokstad era. More press articles on Khotso were produced during the 1960s and early 1970s than at any other time. For instance, the *Daily Dispatch* has a file in its archives labelled 'Khotso Sethuntsa' covering these years alone, indicative of the extent to which the public gaze kept turning to him during that period. Yet paradoxically, the time when Khotso appeared to be at the height of his powers was the point when those powers were in decline.

'When he was in Kokstad,' Lunika remarked, 'he was deeply

associated with such things as supernatural snakes. That's why I say he was very strong when he was in Kokstad because he was associated with certain powers, you know, the spiritual powers.'

Part of the reason why Khotso's potency diminished, Lunika and others have suggested, was that in relocating to Lusikisiki, Khotso had moved away from his pools on the Mzintlava. 'Khotso used to practise with very strong medicines,' Lunika observed. 'He could raise a thunderstorm at will. But when he grew older and came to Lusikisiki he never did those things: he used to do them in Kokstad. His power was not as strong as when he was in Kokstad.'

Although Khotso's Lusikisiki headquarters was the most resplendent of his houses, there was one thing lacking: a river. He began to build a dam beside Kruger House. 'You see, when he left Kokstad and came to Lusikisiki, he found that there was no pool,' said Lunika. 'He wanted to make a pool here.'

But compared to the deep pools on the Mzintlava, what Khotso constructed at Mount Nelson seems as sterile and purposeless as an abandoned quarry. There was no river or spring nearby, so he planned to transport water in drums to fill the dam. But huge quantities of water would have been needed before the pit would have been even half filled, and anyway it leaked.

'He didn't fill it up with water,' Lunika continued, 'so there was no ceremony done here like it was in Kokstad.' Today the derelict crater lies beside the rooms full of tombstones. In a sense, the splendour of Mount Nelson and the deep dry pit beside it symbolise the underlying contradictions of the last twelve years of Khotso's life.

Khotso's new home was in the heart of a region that was very different from the chill, high terrain of Nomansland. As the road winds downhill from Kokstad and eastward towards the Indian Ocean, one enters the lush landscapes of Pondoland, rolling down towards subtropical coastal bush. Even today, this north-eastern part of the Transkei remains closely associated with the mysterious and magical. There is a historical basis to this. The Pondo were the last people to fall under Cape colonial administration, for their territory was only annexed by the Cape government in 1894. In a study of Pondoland published in 1936, Monica Wilson drew attention to the fact that this region had long remained separated from colonial incursion due to its remoteness, the rugged, densely wooded and precipitous nature of its coastal belt, and its heavy rains, all of which hampered transport. 'There are still only two main roads in Pondoland,' she wrote, 'and these are sometimes impassable.' In consequence, there were fewer schools, mission stations and stores in Pondoland than in other reserve areas. Belief in the presence of unseen occult forces persisted without interference from Western colonialism for far longer in Pondoland than in other regions of what is now the Eastern Cape.[8]

The darker dimension of the otherworldly comes to the fore in various outsiders' depictions of Pondoland and some locals' view of the area in which they live. In 1936 Wilson stated: 'Much space has been devoted to witchcraft and magic, but it is commensurate with the part they play in Pondo life. The belief in them ... permeates the whole of life.'

As Wilson herself noted long ago, many Pondoland locals resent the way in which their area has come to acquire a reputation for witchcraft. Nonetheless, even today oral accounts of shadowy malevolent beings and creatures abound in this part of the Transkei. For instance, a river monster that sucks blood and eats brains lurks near the village of Elubaleko, not far from Mount Ayliff, and a few years ago in a village in the vicinity of Port St Johns, a spectral pig, with glowing red eyes and a coal-black body, terrified locals returning home late at night. A snake was recently discovered coiled up inside a loaf of bread from a Flagstaff supermarket, and the person who had purchased the bread died shortly afterwards. These and many other similar stories reinforce the assumption that witchcraft is more prevalent in the northern Transkei than in other parts of the Eastern Cape. To an extent, this perception is rooted in some harsh physical actualities. As Monica Wilson has remarked in her classic study, the extent of suffering and death that has characterised life in poverty-stricken rural regions like the Transkei, obvious even to outsiders from the 1920s onwards, might have strengthened the notion that witchcraft must be practised in such areas.⁹

With such a heightened awareness of the potential menace posed by malign supernatural presences, someone like Khotso, who could call such forces to heel or unleash some more of his own if he felt so inclined, was moving into territory where he could cast a long shadow.

But Khotso was changing. People had been afraid of him in Kokstad, on account of the suspicions of the dark and dangerous dealings that might lie behind his wealth. Khotso himself had encouraged such attitudes through the tales he had spread about his powers, sensing that this would be good for business. But during the latter part of his life, in Lusikisiki, Khotso did attempt to dispel some of the damage that decades of sinister rumours had done to public perceptions of him. At this point in his life, Khotso wanted to be remembered with fondness, not only with fear.

There were gestures of apparently spontaneous charity that showed that since some of Khotso's money was being used to assist the community, it was essentially 'good' and not as suspect as the means by which many alleged it had been obtained. One man, whose father had worked for Khotso in Lusikisiki, recalled the latter's acts of generosity to the community. Khotso assisted destitute families with gifts of food and helped them work the land with his tractors. 'People used to stay in his house,' his employee's son said. 'People would come suffering from poverty. They would work in the garden, or something.'

Khotso continued to give big public donations to charitable causes. One instance of this was provided by Hans Abraham, the commissioner-general of the Xhosa. At Khotso's funeral, he recollected how the man had suddenly intervened, like a jolly, disruptive Santa Claus, at the opening ceremony of the Queen Elizabeth Hospital in Lusikisiki:

> On the platform with me were the Provincial Secretary, the Provincial Director of Health and Chief Botha Sigcau. The Bishop was ready to sprinkle holy water at the door.
>
> At this solemn moment, I felt someone pulling me from the platform. It was Khotso. I said, 'Khotso, you can't pull me out

now, we are about to open this building.' But he insisted: 'Come with me!'

He took me to his Cadillac and brought out a bundle of notes this size. [Mr Abraham cupped his hands.] He said: 'You take this money and give it to the chairman of the hospital board. The priest can wait!'[10]

At this event, as had been the case at many comparable occasions in the past, Khotso hoped to benefit from being a benefactor. In this case, he did so by generating publicity that, as the date of Abraham's anecdote indicates, continued after his death. Thus, Khotso resembles yet again the trickster of African oral tales, whose apparent kindliness is motivated by self-interest.

The latter part of his career was marked by a paradox: the more famous Khotso became, with multitudes of visitors, clients and followers flocking to his house, the more the extent to which he had separated himself from others became apparent. Among the crowds who attended the Kruger Day celebrations, one thing was missing: large groups of friends.

Although many Lusikisiki residents who knew Khotso described him as essentially a kind and jolly man, he was isolated by his wealth and power and the mysterious strangeness of the world that he had created around himself. The old farm worker from Nolangeni recalled: 'There were a lot of people around Khotso most of the time, but they were mostly people working for him. He didn't seem to have a great many friends from the community.'

The bodyguards accompanying Khotso also heightened the sense of separation between himself and the other local people, none of whom could afford guardians of this nature. Quite possibly, Khotso kept bodyguards for this reason: as a way of displaying his wealth, rather than simply a form of protection. One man, who owned a garage in Flagstaff in the 1960s, said: 'In a way Khotso was separate from his friends. For that matter, you would find him alone in his limousine with his driver, right at the back of this long black car. Two other cars with four guys would also be there. These people were his bodyguards.' Khotso seemed a solitary figure, all alone in the back of his black Cadillac.

Some have even described how Khotso tended to keep to himself during the Kruger Day celebrations. One man who frequently attended these festivities described how Khotso would often sit indoors, watching the party take place outside. When the dancing started, which he loved, he would move outside, but he wouldn't mingle with the crowds. Instead, he would sit on a chair placed in the garage, facing the area where the dancers were performing. Even Khotso's children were not permitted to fraternise with the locals. One of his daughters talked about how she and her siblings were not allowed to visit other people's houses in Pondoland, in case they were offered pork to eat, something that Khotso believed would cause bad luck.

Although Khotso thrived on the aura of mystery that he had allowed to develop around him, he paid a price for it in terms of his personal relationships. Trust can never flourish when too much is kept hidden. As Lunika pointed out, an inyanga of Khotso's stature had to be very careful about whom he befriended. What if an individual you trusted and confided in became your enemy? Even Lunika himself, one of the people to whom Khotso was closest, never knew what went on behind the tightly closed door of the one room in Mount Nelson that he, and others, were not allowed to enter.

Khotso still evoked fear in others, both old and young. He took on the proportions of a kind of Transkei bogeyman in the minds of a number of small children in the Lusikisiki area. A woman who grew up during the 1960s in Libode, a town between Mthatha and Port St Johns, remembered this clearly: 'We thought if you said anything bad about Khotso Sethuntsa, even if you just whispered it, he would hear you! And then you would be in trouble!'

While children shivered in terror as they thought of what Khotso could do to them, various adults would, as was the case in Kokstad, continue to exercise extreme caution in their dealings with the man. This account, from the Flagstaff garage owner, indicates how careful Pondoland locals were not to offend Khotso:

> One day he came to fill his car up at my garage and found me out of petrol. He told me that he could make it such that I never had to buy petrol again. But my father heard him and said it was rubbish: everybody had to buy petrol in order to sell it. Khotso was cross, and I had to apologise to him on behalf of my father, because I did not know what he would do, and, without my apology, he could have done anything!

Even those who initially seemed favoured by Khotso might suddenly find themselves on the wrong side of the man – as even Lunika eventually discovered, to his cost. But, as in the past, the stories concerning the alarming extent of Khotso's powers meant that his business continued to reap profits. Among other things, his work as a racketeer continued. Having found it profitable to encourage farmers to take out hail insurance, Khotso turned another aspect of the weather to his advantage in a similar fashion. At times when rain was much needed, he announced that he would be able to bring it about, provided he received individual payments of one rand as 'rain money'. Although the cash began pouring in, the rain did not come pouring down. Just as he had done with the hail protection he offered, Khotso let it be known that this state of affairs had arisen because not everyone in the area had submitted their payment. Obediently, people began to hand in 'rain money' all over again.[11]

Khotso had also been extending insurance coverage to the mines. Probably early in his career he had sensed that migrant mineworkers might be ready to pay for safety before they descended into the dangerous depths that had devoured many lives. The gold mines offered employment for those in areas where job possibilities were scarce, and many men in the Transkei, Lesotho and the Umzimkhulu and Matatiele districts of northern East Griqualand depended on them for that reason.[12] Khotso had let it be known that he offered protection against mining accidents for only a small sum of money. He received many requests for this safeguard.

So, as Khotso established himself in his new kingdom, he was acquiring yet more wealth. Already he had attained the great influence, affluence and renown he had long sought after. As Khotso's world expanded and his fortunes changed, the gap widened between himself and his senior wife, MaDlamini, who had roamed the mountains with him when he was a young jackal hunter seeking his fortune and who had helped set him up in business as a herbalist. While MaDlamini was accorded respect as senior wife, her position in Khotso's household became an increasingly ambiguous one. She was called Mhomkhulu, an abbreviated version of Mama Mkhulu, or 'senior mother', yet it is clear that after the move to Lusikisiki MaDlamini was shifted further and further away from the centre of the household.

She was, humiliatingly, relegated to an outbuilding beside a small store at Mount Nelson, somehow symbolic of her diminished status in her husband's realm. Khotso and various others in his household jokingly referred to this dwelling as *kwaSatan*, taking a dig at MaDlamini's pious Christian conduct and her moral outrage at the goings-on in her husband's house. For her part, MaDlamini objected to Khotso's sexual romps, calling Mount Nelson 'a compound of concubines'. One particular member of this 'compound' was far more unwelcome to Khotso's senior wife than were the derogatory comments and the jokes at her expense. MaDlamini did not get on with Bethinja, perhaps realising that the latter represented a more serious threat to her security, material and otherwise, than any of the other women connected to him.

Unlike a number of Khotso's other wives and concubines, MaDlamini never walked out. This stemmed in part from her innate toughness of spirit and also because, as she told interviewers decades later, she went on loving her husband right until the end. It is also possible that she sensed that turning her back on the Transkei and returning to her family in Lesotho at this late stage in her life would not be an easy option. There she would be regarded as little more than an ageing woman who had crept back to a small, isolated mountainside community, no longer able to hold on to her husband in South Africa. At least in the Transkei she was connected to a famous, wealthy man and she had a house of her own to stay in. Sometimes she could even lay claim to a position of some status, albeit a precarious one.

Chapter 13
Anger in the Hills

Pondoland may strike the visitor as a place of verdant fertility. Driving down the winding, precipitous road from Lusikisiki to Port St Johns after the rains have been bountiful, you are struck by the luxuriance of the hills covered in thick, rippling grass of a hue so bright that it almost overwhelms the eye. Dense tangles of jungle-like forest spill out from kloofs and folds in the hillsides and the greenery is interspersed by tall waterfalls pouring prodigally downhill, as if this natural abundance is overflowing. Birdsong mingles with the sound of rushing water, and as you pause to gaze at the panorama of hills unfolding downwards towards the sea, you might be tempted to believe that the people of Pondoland must be especially blessed.

But when Khotso arrived in Lusikisiki, the downhill slide, which had begun with the annexation of Pondoland by the Cape government near the end of the nineteenth century, had become more marked with the introduction of Bantu Authorities in 1956, and would gather momentum after the Transkei was granted 'self-government' in 1963. Drive through the Transkei today and the raw, red eroded dongas that scar much of the landscape are a visible symbol of the ravages that nearly a century of ever-intensifying, heavy-handed political control and material deprivation has wrought on the economy of the region.

In Pondoland and elsewhere in the Transkei, the damaging effect of those political developments and other policies (such as the land acts) imposed by successive white minority governments was compounded by worsening meteorological conditions. This process has been outlined by historian Clifton Crais. In 1945 the region was struck by severe drought. For the remainder of the 1940s and through the 1950s, the Eastern Cape suffered from lack of rain. With terrible symbolic appropriateness, as the newly elected Nationalist government began implementing apartheid, the rains failed. The drought of 1955 and 1956 was described as 'the greatest within the memory of the present generation'. Where droughts struck rural areas, famines followed.[1]

Beyond Khotso's gilded gates, there lay a region seething with suffering and political turmoil. Khotso settled in Mount Nelson in 1960 – not a good year for someone widely known to be a loyal supporter of the ruling white establishment to arrive in Pondoland. Dissent and disquiet had been smouldering in the Transkei for years after the introduction of the Bantu Authorities, especially in the areas in which government-sponsored land-rehabilitation schemes had been implemented. This programme, which involved livestock control, culling and fencing, resulted in Transkeians losing charge of their livestock and their use of land. Moreover, residents of the region were often expected to abandon their homesteads and form new settlements to facilitate effective land usage, and a system of forced labour took place under the control of the chiefs.[2] The fact that growing anger was being directed at Khotso's friend Botha Sigcau did not help matters. In the latter part of the 1950s, the resistance to the system of Bantu Authorities and the anger directed against Botha and other paramount chiefs who collaborated with the South African government had become apparent. Dissent began welling up in Pondoland during this period, and by 1960 it had risen to the surface in the form of the Pondoland Revolt, described as 'one of the bloodiest chapters in the rural struggle against apartheid'.[3]

Because meetings consisting of more than ten people were not allowed (unless a magistrate granted permission), Pondos held secret meetings, high in the hills and on the ridges. In this way, the movement that became known as *iKongo* ('the Congress') with a hierarchical leadership known as *Intaba* ('the Mountain') was formed. The Mountain Committee developed a separate, independent form of governance, in opposition to that of the Bantu Authorities, with its own taxation and a court system – a 'People's Court'. 'They tell the people that they are the Mountain Court and that there are no Chiefs,' one person stated.[4]

It was at these hilltop meetings that the decision was taken to burn the huts of collaborators. This became a central feature of the Pondoland Revolt. Collaborators included Bantu Authority chiefs, those who had declared themselves in support of the Bantu Authorities and government informers.[5]

In 1960 *Drum* journalist Benson Dyanti described Pondo people giving voice to their sufferings at a commission of inquiry intended to determine the causes of the Pondoland Revolt:

> They said that, after the annexation of Pondoland – which had never been conquered by anybody – the country gradually lost control of its own destiny, because Pondos have no say in the laws which govern them. The whole proceedings left me in agony when a tribesman said that all the Pondos were 'moving dead', and that if the government and its 'Police Chiefs' decided on killing villagers, the villagers had nothing to lose.[6]

Ironically, this commission was composed of Bantu Authorities officials, part of the very establishment against whom the rebels had arisen.

On 6 June 1960, the worst police violence during the Pondoland Revolt occurred. Two aircraft and a helicopter dropped tear gas and smoke bombs on a crowd gathered on Ngquza Hill, while police vehicles closed in on them.[7] People raised a white flag in a desperate attempt to show that their meeting was peaceful, but armed policemen rushed out of the bushes where they had been lurking. They fired on the crowd. According to official records, eleven people were killed; but locals stated that the death toll amounted to thirty, with at least sixty serious injuries. Afterwards, it was discovered that some of the victims had been shot from behind, while they were running away.⁸

The atmosphere of suspicion and fear that gripped Pondoland that year was captured by Dyanti in his *Drum* article published in September 1960:

> When I reached Holy Cross and asked peasants the way to Ngquza Hill, their faces showed hostility until I had to explain that I was looking for an uncle who might either have been arrested or killed during the disturbances at Ngquza Hill. They showed me the village, but I could not help thinking these people, who once liked to sing and joke, who would ask a stranger if during that day he had had a meal, have stopped being hospitable. Nor was this the only shock.
>
> That evening after supper, during the family prayers, my uncle shocked me. I had expected him to thank the Lord for having saved me from death in the terrible jungle that is Johannesburg. Instead, after going through the tribulations of his family, he asked the Lord to look after the black people who are living through times that he likened to Jews in captivity.⁹

During the Pondoland Revolt, special medicines for strengthening warriors would be ritually administered. By a strange twist of circumstances, the rebels were reputed to make use of Khotso's muti for bravery, to assist them in their struggle against the friend of the man who had sold them the medicine, among others. Not only had the tide turned against Botha Sigcau, but the waves of fury and resentment heading his way were threatening to engulf him. So, in his turn, Botha enlisted the aid of the medicine master of Pondoland.

One Eastern Cape man, who has heard accounts of this turbulent period from his uncle who lived in Lusikisiki, observed: 'The Pondos tried to kill Botha Sigcau, but whenever they went to his bedroom at night they would just find a dog or a chicken in the bed . . . and that was Khotso's medicine.'

But even Khotso's powers could not prevent events from catching up with Botha and his family. In November 1960, when a group of Pondos held a meeting on Ngqindilili Hill, the police arrived, accompanied by Chief Vukayibambe Sigcau, Botha's younger brother. Tear gas was fired and, as people fled, the police began shooting. The chief was given a rifle and he fired on his own people. At least one person was killed and a number were injured. The following night, hundreds of people made their way through the mist and rain and converged on Vukayibambe's house. 'Here are the people – they have come,' they said. 'You are going to die.'[10] 'Khotso's medicine didn't work against knives,' someone remarked.

To a certain extent, the killing of Vukayibambe and other acts of violence directed against individuals connected to the authorities had their desired effect: Bantu Authorities ceased functioning in parts of Pondoland, while Botha and the other chiefs were in fear of their lives. A few renounced the government, in a desperate attempt to win popular acceptance and security, but more of them simply abandoned their posts. Some sought protection in refugee camps within the Transkei; others felt they would be safer further away.[11]

In November 1960, a state of emergency was declared, which, as Govan Mbeki put it in his account of rural resistance, *South Africa: The Peasants' Revolt*, 'virtually imprison[ed] the entire population of the Transkei'. The ruling authorities remained in place in this region until the National Party bowed out in 1994 and the Bantustan system was abolished. By January 1961, 4 769 inhabitants of Pondoland had been taken into custody and 2 067 people had already been brought to trial. By April of that year, 524 people were still in detention and 20 people were sentenced to death for their involvement in the revolt. The Transkei was, in effect, under police and army rule, with specific chiefs and sub-chiefs acting as their lackeys. By the end of 1963, most of the resistance had been crushed, but the anger and resentment that had sparked off the Pondoland Revolt was to seethe below the surface for decades. Over forty years later, Pondo people who had lived through those years told their stories to the Truth and Reconciliation Commission, indicating that the anguish surrounding the events persisted and there were still ghosts that needed to be laid to rest.[12]

While the people of Pondoland rose up in rebellion, what was taking place behind the gates of Mount Nelson? Khotso, it is hardly surprising to note, had fallen foul of the Mountain. Towards the end of 1960, he received a letter from this body, ordering him to break off all ties with whites and the paramount chief. In a further attempt to exercise authority over Khotso by diminishing him in an area for which he had become famous, the Mountain commanded him to discard his wives. He was also required to pay two hundred pounds. If he failed to carry out all these things, he was told, he would be killed. Khotso responded by using the letter to generate publicity around himself. He held a press conference at his home at which he announced: 'They only want to rob me. This is only a plan to get £200 out of me. I am not afraid of these Pondos. They are nothing to me. My loyalty is to the Government. As soon as they touch this place I will kill them. They will meet their match. They are *skellums* [scoundrels] and robbers.'

The injunction to relinquish his wives must have annoyed Khotso, because he indicated at the press conference that he still had plans to marry yet another wife.[13]

'It was hard to tell', Blades observed, 'whether Khotso was more contemptuous of the death threat the letter contained or the paltry price it put on his head.' But there was more to the affair than this. We know that Khotso did not take kindly to any attempt to get money out of him. He also resented attempts to order him about, especially by people he regarded as his inferiors. His derogatory reference to 'these Pondos' is expressive of the distance between himself and the surrounding Transkeian populace – a gap that he never truly wished to bridge.

While Botha Sigcau had deemed it best to put some distance between himself and Pondoland, Khotso felt secure in Mount Nelson, protected by his reputation as a formidable worker of magic. Throughout the revolt, he and his establishment remained unscathed: an island of ostentation, conspicuous over-consumption and cunningly calculated, dodgy political alliances in a sea of anger and deprivation.

It seems that Pondoland locals did attempt to capture Khotso when he was travelling through the Transkei, but without success. Lunika told of how Khotso was travelling through a forest in his car one night when a group of Pondos materialised from the shadows to ambush him. 'But he just passed right by them in his car,' Lunika said. 'They didn't touch him – it was like he had hypnotised them.' The fact that Khotso eluded capture throughout the Pondoland Revolt fuelled the stories concerning his ability to magically change his shape, which proliferated during this period. There are even tales of how Khotso turned himself into mist to evade those who sought to catch him.

It is difficult to ascertain what part, if any, Khotso played during the Pondoland Revolt. All we have to go on are hints, speculation and rumours, which add to the obscurity surrounding the nature of his activities during this time. Lunika, for one, thought that Khotso took care not to become overtly involved, in one way or another, in the Pondoland uprising.

CHAPTER 14
Sex, Drugs and the Broederbond

Botha Sigcau's paramount chieftainship continued after the Pondoland Revolt, as did Khotso's connection with him and other black politicians, such as Kaiser Matanzima, who had thrown in their lot with the white political authorities. As had been the case with Botha, Matanzima's rise to political power was hedged with controversy. A keen supporter of the Bantu Authorities system, separate development and the land-rehabilitation scheme, he was elevated to a position of prominence when he was appointed chief of Emigrant Thembuland.

In 1963, the Transkei was declared a self-governing territory and received its first parliament, with Matanzima as its premier. One of the outbuildings at Mount Nelson is called kwaMatanzima, because Matanzima slept there when he visited. Once he slept in his own personal outbuilding with dramatic results. 'That's why he won the elections in 1963,' said Lunika. 'I was there, in Mount Nelson. Khotso pointed to the concrete busts of Chief Victor Poto and Matanzima, and told me that the first of the two who came to consult him would get the premiership of the Transkei. And it was Matanzima.' Poto, the paramount chief of Western Pondoland, was opposed to homeland independence, and Khotso may have chosen not to back someone who did not incline towards his Afrikaner political masters' ideology during the 1963 elections. More to the point, Matanzima may well have owed his premiership to the all-too-material intervention of the white minority regime, rather than to the invisible workings of Khotso's magic.

Five months before the election of the Transkei's chief minister, the South African government had bestowed a farm of 2 630 morgen on Botha Sigcau, who, as paramount chief, had the power to swing the vital upcoming election in the direction of Matanzima, the candidate the Nationalists favoured. There was only one vote for Poto; the rest of the Eastern Pondoland bloc trailed obediently behind Sigcau. After Matanzima's victory, the Sigcau royal family established a 'Great Place', their headquarters, on the farm newly bestowed on their paramount chief. Later on, Sigcau would receive another lavish gift. After the Transkei's 'independence' (which left it no less dependent on its white political overlords) was formalised in 1976, Sigcau would become state president of the Transkei.[1]

It is worth noting that the first elections for self-government were held in the Transkei after the Pondoland Revolt had been crushed. Throughout the territory, emergency regulations were in force, and the two major organisations campaigning for alternatives to the South African political system, the African National Congress (ANC) and the Pan-Africanist Congress (PAC), had been outlawed. In 1963, the year of the first self-government elections, 592 people had been detained. Consequently, Barry Streek and Richard Wicksteed have described the independent Transkei as 'the country that [its people] couldn't refuse'.[2]

Khotso was present at the opening of the Transkei parliament, bearing his gift for Matanzima's government: statues of lions, like those at Mount Nelson. On the day before the first session of the Transkei legislative assembly, Khotso had a gift for the state president of South Africa, C.R. Swart: a bust of himself.[3] During the 1960s, the National Party had a special use for Khotso, so he had no need to bestow an effigy of himself on leading Broederbonders to remind them of his existence. Even if the homelands themselves were not economically viable, self-sufficient states, the Nationalists sought to create the appearance that economic development would, in time, take place in these territories.

They knew that a prominent, wealthy man like Khotso could play a convenient role in this regard.

One example of this can be seen in a newspaper photograph from the 1960s, which displays Khotso polishing his Pontiac, his clean-shaven head gleaming as brightly as his car. The caption, translated from Xhosa into English, reads: 'The government's aim is that we, as a people, should prosper in an area or piece of land that belongs to us. As time goes on, wealthy people like Khotso will become commonplace because eventually these factories and industries will be turned over to us.'[4]

One University of Fort Hare academic, a Xhosa-speaking individual who personally experienced the disruptive effect of the homeland system, as she and her family were compelled to relocate from one part of the Eastern Cape to another, harsher part of that region, commented on the picture and its accompanying caption: 'This is obviously a publicity photo that is meant to justify the creation of a Bantustan by parading Khotso as an indication of what every black man can become if he stays in his "own place", like the Transkei.'

Khotso's farming operations were used to promote the notion that the Transkei had rich agricultural potential which would, in due course, give birth to impressive commercial enterprises. On 27 February 1965, the newspaper *Umthunywa* reported that Khotso had begun growing cotton on his farm at Ntafufu and at Mount Nelson, and that he was planning to start a cotton business in which hundreds of Africans could be employed. According to the article, he had embarked on the cotton-growing project after having been encouraged to do so by the Transkei cabinet. As Khotso's spokesperson in the article, Lunika added that two morgen of castor beans had also been planted. If these proved as successful as the cotton endeavour, Lunika said, Khotso would also start a castor oil business. In actuality, Khotso was reaping disappointment as a result of his cotton-growing operations, rather than a rich harvest.

Lunika explained why this was the case: 'The whole project has been undertaken amid difficulties because of lack of guidance. This has demoralised Khotso. What disappoints him most is the lack of direction from the government.'

Khotso's discouragement may have stemmed from the fact that the political authorities in the Transkei did not pay more attention to his agricultural enterprise. According to the *Umthunywa* article, not one member of the Transkei cabinet – including the minister of agriculture and forestry, C. K. Madikizela, who had been present when Khotso was urged to take up cotton farming – had bothered to visit him to find out how his project was progressing and to offer advice and encouragement.[5] He and his project had been put to temporary use as a showpiece, but they were of as much lasting interest to those presiding over the Bantustan in which he resided as the photograph of himself beside his luxury car.

On the other hand, Khotso continued to reap rewards from his career as an ukuthwala practitioner, which was also proving to have a political aspect to it. He was swelling the ranks of black business people in the Transkei, some of whom would seek security in the white political establishment. A black middle class was needed to underpin the Bantustan system, for during the Pondoland Revolt it had become apparent that the chiefs alone could not provide enough support to sustain the homelands.

According to Govan Mbeki, official reports indicated that in 1962 there were 316 black traders in the Transkei and that approximately 300 Africans were owners of bus services. A considerable number of these entrepreneurs might have sought Khotso's help. While the South African government established bodies to foster the growth of black businesses in the Transkei – the Bantu Investment Corporation, set up in 1959, and the Xhosa Development Corporation in 1966 – in his own way, Khotso was playing a part in the process of economic empowerment.

Khotso discovered that despite the fact that his connection with the white political authorities was apparently congenial, he was not immune to a visitation from the most-feared division of the South African Police. The security branch descended on Mount Nelson in 1965, brandishing a letter with what appeared to be Khotso's signature appended to it. The letter read: 'I am going to fight Dr Verwoerd if women detained for not carrying passes are not released.' Full of righteous indignation, Khotso asked the security policemen to track down those who were responsible for forging his signature. 'In my opinion this is merely the work of cheap political propagandists,' he declared.[6] 'They are silly and unscrupulous tactics of unscrupulous politicians who want me to clash with Dr Verwoerd. That will never happen because Dr Verwoerd is my father.'

When asked who he thought might be responsible for the letter, Khotso contended that it had probably been written by 'silly crooks who frequently visit my place from Johannesburg pretending they want muti. I swear their tactics will never succeed because the truth will always come out.'[7] This calls to mind Khotso's view that the threatening letter from 'the Mountain' emanated from 'skellums' and robbers. In his eyes, left-wing political activists and crooks became quickly conflated. He turned to the security policemen, his tone of injured innocence masking characteristic hyperbole: 'How can I agitate for the release of pass offenders or that women should not have to carry passes when I have lost five of my wives in the past two months to these crooks?'[8]

According to Khotso, one of 'these crooks' struck again the following year, when a wife of his ran off with one of his employees. The wife-stealer 'was a first-class fellow', Khotso conceded, adding, 'but I did not know he was a Communist.' He added that he had lost interest in his wife 'now she has been with the Communists in Johannesburg'. Khotso was well aware that in the eyes of the ruling white establishment, the Communists ranked high in the hierarchy of political demons. So, in denigrating the man with whom a woman who may or may not have been his wife had eloped, Khotso may have deemed it convenient to turn the former into a Communist. He told the press that his runaway wife was one of the few who knew the secret entrance to his strongroom full of cash, below the floor of Mount Nelson. He would have to change the secret entrance to his subterranean vault, he lamented, lest his errant wife return with the Communists and rob him of his fortune.⁹

Although Khotso liked boasting that he was always able to pleasure all his wives and concubines, the truth, according to several sources who knew his household well, was that a number of his women sometimes sought sexual entertainment elsewhere. This would sometimes result in unexpected elopements. A high wire-mesh fence encircled Mount Nelson – to keep wives and concubines in as much as to keep undesirables out. Unfortunately for Khotso, however, the gaps in the mesh were large enough for a woman and a man to sneak up to either side of the fence and have sex through the spaces between the wires. Possibly some of the men concerned remembered this trick from their days as mineworkers, when they were housed in compounds enclosed by wire netting that, while shutting them in, did not necessarily keep their penises prisoner.

But such indiscretions remained concealed behind the high (albeit not all-enclosing) fences of Mount Nelson. Instead, Khotso liked to present himself to the curious, prurient gaze of the tabloid-reading public as Khotso the Bull, the Pondoland superstud. Not only would this be bound to generate the publicity he so loved, but it could also lead to an increase in sales of his high-rise muti: the ever-popular ibangalala.

One newspaper article, tantalisingly entitled 'The Sex Secrets of Khotso Sethuntsa . . . Last of the Red Hot Lovers', contains a story that Khotso must have loved spinning to the press. He showed off his bedroom, which contained four beds, one of them a double. He made it known that he liked to take four wives to the bedroom at eight o'clock in the evening, after which he embarked on a copulation marathon. Each wife would share the double bed with him for three hours, Khotso boasted, and he would make love to her promptly on the hour, changing partners regularly: at 11 p.m., 2 a.m. and 5 a.m. In this way, Khotso sought to create the impression that his libido was as regular and reliable as it was inexhaustible, his sexual impulse raising its head (so to speak) of its own irresistible accord, as regularly as an hourly news bulletin. Possibly, extra beds were carted into the bedroom just before the interview took place.¹⁰ It was a great pity for Khotso that this article was only published two years after his death. He would no doubt have delighted in having it framed, so that it could adorn some prominent part of Mount Nelson.

In 1966 there were not only disruptions to Khotso's affairs of the heart, but a blow was struck at the core of the Afrikaner nation when Verwoerd was assassinated in parliament in September of that year. Some people, recalling how Verwoerd's policies had compelled Khotso to leave Kokstad, claimed that they could see his hand in the prime minister's demise. At one point, Verwoerd's assassin, Dimitri Tsafendas, had insisted that he was inhabited by a giant tapeworm. According to Henk van Woerden's biography of Tsafendas, the assassin was not acting under the orders of his tapeworm when he killed Verwoerd. Still, connections between Tsafendas's inner demon and the serpents controlled by Khotso make for some intriguing flights of imaginative speculation.[11]

Verwoerd's assassination provided the starting point for several stories in which Khotso played a pivotal role. For instance, he told certain family members that Verwoerd had made a mistake when taking the medicine that he had given him and disaster had ensued. Lunika, however, pointed out that Khotso's medicine worked against guns, not knives. That was why David Pratt had not been able to kill Verwoerd when he shot him twice in the face at the Rand Easter Show in April 1961, but Tsafendas had succeeded when he closed in on Verwoerd with a blade.

Thus, in certain quarters Verwoerd's assassination could have reinforced faith in the potency of Khotso's medicines. Business was booming and, as always, his special muti for wealth and luck was especially in demand. An element of sexual testing seemed to be involved in the process of obtaining this medicine. A man was not allowed to have sex, not even with his spouse, while he was in the process of using it. 'If you want to get rich quick, don't sleep with your wife,' said one man from Lesotho, who had heard about this. Khotso sometimes utilised seductive, semi-dressed women to tempt his customers, even after they had left his premises.

The link between sexual abstinence and access to supernatural or even spiritual power is a longstanding, widespread intercultural phenomenon. For example, in African tradition, men and women seeking purification before a crucial undertaking of some kind, whether of a spiritual or military nature, have often been instructed to refrain from sex, while members of Western religious orders have been commanded to embrace chastity in order to attain spiritual purity and strength.

One of Khotso's clients, however, was unable to comply with a single week of self-denial imposed on him. This young man visited Mount Nelson seeking good-luck medicine for his butcher's shop. After he had spent three weeks there, Khotso gave him a small bottle containing a concoction and said, 'All who want meat, they must come to Bennet's butchery. There is no better butchery!' Before his client departed, Khotso told him: 'Don't sleep with a girl for seven days after using the medicine.' He warned the young man that the muti would attract women, but that he should resist them and use its power for his business only. The customer returned to Johannesburg by train. He was all by himself in a compartment when an attractive young woman walked in, flung herself on him and began making love to him. Carried away by the unexpected treat that had literally fallen into his lap, the young man responded eagerly. The bottle containing Khotso's special medicine, which was in his shirt pocket, exploded. The man pushed the woman away, shouting: 'You have spoiled my luck!' He got off the train at the next station and returned, disconsolate, to Khotso. He was more fortunate than some people who did not heed Khotso's instructions, as no supernatural punishments were visited on him. The young man was made to work on Khotso's property for some time, after which the medicine he sought was bestowed on him again.

Khotso made this client describe to Lunika what had befallen him. When it was posited to Lunika that this story might have been merely a yarn that Khotso had made his client memorise, Lunika denied this. 'Khotso called me in to listen to this story as part of my training,' he said. 'It was a true story and a strong warning to me!' If the event on the train did indeed take place, was the lascivious young woman merely a fellow traveller, cruising the compartments for some nocturnal entertainment – or was she perhaps a type of railway succubus, sent by Khotso to tempt his heedless customer? Possibly the bottle was crushed in the excitement of the encounter or, as some have liked to believe, the sudden explosion was a piece of long-range magic on Khotso's part.

Certainly this is one of the stories about Khotso's powers that Lunika found the most memorable. In interviews with two different researchers, this was one of the first narratives that he recounted when asked to relate some of his own recollections of Khotso.

As always, Khotso's magic appeared to be interwoven with both sex and politics: two very powerful forces in the temporal world that he harnessed to further his career. This interconnectedness of the erotic, the political and the paranormal was symbolised by the intricate, personalised staff that he possessed. It had his face engraved on it, in a comparable fashion to Lunika's special walking stick, which displays its owner's face too. But while images of mystical potency are carved on Lunika's staff, Khotso's cane was adorned with the faces of Kruger, Verwoerd and Hans Abraham and with the curvaceous form of a half-naked mermaid woman: Nkosazana among the Afrikaners.[12]

Chapter 15
Tsotsis and Treasure

While the political arena was one area in which Khotso had to exercise craftiness lest he put a foot wrong, he could be secure in the confidence that he was on firm ground when it came to other people's beliefs in his extraordinary powers. In the 1960s, even unremarkable events in his life were being transmuted into testaments to his exceptional capabilities, as the following anecdote from Margaret Barlow indicated:

> One day [my husband] Bruce and I went to look at one of the rivers near the village which had overflowed a bridge, making the road impassable. . . . Shortly after we got there [Khotso] arrived in his enormous new Cadillac and, seeing the condition of the river, he came over to speak to us. . . .
>
> A little while later a commercial traveller arrived and was very anxious to cross the river, so he took the fan belt of his car off and drove across the river. [Khotso], highly impressed, did the same thing. The next day, one of my nurses asked me if I had heard about [Khotso]'s miracle – how he had come to the bridge and, as the waters saw him, they parted just as the Red Sea had done when the Israelites had crossed it.[1]

While Jesus had only walked on water, Khotso had been able to drive his Cadillac over it: a story that would prove, yet again, to his band of believers that he was truly greater than God. Accounts of what Khotso could be capable of took on even more astounding proportions as the 1960s progressed. One of Lunika's most widely reported stories concerns an event that he has narrated to journalists and researchers with fascination since, like the events surrounding Smith's immersion in the Mzintlava, this was something he had witnessed himself.

'Thugs tried to get at Khotso's money,' Lunika said, 'but they failed every time.'

Lunika described how one morning, when he was passing Mount Nelson on his way to work at the magistrate's office in Lusikisiki, Khotso called out to him: 'Come in and have some tea!' Although Lunika said that he couldn't really spare the time, Khotso was so insistent that he joined him inside the house and they sat down together. Suddenly a car drove into the yard, turned around and parked facing out, towards the road. Two men emerged from the vehicle. Khotso looked out at them. 'Those men are robbers,' he told Lunika. 'I can see it from the way their car is parked!'

The men entered the house and introduced themselves. Khotso, as usual, instructed Bethinja to make tea for them. After she had left, one of the visitors leaped to his feet and pulled out a gun. 'Take us to your safe!' he ordered, with his weapon trained on Khotso. Khotso calmly rose to his feet, lightly slapping the man's face as he did so. His would-be assailant collapsed, his gun dropping from his hand and sliding across the floor. His companion grabbed the gun and shakily pointed it at Khotso, shouting his friend's command, only to end up sprawling on the floor beside him after one touch from Khotso's hand. Both men gradually came to themselves, as dazed as if they had just surfaced from a deep sleep full of confusing dreams. Khotso gazed down at them.

'Gentlemen,' he said, 'I'm not going to call the police. Many have tried to rob me, just like you. They have all failed. If you really wanted money, you should have come to me for a consultation, just like everybody else. But don't worry – you can still get something from me, if you really want.'

Khotso took the men to the large glass clock in the outbuilding called kwaMatanzima. 'If you manage to shoot that clock, I'll give you two thousand rands each,' he told the men. They perked up a bit at this. The clock, so big, ostentatious and close at hand, would have been hard to miss. But when each of them tried, the bullets plopped out of the gun onto the floor, as if they were large drops of water falling from a tap. Lunika remembered how much Khotso laughed as he escorted the men out to their car. 'Come back to me for ukuthwala,' he said to them. 'I'll make you rich!'

Lunika tried asking Khotso how he managed to make such things happen. He told Blades that all he got in response was, 'You're still a youngster, you know nothing.'

There are similar stories about Khotso's astonishing ability to thwart would-be thieves. Blades recounted how armed robbers had been challenged by Khotso to fire at a mirror, but then were frozen to the spot; and he had heard a tale of a man who had pressed a knife to Khotso's throat while he lay in bed being turned into a living statue until the police arrived to arrest him. There is also the tale of two men who tried to hold up Khotso's Cadillac as he drove along a lonely road through the mountains. Lunika, among a number of others, describes how these men were invited to shoot at a big boulder beside the road, only to see their bullets plop harmlessly out of their guns onto the dusty road.[2] Blades remarked that 'a man with a fraction of the "petty cash" Khotso kept around the place should have been worried', but Khotso wasn't: he had his magic, or stories such as these which cited sensational examples of his magic, to protect him.

Lunika's first-hand account of the tsotsis and their useless guns has naturally given rise to some conjecture. The power of suggestion might have had enough force to send the tsotsis reeling to the floor. Certain people who have heard Lunika's story have argued that something comparable takes place when people collapse in dead faints during charismatic church services, after having been told that they will be overcome by the Holy Spirit.[3] On the other hand, some have wondered whether the episode that Lunika witnessed might have been deliberately staged by Khotso, so as to impress his prime minister and make him want to describe what he had seen to others. But when the possibility that Khotso's encounter with the tsotsis might have been staged was posited to Lunika, he shook his head firmly, stating that what he saw was genuine wizardry: 'Khotso was tough. He was tough – not physically, but mysteriously. Even today, there's no one to equal Khotso.'

While Khotso appeared to be working his magic on those who sought to snatch his wealth from him, the notion that a great treasure trove lay close at hand, just offshore from one of his properties, seemed to be working its magic on him.

A legend that has gripped the imaginations of a number of fortune hunters both within South Africa and beyond its shores is the story of the sunken treasure of the *Grosvenor*. It is hardly surprising that Khotso, with his fascination for wealth, should have been linked not only to the Kruger millions but also to a venture to uncover this legendary sunken hoard.

True to its name, the Wild Coast, with its tempestuous, treacherous swells and breakers and its hidden reefs and rocks, has destroyed many ships, their European crews unaware that they were negotiating one of the most perilous stretches of coastline in southern Africa. One of the most famous of the vessels that foundered in these waters was the *Grosvenor*, an English East Indiaman which ran aground off Lambasi Bay (later known as Port Grosvenor) on the northern Transkei coast in August 1782. Khotso's Wild Coast cottage at Kilroe Beach lies only a few kilometres to the north.

After it foundered, the *Grosvenor* lay shattered on the ocean floor, smashed by the violence of the waves. However, stories persisted that the ship rested intact beneath the sand, with a precious cargo safely cradled inside it. Popular myths had it that the *Grosvenor* was loaded with jewels and bars of gold and silver. Then the tales of treasure became even more far-fetched, as the story began to circulate that the ship had been transporting two gold peacocks, encrusted with diamonds, rubies and other gems, from the peacock throne of the Mogul dynasty of

Delhi. In actuality, the *Grosvenor* had far fewer riches on board than was commonly believed and the Peacock Throne had been borne off and broken apart after Delhi was sacked by the Persians in 1739. Yet this did not deter fortune seekers or diminish the lustre of tales about the fabulous wealth lying on the seabed. Such yarns were reinforced by the gold and silver coins that were washed up on the shore near the site of the wreck.[4]

In 1963, Khotso met Guido de Backer, a Belgian deep-sea diver and fortune hunter who was convinced that the *Grosvenor*'s treasure lay within his grasp, if only he could raise the money necessary to commence his salvage enterprise, grandiosely entitled the International Technical Development and Research Company of South Africa. So he turned to an individual known to have an inclination for ambitious schemes of his own, the Pondoland millionaire Khotso Sethuntsa. De Backer required one hundred and twenty thousand rands but had only managed to raise half that amount. Lunika said: 'De Backer promised me a new car if I could persuade Khotso to assist him.'

De Backer's mission took several unexpected turns. For a start, he found himself eclipsed by Khotso. Khotso accompanied his would-be partner to the coast to view the site of the shipwreck, providing three of his trucks for the journey. The excursion turned into something of a carnival parade for the press and curious onlookers, with Khotso careering over the Pondoland potholes at the wheel of the truck at the front of the cavalcade. On their return to Mount Nelson, Khotso turned the evening's business into yet another performance starring himself. He appeared before his guests decked in his full regalia, complete with his beaded robe in the South African colours with '*Eendragt maakt magt*' and the national flag worked into the back. The guests were seated in a row along one wall of the long banqueting area, as if they were spectators rather than participants. One journalist provided this description of the event:

> With much ceremony, Mr De Backer presented Khotso with a model of the Grosvenor.

Khotso's face screwed up with joy. He raised the model above his head and led his wives and his secretary around the room in a procession, shouting 'Paul Kruger's Grosvenor, give up your treasure.'

The human crocodile cast shadows across the shining-red polished floor and stark white walls of the room. The wives clapped their hands and chanted as Khotso continued his incantations.[5]

The connection that Khotso established between the *Grosvenor* and Paul Kruger is interesting. It was almost as if the old president's association with wealth loomed so large in Khotso's mind that even a vessel belonging to Kruger's enemies, the English, fell under his powers. On this and various other occasions, the faith that Khotso appeared to have developed in Oom Paul as a spiritual presence, as well as the focal point of a politically expedient publicity stunt, manifested itself. These two attitudes were interwoven, for the fact that Khotso was staging an extravaganza to impress visiting journalists no doubt encouraged him to make sure that Kruger was included in the act, even if only in a supporting role. We have seen that this worked well in the Kruger Day celebrations, in which Kruger could simultaneously serve as publicity drawcard and household god.

Finally, the cavortings came to a halt. Khotso placed the model of the *Grosvenor* on the table and contemplated it in silence for some time. Then he turned to De Backer, declaring that the ship had told him that his enterprise would succeed. 'At last, the *Grosvenor* will give up its wealth,' he pronounced.

Each guest was presented with a beaded tie, which Khotso assured them was a charm for luck and health. Before they departed, Khotso crawled before the seated line of guests, kissing their hands and feet. His wives dutifully followed him, with Lunika at the tail of the procession. The following day, Khotso showed Kruger Park to De Backer and his companions and, in a private meeting with De Backer, he displayed one basket of diamonds and another of gold coins. Whether De Backer was allowed at any time to address the serious business of his visit can only be left open to conjecture. Khotso airily promised to make an unspecified 'substantial investment' in the salvage venture, saying that he could summon up all the men and machinery that would be needed. However, De Backer left Mount Nelson uncertain whether Khotso was actually prepared to deliver the amount he had requested.

It is unlikely that Khotso would have been willing to sink a huge amount of money into a potentially dubious enterprise. He once observed to a journalist: 'I've never seen a rich man who was also a fool and I certainly didn't make all this money just to lose it again.'[6]

The whole episode ended ingloriously for De Backer. His car, like the *Grosvenor*, plunged downwards, descending four hundred and eighty feet over the Magwa Falls, in the region of Lusikisiki. De Backer and his family had parked their vehicle near the edge of the waterfall and then wandered off in order to view the falls from a better vantage point. When they returned, the car had vanished. Several days later, the wrecked car, worth five thousand rands and containing cash, passports and other documentation, still could not be retrieved from the water. Meanwhile, De Backer and his family retreated to Durban.[7] Khotso might well have found the debacle funny. After all, his Cadillacs never went wandering off on their own. Also, it is worth noting that water proved De Backer's undoing. Probably some viewed his defeat at the Magwa Falls as a sign from Khotso that De Backer, with all his expensive possessions, was no match for him – or the Transkei.

During 1964 Khotso talked about buying a luxury yacht that he would keep anchored at the shore of his Wild Coast property, so that he could contemplate it from his modest beach cottage. The vessel in question was a seventy-five-foot twin-engine cruiser with air-conditioning, wall-to-wall carpeting and other modern conveniences, including a cocktail bar (from which Khotso could, presumably, serve orange juice to his guests). The seas around Msikaba are tumultuous and rocky, the wind-whipped shoreline salty and damp with spray. A luxury yacht might have presented an incongruous, perhaps even short-lived, spectacle on such a coastline. But the Department of Inland Revenue, which presented an even greater problem in Khotso's later life than the wild Pondoland ocean and the rough Pondoland roads, blocked the move.[8] Like his dreams of finding the hidden treasure of the *Grosvenor*, Khotso's wish to purchase an opulent yacht that could rival his luxury cars belonged, in the end, to the realm of grandiose fantasies.

CHAPTER 16
King of a Slippery Realm

Even more than hidden treasure and expensive possessions, money in itself would always remain a key consideration in Khotso's life and a subject that he brought up whenever he could, especially with journalists. He liked to describe how much he had earned through his medicine trade. He had received a number of orders from overseas and had made a 'glorious fortune', he told one reporter. 'People from all over the world write to me and ask me to help them solve their problems,' he continued. 'Of course they know that I am the greatest and have helped many here and abroad.'[1]

Khotso informed another journalist: 'I am rich because I sell only high-class magic. I am the most successful medicine man in the world because my charms work and because people all over the world know they work. Sometimes my charges are high and my medicine never fails.'[2]

In 1968, Khotso claimed to have received a multimillion-rand order for muti from a client from the United States.[3] He also displayed a range of letters from desperate people from that country and the West Indies to journalists such as Blades. (Khotso had not fêted busloads of American visitors and even christened one of his outbuildings kwaAmerican Tourist for nothing.) His diverse petitioners, each dwelling on his or her own personal form of anguish, had one thing in common: they believed that their salvation lay in the hands of one man in a small, remote African town, Khotso Sethuntsa. In one letter, a compulsive Chicago gambler bewailed the disastrous turn his life had taken. He had lost twenty-five thousand dollars in twenty-two months, after which he had considered suicide. Then he heard of Khotso: 'When I read of Dr Khotso's unequalled powers I told myself: "Here is a man who can solve my problems and give me a fresh start in my miserable life,"' he wrote. 'I have lost everything I owned and life has become a daily ordeal for me.'

In another missive, a woman from Connecticut turned to Khotso, beseeching him to work miracles in her life: 'I have been ill for years and doctors in America are unable to cure my disease. I appeal to you for help. I am prepared to pay what you demand. My only hope of recovery now depends on you.'[4]

Through exhibiting letters such as these, Khotso presented himself as a muti king whose dominion encompassed not only southern Africa, but extended into Europe and the Americas. But like many kings, Khotso would come to find that some of the domains over which he presided would be subject to instabilities and sudden, unwelcome changes.

Being a rich and powerful Bantustan resident allowed Khotso to indulge in dreams of dominion that would have been impossible to entertain in Kokstad. Urban areas in the Transkei would be declared zones for black occupation and consequently commerce, and white business people could be shifted out of the Transkei so as to create the space for the growth of a black Bantustan business community that would lend credibility and, potentially, support to the system of separate development.[5] As Khotso possibly viewed it, the stage was being cleared to make way for his grand entrance.

In 1965, he hit the headlines when he announced that he planned to buy Mount Frere and Lusikisiki, as soon as they had been proclaimed black areas. Khotso had great ambitions for his small and sleepy kingdoms-to-be, disclosing that he planned to build a factory and shops and flats, which he would let out to Transkei citizens. He said that he had put aside two million rands for this purpose. '[He] may become

Khotso, with James Lunika behind him, sitting upon R 2198 in coins arranged in piles. (©Independent Newspapers)

Southern Africa's biggest entrepreneur if plans he has in mind become a reality,' one journalist enthused.[6] Later, Khotso's dreams of turning the Transkei into his own private fiefdom took on even more grandiose proportions, as he declared that he was going to purchase 'lock, stock and barrel' the ten towns set aside for exclusively black ownership in the Transkei. Khotso went on to add: 'Soon all of it will be mine.'

In January 1966, a government proclamation was passed declaring Lusikisiki a black zone. Khotso and ten of his assistants set about counting what Khotso dismissively called his 'petty cash', in order to buy zoned properties. He made sure that the press was at hand to witness the spectacle. Newspaper photographs depict huge piles of coins with Khotso crouched, beaming, over R2 198 in fifty-cent pieces, all stacked in piles of four. The rows of coins extend far beyond the borders of the photograph. 'This money', Khotso announced, 'I will use only to pay the transfer duty on the places I will buy.'[7]

Shortly thereafter, however, Khotso changed tack, saying that he did not want to 'force' whites to leave the Transkei by buying up all the property they owned – as if he, rather than any government agency, exercised the real control over what took place in that region.⁸ Arguably, Khotso may have felt that, having drawn everyone's attention to the fact that he could rule the entire Transkei if he chose, he could explore other ways of exhibiting his wealth and power. Underlying this, however, was the reality of the situation. Khotso's projected Transkeian kingdom was far more impressive in his initial, wild imaginings than it would have been in actuality. The Nationalists' much-vaunted schemes of self-contained Bantustans into which the majority of the black South African population could be conveniently shunted would collapse into shoddy, messy realities of misery and corruption.

In fact, in terms of the Zoning Proclamation of 1965, complete zoning was only applied to relatively small rural backwaters. This was widely perceived as amounting to an admission on the part of the government that it faced 'undisclosed hazards' in its task of creating entirely black Bantustan areas.⁹ Khotso was able to buy a number of properties in Mount Frere and Lusikisiki cheaply from departing whites, but the larger and more significant urban areas, including the capital Mthatha, were never zoned for complete black occupation.¹⁰ As white settlers began leaving the Transkei, a new wave of white entrepreneurs started moving into the larger towns, such as Butterworth, Dutywa (formerly Idutywa) and Umzimkhulu, as civil servants or in advisory, managerial positions. The awareness had grown that with Transkeian independence under way, some of the funds allocated to that region's bureaucratic and official structures, as part of the process of separate development, would trickle down into the business sector.¹¹

Around the same time as it was becoming evident that his dreams of being lord of the Transkei were no more than high-flown imaginings, Khotso's control over his own personal kingdom appeared to be slipping too.

In 1965, the domestic entourage at Mount Nelson altered in a radical way: Khotso parted company with his prime minister, who was transferred to Mthatha. Lunika's promotion from a clerical position in a Transkeian town to the Department of Finance in the capital itself would lead to significant career developments. As he grew older, he was appointed to influential positions in prominent official bodies. In 1983 and 1984, he served as auditor-general of the Transkei and thereafter, between 1985 and 1988, he was chair of the Transkei Broadcasting Corporation. In later years, from 1988 to 1994, he was a member of the Public Services Commission. The house that Lunika built for himself in Mthatha in 1979, with its spacious front room and large, comfortable items of furniture, is a reflection of the extent to which he ascended into the influential echelons of Bantustan bureaucracy. However, his relationship with his ex-master in Lusikisiki would mean that his move to Mthatha would not simply result in a smooth, gradual progress towards better things.

Initially, Khotso's ex-prime minister retained ties with him, usually visiting him in Mount Nelson on Fridays. Lunika said that Khotso did not seem to appreciate the career opportunities with which his education had provided him, repeatedly asking: 'Are you getting sufficient money at work, in the office?'

In Mthatha, between 1966 and 1968, Lunika sold the herbal medicines that Khotso had trained him to make. He could earn a good income, up to two or three hundred rands a week, selling powdered medicines like intelezi. But Lunika was still dependent on Khotso for his medicine supply. Also, he continued to use Khotso's lucky muti himself, smearing it into his still clean-shaven head. He felt this paid off, because as he made his way down crowded Mthatha streets, people – often total strangers – would greet him as if he was a great friend, offering to assist him or lavishing gifts and privileges on him. Khotso's muti always worked, Lunika said, so he would go back to him for more.

He was foolish, Lunika admitted. Having been trained as a herbalist at Mount Nelson, he wanted to show Khotso that his training had been successful. So he began boasting about making money to his ex-master himself. With hindsight, Lunika acknowledged that this was an unwise move, since, as he would discover, Khotso did not like the idea of competition. Lunika sensed afterwards that Khotso felt that his one-time apprentice was taking his customers away from him and, along with them, the money that was due to him.

Lunika, however, was heedless of this at the time. Whenever his good-luck medicine was used up, he would return to Khotso for more. Once, while he was in Lusikisiki, Lunika heard whisperings that his former master was jealous of his success in Mthatha. But Lunika had once again obtained Khotso's medicine for good fortune and now wanted to use it. Back in Mthatha, he rubbed the medicine in and awaited the usual pleasant developments. But when Lunika walked through town the following day, it was as if Khotso's medicine had turned people in Mthatha against him. Strangers suddenly turned hostile and rushed up to him in the street, abusing him or even threatening him. 'I feel like *klapping* you!' one man yelled.

Lunika returned to Khotso. 'You've given me bad medicine!' he said. Khotso smoothly denied this. Both men stared at each other with mistrustful eyes, the deep-seated mutual dependence and loyalty that had bound them to each other for so many years having been fractured. All Khotso's power could not necessarily guarantee him control over his one-time prime minister; for his part, Lunika knew that Khotso's magic, which he had witnessed himself as a boy in Kokstad and during the course of his duties at Mount Nelson, had now turned against him, of all people. What other disasters might lie in store for him if he ever attempted to get more medicine from Khotso?

The tensions between them erupted into an outright quarrel as Lunika prepared to depart. Khotso wanted him to give a woman in his household a lift, but Lunika did not carry out his wishes, feeling that Khotso was planning to use the woman to tempt him sexually. Khotso did not like being refused, especially by the man who had once called him Morena. He became angry and Lunika returned to his home in Mthatha. That night he had a frightening dream, in which he lay in a dark, narrow space – his own coffin, he realised in dread. The nightmare had been sent by Khotso, so what could he expect next from his former master?

Khotso addresses an array of wives and children. (©BAHA. Photo by Drum photographer)

Probably it would be safest to have as little to do with him as possible, now that he had aroused his wrath, Lunika decided. For the remainder of Khotso's life, the two men never spoke to each other again. The next communication Lunika would receive from his ex-master would be when Khotso was in the spirit world, when he would require Lunika to carry out what could have been a dangerous duty on his behalf.

The press, however, did not take note of the departure of Khotso's prime minister from his life. The arrival of more wives engaged popular interest far more. Khotso played up this side of his affairs to the full. Periodically, throughout the 1960s and early 1970s, he would let it be known that he had acquired yet another spouse; and this would be reported in the newspapers. Little has been reported, however, about one of the most significant connubial additions to Khotso's household. In 1964, Khotso married Eunice Nomantombazana Faye, otherwise known as MaMjoli, formerly a primary school teacher. Like all his marriages, with one notable exception, this was a traditional union.

MaMjoli has inspired admiration in a wide range of people. 'She's like a duchess,' one white inhabitant of Kokstad recently said of her. The meaning of this comparison becomes apparent on meeting MaMjoli. She carries herself in a dignified, graceful way and has a ready smile and an eloquent, confident manner of speaking. Signs of the beauty that she once possessed are still evident.[12] A press photograph taken in the early 1970s, which does not show her at her best, since it catches her squinting into the harsh Transkei sunlight, still cannot obscure her lovely clear features and the finely sculpted planes of her face. MaMjoli and Khotso's first child, their daughter Ma-Six (often called Pretty), was born in 1969.

MaMjoli's family property happened to be next to Khotso's Mount Frere abode, so he was her family's neighbour. With her strikingly attractive appearance and her distinguished bearing, she caught Khotso's roving eye after she took a group of schoolchildren to his house in Mount Frere. 'I was taken by surprise when he sent emissaries to my father, Jackson Faye, asking that I should be his wife,' she told a journalist years later.[13]

After her employment as a teacher, MaMjoli worked in a wholesale store for a while, where she acquired business experience. Following her marriage to Khotso, she began carrying out secretarial duties for her husband, later on taking on more responsibilities. For instance, when her husband's health started failing, she worked full-time as his 'accountant'. She played other roles in Khotso's house as well. While Khotso had always sought to make his children aware of the value of making and saving money, MaMjoli knew that education was important. She would encourage the young ones to make sure they paid attention to their studies at school and would remonstrate with their mothers when this did not happen.

As an illiterate self-made man, Khotso might have wondered why his new consort was so concerned about school attendance. Yet at the same time, after his prime minister's departure, Khotso felt the need to find another person who could carry out at least some of the duties Lunika had performed over the years. MaMjoli was not only literate and numerate and possessed administrative expertise; she was shrewd and sensible as well.

However, while MaMjoli possessed a mature, regal bearing befitting the wife of as eminent a man as the Pondoland muti king, there were certain qualities which she lacked and which her consort continued seeking out in other women: youth, innocence and impressionability. Khotso's inclination to select youthful women as his wives and concubines appeared to intensify the older he became. Many older men pursue women decades their junior partly in the hope that something of their youth will magically infuse their flagging, sagging bodies and spirits with new energy and vitality. Then as the male ego also grows more fragile with age, the concept of a trophy wife or sexual partner becomes more attractive. Even in his latter years, Khotso worked to create the impression that he possessed a youthfulness that did not need replenishing; and with his suitcases of money, luxury cars and assortment of over-ornamented houses he had trophies enough already. Despite all this, he delighted in having even more to boast about. He sensed too that the younger his wives or concubines were (or appeared to be), the more publicity his relationships with them would generate.

Indeed, material concerns might have been the main driving force behind Khotso's preference for very young women. Unlike many ageing men who pretend to a youth that they do not possess as they pursue youthful females, he did the opposite. When he publicly drew attention to the tender years of his prospective brides, most of whom were described as being in – or barely out of – their teens, he would simultaneously emphasise his own advanced years, even adding on several decades to his age.

Decades before cholesterol anxiety, he would tell journalists such as Blades that good fatty meat, combined with ibangalala, was the ideal recipe for inexhaustible youth and masculine potency. 'I mix ibangalala with my gravy and drink it up,' he said to Blades.[14] The lean years of his youth had left Khotso with a taste for fatty meat. He informed Becker that he took his wonder medicine every day. 'That's why my body is young,' he said, 'and my mind gives no thought to age in years.'

In 1970 it appeared that Khotso was going out of his way to emphasise that despite his advanced age, his heart and another vital organ remained eternally youthful. He declared that he was celebrating his ninetieth birthday by bestowing three new wives, young Sotho women aged twenty-two, twenty and nineteen, on himself as a present. Towards the end of the same year, Khotso was reported as saying that he had married yet another teenager, Nogama Msindo, from Lesotho.[15] Another one of Khotso's later wives, Nonkqubela, was also in her teens.

Since Khotso repeatedly lied about his own age, he was quite capable of lying about the ages of some of his wives. But there is no debate about the age of another one of his youthful brides, Selina Sithole. She was fifteen years old when she married Khotso in 1964, although she was even younger when she first caught his attention. She arrived in Kokstad in 1956, when she was seven. Because she was sickly, her father, Samuel Sithole, arranged that she should stay in Khotso's household for a while for herbal treatment. But a brief period of medical care eventually led to far more. When Selina's father wanted to take her home, he found that his daughter's putative healer had now turned into her would-be husband. Selina should stay in his house, Khotso said. When she was old enough, he wished to marry her. Seven years later, when Selina was in her mid-teens, a marriage deal was concluded. But Khotso had obviously started a sexual liaison with her some time before that. Selina was already pregnant.[16]

Before her marriage, Selina accomplished a feat that hardly any of Khotso's wives and host of concubines had succeeded in performing. She provided him with a son: Four Boy, born at 4 p.m. on 21 August 1963.

There are a number of possible reasons why young women like Selina might have been prepared to become part of Khotso's harem. For one, there was Khotso's reputation itself. As a mighty inyanga purported to have tremendous clout in the supernatural world, turning him down might have seemed like a risky prospect to both them and their families.

In other respects too, the power dynamics at work in the situation in which the young women who became physically involved with Khotso found themselves did not operate in their favour. In a social context in which men were usually expected to exercise masculine dominion in all areas of their lives, while the women with whom they came into contact were generally required to submit to male authority, the odds were stacked against women right from the very start. Notwithstanding all the radical political and social changes that have taken place in South Africa since Khotso's day, such deep-seated attitudes are still held dear by some white and black South Africans.

Besides the advantages Khotso's position as a renowned inyanga brought him, his status in the everyday material world carried a great deal of weight too. A number of the youthful women who became sexually involved with Khotso may well have initially felt flattered by the fact that a man of his stature was taking an interest in someone as immature and inexperienced as themselves. Furthermore, in areas as impoverished as the Transkei and Lesotho in the 1960s and 1970s, catching the eye of a millionaire might have been the equivalent of winning the Lotto today.

Then, as we know, Khotso's magic extended to making the unlikely and even the downright incredible seem convincing. So no doubt he succeeded in weaving a spell around some of the young women whose paths crossed his, making them believe that he truly adored them and that life with him would be a source of unending delight. This latter aspect is perhaps reflected in the idyllic, romantic account of her marriage that Selina provided to the press some years after her husband's death:

> Apart from Khotso, I have never known a man, so I cannot compare him with others. But yes, he satisfied me. I believe he truly loved me because he showered me with love – and taught me every aspect of love-making. I still regard him as a great lover. I am still young, but I doubt whether I'll find another man like him. Fate has destined me to be a widow at 26.[17]

Selina might have been indulging in a romanticised re-creation of her relationship with Khotso. Indeed, her depiction of their marriage, which combines true love with tragedy, has popular, sentimental appeal which a more realistic account of their life together might lack. It is worth noting that Selina does not make mention of the fact that her union with Khotso was short-lived, lasting only a couple of years, and that it was she who drew it to a close.

'When I left Khotso to return to my home, it was because he did not treat me well,' Selina said sadly, years after Khotso's death, hinting at the shadows that lurked behind the fairy-tale façade she preferred to proffer to the public gaze. Selina retreated to the security of her family in Donnybrook, Natal, in 1966, leaving her son behind in Khotso's household, just as Ellen had done.[18] Four Boy was cared for by Bethinja. Although Bethinja had not been able to present Khotso with any children, let alone any male offspring of his own, she had become, in effect, the mother of one of his precious sons. As a relative newcomer to a long-established household, Bethinja had been playing her cards carefully, and now suddenly she found that she had been dealt one of the winning cards in the pack. As events would prove, her position in Khotso's household was thus considerably strengthened, because Four Boy was to become Khotso's favourite son.

Khotso liked to boast about his numerous sons and daughters. 'My children are all over the country, as far as Johannesburg and Swaziland,' he would say to visitors such as Blades. 'Yes, there must be 200 or more, about 50 going to school in Lusikisiki, the others at boarding school or too young to go. I've enough sons if they were the right age to form an infantry company. Hundreds . . . and grandchildren and great-grandchildren! You can never finish counting.'

Khotso's allusions to his large numbers of children could fulfil a comparable function to his Cadillacs and suitcases full of money, since they provided proof of his prowess and pre-eminence in another area. Even in his seventies, he still liked to refer to himself as Khotso the Bull. But offspring – above all sons, the manly fruit of his virile loins – could testify to the vigour of Khotso's masculinity in a way that his cars and banknotes could not. Blades described how he once sat with Khotso amid the colour and clutter of the front room at Mount Nelson and suddenly the sound of chanting and drumming began outside. 'Sons,' Khotso muttered non-committally to him, as if a throng of male offspring had come to pay him tribute.

Yet in reality, Khotso had few sons. There were a number of young men connected to his household that outsiders sometimes regarded as his sons. Nyanga, who would become the associate of his eldest son, Langa, was one such example. Although Nyanga's mother had stayed in Khotso's house, his father was someone from outside that establishment.

Khotso's life was characterised by a number of ironies. One that he would have felt deeply was that although he was an internationally renowned purveyor of medicines for good fortune and virility, he seemed dogged by bad luck when it came to his male offspring. By the last decade of his life he had only two boys, one of whom was turning out a bitter disappointment.

A rift gradually widened between Khotso and Langa, in whom he had vested so much. One man who knew Khotso well in the 1960s asserted: 'He liked Langa very much, but this Langa, when he grew up, he started drinking. And he drank like hell! Khotso hated drinking, so he turned to this young boy called Four Boy. He liked Four Boy until he died.'

A number of other informants also maintain that Langa drank heavily.[19] It must have been burdensome having all his father's hopes pinned on him, as the eldest son. As has already been noted, in press photographs taken of him as a child and a teenager, Langa looks uncomfortable or even unhappy. Often he appears awkward in the heavy ornate robes with which his father has bedecked him, eyes downcast and shoulders hunched, as if he finds the regalia too cumbersome to bear.

Langa's childhood circumstances might also have contributed to a sense of inner insecurity. His mother had left when he was a toddler and he had been cared for by a succession of people in a household that

Khotso and Langa on Kruger Day in 1960, with the vierkleur in the background. (© Independent Newspapers)

shifted and swelled, taking on different dynamics as large numbers of people came and went. To an outsider, Khotso's household might have seemed a colourful, exciting place to inhabit, but a small, uncertain boy might have felt himself caught up in a circus of alarming proportions, in which he was expected to be one of the star performers while subject to the whims of a larger-than-life ringmaster. The white Lusikisiki children who attended the lunch party at Mount Nelson for the Nationalist cabinet minister's son did not notice the small stature of the master of the household. Instead, he looked bigger than everyone else around him. For Langa, his father's presence may have loomed so huge in his life (this state of affairs continuing long after Khotso's death) that he felt diminished in comparison.

There might also have been a personality clash between father and son, which could have taken its toll on Langa. Khotso was extroverted, confident, boisterous and goal-directed; his son appeared diffident and withdrawn. It is possible too that Langa might have lacked a clear sense of direction and purpose. Ellen's friend Francina described Langa as sweet and gentle. Just like his mother, Langa was perhaps not sufficiently tough to cope with the situation in which he found himself. To put it more bluntly, though, Langa may have struck some as soft and mild because he was, in fact, weak.

There are other factors that might have played their part in ensuring that even as an adult Langa had something lacking within him. As family members have testified, Khotso was a strict parent in many respects. He hoarded his fortune rather than lavishing it on those around him, including even those close to him, trying instead to instil into his family the importance of working hard and saving money. Yet there was also the fact that Khotso's wealth was often on display. Furthermore, as many photographs in newspapers testify, when press photographers were on hand to record these displays, Langa was often placed centre stage, right beside his father. In consequence, unlike many who went to Khotso for ukuthwala and came away from the ordeal strengthened in their resolve and determined to make their own way in life, Langa may not have felt any necessity for building up his own inner resources and developing firmness of spirit. He was, after all, surrounded by wealth far beyond the reach and comprehension of those in the regions into which Khotso's empire extended and, as his father often emphasised to visitors and journalists, he was the favoured, oldest son.

But although he was the rising star in the household of the richest man in Pondoland, that did not mean that life was easy and comfortable for Langa as he slowly edged towards adulthood. During the course of the inquiry into Khotso's estate that took place after his death, Langa submitted an affidavit in which he sketched his own life story prior to his father's demise. Langa's account, which follows below, illustrates the extent to which the concept of tough love appealed to his parent, especially as far as the upbringing of his eldest son was concerned.

> I worked in our Mount Nelson store. From 1961 to 1965 I managed our shop at Matatiele, and managed the livestock.
>
> From 1965 to 1966, I worked very hard at Mount Frere. First of all, we made bricks, then we built a house from scratch. We

> were pulling hard. . . .
>
> From 1967 to 1971, I went to school and stayed at our farm Ntafufu near Lusikisiki during holidays, when I would fence the farm, weed the mealiefields and harvest cotton.
>
> Sometimes my father instructed me to go to Matatiele (where he had another farm). I stayed at Mount Frere until my father became ill and called me to Lusikisiki.[20]

If Langa's version of events can be relied on, it appears that he did not spend much time at Mount Nelson from his early adolescence onwards. Instead, he carried out onerous duties on several of his father's properties and farms. This was the type of education to which Khotso subscribed: his son was receiving training in a variety of extremely practical areas, all the while, he trusted, learning the value of hard work. For Khotso, this probably represented a character-building exercise. For the son, however, it may have had the reverse effect. From the age of twelve, he was required to take on positions of authority and he was also expected to carry out an assortment of physical tasks that even a fully grown man could have found exhausting. Such duties would have weighed Langa down even more heavily than did the robes in which his father periodically garbed him. His upbringing may also have left him with a sense that the path Khotso was laying out for him was not one that he himself wished to follow.

Langa's account indicates that for a great deal of time he was separated from his father's headquarters. As someone else who knew Khotso's family well put it, 'Langa was let loose at an early age.' Left to his own devices, he went his own way.

Khotso was wounded by the fact that his son was drifting towards alcoholism, in the light of his own rejection of drink. Khotso was, in some respects, a fastidious man, and over-indulgence in alcohol can have messy consequences. He also held that alcohol was incompatible with a fundamentally important part of his lifestyle, sexual activity, because 'you can't do a good job drunk'.[21]

For Khotso, the way in which Langa was turning out was especially

Khotso sunk deep in thought, in 1970. (©BAHA. Photo by Alf Kumalo)

galling as, apart from creating the impression that his medicine for good fortune could not exercise its beneficial effect on his family life, it ran counter to some of his major claims on which he had based his fame. Ever since his youth, Khotso had boasted about his ability to steer the path of the inkanyamba and exercise control over myriad otherworldly forces. He had related that even the mighty spirit of Paul Kruger waited at his side to assist him. Yet he could not exercise his will over one of the most significant people in his life: his eldest son.

There is the belief that sometimes those who practise ukuthwala do not necessarily part with family members, such as children, in a physical sense when death cuts their lives short, but instead they lose them in another way. Their children may become useless, their lives collapsing in ruin. They continue living, but it is as if something vital has expired inside them. Khotso had buried his first-born male child; it was as if, in a sense, he had lost another son.

It was hardly surprising that Khotso turned increasingly to his younger son, Four Boy, to parade him as his heir. Towards the end of Khotso's life, this child, garbed in diminutive ceremonial apparel, features more and more in press photographs.

Interestingly enough, during this latter period in Khotso's life, the boy who would eventually become the master of Mount Nelson and thus, decades later, would appear to some outsiders to be his heir waited not far away, with his mother. By 1968, Masechaba and her son Thabo had moved into MaDlamini's house in Mount Frere. Over the Pondoland hills, in the lush grasslands closer to the coast, Khotso's headquarters lay.

In the latter part of the 1960s, then, Khotso parted company with two of the most important people in his life: his prime minister and also, in a significant sense, his eldest son. There were some who believed that yet another key figure was deserting him: his wife under the water, his serpentine paramour who had lavished fame and good fortune on him for decades.

CHAPTER 17
Nkosazana and Bethinja

The latter part of Khotso's life was characterised by a series of betrayals both real and imagined. He felt that Lunika had betrayed him and it was all too obvious that Langa had let him down. Then there were all the other betrayals that lay in wait for Khotso, both before and after his death, which he could not have foreseen. Yet Khotso himself had initiated a pattern of betrayal long ago. Not only was there his recurrent pattern of extramarital infidelities, but also, if appearances are to be believed, he may have allowed his adoration of money to dominate his life above all else – possibly at the cost of his closest personal relationships. Some have alleged that Nkosazana, the seductive serpentine bringer of great wealth, was the wife who was closest of all to Khotso's heart. The phrase *blood money*, with its connotations of betrayal, suggests the kind of ongoing lobola payment, involving forfeiting the lives or the well-being of family members, that some believe a marriage to her demands. It is said that even if the mamlambo's consort does not physically sacrifice those nearest to him, he is required to put his wife under the water before all others, so that he may have to witness the destruction that his marriage to the mamlambo can wreak within his family. In a sense, then, his own heart's-blood is the offering that sustains his bond with this being.

But, some of the stories maintain, even his passionate love of money did not prevent Khotso from betraying Nkosazana, in the way that a man might be unfaithful to his spouse. Mamlambos become intensely jealous of their owners' sexual partners, and Nkosazana had had to endure decades of Khotso's promiscuity, which tended to take place within the opulent establishments that she herself had helped bring into being. To add insult to injury, as Khotso began approaching the highest point of his career, at Mount Nelson, his sexual profligacy became more flagrant than ever before. Despite the fact that his 'marriage' to Nkosazana was one of the earliest unions that he embarked on, Khotso, never one for monogamy, delighted in taking on more and more spouses and concubines, culminating in an array of teenage brides in the final decade of his career. At this stage, some aver, Nkosazana finally felt she had had enough.

'Nkosazana didn't like Khotso's constant meddling with women,' someone who knew Khotso well in the 1950s and 1960s said. 'He was changing them left and right all the time and she eventually got tired and left him.'

The physical distance between Mount Nelson and the deep pools and rivers to which Khotso was drawn may have symbolically suggested the way in which his wife under the water was drawing away from him, just as he was separating himself from her. In the final years of his life, his career no longer moved 'forward to the stars', as the motto of the Khotso High School[1] near Mount Nelson would eventually put it, but gradually began to curve in a downward trajectory.

A decade earlier, when he was coerced out of Kokstad by Paul Kruger's children, those he had regarded as his special friends and spiritual kin, Khotso's pride had taken a severe blow. He had compensated for this by turning Mount Nelson into a palace of rococo excess. It was, he kept emphasising to outsiders, the hub of his empire, to which he drew hordes of admirers, followers, customers and consorts. In the latter part of his career, however, he began to lose his ability to direct the course of key events in what had once seemed his inviolable domain. As the Pondoland potentate whose fame extended far over the oceans, he needed his prime minister, but the latter had now parted from him. His natural heir, his eldest son, had also deserted him,

Moreover, Khotso and his empire were under attack from redoubtable forces that he had hitherto brushed aside. One of them was a formidable foe: all the mystical monsters Khotso had claimed to have at his disposal were no match for the tax collectors. A number of people who knew Khotso were aware of the extent to which this preyed on his mind. Lunika said: 'All of Khotso's money was in cash at his home, because he had withdrawn it all from the bank in an effort to evade paying tax. He realised that his bank manager used to report to the receiver of revenue about how much he had in the bank.' Khotso's attempt to secure his wealth by removing his money from the bank and stowing it away in Mount Nelson would backfire.

Khotso's fear of having his money taken away from him could reach almost paranoid dimensions. This had been evident, for instance, in the case of the 'Communist' wife-stealer who, Khotso claimed, had made off with the spouse to whom he had entrusted the secrets of his strongroom. But an even worse foe than the Communists was after his money. In what he liked outsiders to regard as his ninetieth-birthday press release, Khotso announced: 'My muti has made me very strong, stronger than I have ever been.' However, it did seem that his medicines could not enable him to defeat the tax collectors. He would have to accumulate 'very much' petty cash to pay income tax, he acknowledged regretfully near the end of the interview.[2]

Earlier on, when Lunika had tried to warn Khotso that publicising the extent of his wealth could have unfortunate consequences, Blades mentioned that Khotso had retorted dismissively: 'James, you know nothing! The taxman won't bother me!' But Khotso was mistaken, Blades recalled: 'They did bother him and thereafter he became suspicious of questions about his wealth. "It's coming in all the time," he told me, purposely vague, long before his death.' Khotso's reluctance to talk about his wealth indicated that he had changed in a major respect.

Also lurking in the shadows was the threat of ageing and physical decline. One of the many paradoxes in Khotso's life was that, despite the enjoyment he derived from adding on decades to his age, he did not want to appear as old as he claimed to be, or even the age that he truly was. Did Khotso manage to convince himself of the fact that he, unlike all other men, would remain immune to the dire, debilitating effects of age? Or did he feel a deep-seated fear of the imminent onset of senescence? Judging from various newspaper articles that appeared during the last few years of Khotso's life, it seems that he began to talk more about ibangalala than Paul Kruger to visiting journalists. Possibly, then, towards the end the wondrous workings of his best-selling medicine were becoming even more important to Khotso than the financial advice Oom Paul could provide.

Yet, in the face of unwelcome changes and potential loss, there was Bethinja. The attractive Pondoland woman who appeared so dependable and diligent had remained a secure part of his establishment, compared to the unpredictability and waywardness of some of the other key figures in his life.

We have seen that it was as if gifts and attributes that held a special appeal for Khotso, including submissiveness, had been bestowed on Bethinja. With her skill in mixing medicines, she could be trained to play a role in Khotso's business, and over time Khotso may have passed on to her some of his private, specialised knowledge of herbs and potions. There was another secret that lay even closer to Khotso's heart, which he shared with Bethinja alone. She was told where his fortune was closeted away and she was provided with the means of accessing it. Khotso handed over the keys of his safe to her care. 'She was, in fact, the one who was entrusted with the safekeeping of all Khotso's things,' said Lunika.

Bethinja and Khotso had certain qualities in common. Like her partner, Bethinja had the knack of finding her way to certain areas of power. As events unfolded towards the end of Khotso's career, Bethinja seemed to possess an almost intuitive aptitude for turning certain circumstances to her advantage. For a while too, she appeared to share something of the tremendous luck with which Khotso claimed to have been so richly blessed. His favourite son had fallen into her care; now she had been granted control over that which lay close to Khotso's heart: his fortune itself.

Bethinja would come to be known as Khotso's senior wife, although that title actually belonged to MaDlamini. In public, the latter preferred not to cross paths with Bethinja. In private, however, she did not keep secret her feelings towards the young woman who was usurping her status as Khotso's chief consort. MaDlamini and her family members and supporters referred to her rival as *moloi*, the 'witch'; or they ridiculed her nickname, Bethinja, calling her 'Beat-the-dog'. When MaDlamini relocated to Mount Frere, she was not so much acknowledging defeat as biding her time.

But at the same time, MaDlamini was aware of the humiliating side of her situation. From the early days on, a recurrent pattern in Khotso's nature had been to turn individuals, objects and circumstances to his advantage. Once, MaDlamini knew, she had been essential to her husband. She had been at his side as he had made the beginnings of his fortune and she had helped set him up in his career as a herbalist. But as someone who met MaDlamini towards the end of her life said of the situation: 'Khotso's stance seemed to have been that of being flattered by younger modern women more in tune with the new – not the older MaDlamini, who had outgrown her use. As Khotso was now "made", he was calling the shots, as it were.' In fact, MaDlamini and her companions once went so far as to quote the Sotho proverb *Mocheka seliba ha a senoe* (The one who prepares a wellspring doesn't drink from it).

But it was not only MaDlamini who had difficulty with the Pondoland woman who had assumed a central position in the household. MaMjoli said that Bethinja did not see eye to eye with the other wives. It is hardly surprising that there should have been clashes, bearing in mind the distinctive, divergent personalities who found themselves flung together at Mount Nelson. MaMjoli, for instance, was educated, accomplished and confident enough to be frank and forthright. There was the strong-willed Gloria, and those with the advantage of having exceptional youth on their side, like Selina, during her short time at Mount Nelson, and the teenage Nonkqubela. From the early days onwards, the recipe for domestic tensions had been there; but in the final years of Khotso's life, the uneasiness, mistrust and outright hostility between his wives and concubines reached a previously unprecedented pitch, fuelled by ever-intensifying questions about the future. Khotso had reached his seventies and, once the old man was gone, what would happen next? Into whose hands would his fortune fall?

Meanwhile, rumours began to simmer and seethe around Bethinja. It was common knowledge that after Khotso's death, she embarked on a public affair with a married man, Saul Ndzumo, who was to become a minister in Matanzima's cabinet. But during Khotso's day, he worked as a clerk at Quma Funeral Parlour in Lusikisiki. Some allege that before Khotso's death, Ndzumo would visit Mount Nelson, desiring not only to purchase medicines. He also wished to be brought tea by the diligent wife who could always be counted on to serve refreshments to Khotso's visitors. Over the tea tray, some of the gossip went, Ndzumo's and Bethinja's eyes could meet and the possibility of private assignations at some point in the future might hover unspoken between them. Some members of Khotso's household said that they tried to drop hints to the master of the house concerning this, but he refused to listen to them.

Yet again the contradictions in Khotso's nature come to the fore. While he was startlingly astute in most ways, there were a few areas of his life in which he seemed almost wilfully blind. He did not, for instance, wish to consider the fact that Paul Kruger's children would apply their policy of racial separation to him. Moreover, he refused to entertain the notion that his special wife could be capable of transgressions. No doubt Khotso wished to overlook any possible failings Bethinja might possess because he was especially drawn to her and he did not want her to be slighted. Criticism of his favourite wife would also reflect badly on his own judgement. If any of Khotso's wives said anything even remotely critical of Bethinja, Khotso would become very angry. So soon

Khotso, Bethinja and Four Boy
(© Sunday Times)

it became widely known that it was best not to say a word against her.

As Bethinja ascended to an influential position in Mount Nelson, Langa still remained in the picture. This was despite the fact that Khotso had no illusions about his son. Lunika expressed the following opinion: 'Khotso knew Langa to be his son, but he did seem to not trust that Langa would look well after his estate.'

We have seen that Langa spent long periods at a distance from his father, staying on his farms and properties. Yet there was a period when he returned home. In 1971 Langa and his first wife, a woman named Elizabeth Ntombile (later Brown) and referred to by one journalist as Langa's childhood sweetheart, moved into Mount Nelson. Elizabeth's description of the first year of her marriage calls to mind some of Ellen's and Selina's rose-tinted recollections of their early lives with Khotso.

'That was probably the happiest year of my life,' said Elizabeth. 'We had everything we could wish for. . . . Langa was such a wonderful man. Kind and gentle and generous. I will never find another man like him,' she said wistfully. But as with Ellen and Selina, the joy Elizabeth derived from her marriage would prove short-lived. 'The only problems that came between us came when he was drunk, and Langa was drinking more and more,' Elizabeth concluded sadly. She parted company with her husband in 1978.[3]

Bethinja was not impressed with Langa. While she may have resented his lack of resolution and the erratic behaviour that stemmed from his alcoholism, her antipathy to Langa may have stemmed from her awareness that he was the long-standing heir to Khotso's estate. One of Khotso's family members who lived in Mount Nelson during that time recalled the battles over Langa that took place between Bethinja and Khotso. 'Your son is a drunkard!' Bethinja would declare furiously. Thus she repeatedly drew attention to the older son's failings, all the while aware that the younger son, Four Boy, was the new favourite who had fallen into her care.

Khotso was angered by Bethinja's attacks on Langa, resenting criticism of those close to him. Their quarrels about Langa would lead into arguments over Khotso's will. Other members of his household would lurk in the corridors, trying to overhear what they could. If they heard enough, would they be able to discover where Khotso's great fortune would go after his death?

Part Four
1971 and thereafter

CHAPTER 18
The Last Days

Even as he turned seventy-two years old, Khotso did not see himself as a frail and doddering septuagenarian. He proudly proclaimed that he had turned ninety. 'Remembering Khotso on the day he celebrated his ninetieth birthday, I believe that he had convinced himself that he would live forever,' Blades recalled in 1970.

Ironically enough, Blades, who marvelled at Khotso's seemingly miraculous capacity to remain youthful in body and spirit despite his advanced years, provided the best account of all journalists of Khotso's sudden decline.[1] In 1971, Blades was present at Khotso's ninety-first (actually seventy-third) birthday party. Khotso would occasionally seem weary and testy, as if the activity around him was becoming too much for him. Then this would pass, as his ebullient spirits and delight in being the centre of attention would reassert themselves. Later on, Blades heard that Khotso had not been well, but no one was willing to divulge any details to him. It was almost as if Khotso had, at this stage, woven yet another web of secrecy around himself. His body was at last beginning to show its age, but this should on no account be revealed to outsiders. However, during the course of his purported ninety-second (in reality, his seventy-fourth) year, it became impossible for Khotso to conceal the fact that old age and illness had closed in on him. He suffered from high blood pressure and heart trouble. His body was becoming swollen and he had grown so feeble that he was having difficulty walking.

One of Khotso's long-standing acquaintances who visited him around this time, the Transkei building contractor, was struck by the change in him. 'He wasn't his usual shiny-faced self,' he said. 'He was very quiet, and that was different too.'

In early 1972, Khotso suddenly became very ill. His eldest daughter, Patricia, told Blades that this had been such a shock to his family that they had succeeded in accomplishing something that seemed unimaginable. The great inyanga, whose medicines could cure every physical ailment, had been bundled into his Cadillac and borne off, protesting, to a local white doctor, who had diagnosed heart trouble. Drawing on her experience as a nurse, Patricia told Blades that she felt that the treatment had helped. For the first time in his life, Khotso was prepared to submit to a white doctor's medicine. 'But he was terrified of it, especially the intramuscular injections and tablets,' Patricia said.

She told Blades that her father wanted to spend more time with his family and get some rest. However, Khotso also instructed his servants to move a huge safe into Kruger House, the dwelling designated to be his final resting place and the spiritual heart of Mount Nelson itself. Thus, in his declining days, Khotso wished to bring two of the most important aspects of his life together, by placing the safe containing some of his fortune inside his personal sanctum.

Khotso's final months were characterised by some important events and surprises. His last child, Ma-Eleven, was born in February 1972, five months before his death. To her mother MaMjoli's relief, she resembled Khotso. MaMjoli recently told Sylvia Tloti: 'The fact that she looked so much like her father when she was a baby saved me! You will understand that she was born towards the end of her father's life. Therefore many people, the hospital staff included, asked me repeatedly if I was sure that Ma-Eleven was my husband's baby!'

Khotso's physical deterioration affected the old energy that he put into maintaining his business. Blades recalled seeing Khotso sitting in his car in Lusikisiki in early 1972. Khotso was waiting for his driver and he was in so much discomfort that he did not want to get out of his car. Passers-by, seeing Khotso within easy reach, tried asking him for muti. The herbalist brushed them off, sounding annoyed. Later that day, when Blades came to visit him, Khotso said had not been able to make his medicines for a whole year because he had been too ill.

At Mount Nelson that afternoon, Blades saw that even some of the people that Khotso delighted in most, press photographers, were not able to revive his flagging body and spirits. The master of Mount Nelson did not welcome his visitors enthusiastically, with a wide grin of welcome wreathing his round face, and none of the welcoming ceremonies that had once been the trademark of Mount Nelson were staged. Instead, Khotso limped laboriously into the room, bundled in a sheepskin jacket, and collapsed wearily into a chair, his wives cosseting him all the while. Eventually he was prevailed upon to pose outside for photographs, but he only managed to do so with pain and difficulty, staggering out into the front yard on his swollen feet and legs, relying on Bethinja's support.

Khotso's old friend Julius Khoapa told Blades: 'Lots of people think he has been bewitched by relatives who are tired of waiting for his money. And others are asking: "How else can an inyanga get so sick that he can't cure himself?" ' When Blades repeated this speculation to Khotso, he roared with laughter. He also treated as a joke the news that premature reports of his death were already doing the rounds. Once, laughing, he even had to limp to the phone to prove that he was still alive, Blades said.

Years later, gossip of another kind arose. Some hearsay still has it that in the end it was venereal disease that struck Khotso down. Given the fact that it was common knowledge that sex had often been like a game of musical chairs for Khotso, it is not inconceivable that at some point, he might have ended up in the hot seat.

The rumours go even further than this. There are various stories describing how Khotso suffered from venereal disease of almost biblical proportions, as if God was finally punishing him for his godless ways. Some grotesque tales maintain that near the end of his life, Khotso's body was not only swollen but also riddled with worms. This is reminiscent of the divine punishment meted out to the wicked King Herod in the Bible. Like certain other tales concerning Khotso, rather than providing a reliable reflection of actual events, these yarns fulfil a compensatory function. They suggest that wealth of the magnitude of Khotso's, which appeared to go hand in hand with an overweening hubris and, some suggested, may have been obtained under dubious circumstances, did not so much shield its owner against the vicissitudes of life, but rather exposed him to disease and decline of extraordinary proportions.

While Khotso himself would not have regarded his illness as a form of divine castigation, it might at times have felt like a form of punishment inflicted purely by the onset of old age, since his sickness was depriving him of that which he valued in life. In May 1972, one newspaper headline proclaimed: 'Khotso Prefers White Muti'. In the article Khotso bitterly complained that his physical decline was robbing him of his customers, who were losing faith in him when they saw that he had turned, in desperation, to white doctors. 'Only a few people are buying herbs now,' he said. 'They have heard that I am sick and that a doctor is treating me. People want to know why I am not treating myself.'

To make matters worse, Khotso was being deprived of something else that he held dear. 'What I miss most is not being able to drive a car,' he said plaintively. 'I get cramps in my leg and consider myself to be a danger on the road.' As he spoke to the journalist, he wrapped a rug over his swollen legs, propping them up on a heap of cushions. In the eyes of this reporter, the dazzling, impressive backdrop that Khotso had created as a reflection of his own public persona was wearing down along with him. 'He sits all day in a gloomy alcove off an inner dining-room surrounded by faded press cuttings, a broken cuckoo clock and gaudy bric à brac,' the journalist wrote.

In the year before Khotso died, although he did manage to conceive a final child, he was also publicly complaining that his sexual capacity was ebbing away.[2] While he loved driving his Cadillac, sexual activity was not simply a pleasure but a vital component of his existence. What would become of Khotso the Bull now that he was losing what had made him a bull? When the above-mentioned press articles produced near the end of Khotso's life are set alongside one another, the decline of his abilities as a medicine man appears to be connected with the dwindling away of his sexual capacity. Viewed from a certain perspective, it is almost as if his magical snakes, with their sexual as well as spiritual associations, were abandoning him.

There is one lurid story that depicts Khotso's loss of sexual potency in graphic detail. One man from the Lusikisiki area related this tale:

> It is believed that someone put muti in herself so as to make Khotso sick. One well-known muti man from Lusikisiki told me that Khotso had called at his place and told him what his problem was. His penis was abnormally long so he had to tie it to his waist. It was clearly a man-made sickness. He had offered to help him, but Khotso never called him back.

A tale like this is still being told partly because of the prurient fascination it arouses. Yet, although it posits the notion that someone close to Khotso destroyed him from within, his fatal illness was taking hold of him at such a rate that it appeared that no assistance was needed from outside (or, in this case, inside) sources.

When he felt that time might be running out for him, Khotso ventured into alien territory, deciding to go through one of the motions that some churchgoers around him would embark on in times of need. In February 1972, he made a confession to the Reverend L. Nkamba, who was in charge of the Palmerton Methodist mission in Pondoland. Khotso's idea of a confession, however, differed markedly from conventional notions of this procedure and would provide an opportunity for penultimate prank-playing.

Reverend Nkamba was one of the many speakers at Khotso's funeral, and at that stage he had no qualms about revealing the strange confession to which he had been treated. His curiosity excited by the idea of hearing the disclosures of the Pondoland millionaire mystery man, it appears that Nkamba had been hoping that Khotso might let slip the hitherto undisclosed secrets of his fortune.

'He did not explain how he became a millionaire,' Reverend Nkamba said, rather plaintively. 'All he kept saying was, "I love money, I love money" and nothing more.' This was a simple statement of truth on Khotso's part, rather than an expression of regret and remorse. Perhaps Nkamba thought that the latter was the case, because he dutifully attempted to persuade Khotso that he should find another object of devotion. 'I told him that he should first seek the Kingdom of Heaven and all other things would be added unto him,' he related.[3]

While such advice made good sense to Nkamba, Khotso probably felt differently. In the past he had not required the assistance of the kingdom of heaven to obtain his wealth. Instead, he had long proclaimed that he was greater than God, and this had proved good for his business. In addition, if he put God's kingdom before his own, this might lead to another dramatic drop in his clientele, comparable to the way his business had suffered when he had turned away from his own medicines to those of white doctors.

By 11 May 1972, Khotso had declined yet further physically, his body growing even more frail, crippled and distorted, yet his strong-willed, vigorous mind and spirit determinedly asserted themselves. MaMjoli, among others, recalled that 'he was spiritually very strong, despite his age and his health condition'. Blades had these final, comparable impressions of Khotso:

> He wore an old pair of trousers belted but with the top two buttons undone. They just wouldn't meet around his swelling middle. He huddled a cream sheepskin over his stomach, though it was a warm day, and his swollen feet, encased in blue and white woolly slippers, rested gingerly on a pillow.
>
> Pain flickered in his eyes, but his face was still smooth and uncreased and he still had that young-old look that always made it hard to tell his real age. His voice was as strong, as raucous, as

ever. He talked fast and his mind was razor sharp as he discussed cattle prices with Carlie Visagie, who had driven out to Mount Nelson with me.

Though we didn't know it, he was holding court for the last time.

Even right near the end, in his combination of feebleness and forcefulness, Khotso seemed not only paradoxical but also enigmatic. No one present guessed that some of the energy he displayed at the gathering might have been generated by the secret that he was concealing from those around him.

A few months later, when reporting the event that had taken place surreptitiously a day before the party at which Blades was present, the *Weekend World* would blaze the headline 'Khotso Secret Wedding Shock'. On 10 May, Khotso clandestinely married Bethinja in the Lusikisiki magistrate's court, bestowing on her the legal status of his wife. All Khotso's other wives, bound to him in terms of customary law, lacked this advantage. The same newspaper would later describe the marriage as Khotso's 'final dying gift to Bethinja'. Incongruously, Khotso describes himself as a bachelor in the marriage register. Bethinja is recorded as being a forty-three-year-old spinster.[4]

The *Weekend World* displayed a photograph of the newlyweds gazing at each other. Khotso is a huddled, shrunken figure, slumped in a chair and clutching a walking stick. Eyes half closed, his swollen face and body clearly visible, his gaze turns upwards, to his new-wedded spouse. Bethinja wears a wide, excited smile that makes her appear younger than she is. Sitting confidently upright, she seems to tower over her husband. A tall, white ornamented turban adds to her height and gives her a certain regal quality. Like a crown, it reminds the viewer that legally she is now queen of Khotso's establishment. In the article, she is referred to as the '*intandokazi*, his favourite wife'. Her expression as she contemplates the ailing man she has just married is both motherly and speculative, as if she is wondering how long her husband will last and what her newly acquired status will bring her. But publicity of this nature was to erupt long after the marriage. At the time, Khotso wanted to keep his new union a secret. In all likelihood, he could guess that it would tear his household apart.

While Khotso's life was full of unexpected twists and turns, some of the most startling of all were connected to his will. His daughter Patricia told Blades: 'When I questioned him about making a will, he said he knew what he was doing. But I always suspected that he was doing nothing about it.' But there had been a will at one stage. Many years before, Lunika said, he had helped Khotso draw up this document. At that time, Langa was the only son and all Khotso's hopes were still pinned on him. Lunika said to Blades:

> Khotso asked me to witness that he was giving Langa the whole of Mount Nelson, and some other property. . . . But what we failed to do was have Khotso lodge the will with attorneys. He said: 'No, it's finished. I'll arrange for other things myself.' I don't know what happened to it.

Khotso did have a copy of this will lodged with Barclays Bank in Kokstad until 1970, when he removed it.[5] There are some who believe that Khotso removed the will because he had had second thoughts about making Langa his heir. Langa disagreed with this, as did Lunika. They both said that there was another copy of the will, which had been kept in Khotso's safe at Mount Nelson.

But in 1971, a year before Khotso's death, a remarkable development took place that would cast its shadow over the years following his demise. The copy of the will at Mount Nelson was removed from the safe where it had been stowed. Who took it? Khotso himself or the person who least wished to see Langa inherit all? Had the will remained where it was and been removed from the safe after Khotso's death? While questions continue to seethe around the fate of this initial will, drawn up in the days when there was still closeness between father and son, there are many who recall that the keys of Khotso's safe had been placed in Bethinja's keeping.

In early July 1972, even as he was gleefully denying reports that he had expired, Khotso began to realise that soon he might not be in a position to deny those reports. A Lusikisiki lawyer, Chris Swartz, was called in to help him make a will. Blades related that Swartz drove to Mount Nelson and met Khotso, but the meeting proved lengthy and inconclusive. The lawyer eventually had to leave for court before anything could be finalised. He assured Khotso he would return as soon as possible so that matters could be brought to a conclusion. In the meantime, he suggested that his client spend time reflecting on their discussion.

Khotso had always preferred action to reflection. Possibly too he decided that since he was a self-made man, he could take matters into his own hands. There are, however, certain individuals who maintain that Khotso was not acting independently at this critical point. At his side there was his intandokazi, whose anxiety about who would stand to inherit Khotso's vast estate had fuelled domestic tensions for some time. It has been alleged that Bethinja might have taken advantage of Swartz's departure to exert her influence over her ailing husband and manipulate the course of events. Some find this idea plausible because Khotso had left the paperwork to others in the past and so, they claim, he might have chosen to delegate decisions concerning his final document to someone else. It has been suggested that Khotso may have thought that if he did as Bethinja suggested, he could put an end to their arguments, put the problem of his estate behind him and not let it clutter what remained of his life.

This has been disputed by others, who argue that Khotso knew exactly what he wanted and would not have allowed himself to be swayed by anyone else. Stubborn and single-minded, he decided that his own affections and desires should dictate his decisions. Blades, for one, was of the opinion that Khotso's preferences tended in Bethinja's direction anyway, since he had bestowed on her a status that would place her in a far stronger position than any of her co-wives. Then there was Four Boy, who had been in Bethinja's care for several years and had become Khotso's favoured son. Yet there was no will to ensure that they would inherit the estate and some believed that Khotso decided he needed to remedy the situation.

Khotso's initial will, naming Langa as his heir, had been professionally printed. 'It was a beautiful thing, in triplicate,' Lunika had said admiringly, recalling it long after Khotso's death. The second will, composed on 7 July, after the meeting with Swartz, was a completely different affair. It was handwritten in an exercise book. Khotso dictated it to his nephew and sometime treasurer, Bethuel Motaung, who acted as scribe. The pages are crammed with Bethuel's spiky, somewhat schoolboyish handwriting, while at the end there is a large, wobbly signature that dominates the page. Nonetheless, there is something deeply impressive about this document. As Blades put it, this final will 'had the majesty of a proclamation by a medieval monarch'.

Khotso's distinctive, forceful voice, its authoritative quality weirdly emphasised by heavy, distorted archaisms as well as rambling, mangled formal pronouncements, comes through firmly in the opening declaration:

> Mr Khotso Sethuntsa, of Mount Nelson Farm. Here is where I put my which or my Will, the one who will be put in the main Will, the names of them are: –
>
> 1) Four Boy Sethuntsa: Date of birth: 21/8/63.
>
> 2) Nomalizo Sethuntsa [Bethinja] she is the herdgirl which is going to look after Four Boy which is the Head, Fourboy is going to be in the career of this Lady.
>
> Here at Mount Nelson Farm is the place for only Four Boy Sethuntsa and Nomalizo Sethuntsa.

The will went on to state that the money kept in the safe at Mount Nelson was intended for Four Boy alone. Throughout the will, this child's name is repeated, entrenching his status as Khotso's heir. Then, alongside his name, Bethinja's proper name is reiterated. 'This woman Nomalizo Sethuntsa is the control of everything which belongs for this boy,' Khotso asserted near the beginning of the will, which went on to emphasise Bethinja's authority. At times, Khotso's ponderous, commanding tone carried an underlying note of warning. It was as if, even after his death, he would remain aware of what took place on his property, and those who did not act in accordance with his wishes would bring the weight of his displeasure down on themselves, as is evident in the following dictum: 'The one who may which to interfere with Nomalizo Sethuntsa. he or she must stay fare from this Erf at Lusikisiki because I give he power at everythings at Lusikisiki this Nomalizo Sethuntsa.'[6]

This handwritten will was Khotso's wedding gift to Bethinja, some believed. It was riddled with strange, convoluted expressions and sprinkled with spelling errors, like a large, sagging wedding cake crammed with dubious bits of fruit of indeterminate age. It would not be entirely unfair to describe it as an ill-made wedding cake, since it had not been signed on every page and was thus not legally valid.

Perhaps the handwritten will was meant to be an outline for a proper, legal document that Swartz could draw up. On the other hand, Khotso might have intended the will he dictated to Bethuel Motaung to stand as it was, as an eleventh-hour means of ensuring that Bethinja and Four Boy would inherit the estate. Whatever the case, it does appear that, having watched his nephew transcribe his words, page after page, into an exercise book, Khotso felt that he had done what was necessary for the time being. He may have believed that he was still the master of his own destiny, with sufficient time at his disposal. This indeed was the impression he created when Swartz phoned him some days later. The lawyer told Blades that he told Khotso that they should meet as soon as possible to continue their business. He conveyed a sense of urgency, but his client did not see the need for haste. 'Oh man! My leg is so painful,' he cried. 'Make it Sunday instead. We'll spend the whole day on the will and finish it.'

But according to Blades, Swartz never saw Khotso alive again. The old man's sufferings intensified, and he was to spend the rest of his days in semi-comatose anguish in a hospital bed in Durban. In this way, the groundwork was laid for the bitter battle that would take place thereafter.

In mid-July, Khotso suffered a heart attack, and he was finally prevailed upon to depart from his beloved mansion to Durban, where he entered the sterile, impersonal realm of Shifa Hospital. This was a step he had resisted for a long time. Despite the increasing seriousness of his condition, he had not wanted to leave Mount Nelson any earlier, because he felt that this could have a damaging effect on his domestic affairs.[7] A few of his wives, including Bethinja and MaMjoli, escorted him. Khotso succeeded, however, in making sure that his journey to Durban would be remembered by all who witnessed it. He did not wish to appear an old, dying man being borne off to hospital, but rather a national dignitary embarking on a state visit to a city. Blades described how Khotso and his entourage departed for Durban in a cavalcade of his favourite cars: a Chevrolet, a Pontiac, a Ford, a Dodge and, of course, his Cadillac.

When Khotso arrived at Shifa Hospital, he was unable to walk to his private ward and his body was so distorted and swollen that he could not be fitted into a wheelchair. Instead, Blades reported, he had to be carried to his bed. The way in which his body had let him down to such an extent may well have been humiliating for Khotso, who had always been proud of his physical might and what he liked to depict as his limitless power to defy age and decrepitude.

While he had sometimes chosen to go barefoot during his career, Khotso was determined to die with his boots on. There is a photograph of him lying semi-conscious in his hospital bed, with the heavy working boots in which he strode across his estates protruding from the bedclothes. Another photograph from the same article depicts Khotso lying sweating and semi-conscious in his bed, while Bethinja, all wifely solicitude, poses for the cameras, her hand on her husband's brow. She smiles, prettily and anxiously, her bright, fresh face the antithesis of the closed, exhausted features of her husband.[8]

As he lay in bed, Khotso remained concerned about his prized possessions, his luxury cars, parked outside the hospital. Apart from the bodyguards he had posted outside his ward and personal aides deputised to stand by on a daily basis in the hospital grounds, even more bodyguards were tasked with the special duty of watching over his cars.[9]

Khotso dying with his boots on in Shifa Hospital in Durban. Bethinja leans on his bed, and MaMjoli stands holding Ma-Eleven. (©BAHA. Photo by Drum photographer)

The cars were so much on Khotso's mind that in defiance of the doctors who had strictly instructed him not to move from his bed, Khotso tried to rise up, wanting to stagger outside to check on them. Blades described how his wives managed to pin him down against the pale blue hospital sheets, convinced that if their husband tried to drag himself outside, this might be the last action he undertook on earth. Khotso worried about his other belongings too, including the livestock on his properties and, above all, his money. He warned Bethinja repeatedly not to remove any of his wealth from the house after his death.

Reporters, Blades included, periodically managed to make their way past Langa and Bethuel, who kept watch outside the hospital, and past Khotso's bodyguards, who stood guard outside the ward, then past his aides, who frequently kept a vigil by his bedside, to the man himself. Some journalists hoped that Khotso's deathbed might be the place where some of the answers to the riddles that had surrounded him all his career would be found. Just as the thought of his cars had galvanised

Khotso into an attempt to take action, so in the presence of journalists he managed to summon up a semblance of his old self-assured persona, even succeeding in cracking a few jokes with them. But in general, visitors were discouraged.

'We try not to let him have visitors because the doctors say it's not good for him,' Bethinja told Blades. 'He loves people so much that he gets excited and wants to jump off the bed.'

Khotso had become so sick that he had to be spoon-fed. He had always loved eating good solid meals, with rich fatty meat and gravy that he liked to claim was laced with ibangalala; now having to swallow small mouthfuls of food seemed little more than an additional form of anguish. An attempt was even made to force-feed him.[10] Then, to make matters worse, Khotso was struck so severely by asthma attacks that he had to have oxygen tubes fastened to his face. Once again Bethinja and MaMjoli had to hold his arms fast, because he hated the tubes so much that he sometimes tried to rip them away. Every now and then, people passing along the hospital corridors would hear bellows of pain from Khotso the Bull in extremis.

Oddly enough, Khotso's element, water, seemed to have turned against him, drowning him rather than charging him with supernatural power. 'The doctor has told us he is full of water inside his body and his heart is sinking in it,' Bethinja said to Blades. 'And he is swollen from the waist down. And the skin has begun peeling from his lower limbs.'

At this stage, as he confronted the prospect of his imminent death, Khotso prepared himself for this in a manner in keeping with the way in which he had lived his life.

CHAPTER 19
Third Death and Final Party

In years long gone by, Khotso had liked to claim that he had died twice and returned from the dead with the aid of his miraculous elixir of life. Now, however, he sensed that his death was imminent and he knew that none of his medicines could bring him back from the grave. So Khotso began planning the last great social gathering over which he would preside: his own funeral. Laughter had been so much part of his life that he did not like to think of people weeping the last time they gathered round him. His funeral should be an occasion where people could bid farewell to him without sadness, he told Bethinja.[1]

In the meantime, there was the physical place over which Khotso had presided and for which he longed: Mount Nelson. Little did he realise that since his departure, his household had begun to change shape. News of his secret wedding to Bethinja had seeped out, shocking and dismaying his wives and concubines. Finally, after years of waiting and wondering, the great question of who stood to inherit Khotso's fortune after his death seemed to have been resolved. Many of the women who had spent years playing out the roles of loyal and submissive wives for Khotso's visitors felt that there was little point in continuing the performance. They staged a mass walkout.

One newspaper went so far as to claim that sixteen of Khotso's twenty-three wives abandoned him as he lay dying.[2] As with the article indicating that Khotso's physical decline led to his loss of potency in both an entrepreneurial and an erotic sense, there is a certain degree of *schadenfreude* in this piece, emphasised by this hyperbole. Like the former article, it conveys an underlying conviction that Khotso's excessive, extravagant lifestyle was bound to end in distress and defeat. Pride always comes before a fall, these articles seem to suggest.

As the evening shadows lengthened into darkness on 25 July, Khotso's serpents deep in the Mzintlava did not stir. Neither did red snow fall in the Malutis; nor did the inkanyamba sweep through the sky on storm wings, wreaking havoc now that the man who had controlled it had let slip its leash. Even Paul Kruger's spirit did not awaken, disturbed, in Kruger House. But there are still those who like to tell how some of these things took place. Khotso's heart began to fail, and he battled for breath to speak. A doctor made it possible for him to gasp a few more breaths before he turned his head, closed his eyes and stopped breathing.[3]

A reporter from *Drum* was in the ward during Khotso's last hours. According to Blades, he did not describe how speech almost failed the old man towards the end, despite the skill with which he had harnessed the magic of words throughout his career. What the reporter swore he recalled, however, was that during his last hours Khotso softly and cryptically murmured, 'Kruger millions . . .', leaving one of his greatest mysteries as a legacy in the minds of those who were at his bedside near the very end.

But there is another, more dramatic account of the way Khotso met his end, a story that some people in Pondoland still tell, often with horrified fascination. Khotso eventually got carried away by his powers, they insist. He paraded around Pondoland, inciting others – especially young innocents – to blasphemy, in order to vaunt himself. One Lusikisiki man related: 'He drove around the countryside, maybe seeing boys who were herding cattle. He'd stop the car, get out and ask the boys: "Who's greater – me or God?" The boys would say, "You!"' Eventually God, wearied of this behaviour, struck Khotso down by lightning.

There is a narrative symmetry here: since the stories started after Khotso used a storm to punish an opponent, it seems fitting that this tale should depict how his career ended with defeat at the hands of a being whose control over the elements was even stronger than his own. This tale, like various other stories concerning the disasters that befell Khotso, suggests that ultimately the average, ordinary individual who lives out his or her life on a more mundane level is less likely to meet so spectacularly disastrous an end.

Khotso himself might well have preferred the dramatic fantasy version of his demise to expiring, old and enfeebled, from heart failure in hospital. He may rather have had it believed that he had been taken out in an epic conflict with the ultimate adversary.

Such were the stories. But Khotso's family concerned themselves with practicalities: his body needed to be laid to rest. Determined to follow his wish that there should be no tears at this event, his family planned what a somewhat bewildered journalist described as 'a swinging funeral', to be held in the colourful splendour of Mount Nelson. Guests were instructed not to wear black, and various female family members planned to don the distinctive orange dresses, a number of which had been left behind by Khotso's departing wives. Although the most colourful person of all would be attending the funeral in his coffin, at least his family could ensure that there would be some brightness at the event.

In terms of scale, Khotso's last big party at Mount Nelson would outstrip the preparatory arrangements for his annual Kruger Day celebrations. Even the local police, who, as the representatives of the Bantustan authorities, would have been excluded from many Transkei events, were drawn into Khotso's feast. They lent a hand, shooting several oxen, which were to be roasted; in addition, a dozen sheep were slaughtered and hundreds of chickens were prepared. A former caterer was called in to assist, since thousands of mourners were expected. 'There is going to be tons of food – tons and tons of it,' she said.[4] Khotso had always made sure his guests' plates were overloaded with food; his family maintained this practice at his funeral.

One of Khotso's most trusted aides, Mr William Golela, the supervisor of Khotso's property at Mngqesha, near King William's Town, and grandiosely described in one newspaper as Khotso's chief induna and head of his vast Ciskei Property Investments,[5] was now at Mount Nelson, assisting with the funeral arrangements. Before his death, Khotso had summoned Golela to his headquarters and entrusted him with the smooth running of the household in his absence.[6] Now that his master's absence had proved to be permanent, Golela's first major task was to see to it that he was laid to rest in a manner he would have wished. Grateful that Khotso had inspired loyalty in an individual as dependable as Golela, some family members welcomed his presence at this time.

Meanwhile, Khotso rested, first in the Kokstad mortuary. Here he was revisiting a friend from his boyhood, French K. Mbotho, long established as a successful undertaker. The day before the funeral, Khotso was brought home, where he lay in state with Golela standing guard at the head of his coffin.[7]

Although Khotso had been the opposite of a devout Christian, there was a flurry of competitive activity among ministers from various dominations, all of whom phoned Mount Nelson, each of them eager to be the one to preside over the funeral of the legendary Khotso Sethuntsa.[8] Finally, possibly guided by the spirit of Khotso, who had always preferred excess to judicious restraint, the family decided that they would invite five ministers, as well as a representative from the Methodist Church, and hold an interdenominational service.[9]

The funeral took place on 6 August. On a day so bright and sunny that Khotso himself might have had a hand in it, thousands of people, both black and white, came streaming to the last big event he had organised. The guests included the commissioner-general, Hans Abraham, and the Lusikisiki magistrate, Nolan Webb. Unsurprisingly, Khotso's old friend Chief Botha Sigcau came to pay his respects as well. Other dignitaries included members of the Transkei government, including the minister of agriculture and forestry, N. P. Bulube, and seconded white officials.

There were also large numbers of journalists, covering what they believed was the final stage in the Khotso saga. Little did they know that there would be plenty of drama to follow.[10]

The funeral was opened with the traditional singing and dancing that Khotso had so loved, performed by 'colourful Pondo tribesmen' (in the words of one newspaper article).[11] As guests poured into Mount Nelson, there were enthusiastic reunions between Khotso's patients and disciples. A number of them were returning after many years to pay their last respects to their one-time healer or teacher. Even Lunika was present, invited to speak at the closing as Khotso's erstwhile great friend and prime minister. As soon as the speeches were over, the feasting started and continued late into the evening.

Khotso lay present in his coffin, which, like his cars, was designed to impress all those who witnessed him travelling past in it. It was an immense, costly, steel sarcophagus, far larger than his short body. President John Kennedy had been buried in a similar casket.[12] Khotso had also presided over a mighty empire. Although he had never attained conventional political power, he had been perceived as a potentate in the phantom realms of the paranormal.

Khotso would have been disappointed that there were only a few wives present at his funeral, clad in their ceremonial orange robes and turbans. At one stage, Bethinja led a group of these women, as if she was asserting her right to preside over household affairs. Most of the time, however, she stayed secluded from public scrutiny behind closed doors.[13]

The speeches at the funeral kept returning, in fascination, to the strange, perplexing aspects of Khotso's life, yet those who knew him well reiterated that he was essentially a kindly, straightforward man. It was apparent that they seemed to find it hard to pin down the 'real' Khotso, underneath the flamboyant persona.

One such case was Botha Sigcau. He began by describing how he had arrived at Khotso's house after having been told many incredible tales about the man, only to discover how far-fetched many of those yarns were. Yet immediately thereafter, he produced an astonishing story of his own. He had sat in Mount Nelson waiting for Khotso, Sigcau said, when a chill wind suddenly arose, freezing his hands. Then Khotso appeared and took his hand, warming it, and the cold breeze vanished, as if by magic. 'He was a very kind man,' Sigcau concluded, '. . . a man of great love.'[14]

In his role as master of ceremonies, C. M. Mancotywa might have attempted to draw together the diverse speeches by providing some kind of authoritative insight into Khotso and his life. Instead, he flung out a number of bewildering questions, compounding the sense that the funeral served to emphasise the riddles surrounding Khotso. The funeral had a strange, disorderly side to it, as if now that Khotso had departed from life, the carefully regulated pattern that he had succeeded in imposing on his eccentric, heterogeneous kingdom was collapsing. At one point, Mancotywa had to remind the crowd that this was a funeral, not a bioscope (movie house), as people jostled around the coffin, hoping to glimpse Khotso's body.[15]

'Khotso Goes to Rest as Police Battle,' one newspaper headline proclaimed. Hundreds of eager, agitated mourners tried to cram themselves into the small interior of Kruger House so that they would be able to tell others that they had witnessed Khotso Sethuntsa's last appearance on the face of this earth. Yelling, pushing and shoving, a crowd of people tried to force their way inside, smashing a window and compelling someone inside Kruger House to bolt the door against them. Shouting just as loudly as the mob, a group of black policemen fought against the wave of people that was threatening to overwhelm them. Meanwhile, inside Kruger House, the face of Paul Kruger gazed on sternly, above the freshly excavated grave his acolyte would occupy.[16]

Even before this chaos had broken out, when pall-bearers carrying the coffin approached Kruger House, the door was found to be locked. A member of the household managed to force open a window and clamber into the building, then unlock the door from the inside. Finally, when the coffin had made its way into Kruger House, to the amazement of many onlookers the undertaker opened the casket and injected Khotso's body with embalming fluid.[17] At the spectacle of his corpse, some tall tales that Khotso had not really died wound down to a halt; but other stories would continue freewheeling through Pondoland and parts of South Africa, right until this day. It was impossible to quench the legends that Khotso had somehow managed to outwit death and that his funeral was a piece of carefully calculated trickery on his part, designed to further his own mysterious purposes.

Before his death, Khotso had told those close to him that he wanted to go to his grave with some of his money. This wish was respected and four thousand rands were placed in the coffin beside him.[18] He had only asked for one thousand rands, but his daughter Patricia felt that this would not be sufficient: 'Since we knew how fond he was of his money, we thought he wouldn't be satisfied in his grave unless we gave him more than he asked for,' she told Blades.

Had Khotso perhaps nurtured the hope that his money would somehow retain its importance in the afterlife? Or maybe, like the Egyptian pharaohs, he could not imagine embarking on the loneliest journey of all without his most precious possessions. The red, blue, white and green beaded coat that Khotso so loved was laid over him. Next, having been draped in the colours of Kruger's republic, the headband of white beads, which Khotso's followers wear to this day, was laid on his forehead and a crystal scarf (which, in the imaginations of some, became transformed into a neckpiece of diamonds) was placed on his chest. Finally, Golela, as one of Khotso's most trusted aides, was accorded the honour of placing Khotso's ceremonial trappings and walking stick in the coffin, before closing the lid.[19]

Even though Khotso's funeral had not convinced everyone that he had expired, news of his demise was sending out ripples to encompass not only his family but the region in which he lived and worked. Lusikisiki's tourist trade would be hard hit, complained Mr Dolf Botha, the manager of the town's only hotel.[20] Proprietors of local shops and cafés were not pleased either. Tour groups to Mount Nelson invariably contained a number of hungry and thirsty people, which had been good for business. But the effect that Khotso's death would have on his herbalist practice engaged the interest of the public even more. Since the business still remained in place, outsiders began wondering which member of his household would take over. In all likelihood, that individual would inherit Khotso's fortune along with his practice. Speculation began to mount in the newspapers. It was almost as if two leading racehorses in a high-profile contest with a great prize at stake were being scrutinised. Unlike certain Durban July races in which Khotso had predicted the winner with ease, there was no clearly established favourite.

Bethinja, ensconced at Mount Nelson with her working knowledge of herbalism, seemed poised to take over from Khotso. Certain journalists felt that, as Khotso's most highly favoured wife, she would be the logical person to inherit his practice. To other reporters, however, the twenty-three-year-old Langa, the eldest son, seemed the firm favourite. The young man told reporters just before his father's funeral that Khotso had taught him medicine from an early age, trying to create the impression that his father intended his mantle to fall on him.[21] Already the battle lines were being drawn, although no one in Khotso's household could foresee the scale of the conflict that lay ahead.

CHAPTER 20
The Boedel

The Afrikaans word *boedel*, meaning 'estate of a deceased person', calls to mind the English slang expression *boodle*, denoting a large amount of money. Whether one opts for the formal Afrikaans term or the casual English idiom, it is almost inevitable that, behind any significant amount of wealth that no longer belongs to its original owner, there follows, like the tail of a comet, a host of the needy and the greedy, the deserving and the undeserving, all clamorously asserting their own claims to the great shining fortune to which they feel attached. For years after Khotso's death, a number of his family members became caught up in a messy, acrimonious scramble for the money, possessions and properties that he had left behind him.

Even before Khotso was laid in the ground, journalists were eagerly asking who had been chosen as Khotso's heir. The family remained tight-lipped, stating firmly that this was a private domestic affair.[1] In fact, the awareness had begun to dawn on many of those connected to Khotso's household that there was no certainty about who exactly stood to inherit the estate. A week before the funeral, it began to be openly reported that Khotso had died without drawing up a proper will. 'This is going to be a tremendous problem to sort out as no conclusions had been reached about the will,' a close associate of the family announced.[2] This was to prove a remarkable understatement. Meanwhile, some of

Khotso's runaway wives had started trickling back to Mount Nelson to await developments. 'Six came back after his death – even those I did not know,' said Bethinja disgustedly.

Even more disastrous news erupted thereafter. Some people firmly believed that Khotso could have been worth as much as R34 million; at the opposite end of the spectrum, others maintained that he probably possessed around R4 million.[3] Yet this was nothing near the truth. As one press headline trumpeted: 'Khotso's Millions Were a Myth.'[4] Other South African papers carried similar news. The inventory of Khotso's estate, drawn up by Chris Swartz and completed on 19 June 1973, indicates that, despite all the farms, impressive houses, flashy cars, gold coins, putative diamonds, suitcases full of bundles of banknotes and heaps of money poured out onto the floor to impress visitors, Khotso was not nearly as wealthy as he had proclaimed.

According to the inventory, Khotso's total assets did not even amount to R1 million. These included firstly his properties, with their furniture, carpets and crockery (all the glassware and chinaware with which Khotso had loved to surround himself was valued at only R294.10); and secondly his vehicles, livestock and cash. Khotso Sethuntsa, the legendary Pondoland millionaire, was worth only a trifling R329 176.45. Just under 80 per cent of this derived from the valuation of his fixed properties with title deeds (twenty-eight in total), although most of these erven were estimated to be worth only a few thousand rands each.[5]

In some quarters, heads began to nod in understanding. The fact that Khotso's estate had amounted to so little after his death was cited as undeniable evidence of his involvement in ukuthwala, proof of the belief that wealth accumulated without the blessing of the ancestors does not survive the accumulator. But as far as many of Khotso's friends and family members were concerned, the conclusion Swartz had arrived at seemed even more incredible than the tall tales the old man had been so fond of spinning. Khotso had publicly flaunted his wealth for decades. He had repeatedly reminded all who visited Mount Nelson that a fortune lay right under their noses, closeted away in the house. How, then, could they accept that most of it had not really existed?

There were those who insisted that nobody could be sure where the Pondoland millionaire, ever anxious that someone might seek to steal some of his money, had stowed away his wealth. It seemed plausible that some of Khotso's riches might have been concealed underground like the legendary Kruger millions. In the course of Swartz's methodical trawl through Mount Nelson in search of Khotso's assets, it did transpire that he had money stashed away in odd, unexpected places. Khotso's daughter Patricia told Blades that she knew of one such place and dropped a hint to the exhausted and bewildered Swartz. His search then took him up into the rafters of Mount Nelson, where he discovered a suitcase full of banknotes tucked away among the beams.

Khotso's brother, Mosala Jack Sethuntsa, knew that Khotso had buried large amounts of money, but he had kept the whereabouts of his fortune a secret: 'I had very little time to visit my brother, and even when I visited him, he never discussed personal matters concerning his moneys, especially his hidden money.'[6]

Yet it was becoming widely agreed that a substantial amount of Khotso's fortune had lain in the most obvious place of all: Mount Nelson, where he had stored his money to prevent it from being taken away by the tax collectors. Lunika and some other informants believe that Khotso's estate amounted to so little because by the time the inventory of his property began, he had already been stripped of a considerable amount of his wealth by far more rapacious hands than those of the receiver of inland revenue. A number of people close to Khotso alleged that there were certain individuals, either members of his household or people who could easily gain access to Mount Nelson, who helped themselves to some of his fortune when Khotso was no longer at hand to prevent them. Lunika said that he had been informed that many of Khotso's Kruger rands had simply vanished.

Even Swartz declared himself mystified by the results of his inventory. He believed there should have been more money, gold coins

One of the best-known and most widely reproduced photographs of Khotso. (©Daily Dispatch)

and diamonds than what he found. He said that there had been diamonds stowed in little bags on shelves in Mount Nelson and gold sovereigns in canvas rolls, but these never turned up when he began his cataloguing of Khotso's assets.[7]

One of the best-known press photographs of Khotso in the 1960s shows him brandishing huge bundles of banknotes and beaming gleefully, enthusiasm dancing in his eyes. Could his delighted grin perhaps have been aroused by the fact that he was successfully pulling off one of his biggest tricks of all: convincing gullible visitors that he possessed wealth on such a grandiose scale that it exceeded their own wildest imaginings?

One person who was not surprised by the fact that Khotso's money fell far short of the millions of which he had boasted was Lunika, who had acquired considerable insight into many aspects of Khotso's financial affairs during his years as prime minister. Khotso's greatest wealth lay in his houses and properties, Lunika said, but when it came to hard cash, that was an entirely different story. 'I would say his money would easily have been in the region of ... let me see ... four hundred thousand rands,' he said.

Yet to this day, this type of judicious, measured assessment of Khotso's financial position has not been widely endorsed. Many who knew Khotso still find it hard to accept that he was never as wealthy as he claimed. He had, for instance, been able to produce suitcases full of banknotes regularly at the Kokstad Agricultural Fair. So, like the tales of the Kruger connection, accounts of the millions that he possessed still remain one of the most persistent and durable parts of the Khotso legend.

Under such circumstances, stories persisted that Khotso had somehow been robbed of his wealth after his death. Bethinja, who had the keys to Khotso's safe and knew exactly where some of her husband's most valuable items were hidden, was especially the target of suspicion. Some did indeed defend her innocence. But both her detractors and defenders still make reference to one particular event when Bethinja found herself an unwitting participant or, a few alleged, a willing accomplice.

Days after the funeral, the event that Khotso had constantly feared ever since he made his fortune came to pass: robbers attempted to make off with his money. To make matters worse, individuals Khotso had deeply trusted, his loyal henchman Golela or, some have alleged, Bethinja herself, were involved in this. But in Bethinja's and Golela's respective versions of what took place, related to the police, in court and to the press, each sought to protect her or his own innocence by pinning the blame on the other.

Firstly, Bethinja related that she discovered that her duplicate key to the main safe had been either lost or stolen. She decided to move the money from this safe to another vault where it could be stored more securely. There were so many bags in the safe, which was located in the garage, that she called on Golela, the gatekeeper at Mount Nelson and his assistant to help her. Bethinja and the three men stuffed banknotes into pillowcases and coins into a trunk, intending to carry them to a safe in Khotso's old bedroom.

Bethinja said that she led the way to the room, carrying the pillowcases full of banknotes. She had turned round to see Golela making his way towards the gate, clutching both pillowcases. She cried out for help and the gatekeeper and his assistant set off after the loyal retainer turned rogue, who was vanishing into the darkness. They caught up with Golela and snatched the pillowcases from him. But then, Golela claimed, the would-be cops turned robbers, making off with the money themselves.

In the meantime, the police had been summoned by Bethinja. Golela informed them that he thought Bethinja was trying to move some of Khotso's wealth into a private hiding place, so that it would not be included in Swartz's inventory of the estate. Because he believed that it was his duty to intervene, he had taken a pillowcase full of money and made away with it for safekeeping.[8]

Despite their protestations of innocence, all three men were accused of theft. They appeared in the Lusikisiki magistrate's court and were found guilty of stealing. Golela was sentenced to two and a half years in jail, the others to twenty-eight months each.[9] The failure of the robbery caused no great surprise, since it was widely believed that Khotso had been monitoring the goings-on in his home from his spiritual panopticon in Kruger House and had taken action against the would-be thieves.

One of the most impressive symbols of Khotso's affluence remained intact at Mount Nelson: his beloved cars. The first major clash between Khotso's favourite wife and the son who had once been all-important to him erupted around the cars. Lunika compiled two scrapbooks of photographs and press cuttings dealing with Khotso and the events that took place after his death. Beneath one photograph, he neatly inscribed in felt-tipped pen: 'Bethinja in luxury'. The picture displays Khotso's Cadillac, with Bethinja's small, sleek face framed in the window, her dark eyes watchful.

Langa verbally and physically attacked the woman he had come to regard as his rival and foe, accosting Bethinja and denouncing her for making private use of his father's cars. She was keeping company with strange men and using Khotso's cars for the convenience of her male consorts, he shouted, all righteous indignation. Then, Langa admitted, he became so angry that he grabbed Bethinja and shoved her against a pole. Worse was to follow, Bethinja maintained. The following month Langa stormed into Mount Nelson with a knife in his hand. Bethinja shrieked for help, and some men who were working in the house came rushing to her aid. Langa was charged with assault, fined and ordered to stay far away from Mount Nelson.[10] The strain was telling on Bethinja too, who was becoming more and more fragile emotionally and physically.

Within Khotso's kaleidoscopic ménage, two more different personalities could hardly have been brought into conflict. Where he could, Langa kept to the shadows. When he moved out of them, he carried within him the shadows of his own insecurities, and these stunted his social and emotional development. Bethinja, on the other hand, who had always thrived in a world of brightness, light and colour, now basked in the limelight as Khotso's purported favourite, his legal wife and the new mistress of Mount Nelson.

Maintaining this position was not proving easy. Bethinja was finding herself the focal point of tensions from other sources apart from Langa. Just as cracks would gradually begin to appear in the blue and white paintwork that had been touched up so carefully in Khotso's day, so long-concealed frictions and antipathies among Mount Nelson's inhabitants were beginning to surface.

'Things were a bit tense in the household,' MaMjoli admitted, 'probably because the person who had brought us together in the first place was not there any more.' In Khotso's day, Mount Nelson had been a place where people converged for large gatherings and celebrations. After her husband's death, MaMjoli said, separation and isolation seemed the order of the day. Like various others, she chose to withdraw into her own part of the house. 'Things were so bad that I stayed in my own room with my children,' she said. 'I used my own kitchen and did my own cooking.'

With its network of winding corridors and honeycombs of rooms, Mount Nelson resembled a hive devoid of its queen – or rather king – bee. Bethinja now wished to establish herself as its queen. During Khotso's lifetime, she had not got on well with many of the other wives, but at this juncture the situation began worsening. Before Khotso's death, Bethinja had managed to hide her real nature, some people have said.

Others speculated that Bethinja might have initially been an essentially innocent and fun-loving woman who had now decided that the time had come to take on a new, forceful and unyielding persona.

Meanwhile, her love affair with Saul Ndzumo had become public. Yet Bethinja persisted in behaving as if her deceased husband was, in a sense, still at her side, in support of her claim to his physical and spiritual inheritance: his estate and his practice as a herbalist. While many who had been close to Khotso were offended by this, certain double standards could have fuelled condemnation of Bethinja's behaviour too. When he was alive, Khotso had thought nothing of engaging in numerous infidelities, but he had never been the target of the type of disapprobation to which Bethinja was being subjected. It was as if Bethinja's affair with Ndzumo was being held up as proof that she was dishonouring Khotso's memory.

As the ornate clocks in Mount Nelson ticked away the months and then the years, tensions were mounting in Khotso's houses and on his properties scattered across Pondoland and East Griqualand. From mid-1973 until early 1974, the inquiry into Khotso's estate and his heirs was postponed month after month. Finally, in mid-March 1974, the inquiry commenced in the Lusikisiki magistrate's court.

At the opening of the inquiry, Bethinja arrived radiating confidence and chanting one of Khotso's favourite songs. She was resplendent in the bright traditional attire that she loved, adorned with beautifully crafted beads. It was as if she was convinced that victory would be hers and she was seeking to instil this conviction in the minds of others.[11] However, her initial self-assurance and finery would not imbue her with the fortitude to carry her through the legal proceedings.

The presiding magistrate, Nolan Webb, announced that, firstly, Khotso's rightful heir had to be established. The inquiry was proceeding according to African custom, in terms of which Khotso's first-born legitimate son would inherit his estate. Next, Khotso's dependants needed to be identified, since they were entitled to support from his assets.[12]

The principal area of uncertainty was the nature of both Ellen's and Bethinja's relationships with Khotso.[13] If Khotso's relationship with Ellen had been yet another of his sexual liaisons rather than a marriage, then Langa's position as the oldest legitimate son and Khotso's heir would be invalidated. On the other hand, if Bethinja's status as Khotso's favourite wife could be proven false, then her claim to the estate would be undermined. The legal waters became murky, because Khotso the Bull had not only been surrounded by a herd of wives and children, but as the subheading of an article in the *Sunday Times Extra* would later put it, there had been a 'continuous circulation of concubines'.[14] This complicated matters, since both Ellen's and Bethinja's positions, as wife and principal wife respectively, were called into question by different witnesses testifying at the inquiry. A number of Khotso's wives and ex-wives were present, some of whom gave evidence, believing that they were entitled to a share of Khotso's worldly goods once they had been established as his dependants or that they stood to gain from supporting either Bethinja or Langa.

Someone who had faded from Khotso's life long ago unexpectedly resurfaced: Ellen Moyce (formerly Ellen Jones). In press photographs, her face is faded and careworn, yet still carrying traces of her delicate youthful prettiness. Not everyone was delighted to see Ellen after her long absence. Some people muttered that it was solely the lure of money that had drawn her back. She had been away from Khotso's household for decades. Ellen's reappearance, just at the point when the possibility of her inheriting wealth as Langa's mother might be imminent, exacerbated the tensions and unhappiness already brewing in Khotso's extended family.

Ellen asserted that she was Khotso's legal wife, married to him by traditional custom, because he had paid lobola for her. Langa was Khotso's legitimate son and, as such, ought to be his heir. Then, to the surprise of some, MaDlamini testified in support of Ellen's claim. She might have chosen to do so in order to oppose her arch-rival, Bethinja, although the fact that she had helped raise Langa could have influenced her decision as well.[15]

Another individual who, like Ellen, had for years been an important member of Khotso's household before setting off in his own direction was present to throw his weight behind Langa's cause. Lunika avowed that MaDlamini, not Bethinja, had been the number one wife.[16] Much later, when asked why he had chosen to support Langa, Lunika stated simply that he had been guided by African tradition.

On the other hand, there were those who supported Bethinja, such as Khotso's brother, Mosala Jack Sethuntsa. He claimed, among other things, that Khotso had presented Four Boy to a meeting of several people, announcing that he was his future heir.[17]

Yet another face from Khotso's past appeared at the inquiry. In a newspaper article covering the inquiry in March 1974, next to a photograph of Ellen, one of Khotso's earliest paramours, there is a picture of a more recent spouse, Selina.[18] A young woman in her mid-twenties, her soft, unlined face wears a slightly puzzled expression. Part of her confusion might have sprung from the fact that one of the key players in the production was the child to whom she gave birth and who was now to all intents and purposes no longer her son.

'Four Boy is my son,' Bethinja declared during the inquiry. 'He was given to me by Khotso and Selina, his natural mother.' Small wonder that Selina looked bewildered. She had not taken a decision to hand Four Boy over to Bethinja permanently, and in 1973, some months after Khotso's death, she had embarked on an unsuccessful legal attempt to recover him. Yet this was a complex issue for Selina. Her son stood to gain if Bethinja's claim to the estate proved successful. Other wives and their representatives took their turn to speak, including Gloria's father, who supported Langa, and MaMjoli.[19]

All the while, as the battle intensified, the racial tensions that Ellen had been aware of when she became part of Khotso's domestic entourage decades ago once again began to take shape around her and her son. These tensions occasionally even extended to incorporate Swartz, the administrator of the estate, because he happened to be a coloured person too in the terminology of the time. Swartz represented Langa in court, exacerbating the racial divisions that were coming to the fore.

Khotso's last marriage of all began to feature in the inquiry. Langa and those testifying on his behalf attempted to use Khotso's last-minute wedding to Bethinja and the subsequent handwritten will as part of their ammunition against her. While the press waxed sentimental about 'the incredible love story of the world-famous herbalist Khotso Sethuntsa and his favourite wife Bethinja', suggestions were made in court that Bethinja had coerced the dying Khotso into a civil marriage. Swartz defended Khotso's ability to be master of his actions right up until the very end of his life, basing this not on circumstantial evidence but on the one part of Khotso that had been very infrequently glimpsed: his handwriting. 'Judging from the signature on the marriage certificate,' Swartz said, 'it is obvious that Khotso was at the time very weak and shaky but it would be wrong to suggest that he was mentally distressed and not sane enough to enter into a marriage contract.' Swartz overlooked the fact that, because Khotso was illiterate, his signature had been wobbly at the best of times.[20]

One of the key players in the drama was becoming shaky too. As the case wore on, Bethinja became so unwell that sometimes she could not even sit properly in her seat in court. There are some photographs taken of her seated outside the courtroom, slumped and sagging, as if bereft of all that could hold her upright, in both body and spirit. When Bethinja was being cross-examined about the validity of her marriage to Khotso, she collapsed in court. Shortly after her husband's death, she complained that her nerves were suffering, but at this point the pressure she was undergoing had worn her down. One of her aides informed the press that she had been under treatment for a nervous breakdown. Continually begging feebly for her pills, Bethinja was rushed to a doctor.[21] Her allies expressed shock and sympathy, while her opponents whispered that Bethinja's emotional and physical collapse was an indication that her case was crumbling too.

Langa also needed support during this period. Like his rival, he was dependent on personal medication of a sort, but one that did not come in the form of pills and that he could not take into court with him. And like Bethinja, he needed his supporters. One of these was Nyanga, the young man whose mother had once been one of Khotso's patients. Although Nyanga liked to be regarded by outsiders as yet another of Khotso's sons, he did not resemble his presumed father in any way and his mother had never attempted to persuade Khotso to acknowledge him as his child. Nevertheless, Nyanga presented himself as a loyal, supportive brother to Langa. Like others, he may have believed that Langa might well feel moved to remember those who had publicly displayed their faith in the rightness of his cause when he finally came into his kingdom.

The inquiry lasted two days before judgment was passed: Khotso had paid one hundred rands as lobola money to Ellen's father. She and Khotso had thus been man and wife, and Langa was to inherit his father's estate, as his oldest legitimate son. He was only twenty-five at the time. Magistrate Webb informed Langa that according to African custom it was his duty as the heir to support and shelter all his father's widows and their children. If he failed to do so, they were legally entitled to act against him.[22]

A press photograph displays the victorious Langa outside the courtroom, hand raised high in victory. Close beside him, Nyanga stands, his arm also in the air and an expression of excitement on his face. Langa appears to be a handsome, confident young man, about to stride into a glowing future.[23]

Bethinja triumphed in one significant respect. She was allowed to remain in Khotso's headquarters at Mount Nelson, while Langa was instructed to reside at Mount Frere, with MaDlamini. His erstwhile temporary foster mother had lived there so long that she did not see the need for any court to inform her that this was her abode.[24] For her part, Ellen had returned to the second, smaller White House, near Bhongweni, where once she had briefly been Khotso's princess. With her son as Khotso's heir, she could now set herself up as a queen in her domain. From 1974 onwards, she stayed in the smaller White House with her husband Victor Moyce. MaMjoli made her home in Khotso's beach house in Msikaba.

The issue of Khotso's estate had not, however, been resolved. A few months later, Bethinja submitted an affidavit to the Mthatha high court alleging that Langa was unfit to be heir. She denounced him for failing in his duties, accusing him of frittering away Khotso's estate. She contended that Langa was always under the influence of alcohol and had a group of 'drinking friends'. Moreover, she claimed that Langa had not only physically attacked her, but had embarked on an ongoing campaign of harassment against her, drawing her into an ongoing war of nerves, which was damaging her health.[25]

The following year, Bethinja cited these accusations when she attempted to have Langa disinherited in the appeal court in Mthatha. She applied for permission to appeal for a re-hearing of the inquiry at which Langa was instated as heir, citing new evidence to submit to the magistrate that would prove that Langa was not Khotso's legitimate son. However, Bethinja's application was turned down on the grounds that it had been made after the stipulated time limit. Thus Langa retained his right to be Khotso's heir.[26]

Langa formally took over the running of his father's estate in 1975.[27] He was twenty-six years old at the time. His inheritance was worth R329 176, but only R70 000 was available in cash. In the meantime, the tax collectors his father had sought to elude were close at hand, demanding R50 000.[28] Langa had also inherited an extensive network of dependants: all his father's widows and children, whom he was now required to support. But most difficult of all were his father's houses and properties themselves, which would have to be maintained. Several years had elapsed since Khotso's death, and the hosts of clients and followers who had laboured on his estates, keeping his farms in order and ensuring that his eccentric mini-mansions remained neat, freshly painted and well cared for, had long since departed, as had many of his loyal retainers. In consequence, the dwellings that had become near-legendary landmarks evoking mingled awe, fascination and fear were beginning to seem less like the impressive abodes of a unique, mysterious millionaire and more like the dilapidated follies of a peculiar dreamer. There was also an assortment of farms that required careful management and extensive maintenance lest they too fall into decay.

Khotso's non-material legacy endured: not only in the form of his estate itself, but also in his very name, which remained redolent with potency and promise. There is, for instance, one man in a mountain village in the vicinity of Quthing, in south-eastern Lesotho, who now calls himself Khotso Sethuntsa, because he believes that this name might serve as a symbolic key unlocking the doorway to fortune and success, through which the original bearer of that name once strode. There are others who have adopted Khotso's name for similar reasons.

His name has also been invoked by those who sought to claim kinship with him because of the direct material benefits that might accrue from this. Khotso had always wanted more sons; now, ironically, it seemed that his death had given birth to them. In January 1975, for example, an eighteen-year-old calling himself Two Boy materialised in the *Sunday Times* offices, claiming to be one of Khotso's favourite sons. It seemed that on a superficial level, Two Boy possessed some of Khotso's distinctive characteristics. Not only did he have an affinity for the press, but he also said that he needed close contact with deadly serpents to develop and maintain his supernatural powers. Two Boy professed to be working as an inyanga, and in order to fortify himself, he said, every year he spent two days and nights in a pit full of poisonous snakes.[29]

It is likely that Two Boy resembled his putative parent most closely in his fondness for spinning tall tales. Blades met him and was not convinced by his story. Likewise, Bethinja and Langa were able to agree on one thing: neither of them had any recollection of Two Boy and they thought he was a fraud. 'We even had children calling themselves Bo-Twoboy, because they knew there was lots of money, millions,' Bethinja grumbled later on, possibly showing her scorn for Two Boy by deliberately distorting his name.[30]

Over the years since Khotso's death a number of other individuals have styled themselves as his sons. For instance, in 1995 a man persuaded some people to part with their money and clothing on the grounds that he was Khotso's son and, equipped with their garments and money, he would be able to draw on his father's magic to produce a fortune for them. After waiting expectantly in a room in their underwear for several hours while the man was supposedly conjuring up wealth outside, the group grew suspicious and emerged only to find that the man had vanished.[31] Even today, however far-fetched and fraudulent some of them may appear, stories that invoke the name of Khotso Sethuntsa still have the power to capture people in their spell.

Chapter 21
Riches Are Like Mist

There were some who believed that Khotso had left a legacy of a very different kind behind him. Khotso was dead, but gossipmongers outside his domestic circle presumed that the malevolent forces unleashed by his practice of ukuthwala had returned to haunt his family. Was Nkosazana's insidious, venomous presence at work, exacting revenge on many of those in the extended household who had been close to Khotso? Fragmented, embattled, the different factions of his family entrenched themselves in their ornate, crumbling houses, isolated cottages and far-flung farms. A number of these individuals' lives seemed poisoned in one way or another: by financial hardship, chronic illness, loneliness, mistrust and enmity.

As they observed the bitter legal battles taking place, some expressed the belief that it was as if a kind of curse was working itself out in Khotso's family, sowing ongoing dissent and psychological and physical anguish. But others argued that legal proceedings have an unpleasant tendency to become protracted and a curse in themselves, without the agency of supernatural forces.

All the while, the winding up of Khotso's affairs dragged on, tying up much of the estate. 'Everything is still in Khotso's name,' Bethinja told a journalist in 1984.[1] Although he could not take his possessions along with him to the world of the dead, Khotso might have approved of the fact that in legal terms everything still belonged to him. Properties still in Khotso's name were recently attached by municipalities (in lieu of property tax arrears).[2]

MaMjoli said that before his death Khotso had spoken to her and other family members, indicating that he wished his estate to be shared among his family after his death. This runs counter to the claims made by both Langa and Bethinja and their supporters that Khotso wanted one specific individual, either his eldest son or his intandokazi, to be his major beneficiary. The puzzle, then, is why Khotso never saw fit to draw up a will formalising his wish that his estate be spread among all those close to him. Never one for the written word, however (unless it came in the form of press articles about himself), Khotso may have felt that a verbal pronouncement would suffice. After her husband had indicated how he wanted his estate to be divided, MaMjoli related, he would then go on to say that if his wish was not carried out, there would be no estate to speak of. With hindsight, Khotso's words had a prophetic ring to them. Although they were the wives and children of a reputed millionaire, Khotso's family seemed to have as much likelihood of laying their hands on any portion of his legendary fortune as did the Pondoland poor beyond the gates of Mount Nelson.

Not only did it appear that the body of Khotso's riches had vanished from (or into) the earth, but it also seemed that he had taken along with him the wealth that he had once bestowed on others. For example, in the Herschel–Sterkspruit area, there were once a number of prosperous people, some of whom had been owners of bus companies. It was avowed that they owed their success to Khotso. Their companies collapsed after his demise, as if the forces from which they had obtained their wealth were calling in to collect their dues. Their family members still do not like to talk about the sudden, startling changes in the family fortunes. There is, for example, a beggar at the Sterkspruit taxi rank, once a rich man who had been to Khotso for ukuthwala, people whisper.

Such stories persist to this day. Having witnessed how all Khotso's wealth and his renowned influence over supernatural forces had not been able to keep suffering, death, family disasters and feuding at bay, people began to put more energy into circulating not only accounts of all the lucky individuals who had made their fortunes through Khotso's agency, but also the tales of those unfortunates who had gained wealth through his arts only to discover that they were involving themselves in a dangerous magic that could eventually turn against them. In this way, a special category of fables relating to Khotso began to evolve, and these were circulated almost as eagerly as the dire cautionary tales for children that were told with horrified fascination during the Victorian era.

One such tale concerns the eventual fate of the woman who stole a pumpkin from Khotso. Eventually she had become destitute. 'Then her business was in disaster afterwards,' said the member of Khotso's household who described what had taken place. 'She was in debt and the money was gone.' While this informant related the account of the talking pumpkin to draw attention to Khotso's powers, as the story was retold by others it emphasised the notion that people obtaining wealth through Khotso were compromising themselves morally and spiritually and would eventually have to pay the price. As such, this narrative represents one example of the way in which stories, which Khotso loved so deeply and relied on to win wealth and fame for himself, could elude his control. There are many comparable examples of how tales that Khotso might well have been responsible for bringing into being were turned against him.

Both Khotso and those who had attained their wealth through his ukuthwala procedure might have been illustrating the Sotho proverb *Monono ke moholi ke mouoane: madiba ho chan a matala* (Riches are like mist and they perish: the greenest pool dries up). This proverb could also be applied to Langa, Khotso's legally proclaimed heir, and the other prominent members of his family. For these individuals, all part of the supporting cast who had been thrust onto centre stage after the death of the lead actor, the metaphorical green pool of affluence and material comfort depicted in the proverb seemed shrivelled and desiccated when viewed from close at hand.

Although Langa had been the victor in court, in various respects he was a loser in life. As heir to his father's properties, he could do little more than watch many of them dwindle in value as they slid into dereliction. Langa retreated to Houston, one of Khotso's farms in the region of Matatiele. The young man might have been happier at a distance from Kokstad and Lusikisiki, the places where his father's presence seemed strongest of all, crowded as they were with people who remembered him well. Possibly Langa did not want people to scrutinise him too closely and declare that he was no Khotso.

On Christmas Eve 1981, a startling event took place. Langa was found dead in his car by the side of the long, lonely road that winds from the farm where he was based to Kokstad.[3] He had set out to visit his mother, wishing to present her with a sheep as a Christmas gift. But man and beast were found lying in the car, side by side in death. Unlike his father, whose departure from life had been floodlit by the glare of the publicity that he so loved, Langa slipped quietly out of the world. He was only thirty-two years old, an age at which his father had been rising to greater and greater heights. Langa, however, had been in a state of decline for years. His death provided fertile ground for stories, which sprouted as wild and rank as weeds, smothering actuality beneath them. For one thing, the rumour that he might have been murdered gained ground.

'They say he had a small wound under his foot,' said Elizabeth Brown, Langa's first wife. When asked by a journalist if she suspected that some kind of foul play had taken place, she fell silent.[4] Ellen also nurtured suspicions about the cause of her son's death. The fact that Langa was a purported millionaire's heir offered a useful starting point for the creation of a murder mystery that could be added to all the other riddling tales entwined around both Khotso and his legacy.

A number of family members believe that Langa's demise was linked to his alcoholic tendencies. He drank himself to death, they say. On the other hand, certain informants contend that the circles within which Langa moved contained shady types with connections in the criminal world, drawn towards him by the alluring combination of an easy flow of alcohol and the belief that he had access to great sums of money. Thus, it is rumoured in some quarters that Langa might have fallen foul of some dangerous individuals who had lain in wait on an isolated road down which they knew he would travel.

As Langa's principal beneficiary, Ellen inherited the fragments of Khotso's estate. Some of the other individuals remembered in his will had been Langa's allies during the tussle for the estate, such as Nyanga; or they had supported him, in one way or another, at various points in his life. One of his foster mothers, MaMjoli, was mentioned in Langa's will, as were her daughters Ma-Six and Ma-Eleven and Gloria's daughter Stella.[5]

Langa was outlasted by his arch-rival. Although Bethinja had lost the legal battle, in certain respects she was the underlying winner. As she had wished, Bethinja was the mistress of Mount Nelson. Moreover, she had succeeded in creating the widespread impression that it was she on whom Khotso's spiritual mantle had fallen. She had taken over her husband's herbal practice and aspirant herbalists were coming to her for training.[6] Bethinja had always exuded a certain charisma; now, within her small kingdom, she succeeded in exercising a degree of power and influence. It is possible that partly as a result of this superficial similarity, Bethinja became widely perceived as the person through whom Khotso's spirit could be contacted. People would seek her out at Mount Nelson because they wished to speak to the man who, though dead, still remained the master of the house.[7]

As Khotso wished, the Kruger Day celebrations continued to take place at Mount Nelson, presided over by Bethinja. There was one marked difference in these celebrations, however. Saul Ndzumo was at Bethinja's side, having moved into Mount Nelson. His career was taking off and he had ascended from Quma Funeral Parlour into the echelons of the Transkei government. In the 1970s he was appointed minister of agriculture, and thereafter he became minister of the interior. On the surface, it seemed as if Ndzumo's move into Mount Nelson was doing him good. In his new abode, he liked to be known as *uTata Omncini,* or 'my father's younger brother'. Various people who had been close to Khotso resented this, feeling that Ndzumo's title reflected the extent to which he had displaced Khotso, in what had been his main house.

Some outsiders might have assumed that Bethinja had landed on her feet, like a cat. But even a cursory glance at press photographs of her face, taken years after her husband's death, indicates that years of bitter conflict and ongoing struggles to maintain an even keel economically were taking their toll. As Khotso's middle-aged bride, Bethinja had managed to radiate a fresh-faced quality and a youthful energy. But in photographs taken years after Langa's appointment as heir, not even the ghost of this woman can be glimpsed. Bethinja has the sagging, dispirited face of a weary matron who has been dealt some bitter blows in life. In one picture she stands apprehensively, hands on hips, as if she expects that onslaughts of one sort or another, whether physical suffering or attacks engineered by her enemies, could strike her without warning.

In 1984, some years after Langa's death, Bethinja complained: 'I suffer from chronic heart trouble because of all this business [of wrangling over Khotso's estate]. . . . I have had enough of all the fighting. I am a sick woman.'[8] The bulk of Langa's estate, including Mount Nelson, had been left to Ellen, although at the time of her son's death these had not yet been transferred into his name. Bethinja was therefore aware that she would eventually become little more than a tenacious tenant in a house over which she would only be able to assert an emotional claim.

Bethinja was not the only one of Khotso's wives whose fortunes waned after their husband's death. Ellen gained little from attaining Khotso's estate after the demise of her son. Someone who met Ellen during the 1990s described her as 'a good-time girl'. Ageing though she was, she was still full of fun and frivolity. For instance, she delighted in being taken to a disco in Kokstad, where she danced as enthusiastically as if she was a young girl at a party. But like her son, Ellen was confronted with burdens too heavy for someone of her nature to handle. She found that the properties that became her own represented more of an economic liability than anything else. Eventually Khotso's houses by the Mzintlava passed into her hands, but as was the case with Bethinja and MaDlamini, Ellen battled to maintain the rambling, derelict dwellings that had fallen to her. Finally, lacking even the amount of money necessary to pay the rates, she fled Kokstad before the creditors closed in on her. Thereafter she declined, eventually passing away in 2003.

Khotso's Kokstad properties were eventually sold by public auction, but Ellen's friend Francina remains in Ellen's special house, the second White House, undeterred by this. She spends time relaxing in the warmth on the front steps. Behind her is the reed-encircled pool, where once hosts of people gathered, led by Khotso, to salute his snake under the water. Francina still cherishes sunny memories of Ellen and her son: two individuals who were sweet-natured and gentle to their friends, yet whose lives ultimately seemed to be filled with more shadow than sunlight.

Bethinja, for her part, sunk into despondency near the end of her life. Beset as she was with heart problems, back trouble and other chronic illnesses, in 1988 she finally collapsed under the weight of her emotional stress and the physical disorders that her anxiety and tension had engendered. MaDlamini's grandson Thabo remembered how she was always complaining of pain – it would start in her back, then move swiftly to her stomach, then on to her head, as if it was roaming around her body, its restlessness somehow expressive of Bethinja's own state of inner disquiet. One story has it that there was something both odd and pathetic about Bethinja's demise. She died in Queen Elizabeth Hospital in Lusikisiki, and some related how, when her corpse was attended to, the nurses found eight thousand rands tied to her waist, concealed under her clothing. It was as if Bethinja was desperately clutching at the scraps of wealth that she could call her own. To all appearances Bethinja had, like her husband, become mistrustful, living in fear that others might rob her.

Four Boy did not live much longer than his erstwhile foster mother. A few years later, almost echoing his half-brother's death on Christmas Eve, he died on Christmas Day 1991. Four Boy's demise also revived widespread speculation around the life of his father. None of Khotso's sons had lived long and contented lives. One had died when he was barely in his teens; another had frittered his life away and been a failure; and both he and Khotso's last son had died while they were young men. Surely this was once again proof, gossipmongers surmised, that the old man's family were still paying the price for his involvement in ukuthwala.

But no account of the eventual fates of the major players in the drama of Khotso's life and legacy would be complete without making mention of the earliest principal figure to arrive on the stage, to remain an important presence throughout the action, albeit sometimes from the wings. MaDlamini remained in the Mount Frere house, a course of action that would require considerable determination on her part.

After Langa came into his inheritance, some members of Khotso's family alleged that he lived an indolent life, was extravagant and dissipated the estate.[9] He began to sell his father's properties in a frantic attempt to gain some economic benefit from them before they collapsed into dereliction. The new owners of some of these places made an unwelcome discovery when they tried to take possession of their recently acquired estates. They found Khotso's family members and individuals who regarded themselves as members of his family ensconced in the houses that had belonged to him, refusing to be dislodged from the dwellings that they had come to view as their own.

One such buyer was Aubrey Zolani Tyali of Umzimvubu Garage, who purchased a property in Mount Frere only to discover he had taken on far more than a run-down plot of land containing a strange, shabby mini-mansion and a conglomeration of outbuildings sliding into mouldering decay. Langa had sold this estate to Tyali without mentioning that along with the transaction there came a one-time foster mother of his. MaDlamini held fast to her belief that because Langa had had no legal or moral right to sell the house at Mount Frere, there was no need for her to move out. In the course of the prolonged legal proceedings that ensued, as Mr Tyali attempted to prove to MaDlamini that she was mistaken in her conviction, the unfortunate man found that he might just as well have tried to shift one of the walls of his new abode by banging his head against it.

The legal wrangle dragged on for years and years from the mid-1980s onwards. By 1990, it had reached the supreme court of the Transkei in Mthatha. In the affidavits she submitted, MaDlamini chose to present herself as a frail, sickly, much put-upon old lady, bewildered by the legal complexities of the situation in which she found herself. In this, she belied her true nature.

MaDlamini did indeed suffer from diabetes and high blood pressure. The latter, she claimed, shot up as soon as she was served with a warrant of ejectment in May 1988. Yet it was not haplessness and feebleness that kept her fixed in the Mount Frere house, but rather her tenaciousness and force of character. As Khotso's longest-established female consort, she had endured decades of challenges to her authority and attempts to humiliate her from much younger rivals who resented her position of pre-eminence. Now, she proved more than a match for Tyali, as obdurate as the mountain rock of her home country.

People who knew MaDlamini say that even at this point in her life she retained a distinguished beauty of her own. Moreover, despite her straitened financial circumstances, the chronic physical ailments that weighed her down and the shabby, ramshackle nature of the place in which she lived, she still exuded a regal, dignified quality. She appeared to transcend her condition and surroundings. Her daughter, Masechaba, also lived in the house, suffering from a complication of the same illnesses that afflicted her mother, for whom she was caring.

It was not so much the force of the law that finally dislodged MaDlamini from Mount Frere as what she may have felt was a heaven-sent opportunity to move away from her position on the periphery into the heart of her deceased husband's empire. In 1992 MaDlamini finally triumphed over the woman she had sometimes called 'Beat-the-dog', when she and her children moved back to Mount Nelson after Bethinja's death. Mistress of an establishment consisting of more than one hundred rooms, she limited herself to only twelve of these chambers, leasing out the rest. Masechaba's son, Thabo, took over as head of the house. The days of hard labour and physical deprivation during which MaDlamini had helped Khotso establish himself in life had no doubt instilled the awareness within her that victories do not necessarily come easily.

In an affidavit submitted during the course of the legal wrangle with Tyali, MaDlamini outlined the costs of maintaining Mount Nelson. The trifling amount of R210 that she gained for the rental of rooms and outbuildings, ten of which were shacks, did not cover maintenance costs for the property and the amount of money owed at Mount Nelson, which included tax in arrears from 1975. MaDlamini concluded with the bleak observation: '[E]ven in spite of the minimum rental that I am collecting in respect of the premises in question, I still fall under the category of indigent people because this rental is consumed substantially by the overheads in respect of these properties.'[10]

Thabo would one day inherit her financial struggle to maintain Mount Nelson. Today, he presides over a kingdom of cavernous, dilapidated rooms and disintegrating outbuildings.

MaDlamini died in 1997, having achieved a measure of victory befitting her status as senior wife. She and her family had attained control of Mount Nelson, and she had outlived her major rival. She remained very strong mentally, emotionally and even physically up until her death, said Thabo, who was with her right at the end. Both she and Bethinja are buried in Kruger House, not far from the special chamber where Khotso himself lies. But while Bethinja rests in an unmarked grave, MaDlamini has an impressive tombstone, a tribute from her grandchildren; Masechaba, who died a scant two years after her mother, rests beside her, with a similar headstone.

The deaths of Khotso's sons, three of his principal wives and his stepdaughter, many of them suffering from long-standing chronic ailments, all had a tragic irony to them. In their various ways they died deprived of the very things that Khotso had been most famed for bestowing on his clients: physical health and material well-being. The wealth that seemed to surround them so securely during Khotso's lifetime had proved to be as ephemeral as mist. As the mirage of financial security shimmered into nothingness, Khotso's wives, his sons and his stepdaughter realised that they all stood, chill and isolated, on bleak and stony ground.

CHAPTER 22
Life After Death

While the wealth that had been a key feature of Khotso's career had vanished and the tombstone in the special antechamber in Kruger House was solid-marble proof that Khotso Sethuntsa was indeed deceased, a range of people remained convinced that Khotso was neither truly dead nor gone. The belief that Khotso continues to make his presence felt at a supernatural level persists in various forms to this day.

For decades after Khotso's death, not only did those individuals whose fortunes had been made through him discover that his demise had brought catastrophe in its wake, but other people, some of whom had never met Khotso, began to feel that they were now vulnerable to dangers that had been kept at bay during his time. Neglected, unpropitiated, some of Khotso's snakes were running wild.

One of the outbuildings at the White House has the cement stripped off half its wall, exposing the raw brickwork beneath. One of the amakhosi came up from the river and did it, Meshack Nogudlu, who currently lives in the White House, explained. It was angry because no one had taken care of it after Khotso's death, so the family had to organise someone to come and appease the snake. Since then, Meshack said, Thabo and other family members come over from Lusikisiki periodically. They eat together in the White House and share their meal with the amakhosi, attending to and placating them.

A few years ago, it was reported that another of Khotso's abodes had been attacked by one of his serpents. In 2004, the *Daily Sun*, a tabloid delighting in sensationalism, ran an article entitled 'Evil Snake Wants Blood'.[1] The report was accompanied by a photograph of a dejected-looking man in front of a damaged building. The individual, one of the people now staying on Khotso's King William's Town property, claimed that Khotso's snake had wreaked havoc because it had not received the offerings it required.

Moreover, rumour had it that one of Khotso's snakes had wandered far away from its pool near the White House to find a dwelling place in another part of the Mzintlava. Near Elubaleko, a Transkei village that clusters along the banks of this river, beyond Mount Ayliff, a strange serpentine creature that some believe had once belonged to Khotso struck terror into the community. In 1997, various South African newspapers carried reports that a hybrid monster, with the head and forelegs of a horse, the tail of a fish and the body of a snake, was lurking near Elubaleko, periodically killing livestock and people. A substantial number of individuals were of the opinion that the river monster could have been one of Khotso's snakes, which had had no one to maintain it since his death. 'And it's hungry now,' one local said.

But although Khotso was no longer able to tend to his serpents himself, the notion had taken hold that he was still physically present. Thousands of people had been in attendance on the day that Khotso was placed in his grave, but appearances might have proved deceptive yet again. Decades after his death, Khotso's body – or something that could have been his body – was very much in evidence. Visitors to Mount Nelson were escorted to a chamber in which a figure that was said to be Khotso could be seen preserved inside a glass-fronted coffin. 'There's a little room there and you go in there, take off your shoes and there's the old man sitting there,' said one man, a Kokstad local who had journeyed to Lusikisiki to see Khotso's body. Sylvia Tloti and a few friends decided to see Khotso's body for themselves. This is Sylvia's account of their experience.

Life After Death

I come from the district of Sterkspruit and heard a lot about Khotso Sethuntsa and his powers, especially his wealth-giving powers. This was due to the fact that a number of very rich people in the area were said to be his followers. This was enhanced by the fact that they all had clean-shaven heads.

It had always been rumoured that, when Khotso died, his body was preserved and placed on display in one of the houses. My two friends and I decided to go and see for ourselves. We travelled to Lusikisiki and went to the house. A guide, who we later discovered was one of the tenants, took us to a separate building called Kruger House. We stood outside the building near a big window. After paying a sum of fifty cents each, we saw through the window what looked like a glass coffin. In it was the body of a man which was in a reclining position. The body was immaculately dressed in a suit and the face looked a bit dry. The guide told us that only those who were already Khotso's followers were allowed to get into the house and perform whatever rituals they needed to.

There are more sensational descriptions of visits to what passed for Khotso's body. Various people found the encounter with what they deemed to be the man himself an unnerving one, evoking mingled fascination and horror. This grouping includes a younger generation of Transkeians, some of whom had been raised on terrifying tales about Khotso's dark deeds of magic. 'When you look at him, your hair stands up here. The eyes, they're eyes like marbles, snake eyes,' said the Kokstad man.

'If you want to see him, you must be prepared, then, for a week or some time, you'll have sleepless nights,' said one young man, now a student, who comes from a village not far from Mount Ayliff. 'I even had a nightmare, the day after I went there.'

Certain people were of the opinion that Khotso's corpse had been preserved so that his body could remain in his home while his spirit continued carrying out its work. Had what remained of the man been transformed into some kind of relic, a corpse able to work wonders of its own accord and inspire deep reverence in the faithful; or had he been turned into some kind of macabre tourist attraction? Each of these possibilities would, no doubt, have appealed to Khotso himself, drawn as he had been to both spirituality and showmanship.

But a number of people swore that the figure in the glass-fronted coffin in Mount Nelson was not the cadaver of its one-time master. Khotso could never have been preserved, they argue, since they saw him being buried themselves. Now that his purported body is no longer on display, it is hard to ascertain what exactly it was that visitors were shown. On the one hand, it is quite possible that they merely saw a waxwork replica; yet on the other hand, some believe that they saw the remains of Khotso himself. Indeed, there are reports that his corpse had been injected with embalming fluid. If we subscribe to that line of argument, it is possible to entertain the notion that long after all the mourners departed, Khotso had been hauled out of his temporary resting place and borne back into the heart of his household. There he could continue to be a source of awe and bewildered speculation.

In death, as in life, Khotso continued to generate riddles and controversies. People closely connected to him, such as MaMjoli and Lunika, assert that what was on display could not have been Khotso's corpse. They had witnessed his burial, and were adamant that his mortal remains had been securely placed underground and could not possibly have been put to commercial use thereafter. MaMjoli provided one pertinent reason why the seated figure that so many visitors had been allowed to glimpse from a distance could not have been that of her husband: 'He would not have wished his body to have been clothed in a suit,' she said. 'He loved his robes. They meant so much to him that he was buried in them.' So she felt that the object in Kruger House had little in common with the real Khotso. Yet Khotso or whatever it was that passed for his corpse continued to draw people to him – whether pilgrims, the morbidly fascinated or the idly curious – before one of the most bizarre spectacles ever staged at Mount Nelson was put to an end.

While Khotso's cadaver could be disposed of, many avow that his spirit remains awake and watchful as he continues to manifest himself in the lives of those he had touched in various ways. To this day there are some who describe how Khotso appears to them in dreams and visions; or they say that they are infused with a strong awareness of his presence as they go about their daily business. This is not unusual in itself, for many people in diverse cultures believe that those who have passed away remain present, in one sense or another, in the lives of those who were close to them. In Khotso's case, it is as if his spirit appears to manifest itself especially in those places that had been important to him at various stages of his life. In Ha Ramokakatlela, for instance, Khotso's niece, a traditional healer, says that her uncle speaks to her in dreams.

Meanwhile, Meshack is not the only occupant of the White House who feels close to Khotso. Ndoda Mgwabashe, the principal resident of this abode, to whom Meshack defers, claims: 'Khotso came to me and gave me a number of rules that I had to obey in order to do his work well. I just go to the pools to talk to him.'

At Mount Nelson, Thabo and the other family members residing on the premises retain an awareness of Khotso's presence in the house that he loved so dearly. Today, people seeking his help still come to Kruger House and sleep in the bed in the front room of this building. According to Thabo, Khotso will appear to them in their dreams, and when they return home what they wish for will be granted. People who wish to commune with Khotso's spirit also spend the night in his inner sanctum. As in MaMjoli's house, the bed is covered with a blanket with a leopard motif. MaMjoli recounted:

> He had told us before his death that people who needed his help would have to be taken to the room where they would spend the night. There was to be a bed next to his tombstone for this purpose. I was the one he chose to prepare a meal for these occasions. The instructions were for me to set a table for four and then leave.

When she was asked who the places at the table were for, MaMjoli laughed and said, 'Only my husband knew that.'

Khotso, some believed, was concerned about what some of the people who had been closest to him in life were doing after his death. There was also a conviction that he was taking careful note of the events happening on the properties that he had cared for so diligently throughout his career. This, it has been related, led Khotso to accomplish an apparently impossible feat: to bring about a reconciliation between two bitter enemies, his favoured wife and the man who had strongly supported his eldest son's cause during the court battle to determine who would inherit his estate.

Knowing what he did about Khotso's powers, Lunika was not surprised to find that his connection with his former master was continuing beyond the grave. In 1974, after judgment had been passed establishing Langa as Khotso's heir, Lunika had dreams that he still recollects vividly decades later.

'I dreamed that there were Khotso's beautiful cars, crashing into one another,' Lunika said. 'And then, in my dream, Khotso said to me: "Do you see what Langa is doing to my cars? That's what Langa is going to do to my estate. I know you are fighting [alongside] him, but I know this little child will not keep my property." '[2]

Lunika dreamed again on that night. 'Khotso was asking me: "Why don't you go to my place any more?" ' As far as Lunika was concerned, the answer seemed obvious. To venture into Mount Nelson seemed a risky enterprise. He had set himself against Bethinja by giving legal evidence in support of Langa, so it seemed best to steer clear of the place where she was now established. But in the dream, Khotso showed Lunika how Bethinja and other people were preparing for Kruger Day at Mount Nelson, which was due to take place that weekend. 'You must go to the Kruger Day celebration,' Khotso told him.

'I knew Bethinja didn't like me,' Lunika said. 'So I thought: how can I go?'

Troubled in his heart, Lunika went to his house in Caquba for the weekend. Because the village was near the coast, it seemed a safe distance from Lusikisiki. But it was as if Khotso was steering events, making sure

LIFE AFTER DEATH

that his erstwhile prime minister carried out his wishes. Lunika's wife informed him that his chief had called him. Bethinja had invited the chief to the Kruger Day celebrations, so he wanted Lunika to drive him to Mount Nelson on 10 October. Lunika reluctantly undertook to be of assistance. On Kruger Day, when they arrived at the house, the chief got out of the car and walked through the gates, still adorned with the golden letter *K*. Lunika was left sitting alone in the car, looking at the house and the crowd of people that had already gathered in the yard, Bethinja among them. As he steeled himself to abandon the security of his car and enter the place where people regarded him as an enemy, a bee flew through the open window of the car and into his hand. It gently settled in his palm, without stinging him.

Lunika believed that this was no ordinary bee. Khotso had always maintained that these insects are messengers of the ancestors, so Lunika felt that the bee had been sent as a sign. Khotso was grateful that Lunika had returned to visit his home at last and he was assuring Lunika that everything at the feast would go well for him. So Lunika left the car and walked through the gates and into the yard. Then he received the greatest surprise of all.

'Bethinja welcomed me joyfully!' Lunika exclaimed. She told everyone: 'This man was my husband's great friend. Now the gathering is complete.'

Lunika, still incredulous, was asked to address the crowd. Although Khotso was dead and Bethinja had viewed him as her foe, Lunika was made to feel that there was still a place for him on what Khotso had regarded as the most important day of the year, at the place that had been his headquarters. This, Lunika was convinced, had come about because Khotso's spirit was at work among those closest to him.

Lunika resembled many others in his belief that Khotso's influence was making itself felt in other, more disturbing ways. It was claimed that his ever-vigilant spirit was visiting vengeance on anyone who had been connected to him during his lifetime or shortly thereafter and who strayed from the path that he wished that person to follow. 'Any person who tried to rob Khotso of his money would end up in disgrace, or would die a disgraceful death,' Lunika asserted.

Some have even said that Khotso's element, water, reached out to claim the life of Chris Swartz, who drowned while trying to cross the Mngazi River near Port St Johns. They wondered if Swartz had in some way incurred Khotso's displeasure in his handling of the estate. The emotional trauma and physical anguish that Bethinja underwent after Khotso's death, which led her to an early grave, were viewed in some quarters as a form of punishment visited on her by her departed husband.

Bethinja's lover, Saul Ndzumo, departed from life in a dramatic manner. In a speech in September 1980, he divulged news of what he claimed was a plot to depose Kaiser Matanzima. Although Ndzumo professed to have opposed the conspiracy, he was dismissed from his position in Matanzima's cabinet and detained, purportedly 'to put the record straight'. He died in detention, officially of natural causes. The Transkeian prime minister and the premier's brother, Chief George Matanzima, stated: 'It was unfortunate that at the peak of his career [Mr Ndzumo] fell into a trap which led to his dismissal.'[3] Some argued that his downfall arose not so much from political machinations, but because he had installed himself alongside Bethinja at Mount Nelson. Thus the impression took hold that death had not prevented Khotso from going about his business.

At Khotso's funeral, on the other hand, several speakers had expressed the belief that although he was not present in this world any more, the master of Mount Nelson was now rejoicing in another. When it was his turn to address the crowd, Botha Sigcau declared that Khotso had most certainly ascended to a higher realm. Later, Sigcau's assertion was corroborated by someone who claimed to have witnessed the event, a woman from Ntabankulu who described herself as a clairvoyant. She had known Khotso for many years and listened eagerly while he shared his knowledge of matters supernatural with her. She told the assembled mourners that she had dreamed that she saw Khotso on his way to heaven long before his death had been announced on the radio. In her dream, there Khotso stood, surrounded by a line of long-dead chiefs, his companions in the afterlife. The chiefs formed a stately procession, while Khotso was anything but sedate. '[He] was wearing white robes and he looked very happy,' she said. 'He was so happy that he was doing a little dance.'[4] In her dream, death did not seem to have subdued Khotso's irrepressible lively spirit.

Chapter 23
The Last Laugh

On the one hand, it appeared that death could not put a stop to Khotso's career, irradiated as it was with the gleaming light of fame and publicity and wreathed in the shadows of secrets and mysteries. But on the other hand, it is sometimes as if the man who was Khotso Sethuntsa never existed. He may have been one of the most well-known and influential figures of his day in his particular corner of Africa, yet history has passed him by.

Just as the National Party's policies turned Khotso into a second-class citizen, costing him the right to reside on his great house on the Mzintlava, so his white political overlords would diminish him in another area he held dear: his fame. According to their political ideology, which they sought to impose on all those they governed, South Africa's past and present were presided over by whites, with black people consigned to the shadows. In consequence, this gave rise to this country's hidden histories: the people and events that became obscured during the days of white minority rule, Khotso's story among them. Who would wish to remember a Transkei 'witchdoctor' that some of the most renowned leaders of the Afrikaner nation had regularly visited? So Khotso was dismissed, along with a multitude of others.

Now, in a changed political climate, notions of our country's history, culture and heritage are being redefined and recorded. Yet Khotso has not been included in this process. Many of those who knew him well and cared for him deeply are saddened by this. 'It makes me unhappy,' MaMjoli said. 'Even today, it looks like people like my husband are not taken as part of our history and culture.'

This might be seen to be due to a deliberate omission, stemming from one controversial aspect of Khotso's life: his association with representatives of the old apartheid establishment. The chronicles of the past are compiled by the winners, but despite his successful predictions at the horse races, when it came to the field of politics Khotso backed the wrong steed in the end. But matters might have been different had he still been alive after the demise of white minority rule. Many allies of the old regime refashioned themselves, becoming loyal ANC supporters, some members of the Sigcau family among them. Having adapted his hue to match the political establishment of his time, Khotso might have repositioned himself too.

Other factors in Khotso's career, apart from his political affiliations, have brought about his neglect. For instance, his extravagant, ostentatious lifestyle gave rise to lingering resentment. Khotso is remembered with a degree of bitterness in certain quarters because he kept his money dammed up inside his large estates instead of allowing some of it to flow back into the local community. One ANC representative in the Transkei once suggested that this might have been one reason why Khotso's houses and his legacy have been allowed to fall into decay, when they could have received official care as part of the local cultural heritage. Moreover, the sense of apprehension and dread that Khotso inspired during his lifetime still hovers around many people's recollections of him and, arguably, may make them reluctant to dwell on him today.

In consequence, some might conclude that Khotso's memory has gradually become as faded as the blue and white paintwork on his houses and as tarnished as the golden letter K on the gates of Mount Nelson. However, this would not be an adequate reflection of the man's legacy. Khotso's history is worth remembering not only on account of its fascinating nature, but also because it reveals how he came to possess power over the South African imagination and the convoluted and varied depths of the South African psyche. This he wielded especially through the tales that he told. Stories still draw us to Khotso today, as in the past, when accounts of the man and his powers attracted people to him, whether drawn by amusement, amazement, curiosity, cynicism, conviction or a compelling combination of these. Some of these tales were even given a new lease on life by his death. As he indicated in the confession he made in his dying days, Khotso chose this world, and remains present in it in the stories that are told and retold, even if not in the official chronicles of the South African past.

Khotso's delight in things of this earth, evident in his material and sexual profligacy, his love of ostentation, self-conscious excess and tongue-in-cheek spectacle, gave his life a carnivalesque quality, heightened by the darkness of the times in which he lived. As his sociopolitical context became increasingly dire and oppressive, the quirky, flamboyantly colourful aspects of his life stood out all the more brightly. This irreverent, audacious aspect of Khotso's character came to the fore in his delight in trickery. Through the public persona he presented and the stories he spread about himself, all too often Khotso was concocting a series of extended jokes; at the expense of not only many of his listeners and spectators, but also those who might seek to define and interpret him after his death. Thus he reinforced the mystique that he cultivated around himself, which would capture the imaginations of many during his lifetime and shortly thereafter. However, he could not have foreseen how the secrets and riddles that surrounded him would play their part in reducing his renown in posterity. By giving rise to more questions than answers and clouding many of the details of his life, they have veiled much of his story, and many significant parts of it have begun slipping away towards obscurity. In fact, the mysterious nature of Khotso's life may have been one reason why, despite his extraordinary career, it has taken over thirty-five years for his biography to be produced.

A contradictory, capricious figure, who found comedy at the most incongruous of times, Khotso went out of life in the spirit in which he had lived it. His tantalising whisper 'Kruger millions . . .' offered a teasing hint that he knew would linger, fascinatingly and frustratingly, around his memory after he departed. But even more importantly, it has been said that he went to his death laughing loud and long.

Ellen has this story to offer: 'In the Durban hospital, he told everyone around him that he was going to have his last laugh. And he went ahead and had a good long laugh, despite his pain and imminent death. He laughed so that the world might remember the good times and the lively joking medicine man who loved money, sex and laughter.'

This tale seems appropriate. Because Khotso believed that above all life was to be enjoyed, succumbing to sorrow and sobriety at the end would have amounted to an admission of defeat for him. He wanted his funeral to be a party, so he did not want his deathbed to be an occasion for tears.

This anecdote is, however, one of the many free-floating narratives concerning Khotso that drift away into the airy terrain of myth once they are closely scrutinised. Ellen may have related either a tale that someone else had told her or a description of something that she felt should have occurred. On the other hand, MaMjoli, who was present in Shifa Hospital when her husband died, stated that the event that Ellen related never took place. Various family members, such as Thabo, agree with her. Blades, on the other hand, who was one of the journalists present at Khotso's hospital bed near the end, offers instead a somewhat poignant variation of Ellen's story. He described how Khotso did attempt to laugh loudly before he died, but he lacked sufficient breath to give a good hearty laugh.

Myths, it is known, contain underlying truths. The tale that Khotso did laugh in his dying moments does highlight a key aspect of the man's character and career. Thus Ellen's story has an aptness to it that gives it an established place in the legends surrounding Khotso.

Because death did not seem to be the end for Khotso, it would be inapposite to conclude his story with his deathbed. In closing, then, let us return to the man at the height of his career. We are back at Mount

Nelson in 1970, beside the group of visitors waiting in the yard, as the drums fall into silence and the dancers make way for the great man to take centre stage. At last the great Khotso Sethuntsa himself is to appear before us, the visitors think. Then they see an ebullient figure come bounding out of the house, arrayed in a splendid beadwork robe, a gaudy bead tie fanning out over his torso. Diamonds gleam in his ears, while his eyes sparkle like his gemstones. An ornate, imposing headdress crowns him monarch not only of Mount Nelson but of a far greater kingdom. In the place of a sceptre, he flourishes an intricately carved staff that gives him an air of regal authority. He compels awestruck attention from his visitors, and as he does so, some people find themselves believing even the most incredible tales they have been told about Khotso. Yet others are silently asking: who is the man beneath the dazzling robes?

Glossary

Note: In various cases, anglicised versions of specific words (sometimes omitting the Xhosa or Zulu *i-* and *u-* prefixes) are used in this book. The terms that appear recurrently are listed and defined here; where necessary, their correct, formal spelling is also provided.

abantu bomlambo: the Xhosa name for 'the people of the river'. These presences, sometimes associated with the ancestors, live in a world at the bottom of rivers or deep pools.

amakhosi: protective ancestral spirits, in Xhosa and Zulu traditions. They can manifest themselves in the form of snakes.

bayete: the royal salute.

ibangalala: a traditional South African herbal medicine for sexual potency and fertility; an aphrodisiac. (The correct Xhosa term is *ubangalala*, but Khotso's medicine was known as *ibangalala*.)

igqirha: the term used by Xhosa-speaking peoples to denote a spiritual healer and diviner who has received a special calling and undergone a process of initiation. (Plural: *amagqirha*)

inkanyamba: the tornado spirit, which often takes the form of a flying snake.

intandokazi: the favourite wife.

intelezi: a medicine for protection and purification, also offering short-term material prosperity and good fortune. It can also be used to heal physical ailments, such as skin irritations and stings.

inyanga: the Zulu word for 'herbalist', often used by Xhosa-speaking peoples in the areas of the Eastern Cape adjoining KwaZulu-Natal, a region inhabited by both Zulu- and Xhosa-speaking peoples. Consequently, languages intermingle; and the term *inyanga* can take on other meanings for various non-Zulu speakers. For Khotso, and for a number of people who knew him, such as Lunika, an inyanga denoted a specialised and skilled traditional practitioner with a knowledge of herbalism and authority over various areas of the supernatural, rather than simply a herbalist. In English, the phrase 'medicine man' is periodically used to indicate an inyanga.

inyoka: the Xhosa word for 'snake'.

isipili: from the Xhosa, denoting a herbal concoction by means of which one can commune with the spirit world, making it possible to speak to the ancestors. By taking isipili, one can obtain visions, insights and answers to questions. This mixture has hallucinogenic properties, and its name derives from the Afrikaans word *spieël* (mirror).

khanyapa: the Sotho term for the tornado snake (*inkanyamba* in Xhosa).

kwa-: Xhosa prefix denoting the locative. (For instance, the outbuilding where Khotso entertained his foreign visitors was dubbed kwaAmerican Tourist.)

lobola: the bride price paid in terms of traditional southern African

Glossary

custom, which can take the form of cattle or money. The correct form of the term is *ilobola*.

mamlambo (*uMamlambo*): a wealth-giving serpentine being, from the Xhosa: *u-Ma-Mlambo* (the mother of the river). The mamlambo can take on a variety of forms, although she has often been depicted as a mermaid: half woman and half snake. Through the process of *ukuthwala*, one can enter into a pact with a mamlambo, who bestows great wealth but at a great price. Comparable figures occur in other parts of Africa, such as the West African mermaid woman, Mami Wata.

mamolapo: the Sotho name for the *mamlambo*, also meaning 'the mother of the river'.

morena: this title means lord, king or chief in Sotho. Also, in the Christian context it is a term for God.

ngaka: the term for spiritual healer and diviner in the Sotho tradition; an individual who has received a special calling and undergone an initiation process enabling him or her to become a spiritual practitioner. (Plural: *dingaka*)

nkosazana: (*iNkosazana*) literally 'princess', in Xhosa and Zulu. This name is sometimes bestowed on the *mamlambo*, as a euphemistic title.

ntekwane (intekwane): a rare and special plant, which Khotso utilised in his good-luck medicines.

sangoma: the term for a spiritual healer and diviner in the Zulu tradition; an individual who has received a special calling and been initiated into her or his profession. (Plural: *izangoma*.)

tokoloshe: South African English for the Xhosa word *uthikoloshe*, a mischievous dwarf-like being.

ukuthwala: the Xhosa term for ownership of a wealth-giving creature, often a snake. This can also denote a powerful and hazardous procedure for obtaining wealth on a sustained basis. Not to be confused with the Xhosa word *ukuthwasa*, which denotes the special period of initiation and training that an individual who receives a calling to be a spiritual healer and diviner (an igqirha) is required to undergo in order to be initiated into her or his profession.

Informants

Interviews with the following individuals were conducted by Felicity Wood, Michael Lewis and Sylvia Tloti, as indicated by their initials. (The list excludes informants who do not wish to be mentioned by name.)

Mthatha, Lusikisiki and elsewhere in Pondoland

Anele Mabongo *(FW)*
Bonga Vika *(FW)*
Emmanuel Shete *(ML)*
Fanele Sicwetsha *(FW)*
James Lunika *(ML/FW/ST)*
Joseph Underwood Ramathleka *(ML)*
Kayakazi Sigwili *(FW)*
Khanyisa Madyibi *(FW)*
Lunathi Kwinana *(FW)*
Lwazi Mahlaka *(ML)*
MaDlamini Catherine Sethuntsa *(ML)*
Mametsi-a-Leoatle Sethuntsa *(FW/ML)*
MaMjoli Eunice Nomantombazana Sethuntsa *(ST/FW)*
Mbeko Sigwili *(FW)*
Nomzamo Mpeta *(FW)*
Roseberry Maloi *(FW)*
Thabo Sethuntsa *(FW/ST)*

Tsolwana Mpayipheli *(FW)*
Vuyo Sijentu *(FW)*

Kokstad

Barry Elliot *(ML/FW)*
Bim Stanford *(FW)*
Ellen Jones *(ML)*
Faith Mpofu *(ST/FW)*
Francina Greeves *(FW/ST)*
Ganiko Radebe Mgijima *(ML)*
Haldane Basson *(FW)*
Isaac Godden *(ML)*
Isaac Tuku *(FW)*
Jack Lewis *(ML)*
Janice Willemse *(FW)*
Jill and Elizabeth Scott *(FW)*
Jimmy R. Smith *(ML)*
Maria Edwards *(FW)*
Meshack Nogudlu *(ST/FW)*
Miriam July *(ST/FW)*
Ndoda Mgwabashe *(ST)*
Pie Dorning *(FW)*
Robin Scott *(ML)*
Thandeka Jonas *(ST/FW)*
Theo Christodoulou *(FW)*
Trevor Strachan *(FW)*

Matatiele and elsewhere in East Griqualand

John van Niekerk *(FW)*
Mrs Njongwe *(ML)*
Nthoa Bohlokoa Moeshoeshoe *(ML)*
Tsepo Letsie *(ML)*

Informants from elsewhere in South Africa
Alf Marsburg *(FW)*
Andile Zeka *(ML)*
Billy Selili *(ML)*
Credo Mutwa *(FW)*
Darlington Nyankuza *(ML/FW)*
Fabio Petronio *(FW)*
Henry Siebert *(ML)*
Joe Jordan *(ML)*
Lala Yako *(ML/FW)*
Leholisa Qina *(FW)*
Madiba Sethuntsa *(FW)*
Ma-Ngconde (Joyce Makiwe Mali) *(ST/FW)*
Ma-Six Pretty Sethuntsa *(ST)*

Qacha's Nek and the Hermitage
Antonia Mpeoane Matsipsa *(FW/ST)*
Lekhotla Tseane *(FW/ST)*
Mampheteng Tshiame *(FW/ST)*
Mapheelo Mahaseli *(FW/ST)*
Martin Qacha *(FW)*
Mostat Taole *(FW/ST)*
Motloi Motloi *(FW/ST)*
Pascal Makeka *(ML/FW)*

Ha Ramokakatlela
Lazarus Rabukana *(ML/FW)*
Lefu Ma-Thabo Motumi *(ML/FW)*
Mafihlela Motsi *(ML/FW)*
Mkethwa Ponya *(ML/FW)*
Teboho Mokakatlela *(ML/FW)*

Maseru and elsewhere in Lesotho
Anthony Nkosana Faro *(ML)*
James Allah *(ML)*
Motsapi Moorosi *(ML)*

Notes

Prologue
1. Transkei's Richest Native: The Incredible Dr Khotso.' *Daily Dispatch*, 17 July 1954.
2. Crous, Con. 'Khotso Lives!' *Scope*, 11 May 1973: 80.
3. *Daily Dispatch*, 7 August 1972; *Natal Witness*, 7 August 1972.
4. Cited in Blades, Jack. 1982. Unpublished work on Khotso Sethuntsa. (Hereafter, unless otherwise indicated, information provided by Blades derives from this source.)
5. Italics are used the first time that words from Xhosa, Sotho, Zulu and certain other languages are included in the text. Thereafter, the meaning of these words is explained and they are not italicised in later instances. Several of these words are used frequently, constituting important features of Khotso's story, and in many cases they are terms for which no concise English equivalent exists. (Definitions of such recurring terms are also included in the Glossary.)
6. A range of informants, including James Lunika, two of Khotso's daughters, and his wives MaMjoli Eunice Sethuntsa and Ellen Jones, testify to this, as does the journalist Jack Blades.

Chapter 1: In the Land of the Red Snow
1. Jack Blades is the source of this story.
2. Contemporary southern African place names are used, such as *Lesotho* rather than *Basutoland*.
3. This phrase is taken from Robert C. Germond's *The Chronicles of Basutoland* (Morija Sesoto Book Depot, 1967: 19), in which Lesotho is described as 'the land of the hidden rivers'.

4. This cavern would be the Luma-Luma cave in Sotho, since the letter *l* when followed by an *i* or a *u* is pronounced as a *d* in this language. However, for purposes of simplicity, the name of this cave and the term *dingaka* (which is periodically used in the course of this book) are spelled phonetically, with a *d* rather than an *l*. In other cases, the correct Sotho spelling is retained.
5. Traditional healers and diviners, termed *dingaka* in Sotho, are known as *amagqirha* in Xhosa tradition and *izangoma* in Zulu tradition. (The singular forms of these terms are *ngaka*, *igqirha* and *sangoma* respectively.) These are spiritual practitioners with special powers of healing and insight into the unseen, the unknown and the future, who have received a calling and undergone a process of initiation into their profession. Forms of divination vary. For instance, a diviner might throw the bones and take note of the way in which they fall. Another way in which a diviner might be enlightened is through communication with or a visitation from the ancestors, which could take the form of a dream. A diviner could provide answers to questions or discern the cause of illness or misfortune, discern that which is hidden or that which is yet to take place, or interpret the wishes of the ancestors.
6. Donnelly, Simon. 1999. 'Southern Tekela Nguni Is Alive: Reintroducing the Phuthi Language.' *International Journal of the Sociology of Language* (136): 97–120. Germond: 330.
7. Anglicised versions of the names of southern African peoples and their languages are used, omitting the Xhosa, Zulu and Sotho prefixes. For example, the word *Sotho* denotes both the people and their language, instead of *Basotho* and *Sesotho* respectively. Similarly, the term *Xhosa* indicates the language isiXhosa, and the Baphuthi people are referred to as the *Phuthi*.
8. These points concerning the Phuthi have been made by the historian Jeff Peires.
9. Ideas and information in this paragraph and in various parts of this book have already been published in academic articles by Felicity Wood in *Kronos*, *Indilinga*, *International Journal of the Humanities* and *Journal of South African Literary Studies*. (Full details appear in the Bibliography.)
10. Scheub, Harold. 1996. *The Tongue Is Fire: South African Storytellers Under Apartheid*. Madison: University of Wisconsin Press: 300–303.

11. Peires, J. B. 1989. *The Dead Will Arise: Nongqawuse and the Great Cattle-Killing Movement of 1856–7.* Johannesburg: Ravan; Bloomington and Indianapolis: Indiana University Press; London: James Currey: 125.
12. Various points in this and the preceding paragraph have been made by Manton Hirst. 1997. 'A River of Metaphors: Interpreting the Xhosa Diviner's Myth' in McAllister, Patrick (ed). *Culture and the Commonplace: Anthropological Essays in Honour of David Hammond-Tooke.* Johannesburg: Witwatersrand University Press: 219–220.
13. The rock art expert Frans Prins has drawn attention to these points. More broadly, he provided much of the information in this chapter concerning the San. (Where indicated, some of the information of this nature was also derived from interviews with specific informants.)
14. The account of Moorosi's confrontation with the British in this and the following paragraph draws on Germond: 332–337, 339, 340.
15. Couzens, Tim. 2003. *Murder at Morija.* Johannesburg: Random House: 129–130.
16. Kruger, Paul. 1902. *The Memoirs of Paul Kruger.* London: Unwin: 66–70.
17. Michael Lewis and Sylvia Tloti: discussions with David Ambrose.

Chapter 2: Into Nomansland
1. The Griqua were a people of mixed-race descent who originated in the Northern Cape. In the early nineteenth century, they established territories of their own in the Orange River region, in what would be known as Griqualand West. But they became engaged in a struggle for land with white farmers, so in 1861, under Adam Kok III, they relocated to what would become East Griqualand.
2. Davenport, T. R. H. 1977. *South Africa: A Modern History.* Johannesburg: Macmillan: 103–104. Beinart, William and Bundy, Colin. 1987. *Hidden Struggles in Rural South Africa: Politics and Popular Movements in the Transkei and Eastern Cape, 1890–1930.* London: James Currey; Johannesburg: Ravan: 46.
3. Beinart and Bundy: 46, 48, 55. Beinart, William. 1986. 'Settler Accumulation in East Griqualand from the Demise of the Griqua to the Natives Land Act' in Beinart, William and Delius, Peter and Trapido, Stanley (eds). *Putting a Plough to the Ground: Accumulation and Dispossession in Rural South Africa, 1850–1930.* Johannesburg: Ravan: 259, 283.

4. *Kokstad Advertiser*, 30 October 1925.
5. References to Govan Mbeki are taken from the online version of his 1964 work *South Africa: The Peasants' Revolt* (http://www.anc.org.za/books/peasants.html).
6. Roux, Edward. 1964. *Time Longer than Rope: A History of the Black Man's Struggle for Freedom in South Africa*. Madison and London: University of Wisconsin Press: 88. Bundy, Colin. 1979. *The Rise and Fall of the South African Peasantry*. Cape Town: David Philip; London: James Currey: 110, 114–115.
7. The National Party (NP) was founded in 1914 to advance the interests of the Afrikaners. After winning the 1948 elections under the leadership of D. F. Malan, the Nationalists began implementing their policy of *apartheid* (literally 'apart-ness'), a legalised form of racial segregation intended to benefit white South Africans, especially the Afrikaans-speaking members of the NP. The Nationalists remained the ruling party until the first democratic elections took place in South Africa in 1994.
8. Beinart and Bundy: 25–32, 191–196.
9. When Khotso Was Kokstad Shoeshine Boy.' *Daily Dispatch*, 4 August 1972.

Chapter 3: Hunting for Jackals and Dwarves
1. Mantsopa predicted, for instance, that King Moshoeshoe would triumph over the British forces near Modderpoort in 1851 and at Berea in 1852. At the very same time, she also prophesied the coming of a great rain that would break the drought that gripped the area. All these prophecies came true. (Ambrose, David. 2002. ''Mantsopa, Prophetess of the Sotho Nation.' Speech delivered at Modderpoort on 9 August 2002 to commemorate International Women's Day and the renaming of the Ladybrand District as Mantsopa Municipality: 3. Coplan, David. 2003. 'Land from the Ancestors: Popular Religious Re-appropriations Along the South Africa–Lesotho border.' *Journal of Southern African Studies* 29 (4): 977–993. Rademeyer, Julian. 'Resolute Prophet Lives On as a "Saint".' *Sunday Times*, 5 November 2006: 33.)
2. Ambrose: 4.
3. Sylvia Tloti: discussion with David Ambrose.
4. The oral narrative theorist Isidore Okpewho discusses this aspect of trickster stories in *Myth in Africa*. 2003. Cambridge: Cambridge University Press: 33.

5. This information is based on an interview conducted by Michael Lewis.
6. Beinart, William. 2003. *The Rise of Conservation in South Africa: Settlers, Livestock and the Environment, 1770–1950.* Oxford: Oxford University Press: 195.
7. Beinart: 227.
8. Beinart: 195.
9. Julius Khoapa, speech delivered at Khotso Sethuntsa's funeral. Cited in Blades.
10. Beinart: 205–206.
11. Before decimal currency was introduced into South Africa in 1961, the *tickey* (or *tickie*, or *ticky*) was the colloquial term for a little coin, the threepenny-bit.
12. Informants who confirm this include one direct descendant of Moorosi as well as Stephen Gill, curator of the Morija Museum, Lesotho. See also How, Monica Walsham. 1962. *The Mountain Bushmen of Basutoland.* Pretoria: Van Schaik: 22.

Chapter 4: The Snake in a Whirlwind
1. 'The Cyclone Which Set Khotso on the Road to Success.' *Kokstad Advertiser*, 1 February 1973. *Natal Mercury*, 27 July 1972.
2. Jill and Elizabeth Scott are the sources of this information.
3. 'Destructive Cyclone Near Kokstad: Mr Eric Scott's Homestead Devastated.' *Kokstad Advertiser*, 13 November 1925.
4. 'The Cyclone Which Set Khotso on the Road to Success.' *Kokstad Advertiser*, 1 February 1973.
5. Julius Khoapa, speech delivered at Khotso Sethuntsa's funeral. Cited in Blades.
6. Felicity Wood. Telephone conversation with Manton Hirst. Although this phrase was not being applied to Khotso, it seems appropriate here.
7. Niane, D. T. 1965. *Sundiata: An Epic of Old Mali.* Harlow: Longman: 84
8. Mitchell, Peter. 2002. *The Archeology of Southern Africa.* Cambridge: Cambridge University Press: 166, 214, 220. In 1964, the anthropologist Mircea Eliade once went so far as to declare that 'quartz crystals are universally recognised as possessing magical qualities' (cited in Mitchell: 220).
9. Breyer-Brandwijk, M. G. and Watt, J. M. 1932. *The Medicinal and Poisonous Plants of South Africa.* Edinburgh: E & S: 116.

10. Fanele Sicwetsha grew up surrounded by stories about Khotso, and as a student he became fascinated by the oral narratives in his area, conducting independent research into them. Where indicated, some of his findings are included in this book.
11. Blades provides this account.
12. Sylvia Tloti gives this description of *ukuvutha*.

Chapter 5: The Wife Below the Water
1. '*Indodakazi kaKhotso Ngempilo Kayise.*' *Ilanga*, 19 August 1972: 1.
2. *Ukuthwala* should not be confused with *ukuthwasa*. This latter word has a very different meaning, denoting the period of initiation and training that an individual who has received a special calling to be an *igqirha* (the Xhosa term for a traditional healer and diviner) is required to undergo.
3. Wilson, Monica Hunter. 1936. *Reaction to Conquest*. London: Oxford: 287. It has been argued by, for example, the anthropologist Penny Bernard that the negative aspects of the snake, in the form of wealth-giving 'muti' snakes, developed through contact with modern economic forces, specifically the pressure to accumulate individual wealth (Bernard, Penny. 2000. 'Negotiating the Authenticity of Traditional Healers in Natal.' English version of an article published as '*Guérisseurs traditionnels du Natal: une authenticité negociée*' in Faure, V. (ed). *Dynamiques religieuses en Afrique australe*. Paris: Kathala: 13). This ties in with the way belief in the mamlambo was spread among southern African peoples through the migrant-labour system. This method of employment was indicative of the fact that individuals had lost the capacity to sustain themselves through their traditional lifestyle and had become dependent on white-owned operations, such as mining and commercial farming, in order to support themselves and their families (Niehaus, Isak. 2001. *Witchcraft, Power and Politics: Exploring the Occult in the South African Lowveld*. Cape Town: David Philip; London: Pluto: 46, 56).
4. Morrow, Sean and Vokwana, Nwabisa. 2004. ' "Oh Hurry to the River": The Meaning of *uMamlambo* Models in the Tyumie Valley, Eastern Cape' in *Kronos* 30. November: 192.
5. Niehaus: 58–59. The mamlambo can also appear in the form of bright, shiny objects. She is associated with things that shimmer and glisten, like water, lights and the gleaming scales of a snake. This,

anthropologist Isak Niehaus has pointed out, links her to symbols of wealth, such as coins, which sparkle and shine. Money and water, he also observes, share similar attributes. Both are viewed as essential for survival in today's society, yet they possess hazardous aspects (58–59).
6. Niehaus: 56.
7. D'Oliveira, John. 'Millionaire Medicine Man.' *Sunday Tribune*, 10 October 1965: 4. All subsequent references to D'Oliveira derive from this source.
8. Julius Khoapa, speech delivered at Khotso Sethuntsa's funeral. Cited in Blades.
9. Southall, Roger. 1983. *South Africa's Transkei: The Political Economy of an 'Independent' Bantustan*. New York: Monthly Review Press: 20.
10. Peires has drawn attention to this point.
11. Scheub: 300.

Chapter 6: At the White House

1. 'Transkei's Richest Native: The Incredible Dr Khotso.' *Daily Dispatch*, 17 July 1954.
2. Becker, Peter. 1975. *Trails and Tribes in Southern Africa*. London: Clowes: 141–142. All subsequent references to Becker are taken from pp. 137–145 of this book.
3. Mohlomi, Godwin. 'Eunice: Wife Parade Was Just a Gag.' *Sunday Times Extra*, 31 March 1974: 2.
4. 'Transkei's Richest Native: The Incredible Dr Khotso.' *Daily Dispatch*, 17 July 1954.
5. Ngcobo, Duke. 'Our Only African Millionaire Medicine Man ... Khotso Sethuntsa.' *Drum*, August 1958: 53. All subsequent references to Ngcobo derive from this article, pp. 48–55.
6. This account is based on Jack Blades's description.
7. Coulter, Jean. 'The Mystery of Khotso and the Kruger Millions.' *Daily Dispatch*, 22 September 1989.
8. Mosimane, Maleho. 'What Happened to the Khotso Millions?' *Pace*, September 1984: 51.
9. Hirst, Manton. 2001. 'Khotso: Legendary Herbalist.' *Imvubu: Amathole Museum Newsletter* 13 (3): 1.
10. Sethuntsa, Mosala Jack. 1975. Affidavit submitted to the Appeal Court, Mthatha.
11. Mohlomi, Godwin. 'Ellen: He Was So Charming, I Loved Him.'

Sunday Times Extra, 31 March 1974: 2.
12. Jones, Ivy. 1975. Affidavit submitted to the Appeal Court, Mthatha.
13. Jack Blades; also cited in submission from Nomalizo Sethuntsa to the Appeal Court, Mthatha, in 1975. Ellen's statement two paragraphs below is taken from the same sources.
14. Sethuntsa, Gloria. 1990. Affidavit submitted to the Magistrate's Court, Mount Frere.
15. Du Preez Bezdrob, Anne Marie. 2003. *Winnie Mandela: A Life*. Cape Town: Zebra: 36.

Chapter 7: From Ibangalala to Ukuthwala

1. 'Transkei's Richest Native: The Incredible Dr Khotso.' *Daily Dispatch*, 17 July 1954.
2. D'Oliveira: 4.
3. A press cutting in which this is reported was framed and displayed, among many other press cuttings, at Mount Nelson. It still hangs in the front room today.
4. Newman, Bernard. 1965. *South African Journey*. London: Travel Book Club: 85–86. All subsequent references to Newman are taken from pp. 84–88 of this book.
5. Ngcobo: 53–55.
6. Historically, Limba's church was known as the Bantu Church of Christ. Baines, Gary. 1992. ' "In the World But Not of It": "Bishop" Limba and the Church of Christ in New Brighton. c. 1929–1949.' *Kronos* 19: 102–134.
7. This point and the ones concerning Limba in the previous paragraph were made by Baines: 123–126.
8. In 1962, the anthropologist W. D. Hammond-Tooke stated that the Bhaca people, in East Griqualand and the northern Transkei, maintained that two men, one in Durban and the other in Kokstad, were famous sellers of *intlathu*, wealth-giving snakes (*Bhaca Society*, Cape Town: Oxford University Press: 265). It is most probable that Khotso was the second man in question.
9. This was noted by the economic historian Harold Wolpe, among others. He made the following points: 'By the 1920s attention was already being drawn to the deterioration of the situation in the African areas and in 1932 the Native Economic Commission report (1930–1932) commented at length on the extremely low productivity

of farming in the Reserves, on the increasing malnutrition and on the very real danger of environmental destruction through soil erosion. Every subsequent Government Commission dealing with the Reserves reiterated these points and drew attention to the decline in output.' (Cited in Simpkins, Charles. 1981. 'Agricultural Production in the African Reserves of South Africa, 1918–1969.' *Journal of Southern African Studies* 7 (2) April: 256.)

10. A. P. Walshe, cited in Copelyn, John. 1974. *The Mpondo Revolt, 1960*. Unpublished dissertation. University of the Witwatersrand: 4–5.
11. Redding, Sean. 1996. 'Government Witchcraft: Taxation, the Supernatural and the Mpondo Revolt in the Transkei, South Africa, 1955–1963.' *African Affairs* 95 (381) October: 567.
12. Some of the basic recommendations in this report were rejected by the government in 1956 (Carter, Gwendolyn M. and Karis, Thomas and Stultz, Newell M. 1967. *South Africa's Transkei: The Politics of Domestic Colonialism*. London: Heinemann: 42–45).
13. Peires has observed that the chief in question might have been King Mhlontlo of the Mpondomise, who spent nearly twenty years in exile near Khotso's home terrain in Lesotho. As with a number of other prominent figures, including Mantsopa, the king became drawn into the legends surrounding Khotso.
14. Gcina Mhlope's story 'Nokulunga's Wedding' (1983), which is set in the Transkei, depicts one instance of female abduction, protesting against this practice.
15. Peires: 131–132. Hodgson, Janet. 1982. *The God of the Xhosa*. Cape Town: Oxford University Press: 23, 18.
16. The older Sotho spelling of the word 'sea' is *leoatle*. Khotso's daughter's name is spelled Mametsi-a-Leoatle, in full.
17. Hammond-Tooke, W. D. 1975. 'The Symbolic Structure of Cape Nguni Cosmology' in Whisson, Michael G. and West, Martin (eds). *Religion and Social Change in South Africa*. Cape Town: David Philip; London: Collings: 22.

Chapter 8: Greater than God

1. D'Oliveira: 4. The references to press articles in the rest of this chapter also derive from this source.

Chapter 9: The Kruger Connection
1. Sethuntsa, Khotso and Fortein, C. J. R. 1956. Deposition to Kruger House.
2. 'A Man Goes on His Knees to Preserve Kruger House.' *Pretoria News*, 12 September 1956. The quotation from the *Pretoria News* later in this chapter is also taken from this article.
3. Mutwa, Credo. 1998. *Indaba My Children*. Edinburgh: Canongate: 610.
4. The discussion of the Kruger millions in this section draws on information contained in *The Smuts Papers* (Oxford University Press, 1960), cited by Blades.
5. Strauss, Gehri. 'Khotso: Millionaire Herbalist, Fascinating Character.' *South African Panorama*, April 1961: 19.
6. Coulter, Jean. 'The Mystery of Khotso and the Kruger Millions.' *Daily Dispatch*, 22 September 1989. 'When Khotso Was Kokstad Shoeshine Boy'. *Daily Dispatch*, 4 August 1972.
7. Blades, Jack. 'The Story Khotso Told the Clairvoyant: How I Found the Kruger Millions.' *Sunday Times*, 27 August 1972: 6.
8. This information and the point in the last sentence of the preceding paragraph derive from Blades, Jack. 'The Secret of Those July Tips.' *Sunday Times News Magazine*, 13 August 1972: 1.
9. 'Khotso's Bones Tip "July" Winner.' *The Post*, 29 June 1969.
10. Blades, Jack. 'The Secret of Those July Tips.' *Sunday Times News Magazine*, 13 August 1972: 1. Duffield, Ernie. 1992. *The History of the Rothmans July Handicap*. Cape Town: Struik: 107–108.
11. *Natal Mercury*, 11 October 1961.

Chapter 10: Verwoerd's Inyanga
1. The description of the meeting between Khotso and H. F. Verwoerd is derived from information provided by Michael Lewis, based on his own conversations with Ellen.
2. The correspondence between Khotso Sethuntsa and Verwoerd, entitled 'Mr Khotso Sethuntsa Writes to the Minister for Native Affairs', was published in *Umthunywa*, 1 March 1958: 3.
3. Roux: 370.
4. Cited in Baldwin, Alec. 1975. 'Mass Removals and Separate Development.' *Journal of Southern African Studies* 1 (2) April: 221.
5. Carter, Karis and Stultz: 36–37; Roux: 419.
6. Michael Lewis is the source of this information.
7. Michael Lewis has this picture, sent to him by Danie Verwoerd.

8. Barlow, Margaret and Buchan, Bruce. 1995. *The Last of the Lotus Lands: Being an account of twenty-four years spent in Pondoland.* Natal: Kohler Carton and Print: 147–148.
9. Cited in Strauss, Gehri. 'Khotso: Millionaire Herbalist, Fascinating Character.' *South African Panorama,* April 1961: 19.
10. Monica Wilson mentions this in her 1936 study of Pondoland. 'All *ubuthi* [materials for sorcery] come from Europeans. They are the real *amagqwirha* (witches or sorcerers). They do not use it but keep it and sell it to people,' one of Wilson's informants said (316–317).
11. Redding: 555–579.
12. For example, anthropologist Adam Ashforth argues that a commonly held perception in Soweto during the apartheid era was that the government, in its oppressive, exploitative actions, was seen as 'an unmitigated source of evil'. Ashforth continues: 'Beyond the apparent face of political power . . . people perceived an originary source of evil power. The hidden, secret, nature of this power fostered fantasies about an enormous capacity for causing misfortune' (1998. 'Witchcraft, Violence and Democracy in the New South Africa.' *Cahiers d'Etudes Africaines* 150–152 [2–4]: 527).
13. Redding: 555–579.
14. Finnegan, Ruth. 1970. *Oral Literature in Africa.* Nairobi: Oxford University Press: 345.
15. This is evident today – so much so that on 31 August 2006, on the home page of the Afrikaner NGK (the Nederduitse Gereformeerde Kerk [Dutch Reformed Church]) website, it is noted with alarm that some Afrikaners go so far as to consult 'sangomas, witchdoctors and traditional healers'. Grobler, Japie. *'Die "New Age" Movement'* (http:// www.gksa.org.za/kies/Artikels/artikel_11.htm).
16. Blades, Jack. 1972. 'Strange Stories They Tell About the Most Famous of All Muti-men.' *Sunday Times News Magazine,* 13 August 1972: 1.
17. Redding: 565; Southall: 109.

Chapter 11: Hubris to Nemesis
1. *Kokstad Advertiser*, 4 April 1957.
2. *Kokstad Advertiser*, 31 August 1950.
3. Baptismal Certificate. Peace Doctor Khotso Sethuntsa. Baptised 27 October 1922, Kokstad. Born 7 January 1898.
4. Cited in Blades.

5. The description of the rocking horse was provided by Peires.
6. Ngani, Marcus. 'Khotso's Love-Life: Marriage Was His Dying Gift to Bethinja.' *Weekend World*, 21–23 March 1974: 5.
7. Tloti, Sylvia. 2005. 'The Women in Khotso Sethuntsa's Life: A Study of How They Epitomise the Role of Women in African Society.' Unpublished paper. Presented at Govan Mbeki Seminar, University of Fort Hare.

Chapter 12: Bantustan Fantasia
1. This writer has subsequently noticed that a 1960 article by John Niewenhuysen in *Africa South* IV (2) January–March: 36–41 also makes use of this chapter's title, although in a different context. Apparently, the two words that compose this chapter heading lend themselves to being placed in conjunction.
2. *Scope*, 10 October 1966.
3. Bennet, Leon. 'Millionaire Medicine Man Is Lord of Transkei.' *Sunday Times News Magazine*, 2 June 1963: 1.
4. 'I Count Petty Cash – There Is R4m of It.' *Sunday Tribune*, 9 January 1966.
5. *Territorial News*, 6 January 1966.
6. Mohlomi, Godwin. 'Eunice: Wife Parade Was Just a Gag.' *Sunday Times Extra*, 31 March 1974: 2.
7. Photograph belonging to James Lunika; source not indicated.
8. Smuts, J. C. 1936. Foreword in Wilson: vii, for points in the earlier part of this paragraph. Wilson: 7.
9. Wilson: 319, 539–540.
10. Blades, Jack. 'Strange Stories They Tell About the Most Famous of All Muti-men.' *Sunday Times News Magazine*, 13 August 1972: 1.
11. 'Khotso.' *Friends of East Griqualand Museum*, 8 February 2003: 15.
12. Bundy: 124.

Chapter 13: Anger in the Hills
1. Crais, Clifton. 2002. *The Politics of Evil: Magic, State Power and the Political Imagination in South Africa*. Cambridge: Cambridge University Press: 148.
2. Redding: 555; Southall: 107.
3. *Daily Dispatch*, 24 March 1997.
4. Carter, Karis and Stultz: 25; Crais: 203–204.
5. Crais: 204. Dyanti, Benson. 'Trouble in the Bantustans.' *Drum*,

September 1960: 24. *Daily Dispatch*, 24 March 1997.
6. Dyanti: 25.
7. *Daily Dispatch*, 24 March 1997; Mbeki.
8. Southall: 112; Dyanti: 24; Copelyn: 70.
9. Dyanti: 21–22.
10. The information concerning the killing of Vukayibambe Sigcau is based on Crais's account: 178–180; also drawing on Copelyn: 44 and Southall: 110.
11. Copelyn: 75; Southall: 110–111.
12. Mbeki; Carter, Karis and Stultz: 26; Southall: 113; Crais: 206–208; *Daily Dispatch*, 24 March 1997.
13. This was reported in 'Troubled Pondoland.' *Umthunywa*, 3 December 1960: 3. The information and the quotation in the preceding paragraph are taken from this article and also from 'A Millionaire's Life Is Menaced by Pondos'. *Sunday Tribune*, 27 November 1960.

Chapter 14: Sex, Drugs and the Broederbond
1. Streek, Barry and Wicksteed, Richard. 1981. *Render unto Kaiser: A Transkei Dossier*. Johannesburg: Ravan: 235–236.
2. Streek and Wicksteed: 3, 10.
3. *Daily Dispatch*, 12 May 1964.
4. The photograph and caption are taken from a newspaper clipping belonging to James Lunika; source not indicated.
5. '*UKhotso Ujonge Ukuvula, Ishishini Lomqhaphu.*' *Umthunywa*, 27 February 1965.
6. 'S.A.P. Visit Wealthy Herbalist.' *Natal Witness*, 24 December 1965.
7. Cited in Blades.
8. 'S.A.P. Visit Wealthy Herbalist.' *Natal Witness*, 24 December 1965.
9. 'Millionaire Sethuntsa Loses Wife to Red.' *Natal Mercury*, 10 January 1966.
10. Blades, Jack. 'The Sex Secrets of Khotso Sethuntsa . . . Last of Red Hot Lovers.' *Sunday Times Extra*, 31 March 1974: 2.
11. Van Woerden, Henk. 2000. *A Mouthful of Glass*. Johannesburg: Jonathan Ball.
12. This walking stick is described in '*Uphoswe Ngama – R329,176 uBethinja Khotso, Waf'isiqaqa.*' *Intsimbi*, 30 March 1974: 5.

Chapter 15: Tsotsis and Treasure
1. Barlow: 146.

2. Lunika recounted the events described in the first part of this chapter during interview sessions. Blades also describes these episodes in his unpublished work on Khotso and in an article entitled 'I Saw Khotso's Magic Stop Bullets.' *Sunday Times Extra*, 5 October 1975: 5.
3. Blades mentions this in his article in the *Sunday Times Extra*, cited above.
4. Crampton, Hazel. 2004. *The Sunburnt Queen*. Johannesburg: Jacana: 285. Kirby, Percival R. 1960. *The True Story of the Grosvenor*. Cape Town: Oxford University Press: 181–183, 207–212. Taylor, Stephen. 2004. *The Caliban Shore*. London: Faber: 255–257.
5. The account of De Backer's visit to Khotso in this chapter is based on Leon Bennet's 1963 report in the *Sunday Times News Magazine*: 1, 7; also on interviews with James Lunika.
6. D'Oliveira: 4.
7. *Daily Dispatch*, 17 June 1963.
8. *Daily Dispatch*, 27 July 1972.

Chapter 16: King of a Slippery Realm
1. 'Khotso, Man with Million Dollar Smile.' *Daily Dispatch*, 20 July 1968.
2. D'Oliveira: 4.
3. Khotso, Man with Million Dollar Smile.' *Daily Dispatch*, 20 July 1968.
4. Blades gives an account of this letter and the other correspondence mentioned earlier in this chapter.
5. Southall: 146–148, 164.
6. 'Khotso May Buy Transkei Towns.' *Daily Dispatch*, 23 February 1965. *Daily Dispatch*, 26 March 1965.
7. Information in this and much of the preceding paragraph derives from *Daily Dispatch*, 8 January 1966 and 6 October 1966. 'I Count Petty Cash – There is R4m of It.' *Sunday Tribune*, 9 January 1966. *Territorial News*, 6 January 1966.
8. *Daily Dispatch*, 8 January 1966.
9. 'I Count Petty Cash – There is R4m of It.' *Sunday Tribune*, 9 January 1966.
10. On 8 January 1966, however, the *Daily Dispatch* reported that Lusikisiki had been zoned entirely black, but Mount Frere had not been. (The information concerning Khotso's properties is taken from the Inventory of the Estate of Khotso Sethuntsa, compiled by J. J. Swartz, 19 June 1973.)
11. Southall: 165–168.

12. This description is based on Sylvia Tloti's first impressions of MaMjoli.
13. Mohlomi, Godwin. 'Eunice: Wife Parade Was Just a Gag.' *Sunday Times Extra*, 31 March 1974: 2.
14. Blades, Jack. 'The Sex Secrets of Khotso Sethuntsa ... Last of Red Hot Lovers.' *Sunday Times Extra*, 31 March 1974: 2.
15. 'Khotso, 90, Takes New Wives.' *Daily Dispatch*, 8 January 1970. *Daily Dispatch*, 12 October 1970. *Pretoria News*, 12 October 1970.
16. Duma, Enoch. 1974. 'Selina: I Will Never Find Another ...' *Sunday Times Extra*, 31 March 1974: 2. '*Uphoswe Ngama – R329,176 uBethinja Khotso, Waf'isiqaqa.*' *Intsimbi*, 30 March 1974: 5.
17. Duma: 2.
18. Duma, Enoch and Mohlomi, Godwin. 31 March 1974. Newspaper clipping given to Michael Lewis; source not indicated.
19. Various family members testify to this, including MaDlamini and Langa's first wife, Elizabeth Brown. (Sethuntsa, Catherine. 1990. Affidavit submitted to the Supreme Court, Mthatha. Du Buisson, Louis. 'The Wife Who Was Left Out in the Cold.' *Pace*, September 1984: 56.)
20. Cited by Blades.
21. Jack Blades. 1974. 'The Sex Secrets of Khotso Sethuntsa ... Last of Red Hot Lovers.' *Sunday Times Extra*, 31 March 1974: 2.

Chapter 17: Nkosazana and Bethinja
1. The Khotso High School was started in 1981. Bethinja contributed towards the building of the first classrooms using endowments from Khotso's estate.
2. 'Khotso, 90, Takes New Wives.' *Daily Dispatch*, 8 January 1970.
3. The points in this and the preceding paragraph derive from Du Buisson: 56.

Chapter 18: The Last Days
1. The description of Khotso's last days contained in this chapter draws on Blades's account of this final part of Khotso's life.
2. The information contained in this and the preceding paragraphs is based on 'Khotso Prefers White Muti'. *Daily News*, 15 May 1972. It is also based on 'Khotso, 92, Loses His Sex Power.' *Daily Dispatch*, 20 May 1972.
3. *Daily Dispatch*, 7 August 1972.

4. Information in this paragraph is based on Ngani, Marcus. 'Khotso Secret Wedding Shock.' *Weekend World*, 6 August 1972: 1. The photograph described in the following paragraph illustrates this article. Information also derived from Ngani, Marcus. 'Khotso's Love-Life: Marriage Was His Dying Gift to Bethinja.' *Weekend World*, 21–23 March 1974: 5. Information also based on Abridged Marriage Certificate: Khotso Sethuntsa and Nomalizo Grangxa. 10 May 1972. The details on the marriage register are reported by Ngani, 1972: 1.
5. *Natal Witness*, 15 March 1974; also Blades.
6. Will of Khotso Sethuntsa. 7 July 1972. Handwritten document dictated to Bethuel Motaung.
7. *Daily Dispatch*, 1 May 1972.
8. The photographs described in this paragraph appeared in an article entitled 'Khotso Dies with Secret of Kruger Millions.' *Drum*, 8 September 1972: 61–63.
9. 'R2m Secret of Life Khotso Dies at 92.' *Daily Dispatch*, 26 July 1972.
10. *Daily News*, 22 July 1972.

Chapter 19: Third Death and Final Party
1. 'Khotso's Family Plan a Swinging Funeral.' *Daily Dispatch*, 5 August 1972. Blades also makes mention of this.
2. *Daily Dispatch*, 27 July 1972.
3. 'Khotso Dies with Secret of Kruger Millions.' *Drum*, 8 September 1972: 61. Also Blades.
4. Points in this and the preceding paragraph derive from 'Khotso's Family Plan a Swinging Funeral.' *Daily Dispatch*, 5 August 1972.
5. *Pretoria News*, 28 August 1972.
6. Information in this and the preceding paragraph draws on the *Daily Dispatch*, 3 August 1972, and Blades.
7. Blades, Jack. 'Khotso Will Rise from the Dead . . . Claim Men Who Believe Him a God.' *Sunday Times News Magazine*, 13 August 1972. *Daily Dispatch*, 3 August 1972. *Daily Dispatch*, 7 August 1972.
8. *Daily Dispatch*, 29 July 1972.
9. Order of Service. Funeral of Khotso Sethuntsa. 6 August 1972.
10. *Natal Mercury*, 7 August 1972.
11. *Weekend World*, 13 August 1972.
12. *Daily Dispatch*, 28 July 1972.
13. *Weekend World*, 13 August 1972.

14. Blades, Jack. 'Strange Stories They Tell About the Most Famous of All Muti-men.' *Sunday Times News Magazine*, 13 August 1972: 1.
15. *Daily Dispatch*, 7 August 1972. *The World*, 7 August 1972.
16. *Pretoria News*, 7 August 1972.
17. *Daily Dispatch*, 7 August 1972.
18. Mosimane, Maleho. 'What Happened to the Khotso Millions?' *Pace*, September 1984: 50.
19. Blades, Jack. 1972. 'Khotso Will Rise from the Dead . . . Claim Men Who Believe Him a God.' *Sunday Times News Magazine*, 13 August 1972: 1, 10.
20. *Pretoria News*, 27 July 1972.
21. *Daily Dispatch*, 8 August 1972.

Chapter 20: The Boedel

1. *Pretoria News*, 26 July 1972.
2. *The Star*, 27 July 1972.
3. This point, and Bethinja's statement in the preceding paragraph, derive from Mosimane, Maleho. 'What Happened to the Khotso Millions?' *Pace*, September 1984: 54, 50.
4. *Pretoria News*, 15 August 1972.
5. Inventory of the Estate of Khotso Sethuntsa. Compiled by J. J. Swartz. 19 June 1973.
6. *Daily Dispatch*, 29 July 1972.
7. Blades makes mention of this.
8. Bethinja's description of the events that took place appears in *Daily Dispatch*, 12 August 1972. Golela's version is provided by Blades.
9. *Pretoria News*, 28 August 1972; *Daily Dispatch*, 12 August 1972. Blades provides details about the sentences meted out by the court.
10. *Daily Dispatch*, 28 June 1974; also Blades quotes from an affidavit submitted by Langa; and *Weekend World*, 20–22 June 1974.
11. 'Bethinja Collapses in Court.' *Weekend World*, 21–23 March 1974: 5. *Intsimbi*, 30 March 1974: 1, 5.
12. *Daily Dispatch*, 15 March 1974.
13. *Weekend World*, 21–23 March 1974: 5. Ngani, 1974: 5.
14. This subheading appeared in Blades's article 'The Magician, the Girl and the Frightened Father.' *Sunday Times Extra*, 14 September 1975: 5. Mosala Jack Sethuntsa. 1975. Affidavit submitted to the Appeal Court, Mthatha.

15. Duma and Mohlomi. 31 March 1974. Newspaper clipping given to Michael Lewis; source not indicated.
16. *Weekend World*, 21–23 March 1974: 5.
17. Duma and Mohlomi. 31 March 1974. Newspaper clipping given to Michael Lewis; source not indicated.
18. *Intsimbi*, 30 March 1974: 1, 5.
19. Duma and Mohlomi. 31 March 1974. Newspaper clipping given to Michael Lewis; source not indicated. Blades makes reference to Selina's legal attempt to regain Four Boy. But it was also reported that while Bethinja tried to claim to be Four Boy's mother in court, Selina did make it clear that she wanted her son back. *Intsimbi*, 30 March 1974: 1, 5.
20. Ngani, 1974: 5.
21. *Weekend World*, 21–23 March 1974: 5. *Intsimbi*, 30 March 1974: 1, 5.
22. *Daily Dispatch*, 16 March 1974.
23. The photograph of Langa appeared in *Intsimbi*, 30 March 1974: 1.
24. *Daily Dispatch*, 10 August 1974.
25. *Weekend World*, 20–22 June 1974; *Daily Dispatch*, 28 June 1974; *Natal Mercury*, 28 June 1974. Sethuntsa, Nomalizo [Bethinja]. 1975. Submission to the Appeal Court, Mthatha.
26. Blades, Jack. 'The Magician, the Girl and the Frightened Father.' *Sunday Times Extra*, 14 September 1975: 5.
27. Du Buisson, Louis. 'The Wife Who Was Left Out in the Cold.' *Pace*, September 1984: 56.
28. This is indicated by Blades.
29. Blades, Jack. 'Khotso's Magic Snake.' *Sunday Times Extra*, 12 October 1975: 5.
30. Mosimane: 54.
31. *Daily Dispatch*, 2 June 1995.

Chapter 21: Riches Are Like Mist
1. Mosimane, Maleho. 'What Happened to the Khotso Millions?' *Pace*, September 1984: 54.
2. Michael Lewis. Interview with Kokstad attorney Barry Elliot.
3. Death Notice. Langa Khotso Sethuntsa. 25 January 1982.
4. Du Buisson, Louis. 'The Wife Who Was Left Out in the Cold.' *Pace*, September 1984: 56.
5. Will of Langa Khotso Sethuntsa. 29 May 1980.

6. Mosimane: 54–55.
7. Crous, Con. 'Khotso Lives!' *Scope*, 11 May 1973: 80.
8. Mosimane: 54. The photograph described in the previous paragraph appears in the same article, p. 52.
9. For example, this is claimed in an affidavit from MaDlamini submitted to the Supreme Court, Mthatha, in 1990, and in a submission from Bethinja to the Appeal Court, Mthatha, 1975.
10. Information in this and the preceding two paragraphs derives from affidavits submitted by MaDlamini to the Magistrate's Court, Mount Frere, in 1988, and to the Mthatha Supreme Court in 1990 and 1994.

Chapter 22: Life After Death
1. *Daily Sun*, 5 July 2004.
2. This account of Lunika's dream and its aftermath is based on interviews with Lunika, conducted by Sylvia Tloti and Felicity Wood. It also draws on Blades.
3. Streek and Wicksteed: 353–355.
4. Blades, Jack. 'Khotso Will Rise from the Dead . . . Claim Men Who Believe Him a God.' *Sunday Times News Magazine*, 13 August 1972: 1.

Bibliography

Books, journal articles, presentations and Internet sources

Ambrose, David. 2002. ''Mantsopa, Prophetess of the Sotho Nation.' Speech delivered at Modderpoort on 9August 2002 to commemorate International Women's Day and the renaming of the Ladybrand District as 'Mantsopa Municipality.

Ashforth, Adam. 1998. 'Witchcraft, Violence and Democracy in the New South Africa.' *Cahiers d'Etudes Africaines* 150–152 (2–4): 505–532.

Baines, Gary. 1992. ' "In the World But Not of It": "Bishop" Limba and the Church of Christ in New Brighton, c. 1929–1949.' *Kronos* 19: 102–134.

Baldwin, Alec. 1975. 'Mass Removals and Separate Development.' *Journal of Southern African Studies* 1 (2) April: 215–227.

Barlow, Margaret and Buchan, Bruce. 1995. *The Last of the Lotus Lands: Being an Account of Twenty-four Years Spent in Pondoland*. Natal: Kohler Carton and Print.

Becker, Peter. 1975. *Trails and Tribes in Southern Africa*. London: Clowes.

Beinart, William. 1986. 'Settler Accumulation in East Griqualand from the Demise of the Griqua to the Natives Land Act' in Beinart, William and Delius, Peter and Trapido, Stanley (eds). *Putting a Plough to the Ground: Accumulation and Dispossession in Rural South Africa, 1850–1930*. Johannesburg: Ravan: 259–310.

Beinart, William. 2003. *The Rise of Conservation in South Africa: Settlers, Livestock and the Environment, 1770–1950.* Oxford: Oxford University Press.

Beinart, William and Bundy, Colin. 1987. *Hidden Struggles in Rural South Africa: Politics and Popular Movements in the Transkei and Eastern Cape, 1890–1930.* London: James Currey; Johannesburg: Ravan.

Bernard, Penny. 2000. 'Negotiating the Authenticity of Traditional Healers in Natal.' English version of an article published as '*Guérisseurs traditionnels du Natal: une authenticité negociée*' in Faure, V. (ed). *Dynamiques religieuses en Afrique australe.* Paris: Kathala: 1–16.

Blades, Jack. 1982. Unpublished work on Khotso Sethuntsa.

Breyer-Brandwijk, M. G. and Watt, J. M. 1932. *The Medicinal and Poisonous Plants of South Africa.* Edinburgh: E & S.

Bundy, Colin. 1979. *The Rise and Fall of the South African Peasantry.* Cape Town: David Philip; London: James Currey.

Carter, Gwendolen M. and Karis, Thomas and Stultz, Newell M. 1967. *South Africa's Transkei: The Politics of Domestic Colonialism.* London: Heinemann.

Copelyn, John. 1974. *The Mpondo Revolt, 1960.* Unpublished dissertation. University of the Witwatersrand.

Coplan, David. 2003. 'Land from the Ancestors: Popular Religious Re-appropriations Along the South Africa–Lesotho Border.' *Journal of Southern African Studies* 29 (4): 977–993.

Couzens, Tim. 2003. *Murder at Morija.* Johannesburg: Random House.

Crais, Clifton. 2002. *The Politics of Evil: Magic, State Power and the Political Imagination in South Africa.* Cambridge: Cambridge University Press.

Crampton, Hazel. 2004. *The Sunburnt Queen.* Johannesburg: Jacana.

Davenport, T. R. H. 1977. *South Africa: A Modern History.* Johannesburg: Macmillan.

Donnelly, Simon. 1999. 'Southern Tekela Nguni Is Alive: Reintroducing the Phuthi Language.' *International Journal of the Sociology of Language* (136): 97–120.

Duffield, Ernie. 1992. *The History of the Rothmans July Handicap*. Cape Town: Struik.

Du Preez Bezdrob, Anne Marie. 2003. *Winnie Mandela: A Life*. Cape Town: Zebra.

Finnegan, Ruth. 1970. *Oral Literature in Africa*. Nairobi: Oxford University Press.

Germond, Robert C. 1967. *The Chronicles of Basutoland*. Morija: Morija Sotho Book Depot.

Grobler, Japie. '*Die "New Age" Movement*.' Home page, Nederduitse Gereformeerde Kerk. http://www.gksa.org.za/kies/Artikels/artikel_11.htm. 31 August 2006.

Hammond-Tooke, W. D. 1962. *Bhaca Society*. Cape Town: Oxford University Press.

Hammond-Tooke, W. D. 1975. 'The Symbolic Structure of Cape Nguni Cosmology' in Whisson, Michael G. and West, Martin (eds). *Religion and Social Change in South Africa*. Cape Town: David Philip; London: Collings: 15–33.

Hirst, Manton. 1997. 'A River of Metaphors: Interpreting the Xhosa Diviner's Myth' in McAllister, Patrick (ed). *Culture and the Commonplace: Anthropological Essays in Honour of David Hammond-Tooke*. Johannesburg: Witwatersrand University Press: 217–250.

Hodgson, Janet. 1982. *The God of the Xhosa*. Cape Town: Oxford University Press.

How, Monica Walsham. 1962. *The Mountain Bushmen of Basutoland*. Pretoria: Van Schaik.

Kirby, Percival R. 1960. *The True Story of the Grosvenor*. Cape Town: Oxford University Press.

Kruger, Paul. 1902. *The Memoirs of Paul Kruger*. London: Unwin.

Mbeki, Govan. 1964. *South Africa: The Peasants' Revolt*. http://www.anc.org.za/books/peasants.html.

Mitchell, Peter. 2002. *The Archeology of Southern Africa*. Cambridge: Cambridge University Press.

Morrow, Sean and Vokwana, Nwabisa. 2004. ' "Oh Hurry to the River": The Meaning of *uMamlambo* Models in the Tyumie Valley, Eastern Cape.' *Kronos* 30 (November): 184–199.

Mutwa, Credo. 1998. *Indaba My Children*. Edinburgh: Canongate.

Newman, Bernard. 1965. *South African Journey*. London: Travel Book Club.

Niane, D. T. 1965. *Sundiata: An Epic of Old Mali*. Harlow: Longman.

Niehaus, Isak. 2001. *Witchcraft, Power and Politics: Exploring the Occult in the South African Lowveld*. Cape Town: David Philip; London: Pluto.

Okpewho, Isidore. 1983. *Myth in Africa*. Cambridge: Cambridge University Press.

Peires, J. B. 1989. *The Dead Will Arise: Nongqawuse and the Great Cattle-Killing Movement of 1856-7*. Johannesburg: Ravan; Bloomington and Indianapolis: Indiana University Press; London: James Currey.

Redding, Sean. 1996. 'Government Witchcraft: Taxation, the Supernatural and the Mpondo Revolt in the Transkei, South Africa, 1955–1963.' *African Affairs* 95 (381) October: 555–579.

Roux, Edward. 1964. *Time Longer than Rope: A History of the Black Man's Struggle for Freedom in South Africa*. Madison and London: University of Wisconsin Press.

Scheub, Harold. 1996. *The Tongue Is Fire: South African Storytellers Under Apartheid*. Madison: University of Wisconsin Press.

Simpkins, Charles. 1981. 'Agricultural Production in the African Reserves of South Africa, 1918–1969.' *Journal of Southern African Studies* 7 (2) April: 256–283.

Smuts, J. C. 1936. Foreword in Wilson, Monica Hunter. *Reaction to Conquest*. London: Oxford University Press: vii–ix.

Southall, Roger. 1983. *South Africa's Transkei: The Political Economy of an 'Independent' Bantustan*. New York: Monthly Review Press.

Streek, Barry and Wicksteed, Richard. 1981. *Render unto Kaiser: A Transkei Dossier*. Johannesburg: Ravan.

Taylor, Stephen. 2004. *The Caliban Shore*. London: Faber.

Tloti, Sylvia. 2005. 'The Women in Khotso Sethuntsa's Life: A Study of How They Epitomise the Role of Women in African Society.' Unpublished paper. Presented at Govan Mbeki Seminar, University of Fort Hare.

Van Woerden, Henk. 2000. *A Mouthful of Glass*. Johannesburg: Jonathan Ball.

Wilson, Monica Hunter. 1936. *Reaction to Conquest*. London: Oxford University Press.

Wood, Felicity. 2004. 'Snakes, Spells, Cadillacs and Kruger.' *Kronos* 30 (November): 167–183.

Wood, Felicity. 2005. 'Blood Money: An Analysis of the Socio-economic Implications of Oral Narratives Concerning Wealth-Giving Snakes in the Career of Khotso Sethuntsa.' *Journal of South African Literary Studies* 21 (1–2): 68–92.

Wood, Felicity. 2005. ' "The Snake Will Swallow You": Supernatural Snakes and the Creation of the Khotso Legend.' *Indilinga* 4 (1) June: 347–357.

Wood, Felicity. 2007. 'The Shape-Shifter on the Borderlands: The Trickster Figure in African Orality and in Oral Narratives Concerning One South African Trickster, Khotso Sethuntsa.' *International Journal of the Humanities* 4 (7): 19–26.

Primary newspaper and magazine articles

Some of the following articles are referred to repeatedly or quoted from substantially. Certain articles cited below draw attention to significant aspects of Khotso's life or contain photographs that are discussed in this book.

1925–1958

'Destructive Cyclone Near Kokstad: Mr Eric Scott's Homestead Devastated.' *Kokstad Advertiser*. 13 November 1925.

'Transkei's Richest Native: The Incredible Dr Khotso.' *Daily Dispatch*. 17 July 1954.

'A Man Goes on His Knees to Preserve Kruger House.' *Pretoria News*. 12 September 1956.

'Mr Khotso Sethuntsa Writes to the Minister for Native Affairs.' *Umthunywa*. 1 March 1958: 3.

Ngcobo, Duke. 'Our Only African Millionaire Medicine Man . . . Khotso Sethuntsa.' *Drum*. August 1958: 48–55.

1960–1965

Dyanti, Benson. 'Trouble in the Bantustans.' *Drum*. September 1960: 21–27.

'A Millionaire's Life Is Menaced by Pondos.' *Sunday Tribune*. 27 November 1960.

'Troubled Pondoland.' *Umthunywa*. 3 December 1960: 3.

Strauss, Gehri. 'Khotso: Millionaire Herbalist, Fascinating Character.' *South African Panorama*. April 1961: 18–19.

Bennet, Leon. 'Millionaire Medicine Man Is Lord of Transkei.' *Sunday Times News Magazine*. 2 June 1963: 1, 7.

'Stained Glass for Transkei.' *Natal Mercury*. 11 February 1964.

'Khotso May Buy Transkei Towns.' *Daily Dispatch*. 23 February 1965.

'*UKhotso Ujonge Ukuvula Ishishini Lomqhaphu.*' *Umthunywa*. 27 February 1965.

D'Oliveira, John. 'Millionaire Medicine Man.' *Sunday Tribune*. 10 October 1965: 4.

'S.A.P. Visit Wealthy Herbalist.' *Natal Witness*. 24 December 1965.

1966–1970

'I Count Petty Cash – There Is R4m of It.' *Sunday Tribune*. 9 January 1966.

'Millionaire Sethuntsa Loses Wife to Red.' *Natal Mercury*. 10 January 1966.

'Khotso, Man with Million Dollar Smile.' *Daily Dispatch*. 20 July 1968.
'Khotso's Bones Tip "July" Winner.' *The Post*. 29 June 1969: 1.
'Khotso, 90, Takes New Wives.' *Daily Dispatch*. 8 January 1970.

1972

'Khotso Prefers White Muti.' *Daily News*. 15 May 1972.
'Khotso, 92, Loses His Sex Power.' *Daily Dispatch*. 20 May 1972.
'R2m Secret of Life Khotso Dies at 92.' *Daily Dispatch*. 26 July 1972.
'When Khotso Was Kokstad Shoeshine Boy.' *Daily Dispatch*. 4 August 1972.
'Khotso's Family Plan a Swinging Funeral.' *Daily Dispatch*. 5 August 1972.
Ngani, Marcus. 'Khotso Secret Wedding Shock.' *Weekend World*. 6 August 1972: 1.
Blades, Jack. 'Khotso Will Rise From the Dead . . . Claim Men Who Believe Him a God.' *Sunday Times News Magazine*. 13 August 1972: 1, 10.
Blades, Jack. 'The Secret of Those July Tips.' *Sunday Times News Magazine*. 13 August 1972: 1.
Blades, Jack. 'Strange Stories They Tell About the Most Famous of All Muti-men.' *Sunday Times News Magazine*. 13 August 1972: 1.
'Indodakazi kaKhotso Ngempilo Kayise.' *Ilanga*. 19 August 1972: 1.
Blades, Jack. 'The Story Khotso Told the Clairvoyant: How I Found the Kruger Millions.' *Sunday Times*. 27 August 1972: 6.
'Khotso Dies with Secret of Kruger Millions.' *Drum*. 8 September 1972: 61–63.

1973–1975

'The Cyclone Which Set Khotso on the Road to Success.' *Kokstad Advertiser*. 1 February 1973.
Crous, Con. 'Khotso Lives!' *Scope*. 11 May 1973: 76–77, 80–82.
'Bethinja Collapses in Court.' *Weekend World*. 21–23 March 1974: 5.
Ngani, Marcus. 'Khotso's Love-Life: Marriage Was His Dying Gift to Bethinja.' *Weekend World*. 21–23 March 1974: 5.
'*Uphoswe Ngama – R329,176 uBethinja Khotso, Waf'isiqaqa.*'

Intsimbi. 30 March 1974: 1, 5.

Blades, Jack. 'The Sex Secrets of Khotso Sethuntsa ... Last of Red Hot Lovers.' *Sunday Times Extra.* 31 March 1974: 2.

Duma, Enoch. 'Selina: I Will Never Find Another ...' *Sunday Times Extra.* 31 March 1974: 2.

Mohlomi, Godwin. 'Ellen: He Was So Charming, I Loved Him.' *Sunday Times Extra.* 31 March 1974: 2.

Mohlomi, Godwin. 'Eunice: Wife Parade Was Just a Gag.' *Sunday Times Extra.* 31 March 1974: 2.

Blades, Jack. 'The Magician, the Girl and the Frightened Father.' *Sunday Times Extra.* 14 September 1975: 5.

Blades, Jack. 'I Saw Khotso's Magic Stop Bullets.' *Sunday Times Extra.* 5 October 1975: 5.

Blades, Jack. 'Khotso's Magic Snake.' *Sunday Times Extra.* 12 October 1975: 5.

1984 on

Du Buisson, Louis. 'The Wife Who Was Left Out in the Cold.' *Pace.* September 1984: 56.

Mosimane, Maleho. 'What Happened to the Khotso Millions?' *Pace.* September 1984: 50–55.

Coulter, Jean. 'The Mystery of Khotso and the Kruger Millions.' *Daily Dispatch.* 22 September 1989.

Hirst, Manton. 2001. 'Khotso: Legendary Herbalist.' *Imvubu: Amathole Museum Newsletter* 13 (3): 1, 6–8.

'Khotso.' *Friends of the East Griqualand Museum.* 8 February 2003: 13–16.

Rademeyer, Julian. 'Resolute Prophet Lives On as a "Saint".' *Sunday Times.* 5 November 2006: 33.

Secondary newspaper and magazine articles
Daily Dispatch
17 June 1963

12 May 1964

26 March 1965
8 January 1966
6 October 1966
12 October 1970
1 May 1972
27 July 1972
28 July 1972
29 July 1972
3 August 1972
7 August 1972
8 August 1972
12 August 1972
15 March 1974
16 March 1974
28 June 1974
10 August 1974
2 June 1995
24 March 1997
Daily News
22 July 1972
Daily Sun
5 July 2004
Kokstad Advertiser
30 October 1925
27 November 1925
31 August 1950
4 April 1957
Natal Mercury
11 October 1961
27 July 1972
7 August 1972
28 June 1974

Natal Witness
7 August 1972
15 March 1974
Pretoria News
12 October 1970
26 July 1972
27 July 1972
7 August 1972
15 August 1972
28 August 1972
Scope
10 October 1966
The Star
27 July 1972
Sunday Tribune
27 November 1960
Territorial News
6 January 1966
Weekend World
13 August 1972
20–22 June 1974
The World
7 August 1972

Other Documentation

Abridged Marriage Certificate: Khotso Sethuntsa and Nomalizo Grangxa. 10 May 1972.

Baptismal Certificate. Peace Doctor Khotso Sethuntsa. Baptised 27 October 1922, Kokstad. Born 7 January 1898.

Death Notice. Langa Khotso Sethuntsa. 25 January 1982.

Inventory of the Estate of Khotso Sethuntsa. Compiled by J. J. Swartz, 19 June 1973.

Jones, Ivy. 1975. Affidavit submitted to the Appeal Court, Mthatha.

Order of Service. Funeral of Khotso Sethuntsa. 6 August 1972.

Sethuntsa, Catherine [MaDlamini]. 1988. Affidavit submitted to the Magistrate's Court, Mount Frere.

Sethuntsa, Catherine. 1990. Affidavit submitted to the Supreme Court, Mthatha.

Sethuntsa, Catherine. 1994. Affidavit submitted to the Supreme Court, Mthatha.

Sethuntsa, Gloria. 1990. Affidavit submitted to the Magistrate's Court, Mount Frere.

Sethuntsa, Khotso and Fortein, C. J. R. 1956. Deposition to Kruger House.

Sethuntsa, Mosala Jack. 1975. Affidavit submitted to the Appeal Court, Mthatha.

Sethuntsa, Nomalizo [Bethinja]. 1975. Submission to the Appeal Court, Mthatha.

Will of Khotso Sethuntsa: 7 July 1972. Handwritten document dictated to Bethuel Motaung.

Will of Langa Khotso Sethuntsa. 29 May 1980.

INDEX

a*bantu bomlambo* 10, 11
Abraham, Hans 166, 177, 205–6, 226, 280
African National Congress (ANC) 167, 219, 321
amakhosi 85, 134, 311
Ambrose, David 16
ancestors 9, 10, 16, 52, 56, 74, 103, 116, 123, 156, 286, 317; *see also amakhosi*
apartheid 23, 70, 75, 109–10, 148, 159, 169, 175–6, 183, 212, 221; *see also* segregation

Bantu Authorities 172, 211–12, 215
Bantu Investment Corporation 221
Bantustans 75, 109, 164, 165, 184, 215, 218–20, 236, 238
Barnato, Barney 190
Beaconsfield 20, 26, 40
Beinart, William 33
Bethinja, *see* Sethuntsa, Bethinja
betterment 24–5, 118

Bhongweni 22, 25, 110, 183–4
Broederbond xxii, 166, 169, 219
Brown, Elizabeth 259–60, 303
Bulube, N. P. 280

Caquba 316
Cadillac xxii–xxiii, 183, 200–2, 206, 227, 229, 233, 264, 267, 274, 290
Christianity, *see* Sethuntsa, Khotso: religion
Church of the Nazarites 107
Churchill, Winston 161
Crais, Clifton 212

De Backer, Guido 231–3
diamonds 76–8, 195, 288
Dibopuoa, Chief 54
Drakensberg 4, 7, 11, 18, 20
Duma-Duma cave 4, 5
Durban July 143–4, 156–7, 284
Dutywa (former Idutywa) 238

East Griqualand 17–19, 22, 23, 68, 110, 203, 208

Faye, Eunice Nomantombazana, see Sethuntsa, MaMjoli
Finnegan, Ruth 168
FitzSimons, V. 148, 151
Flagstaff 32, 88, 102, 113, 132, 204, 206
Four Boy, see Sethuntsa, Four Boy

Gloria, see Sethuntsa, Gloria
Golela, William 280, 283, 289–90
Grangxa, Nomalizo, see Sethuntsa, Bethinja
Greeves, Francina 98, 249, 306
Griquas 19
Grosvenor 230–4
Group Areas Act (1950) 176
Group Areas Amendment Act (1957) 183
Gun War 14–15

Ha Mapote 56
Ha Ramokakatlela 3, 4, 5, 9, 12, 17, 52, 58, 158, 315
herbalism 17, 27–32, 44–50, 54, 56, 57, 73, 76, 87, 103–5, 122, 166, 175, 179–80, 183, 196, 244, 284, 292, 304
Herschel 2, 7
Hirst, Manton 48
homelands, see Bantustans

ibangalala xx, 52–3, 105, 223, 243, 256
igqirha (pl. amagqirha) 10, 170
inkanyamba xxiv, 11, 43–4, 58, 67, 130, 132
intandokazi 269

intelezi 12, 51, 96
inyanga xxiii, 49–50
isibunge 107
isipili 52, 122
ixhwele 49

Jameson Raid 146–7
jackal hunting, see Sethuntsa, Khotso: as hunter
Jones, Ellen 30, 39, 66, 68, 88, 96, 98–101, 103, 126, 293–4, 296, 304–6, 323

khanyapa 3, 11
Khoapa, Julius 57, 73, 265
Kilroe Beach 127–9, 175, 230
King William's Town 15, 86, 157, 312
Kokstad 20–5, 29, 58, 69–70, 72, 82–3, 159–60, 174, 182–5, 205, 306
Kruger rands 77, 139, 153
Kruger millions 151–4, 278
Kruger, Paul xxi–xxii, 15–16, 139–58, 226, 232, 316
Kruger Day celebrations 139, 189, 200–1, 206–7, 316–17
Kruger House (Mount Nelson) 199–200, 264, 282–3, 309, 311
Kruger House (Pretoria) 145, 148, 190
Kruger House deposition 144–9, 155

Langa Lase-Afrika, see Sethuntsa, Langa
ledumela 3
Lefu, see Motumi, Ma-Thabo Lefu

Lekganyane, Ignatius 107
Lesotho 1–18, 58, 76, 96, 109–10
Limba, 'Bishop' James 107–8
Lunika, James 30–1, 47, 50–1, 56–7, 78, 79, 90–1, 106–7, 116–19, 121, 133, 134, 153, 158, 180, 196–7, 207, 217, 218, 225, 228–30, 232, 238–41, 253, 255, 281–8, 316
Lusikisiki xvii, xix, 116, 184, 205–7, 236–7, 283

Macotha 32
Madikizela, C. K. 221
Magwa Falls 233
Makeka, Pascal 47–8, 57, 71, 88, 92, 105, 115, 138, 202
Malan, D. F. 161, 165, 167–8, 191
Maluti Mountains 1, 2, 3, 7, 11, 22, 27, 37
Mametsi, *see* Sethuntsa, Mametsi
Mami Wata 65
mamlambo 3, 43, 66–7, 112–15, 253–4
mamolapo, see mamlambo
Mancotywa, C. M. xviii, 282
Mandela, Winnie 102
Mantsopa 27–31, 45
Maphasa 147
Marsburg, Alf 90, 92–3, 128, 158, 161, 180, 194
Matanzima, George 318
Matanzima, Kaiser 218–19, 258, 318
Matatiele 18, 21, 23, 34, 54, 303
Matsieng 96
Mbeki, Govan 23, 172, 215, 221
Mdantsane 57

Melikane 4
Mngqesha 157, 280
Modderpoort 28
Moshoeshoe, King 1
Moshoeshoe, Nthoa Bohlokoa 47, 54–5, 78, 87, 127
Mokholitsoane 13, 17–20
Montgomery, Bernard Viscount 166
Moorosi 1, 14–16, 37
Motaung, Bethuel 272, 275
Motumi, Lefu Ma-Thabo 7, 52, 59
Motumi, *see* Ramokakatlela, Motumi
Mount Ayliff 20, 204, 312
Mount Frere 133, 157, 191, 236, 238, 242, 249–50, 252, 257, 307
Mount Moorosi 14–16
Mount Nelson xx–xxvi, 29, 77, 133, 139, 184, 189, 209, 216, 220, 222, 223, 238, 254, 277, 305, 308–9, 312, 321
Msikaba 127, 233
Msindo, Nogama, *see* Sethuntsa, Nogama
Mthatha (formerly Umtata) 238
Mutwa, Credo 149–50, 170
Mzintlava River xxiv, 21, 67, 82, 84, 110, 124–7, 129, 132, 203, 305

National Party (NP) 150, 161, 167–9, 171, 219, 320
Natives Land Act (1913) 22–3, 69, 75
Native Trust and Land Act (1936) 75
Natives (Urban Areas) Act (1923)

69, 75, 175, 183
Ndzumo, Saul 258, 292, 304–5, 318
Nel, M. D. C. de Wet 177
Newman, Bernard 106, 194, 198
ngaka (pl. dingaka) 4–5, 48
Ngquza Hill 213
Nkamba, Reverend L. 266–7
Nkosazana 80–1, 226, 253–4; see also mamlambo
Nogudlu, Meshack 84, 311
Nomansland, see East Griqualand
Nonkqubela, see Sethuntsa, Nonkqubela
Ntafufu 160, 177–8, 220
Ntafufu River 179
ntekwane 56, 163

oral narratives, see stories

Palmerton Methodist Mission 267
Pan-Africanist Congress (PAC) 219
Peires, Jeff 18
Phuthi 7, 8, 14–15, 69
Pondoland 203–4, 211–15; see also Pondoland Revolt
Pondoland Revolt 168, 172–3, 212–19, 222
Port St Johns 30
Poto, Victor 218–19
Pretoria 145–8, 152, 158

Qacha, Chief 37, 46
Qacha's Nek 2, 5, 11, 17–18, 37, 96
Queen Elizabeth Hospital 205, 306

Ramokakatlela, Motumi 7, 17, 27, 32, 45, 59
Redding, Sean 109
Reitz, Deneys 152
Representation of Natives Act (1936) 75

San 4, 5, 7, 10–13, 44
sangoma (pl. izangoma) 10, 170
Scheub, Harold 8, 79
Scott, Eric 20, 26, 41–4, 131
Scott family 19, 32, 97
'Section 10' law 183–4
segregation 22–4, 69–70, 75, 108–10, 161, 164–5, 169, 182–5, 212, 236–8, 254, 258, 320; see also Bantustans
Senqu River 2–4, 11–13, 56, 127
separate development, see segregation
Sethuntsa, Bethinja 179–82, 228, 246, 256–60, 269–76, 281, 284, 289–98, 304–6, 309, 316–18
Sethuntsa, Four Boy 199, 244, 251, 271–3, 294, 306
Sethuntsa, Gloria Manuku Lesala 101–2, 258
Sethuntsa, Khotso:
  early life in Lesotho 1–17
  growing up in East Griqualand 18–35
  as herder 20, 26, 30, 41
  as hunter 12, 19, 33–5, 38–9, 45, 95
  and horses 18, 32, 39, 41, 45, 138, 143–4, 155–7
  training as herbalist 12–13, 27–9, 44–59

career as a herbalist in Kokstad
41, 45–59, 72, 105–30, 174–6
wives and concubines 35–40,
98–103, 191, 197–8, 241–5,
254, 277–9, 291–7, 304–10; *see
also under names of individual
wives*
sexuality xx, xxiv, 31, 32, 38, 43,
98, 106, 197–8, 223–6, 243–5,
265–7; *see also ibangalala*
children 246–7; see *also under
names of individual children*
followers xxiv–xxv, 29, 90–1, 97,
103, 175–8, 196, 239–40
visitors xix–xxi, 86, 88–90, 93,
96–7, 103–5, 140–5, 161–8,
171, 177–8, 193–6, 198–202,
206–7, 209, 235, 265
religion 9, 25, 64, 107–8, 135–7,
209, 227–8, 229, 268, 278, 289
wealth and money xviii–xix,
30, 66–8, 70, 73–8, 86, 91,
93–6, 150–4, 195–6, 205,
232–3, 235–55, 283, 286–90;
see also Kruger millions
motor cars 75, 94, 141, 183,
220–1, 227, 229, 274–5, 290;
see also Cadillac
income tax 234, 255, 286
old age 263–76
death 277–9, 323
funeral xvii, 26, 279–84
will 270–4, 285–99
manifestations after death
311–19
Sethuntsa, Langa 99–100, 134,
178, 193, 247–52, 259–60, 270,
284, 290–8, 302–5, 307

Sethuntsa, MaDlamini 36–40,
46–7, 57, 65–6, 74, 82, 100–2,
136, 157, 165, 176, 199, 209–10,
257, 293, 296, 307–9
Sethuntsa, MaDzanibe 36, 65
Sethuntsa, Ma-Eleven 264, 304
Sethuntsa, Mametsi (Mametsi-a-
Leotle) 45, 130, 133
Sethuntsa, MaMjoli 13, 69, 87,
101, 105–6, 128, 198, 241–3, 257,
264, 268, 274, 276, 291, 294, 300,
314, 315, 323
Sethuntsa, Masechaba 36, 163,
165, 199, 252, 309
Sethuntsa, Ma-Six 304
Sethuntsa, Mosala Jack 98, 294
Sethuntsa, Motiki 36, 79–80
Sethuntsa, Nogama 244
Sethuntsa, Nonkqubela 258
Sethuntsa, Patricia 36, 65, 128,
264, 282, 287
Sethuntsa, Selina 244–6, 258, 294
Sethuntsa, Thabo 39, 46, 252, 306,
308, 315
Shembe, Isaiah 107
Shifa Hospital 274, 323
Sigcau, Botha 128, 171–3, 214,
216, 218–19, 280–2, 318
Sigcau family 171, 321
Sigcau, Vukayibambe 215
Sithole, Selina, *see* Sethuntsa,
Selina
snakes 3, 11, 13, 43–4, 55–7, 64–7,
85, 110–15, 117–18, 129, 132–5,
224, 253–4, 312; *see also inkan-
yamba, mamlambo*
South African War 22–3, 75, 164
Stallard Commission 69

statuary 83–4, 139, 141, 190–1, 218
Sterkspruit 86, 301, 313
stories 3, 11, 13, 43–4, 55–7, 64–7, 85, 110–15, 117–18, 129, 132–5, 224, 253–4, 312
Strachan, Boy 167, 191
Streek, Barry 219
Strijdom, J. G. 161, 165, 176, 191
Swart, C. R. 219
Swartz, J. J. (Chris) 271–3, 286–7, 290, 294, 318

Telle Bridge 5
Teyateyaneng 88–9, 96, 111
Thaba Bosiu 15–16
tokoloshe 130
Tomlinson Commission 109
tornado 41–3, 49
Transkei 23, 108–9, 174, 211–12, 218–21, 236–8
trickster 8, 30, 35, 78–80, 206, 322
Truth and Reconciliation Commission (TRC) 215
Tsafendas, Dimitri 224
Tsoelike River 5
Tyali, Aubrey Zolani 307

uHlanga 126
ukuthwala xxiv, 64, 66–7, 80, 86, 108, 110–24, 221, 249, 286

ukuthwetyula 10
ukuvutha 58
Umzimkhulu 36, 75, 208, 238
Urban Areas Act, *see* Natives (Urban Areas) Act

Verwoerd, Danie 166
Verwoerd, H. F. xxii, 161–3, 191, 222, 224, 226
vierkleur 139, 159

water 2–3, 4, 9–11, 13–14, 54–6, 58, 65, 110, 115, 116–18, 124–30, 203, 276, 318; *see also* Mzintlava River, *ukuthwala*
Waring, Frank 200
Wilson, Monica Hunter 204
witchcraft 25, 43, 137, 204–5
White House 82–92, 111, 133, 139–40, 143, 161, 190, 311, 315

Xhosa Development Corporation 221

Yako, Lala 57, 75–6, 107, 120, 129, 202

Zion Christian Church 107
Zoning Proclamation (1965) 238